RADICAL INNOCENCE:

STUDIES IN THE CONTEMPORARY
AMERICAN NOVEL

Where *is* this new bird called the true American? Show us the homunculus of the new era. Go on, show us him. Because all that is visible to the naked European eye, in America, is a sort of recreant European. We want to see this missing link of the next era.

D. H. LAWRENCE, *Studies in Classic American Literature*

RADICAL INNOCENCE:

STUDIES IN THE CONTEMPORARY AMERICAN NOVEL

BY IHAB HASSAN

PRINCETON, NEW JERSEY
PRINCETON UNIVERSITY PRESS

L.C. Card 61-7416

ISBN 0-691-01301-2 (paperback edn.)

ISBN 0-691-06107-6 (hardcover edn.)

Publication of this book
has been aided by a grant from the
John Simon Guggenheim Memorial Foundation
and by the Ford Foundation program
to support publication, through
university presses, of work in the
humanities and social sciences.

Printed in the United States of America
by the Princeton University Press,
Princeton, New Jersey

First Princeton Paperback Printing, 1971

Fourth Hardcover Printing, 1971

FOR MY SON
GEOFFREY KARIM HASSAN

ACKNOWLEDGMENTS

I AM grateful to the John Simon Guggenheim Foundation for grants which made the writing and production of this book possible; and to the Wesleyan Research Fund for helping defray clerical and research expenses.

Certain parts of this work have appeared in periodicals. I am grateful to the editors and publishers of the following journals for allowing me to use (sometimes a large part of an article, more often only a few paragraphs) these earlier writings: "The Pilgrim as Prey: The World of Paul Bowles," *Western Review* (Fall, 1954); "Jean Stafford: The Expense of Style and Scope of Sensibility," *Western Review* (Spring, 1955); "Rare Quixotic Gesture: The Fiction of J. D. Salinger," *Western Review* (Summer, 1957); "The Idea of Adolescence in American Fiction," *American Quarterly* (Fall, 1958); "Carson McCullers: The Alchemy of Love and Aesthetics of Pain," *Modern Fiction Studies* (Winter, 1959-1960); "The Anti-Hero in Modern British and American Fiction," in W. P. Friedrich, ed., *Comparative Literature, Proceedings of the ICLA Congress in Chapel Hill* (Chapel Hill, 1959); "Love in the Modern American Novel," *Western Humanities Review* (Spring, 1960); and "Truman Capote: The Daydream and Nightmare of Narcissus," *Wisconsin Studies in Contemporary Literature* (Spring-Summer, 1960).

For permission to quote from the ensuing works, I am much indebted to these authors and their publishers: William Styron, *Lie Down in Darkness*, The Bobbs-Merrill Company, Inc.; Bernard Malamud, *The Assistant*, Farrar, Straus and Cudahy, Inc.; John Cheever, *The Wapshot Chronicle*, Harper and Brothers; Norman Mailer, *The Naked and the Dead*, Holt, Rinehart and Winston, Inc.; Carson McCullers, *The Ballad of the Sad Café*, Houghton Mifflin Company; Frederick Buechner, *A Long Day's Dying*, Alfred A. Knopf, Inc.; Herbert Gold, *The Optimist*, Little, Brown and Company; Granville Hicks, ed., *The Living Novel*, Macmillan Company; J. P. Donleavy, *The Ginger Man*, Ivan Obolensky, Inc.; Truman Capote, *Other*

ACKNOWLEDGMENTS

Voices, Other Rooms, A Tree of Night and Other Stories, The Grass Harp, Breakfast at Tiffany's, and Ralph Ellison, *Invisible Man,* Random House, Inc.; Saul Bellow, *The Adventures of Augie March, Seize the Day, Henderson the Rain King,* and Harvey Swados, *Out Went the Candle,* The Viking Press, Inc.

My interest in the generation of novelists to which this study is addressed was stimulated by the Examination of New Writers Series sponsored by the *Western Review* under the editorship of Ray B. West, Jr. It was formed by my readings in American literature, the modern European novel, Freudian and Existentialist thought. The criticism of D. H. Lawrence, in *Studies in Classic American Literature,* proved to be both a hindrance and a creative irritant.

John Cheever, Harvey Swados, and William Styron have very kindly given me the opportunity to exchange opinions with them in conversation; and Truman Capote, Herbert Gold, and Flannery O'Connor have graciously responded to my queries with valuable letters. I am indebted to them all.

Though the responsibility for the errors and omissions in this book are solely mine, I wish to thank Norman Holmes Pearson, Loren Baritz, and particularly Alexander Cowie for their careful reading of my manuscript, and for their generous and helpful suggestions. Professor Cowie's interest in my work, throughout its evolution, has been steadfast as his friendship. Malcolm Cowley, who saw an outline of my project, has helped to give it form and direction. Miss R. Miriam Brokaw, and Mrs. James Holly Hanford, both of the Princeton University Press, have provided me with constant encouragement and courteous editorial guidance. To Nathan Shapira I am grateful for a sensitive design of the dust jacket.

My most profound debts, however, must remain unacknowledged. They are fit subject for personal knowledge and silence.

IHAB HASSAN

Wesleyan University
Middletown, Connecticut
August 1961

CONTENTS

RADICAL INNOCENCE:

STUDIES IN THE CONTEMPORARY

AMERICAN NOVEL

PROLOGUE

I

IT is the privilege of every age to consider its predicament
unique, and it is its hope that the predicament may prove
the most gravid history has known. Such illusions are not
always idle; for they are the stuff of which men make the record
of their speeding days, heightening their moment with some
articulate show of pride, wonder, or despair. In the end, such
illusions are but the human way of stating: "We are here!"

We are indeed here, past the meridian of the twentieth
century, a devastating war behind us, and a war we dare not
call by any name lowering ahead. Yet it is time, perhaps, we
called a halt to the melodrama of fission and fusion, of grim
threats and endless lamentation. Poised at the edge of the Space
Age, we have no recourse but to choose life over death, turning
our attention to this time and to this place, to the actions of
man and to his works which make time and place an habitation
for his spirit.

We are here: precisely the cry literature has articulated with
the fullest resonances throughout the ages. If that were the
only statement contemporary American fiction made, it should
have been reason enough to rescue it from the vulgar interest
or stylish indifference with which it is greeted. But the contemporary American novel does not only aver our presence: it
explores and enlarges the modalities of our *being*. "To be alive,
to be the whole man alive: that is the point," D. H. Lawrence
wrote with the wisdom that qualifies itself by excess. "And at
its best, the novel, and the novel supremely, can help you. It
can help you not to be a dead man in life."[1] Professors of the
view that the novel is defunct—professors, that is, of their own
weary sophistication—condemn current fiction as a spent form,
irrelevant to the goals of a Supersociety committed to a galactic
adventure, and therefore no longer receptive to the piteous

3

heroics of the individual soul. Such a view reveals that myopia is indeed the most pronounced trait of utopian vision; and though we can no more refute it than we can refute a nightmare or a prophecy, we can put its judgment to question by inquiring into a more vital matter: the nature of the contemporary self in action and reaction, in stress and freedom, in assent and denial, sallying forth to confront experience and recoiling again to preserve its sanity or innocence.

The actions and recoils of the contemporary self engage that dense area of reality wherein our epochal consciousness and our literary forms meet. The movements of the self suggest the regions of tension and repose in our cultural life. Such movements have been the primary business of the novel since the Knight of the Mournful Countenance jogged down the road with fat Sancho by his side. The hero, while life still beats in his fictive heart, mediates between self and world in that imaginative dialectic form we have agreed to identify as the novel.

But what image of the hero does contemporary American fiction project, giving the novel its shape and our world its particular substance? No single answer, of course, will tell the whole story. Still, a beginning may be made by imagining the reactions of a venerable and literate Martian to some current titles—merely the titles—on our bookshelves: *The Victim, Dangling Man, The Naked and the Dead, The Heart Is A Lonely Hunter, Invisible Man, A Long Day's Dying, The Color of Darkness, A Good Man Is Hard to Find, The End of Pity, A Tree of Night, Lie Down in Darkness,* etc. We should not hold it entirely against our visitor if his initial reaction should be that the Planet Earth is on the way to self-demolition. Obviously, a dark impulse of *resistance* permeates contemporary letters. Novelists are not afraid to admit it. A Christian writer like Flannery O'Connor and a radical novelist like Norman Mailer concur that violence and distortion must be the means of projecting a vision to which society is hostile.[2] They would further agree that the contemporary world presents a continued affront to man, and that his response must therefore be the response of the rebel or victim, living under the shadow of death.

Such a response goes far beyond the assumptions of mere opposition, and it bears no witness to the charges of neutrality or disaffiliation. The contemporary "opposing self," to be sure, has the powers of indignant "perception," has the "intense and adverse imagination of the culture in which it has its being" that Lionel Trilling astutely perceived in the novel of the last hundred and fifty years.[3] But the contemporary self is also post-Romantic. It was not only born, like Little Dorrit, in a prison, and it has not only made of its prison, like Axel, a fortress and mausoleum. It has been also discovering the strange secrets of all prisons: that though their doors are never locked, no prisoner wishes to escape; that all avenues of escape lead to the same cell; that nothing may really exist beyond prison walls; that every gaoler is merely another prisoner in disguise. The contemporary self recoils, *from* the world, *against* itself. It has discovered absurdity. The parable used by Saul Bellow as an epigraph to his novel, *The Victim*, sums up this terrible recognition. The story is that of the wealthy merchant in the *Arabian Nights* who sat down under a tree to eat his dates in peace.

When he had ended eating the dates he threw away the stones with force and lo! an Ifrit appeared, huge of stature and brandishing a drawn sword, wherewith he approached the merchant and said, "Stand up that I may slay thee even as thou slewest my son!" Asked the merchant, "How have I slain thy son?" and he answered, "When thou atest dates and threwest away the stones they struck my son full in the breast as he was walking by, so that he died forthwith."[4]

Yet if the contemporary self is in recoil, it is not, we hope and believe, cravenly on the run. Its *re-coil* is one of the resources of its awareness, a strategy of its *will*. As we shall have occasion to see, its most tortured gestures of opposition proclaim its involvement in the world it opposes, and its most desperate forms of surrender probe the heart of the religious life in our time. "If the modern temper, as distinct from the romantic, lies in the admission that men are mortal," Wright Morris says, "this admission determines the nature of the raw material with which the artist must work. An element of despair, a destructive element, is one of the signs by which we shall know him—the other is the constructive use to which this element is put."[5]

Both elements, we believe, emerge in the new figure of the hero in contemporary American fiction. Precisely what the new hero stands for, no one can yet define. He is not exactly the liberal's idea of the victim, not the conservative's idea of the pariah, not the radical's idea of the rebel. Or perhaps he is all of these and none in particular. Sometimes one aspect of his makeup is underscored, sometimes another. His capacity for pain seems very nearly saintly, and his passion for heresy almost criminal. But flawed in his sainthood and grotesque in his criminality, he finally appears as an expression of man's quenchless desire to affirm, despite the voids and vicissitudes of our age, the human sense of *life*!

It is this quality of his passion, of his awareness, that we have chosen to call *radical innocence*. Radical, first, because it is inherent in his character, and goes to the root or foundation of it. But radical, too, because it is extreme, impulsive, anarchic, troubled with vision. The new hero brings the brilliant extremities of the American conscience and imagination to bear on the equable tenor of our present culture. His stance questions the "mystic centrality" of our day, which Richard Chase so ably condemned in *The Democratic Vista*, and his fate testifies to the continuance of "the vivid contradictions and anomalies that in the past have engaged the American mind."[6] His innocence, therefore, does not merely revert to those simplicities which, rightly or wrongly, have been identified with vision in America. His innocence, rather, is a property of the mythic American Self, perhaps of every anarchic Self. It is the innocence of a Self that refuses to accept the immitigable rule of reality, including death, an aboriginal Self the radical imperatives of whose freedom cannot be stifled. There is something in the quality of that in-

6

nocence to remind us of the *ignoble* savage, the archaic and roguish character, say, of the Winnebago Trickster who, as Jung described him, "is a faithful copy of an absolutely undifferentiated human consciousness, corresponding to a psyche that has hardly left the animal level."[7] But the innocence we speak of also has a divine element in it; has, like Dionysus, that inner energy of being, creative and sacrificial, which D. H. Lawrence hoped to find in the American Adam. The disparity between the innocence of the hero and the destructive character of his experience defines his concrete, or existential, situation. This does not add up to an orthodox notion of American innocence—the notion is radical—but it is one, we believe, that can help to make the new hero more intelligible.

I I

If the foregoing remarks amount to something of a doctrine, they are all the doctrine we shall dare maintain. Dogmas sometimes survive the ravages of time, but critics have no business with Eternity. A theme, nonetheless, may be discovered in this study, and a view of some kind—it might be labeled broadly existential—may lie behind it. The metaphor of "radical innocence" hopefully suggests both theme and view.

But the metaphor can serve, in the end, only to unmask the hero's face. The heroes of fiction are made, not born. Though the subtle substance of the ages flows in their veins, heroes do not only incarnate our history but recreate it with artifice. The hero is one mirror fiction uses to surprise reality—and identify its forms.

Our view of the recent American novel evolves in three continuous stages, each corresponding to a major subdivision of this work. The movement, on the whole, is from hypothesis to example, from the general to the specific. The concepts we may have pressed too hard in the beginning we have allowed purposely to spread, engaging concrete literary facts, toward the end. The three parts may be anticipated in the following outline:

I. The Hero and the World: A historical perspective of the changing image of the hero in the modern novel, in Europe and America.

II. The Forms of Fiction: A formal analysis of the way the novel, as genre, responds to the shifting vision of man in contemporary American fiction. Nine novels, reflecting a variety of fictional types, are used as the basis for a definition of a new ironic form.

III. The Individual Talent: An exemplary view of four writers —McCullers, Capote, Salinger, and Bellow—who have brought some of the most pressing novelistic concerns since the last war to the condition of performance.

The dialectic forces of history and society (the World) affect our idea of the self (the Hero). A new type of hero emerges, and from the two critical moments in his encounter with experience, the moments of initiation or defeat, the form of fiction takes its shape. The ensuing problems of form express the problems of vision which the best of the new writers face. This, in brief outline, is the logic of our exposition.

A few words of definition more. The novelists who concern us in this book, and to whom we refer as *contemporary*, were all born after 1910. A good many of them were born much later. They are *some* of the novelists—there is no claim to inclusiveness here, and no conscious attempt to estimate reputations in the literary stockmarket—whose achievement came to public attention after World War II, and whose efforts, however various or distinct, suggest a new tenor of American writing. Older critics, some of whom prefer to remain boys in Hemingway's boyhood, have not heeded them much; others enjoy making them the butt of their Olympian or Chthonian wit. We have no bones to pick with critics, no preconceived norms to impose on a writer's struggle with his art, no eschatologies to prescribe for the salvation of the novel. It is enough for critics if, by some miracle or chance, they can discover that mode of speech which allows authors to speak for themselves.

PART I

THE HERO AND THE WORLD

As the relation of the Hero to his World changes, so does the form of fiction. The Hero, who once figured as Initiate, ends as Rebel or Victim. The change in his condition implies destruction—and presages rebirth.

The destructive element has an objective reality in our age. It is not a product of the eccentric vision, the enervated sensibility, or the alienated condition of the "writer in America." The image of the rebel-victim we shall persistently examine is not that of the novelist described by the editors of *Life* (September 12, 1955) as "an unemployed homosexual living in a packing-box shanty on the city dump while waiting admission to the county poorhouse." It is rather the image of man—modern and strictly contemporary too—which the lackeys of our culture cannot bring themselves to recognize.

Nor is the concept of man we hope to understand a wayward product of the recent American novel, a sort of excrescence to be hidden or cauterized. Quite to the contrary: the paradox of American literature in our time is that to the extent it has become a unique expression of American life, it has also engaged the most vital issues Europe confronts. The ideas of victimization, rebellion, and alienation remain at the center of Western literature since—and perhaps before—the turn of our century. They are, moreover, implicit in the relentless dialectic of innocence and guilt which informs the process of initiation in America.

Our concern is with the novel, *contemporary* and *American*. But the contemporary sensibility is a development of the modern mind in which *both* Europe and America have a large stake. This is a fact no methodology of American Studies can afford to ignore.

CHAPTER 1

THE MODERN SELF IN RECOIL

The purpose of the historical analysis . . . is to trace back modern world alienation, its twofold flight from the earth into the universe and from the world in the self. . . .—HANNAH ARENDT, *The Human Condition*

I

THE imperatives of suffering and rebellion constitute the modern response to some grim events and strange developments of our century. History, social and political science, psychology, and philosophy have inquired seriously into the cause of the modern distemper. While it is quite beyond our scope to review the contribution each of these disciplines makes toward understanding the human predicament, it may be necessary to recall some critical facts adduced by each. The prospect we shall unfold is not balanced and far from comprehensive. If it seems rather heavily weighed in favor of man's adverse response to his condition, it is because we must carefully gauge those threats to his humanity which have awakened the literary imagination of our time to its full and passionate utterance.

Man's awareness of his history has seldom caused him great jubilation. There are records on papyrus decrying the evil times fallen upon Egypt, and Thucydides, we know, imposed on history the pattern of tragedy. Today our awareness of history tends to be still more acute. The mighty pageants of Spengler and Toynbee do not bolster our confidence; a barrage of anti-utopias —Wells's, Huxley's, Orwell's—blots the horizon. The story is nearly always the same: spirit is exhausted, civilization is over-extended, the individual must move on surfaces or be crushed inward. History, we learn from Spengler's *Decline of the West*, is the relative process of human societies, evolving from Culture to Civilization, from a dream-heavy awakening of the soul, through a great moment of creative and ripening consciousness, to cosmopolitan, practical, and irreligious decadence. Imperialism and urbanization on a giant scale are the precursors of dissolution. From our point of view the interest of Spengler's work does not depend on its prophecy of doom; it lies rather in its vision of man fulfilling his destiny in cycles, not in progressions, and in its discovery of "the *opposition of History and Nature* through which alone it is possible to grasp the essence of the former."[1] The idea that man must always work *against* Nature, and work in a cyclical process which has no *final end*, is one that defines his predicament in radical terms. History, that is to say Destiny, so conceived cannot encourage man to look behind or ahead; it merely prompts him to live his moment.

It is not impertinent, perhaps, to note that Spengler wrote his work in the midst of one world war and Toynbee in the midst of another. Toynbee's faith in the redeeming powers of Christianity, however, mitigates his sense of catastrophe. Western civilization is seen allegorically in the long voyage of the *Kon-Tiki* headed finally toward a coral reef which it has no power to avoid. Will it ride the tide or shatter itself to splinters? No one can foreknow the outcome. But the ordeal is there: "This unavoidable danger ahead was the perilous transition between the World partitioned into an American and a Russian sphere and a World united under a single political authority. . . ."[2] Again, it is not the prophecy of Toynbee that commands our interest but his analysis in the sinister light of our present condition. The emergence of a creative minority and an alienated "proletariat"—those who do not belong spiritually to the society within which they are physically included—is, in Toynbee's system, the most conspicuous mark of impending disintegration. Toynbee notes symptoms both of alienation and reconciliation in our society. His stand, however, becomes clearer when he infers that "the regimentation that was now being imposed on the Western society's economic and political life would be likely to liberate Western souls for fulfilling the true end of Man by glorifying God and enjoying Him once again."[3] The reaction against external regimentation converts itself into a religious impulse working inward and upward—still a form of recoil, albeit one of the most significant.

The grand designs of both Spengler and Toynbee locate modern man at a critical juncture of history and attest to his growing alienation from his "true" self. The vision of utopians and anti-utopians seems equally dreadful. "Consciousness will gradually evaporate and disappear in this posthistoric period," Roderick Seidenberg observes not without some relish, "very much as it condensed step by step into ever sharper focus during man's prehistoric period. In the ultimate state of crystallization to which the principle of organization leads, consciousness will have accomplished its task, leaving mankind sealed, as it were, within patterns of frigid and unalterable perfection."[4] A pretty picture to hold against another suggested by Orwell's *Nineteen Eighty Four*: "If you want a picture of the future, imagine a boot stamping on a human face—forever."[5] Yet the abolition of the self is not at hand. Its recoil confounds that end. The prominent role played by terrorism and rebellion in the last hundred years of Western history must persuade us that man is no willing victim to his future. Even nihilism wears the ravaged face of human protest. The nihilist's revulsion against the present confirms the prophet's revulsion against that future the present contains.

Revulsion has indeed become a modern attitude toward history. It finds expression in such current phrases as the "terror" or the "nightmare of history." It is a confession that man finds no redemption in history. Eden is far behind, the millennium not appreciably nearer. The prevalent sense is one of cataclysm or else of transience. And the pattern of human actions in time yields no recognizable meaning. The political experience of our century can be evoked by stark names: Sarajevo, Versailles, Abyssinia, Munich, Danzig, Dachau, Pearl Harbor, Hiroshima, Yalta, Little Rock, Bandung, Suez.

The political and social experiences of our century reveal two opposite tendencies at work: the unremitting organization of society and the unleashing of vast destructive energies against civilization. Both tendencies are incarnated by the superstate which is at once utopian and demonic. Both have been abetted by the incredible development of technology.

Technology has made improvements possible in the fields of social justice and economic planning. Culture and education are in its debt. In large parts of the world men enjoy social and material benefits their forefathers could not dream of. These are gifts easy to deprecate, hard to renounce. Renunciation, however, is not in question. It is rather the capacity of human beings to retain and develop them that must concern us. Chaplin's image of a man impaled between two giant cogwheels, in "Modern Times," has begun to lose its ironic pathos. It is a possibility daily becoming more probable. Friedrich Juenger may sound a little superstitious when he claims, in *The Failure of Technology*, that "the surplus of elemental power that man has obtained by his destructive exploitation of nature thereby turns against him and threatens to destroy him."[6] But his analysis of the demonism of the machine, that nonhuman and truly nonrational lifelessness which permeates life, must give us pause. For the demonic resides as much in human irrationality as it does in inhuman regularity. The one like the other works toward the abolition of man. Indeed, we are told by scientists who attended an international congress on "The Mechanization of Thought Processes" in Britain that "whatever a human being can do an appropriate machine can do too."[7] (What, not better?) Evidently, utopians are quite resolved to put an end to that nuisance: human consciousness. But in whose interest will total lobotomy be performed?

14

The "brain eaters" of coming utopias are not yet in power. When lobotomy is performed by technology nowadays, it is usually performed in the name of the State. But technology has not only reduced individual freedom, it is taking over the State itself. "The outstanding feature on the economic-social plane was the tug of war between a regimentation imposed by mechanized industry and an obstinate human reluctance to be regimented," Toynbee writes. "The crux of the situation was the fact that mechanization and police were unfortunately inseparable."[8] Regimentation can be benevolent as well as infernal, and "police" may seem a harsh word to apply to the democracy we conceive ourselves to be. Yet even in democracy, regimentation for the common good has tended to be reckless of the rare, unique, and infrangible. Political participation, which is the foundation of democracy, becomes tenuous. The individual's sense of his own potency, his power to effect change and mold events, seems in steady decline. It is no great wonder that men choose to withdraw from the public realm of action, though their withdrawal from the world compels them into a fragile or futile relation to themselves. Instead of action, *behavior* reigns, and instead of authority, covert persuasion or systematic coercion.[9] Human energy is assessed in terms of abstract *functions*, and human qualities dealt with as *commodities*. The only victor, we all seem blandly to agree, is Society which in an age of technocracy and totalitarianism becomes tantamount to the State.

"Today, America is simply the most accomplished exponent, the most advanced outpost of that ever-broadening general trend of Western civilization which may be characterized as *the extraversion of man*," Erich Kahler notes in *The Tower and the Abyss*.[10] The possibilities of rebellion against that trend are still viable in mass democracy and the welfare State, as the works of the so-called Beat and Angry writers suggest. Rebellion against the unrelieved terror of the Fascist and Communist State, however, can only result in self-annihilation. In fascism or naziism,

15

terror is not a means; it is an end. Man is not only extraverted; he is utterly identified with the irrational force of the State. Power dismisses justice and reason. "Nothing beyond the State, above the State, against the State. Everything to the State, for the State, in the State," was the insane war cry of Mussolini.[11] When technology is put in the service of such an ideal, the refinements of mass terror, mass torture—sometimes performed in the name of experimental medicine—and mass hysteria become virtually inexhaustible. But the most diabolic perversion of this ideal is witnessed when the victim adopts the values and prejudices of his tormentor in the very act of torment, and when contrition is created in the victim to excuse the guilt of his oppressor. The Nuremberg trials of war criminals present gruesome illustrations of these techniques which Koestler's *Darkness at Noon* and Orwell's *Nineteen Eighty Four* show to be the staple method of any thoroughgoing totalitarianism. There are, to be sure, differences between the Nazi and Communist philosophies of torture. But in either case the individual as we have known him for thirty centuries in the West must vanish. Against the Nazi mystique or Communist science of terror, against demonic statism or demonic utopianism, the powers of individual rebellion are tried to their shattering limit.

The powers of human resistance find expression in a great number of documents written in the extremity of twentieth century despair; the limits of these powers are suggested by psychoanalytic theory which attempts to infer the central predicament of the self.

Works like Koestler's "Scum of This Earth," in *The Yogi and the Commissar*; Michel del Castillo's *A Child of Our Time*; *The Diary of Anne Frank*; John Hersey's *Hiroshima* or *The Wall*; C. Virgil Gheorghiu's *The Twenty-Fifth Hour*; and the Air Force transcripts on American war prisoners in Korea give forth the collective *de profundis* cry of our century, and reveal their share of stark outrage and ironic acceptance. The human response to outrage, however, strains our capacities for vicarious-ness. Its limit is madness. Dr. Bruno Bettelheim, himself an inmate of a Nazi concentration camp for many years, has observed how the self seeks refuge in schizophrenia when "reality" becomes unendurable. Indeed, he was able to preserve his own sanity only by allowing his consciousness to split up into subject and object, and by assigning to the first a genuinely human role which the indignities of the second could not subvert.[12] The significance of this act reaches far beyond pathological behavior; it confronts us with the unspeakable fact of *pain* in the world. Schizophrenia, insofar as it entails the withdrawal of libido from real objects and its reversion back to the ego, constitutes the ultimate form of recoil. But if the withdrawal results sometimes in madness, it can also afford distance and high lucidity. It offers a way, this side of madness, of rising above the inexorable realm of necessity, of pain, to a higher ground from which necessity may be understood in *human* terms.

The conflicts between pain and pleasure, between reality and the self, between power and love—those same conflicts which have been the steady concern of literature for many centuries—receive full recognition in Freud's *Civilization and Its Discontents*. Freud's somber conclusion is that "the price of progress in civilization is paid in forfeiting happiness through the heightening of the sense of guilt."[13] For civilization is built on acts of instinctual renunciation required by Necessity, or *Ananke*. But every act of instinctual renunciation begets another. Conscience becomes more intolerant, repression stronger, guilt harsher. Guilt produces aggression toward the self: "Every impulse of aggression which we omit to gratify is taken over by the super-ego and goes to heighten its aggressiveness [against the ego]."[14] When guilt is swollen to an intolerable degree, aggression breaks loose. The ultimate result is either mass murder or mass suicide. The basic and perhaps irreconcilable struggle, however, is not between man and society. The basic struggle is between the primal instincts of Life and Death, between love and aggression in their manifold disguises. Freud's idea of the death instinct, an idea that has been seriously questioned, suggests that the self is not only opposed to the world but also divided in its own house. Man, in this pessimistic and perhaps ultimately religious view, is as much his own victim as he is the victim of society. Suicide, which Emile Durkheim found to be constantly on the rise through the latter part of the nineteenth century, and which he identified as an extreme symptom of the ego's estrangement from the collective conscience, suicide reminds us that human violence may strike back at its own roots. This is precisely the way a masochistic ego chooses to achieve victory in defeat. Masochism, that malady of modern man, as Theodore Reik has argued, compounds fantasy with rebellion; it is really spite seeking to transcend itself. "Both in the lives of individuals and of communities," Reik observes, "masochism represents an unavoidable transitory phase from the development of unmastered sadistic instincts to their domestication in the service of culture."[15] But just how transitory can any phase of history be for which men are compelled to forsake their humanity?

The difficulties of the ego outlined by psychoanalytic theory in many ways correspond to the experience of the self as apprehended by Existentialist thought. This is to be expected. Nietzsche and Kierkegaard, the great nineteenth-century precursors of modern Existentialism, are also considered the most brilliant psychologists of that century; and the views of both men find current and common expression in existential psychoanalysis.[16] In its recoil the modern self has once again discovered that all truths must be bloody and personal truths, truths, that is, *experienced* in anguish and action. "What every reporter on the present human condition has, indeed, to take into account is the sense that men have today of being thrust into the nudity of their own isolated individual existence," Nathan Scott has observed.[17] This statement is supported by a company of varied and distinguished thinkers, most of whom have been recently coopted to the swelling ranks of Existentialism: Nietzsche, Kierkegaard, Feuerbach, Jaspers, Heidegger, Unamuno, Ortega Y Gasset, Maritain, Marcel, Berdyaev, Buber, Tillich, Sartre, Camus. The statement is furthermore elaborated by the major writers of our century for whom the idea of man's alienation is axiomatic and the ontological problem of man's being—not merely his struggle or defeat, but the stark encounter with nothingness—is the cardinal question. In this urgent and particular sense, our awareness of the modern experience can be called supremely existential.

The baffling contradictions of Existentialism, which its current faddishness in America must seem to aggravate, need not deter us from perceiving its relevance. Contradictions are sometimes put in the service of truth. That much Nietzsche knew. And it was Nietzsche who forecast the advent of nihilism in our century "because nihilism represents the ultimate logical conclusion of our great values and ideals—because we must experience nihilism before we can find out what value these 'values' really had."[18] The recoil of the self in passion (from which new values may be created) and its extension in gratuitous actions which refer to no accepted norm (the need to act precisely because action is no longer intrinsically meaningful) constitute the means by which modern man is forced to cope with the fact of nihilism. Man reclaims the devil in him to transcend the death of God and escape the death of man, to become at once better and more evil than himself.[19] This is an extreme measure, but so is our literature reputed to be a literature of extreme situations. This, too, is the ultimate meaning of individualism as Kierkegaard, playing a Christ to Nietzsche's Anti-Christ, saw it. "The crowd is untruth. Therefore was Christ crucified. . . . And hence every one who truly would serve the truth is *eo ipso* . . . a martyr."[20] Between nihilism and sainthood, the modern self wavers, seeking still the meaning of life. In its concrete encounter with absurdity, with dread and the obscene corporeality of death, with mystical anarchy and organized nothingness, with abstract truth and experienced reality, the modern self discovers ways of affirmation that heroes of yore did not envision. For better or worse, man's fate is now a *human* fate; and as Camus said in his conclusion to the *Myth of Sisyphus*, "One does not discover the absurd without being tempted to write a manual of happiness."[21] If Existentialism is a symptom of an industrial society in process of dissolution, the existential self which modern literature reveals is one that reaches out to new conditions while recoiling to preserve a radical kind of innocence.

The alienation of the self, its response in martyrdom or rebellion or both to the modern experience, has been briefly observed in history, in the body politic, in man's psyche, and in his existence. History predicts no salvation for man and accords no meaning retrospectively to his efforts. The dominant political trend of the age fortifies the collective and technical organization of society. Freudian psychoanalysis reveals that the antagonism between instinct and civilization is founded on the more hopeless opposition between love and aggression. Existentialist philosophy exposes the absolute nudity of the self in a world devoid of preconceived values or significance. Is it proper, then, to infer that what the world may face is not only an end to individualism but a breakdown of the human form itself? What the world faces ultimately depends on man's response to the destructive elements in his experience. Nowhere is that response more richly articulated than in the modern novel, to which we must now turn.

II

"In its essence literature is concerned with the self," Lionel Trilling writes in *Freud and the Crisis of Our Culture*, "and the particular concern of the literature of the last two centuries has been with the self in its standing quarrel with culture."[22] The image of the self in its standing, and recently embittered, quarrel with culture—indeed in its quarrel with itself, as Mr. Trilling neglects to say—comes to focus in the figure of the anti-hero.

In fiction, the unnerving rubric "anti-hero" refers to a ragged assembly of victims: the fool, the clown, the hipster, the criminal, the poor sod, the freak, the outsider, the scapegoat, the scrubby opportunist, the rebel without a cause, the "hero" in the ashcan and "hero" on the leash. If the anti-hero seems nowadays to hold us in his spell, it is because the deep and disquieting insights revealed to us by modern literature often require that we project ourselves into the predicament of victims.

The gradual process of atrophy of the hero may have begun with Don Quixote, or perhaps even Job, Orestes, and Christ. It enters the critical phase, however, only late in the eighteenth century. Goethe's Werther introduces the "tragic" Romantic hero who, in his inordinate conception of himself, severs the traditional bond between the hero and his society, and points the way to such extreme stances of alienation as were to find expression in the Byronic and Sadist hero, in the gothic and demonic protagonist, in werewolf, ghoul, and vampire. But as the new bourgeois order, which the Romantic hero rejected, became a powerful social reality, the strategy of opposition changed. The characters of Stendhal, Balzac, and Flaubert often seem, as Raymond Giraud has recognized, "heroes of ironies" whose "ideals, desires, and feelings are in disharmony" with their "adult conception of reality."[23] Similarly, the subtitle for *Vanity Fair: A Novel Without a Hero*, suggests that Victorian fiction was quietly disposing of the heroic protagonist. The ambivalences of a bourgeois hero in an overwhelmingly middle-class society raise for him problems of estrangement and communion, sincerity and simulation, ambition and acquiescence, which we recognize as the patent themes of the great novels of the last century. The wretched fate of the lower-class hero, caught between malignant Heredity and crushing Environment in the *roman experimental* of Zola, and in the less experimental but more benign novels of the brothers Goncourt, reflects the familiar bias of Naturalism and marks a further stage in the disintegration of heroism. Victim to immitigable "cosmic laws," with little or no control over his fate in the world, man turns inward again. The next development is predictable. "The way was open from the realist to the intimist novel," Mario Praz concludes in *The Hero in Eclipse in Victorian Fiction*. "Disillusioned observation of life as it really was, led to the eclipse of the hero and the disclosure of man's swarming interior world, made up of disparate and contradictory things."[24]

With the retrenchment of the individual, the drama of good and evil which the hero and villain once objectified in society becomes blurred. The traditional forms of moral conflict are so internalized that no victory or defeat, where self is divided against itself, can claim to be more than pyrrhic. Cunningly introspective, the modern novel redefines the identity of its central character and redirects his energies toward the virtues of love or self-discovery, virtues that are a good deal more personal than social. To become someone, to know who or what one is, to reach finally another human being with love, and to do so in terms that society may censure, this is the passionate, bitter concern of the modern anti-hero. But the modern identity proved an elusive thing to capture. "You mustn't look in my novel for the old stable *ego* of the character," D. H. Lawrence wrote to Edward Garnett. "There is another *ego*, according to whose action the individual is unrecognizable, and passes through, as it were, allotropic states. . . ."[25] A new shifty ego, a new concept of man. The sad history of the anti-hero is nothing more than the history of man's changing awareness of himself. It is the record of his recoil.

The encounter between the new ego and the destructive element of experience, we have insisted, lies at the dramatic center of the modern novel in Europe and America. The en-

22

counter is further illumined by some striking European images which define the modern idea of the self and clarify its responses. We shall view some concrete instances of the anti-hero—whom in hope and charity we may simply call "hero." These instances are taken from writers of very different age and background, yet they add to a remarkably persistent theme.

To consider Dostoyevsky's *Notes from Underground*, 1864, modern is perhaps to stretch the idea of modernity to its permissible limit. The document so shrill and anxious, so full of spite and spleen, reveals, in any case, what the modern soul likes most to gnaw upon: itself. The dagger is turned inward, the most refined tortures are reserved for the self. Whom else are we really interested in? Listening for forty years from the crack under his floor, Dostoyevsky's hero looks at existence with a cringe and a snarl. He knows the intense pleasure of degradation and of despair, and knows, while gnashing his teeth, that "there is no one even for you to feel vindictive against, that you have not, and perhaps never will have, an object for your spite. . . ."[26] Precisely the condition which Albert Camus calls, in *The Rebel*, metaphysical rebellion, and which our hero understands as a revolt against "the whole legal system of Nature."[27] But no one is to blame; "consequently there is only the same outlet left again—that is, to beat the wall as hard as you can."[28] This frenzy is not only meant to be a protest against the whole order of Nature, the terrible fact that "every sort of consciousness . . . is a disease," or merely a protest against the historical enemies of Dostoyevsky—rationalism, meliorism, and science, the coxcomb fact that two plus two equals four.[29] The frenzy, in the form of caprice, is also directed against our individuality. That Dostoyevsky's "insect" can establish his identity only by forcing himself to collide ignominiously with an arrogant officer who does not even recognize his existence is of no importance. The important thing is that it is *he* who *forces* the recognition. This is freedom.

The grotesque image of this strange creature haunts modern literature and remains at the center of our dread. Its cracked reflections in some way or other penetrate the works of most European novelists. And its perverse truths, almost insupportable, infiltrate recent American fiction which does not stem only, as Hemingway claimed, from a book by Mark Twain called *Huckleberry Finn* but also from another, it may be argued with equal pertinence, by Dostoyevsky called *Notes from Underground*. The image, taken up, modified, and recreated by later novelists deserves further attention.

Conrad, we know, shared with Dostoyevsky more than the dubious heritage of a Slavic temper. His metaphysical romances of the seven seas subject the idea of heroism to an ironic rhetoric which is peculiarly modern, and his abiding interest in the theme of the double—his *Secret Sharer* and Dostoyevsky's *The Double* come to mind—probes the distempers of the modern self in a way that seems now familiar. While no character of his strictly reminds us of the hero of the *Notes*, the state of immersion, the desperation felt in the heart of darkness or in the underground habitations of consciousness, the surrender to the "destructive element," compel our terrified assent in the novels of both authors. Kurtz, in *Heart of Darkness*, had perhaps immersed himself too deeply, there where victim and victimizer become one, till he could distinguish only the horror. But Kurtz creeping on all fours in the night-time jungle and Lord Jim erect and dazzling in spotless white are still two sides of the same image, two sides separated really by the enormous distance between action and heroic intention. Conrad does not repudiate human striving. In a celebrated passage from *Lord Jim* he simply points to the way of fulfillment. "A man that is born falls into a dream like a man who falls into the sea," Conrad writes. "If he tries to climb out into the air as inexperienced people endeavor to do, he drowns. . . . The way is to the destructive element submit yourself. . . ."[30] The unintelligent brutality of existence leaves man no other choice.

It is, of course, the unintelligent brutality of existence that dominates the Dublin of Joyce's *Ulysses*; the city becomes a focus, in Eliot's famous words, to "the immense panorama of futility and anarchy which is contemporary history."[31] The proportions of the hero are further shrunken, his self pushed further underground in the world of memory and fantasy. The element to which Bloom submits himself, in humor and humility, is the ignominious element. Insult and pathos, loneliness and failure, are his familiars. Leopold Bloom, wandering Jew, mock Odysseus, and lowly Christ, finally appears to us, above all, as "Everyman or Noman."[32] He stands between Stephen Dedalus and Molly Bloom, between intelligence and nature, as a bathetic monument to the generosity of suffering. For intelligence, in the person of Stephen—he is Lucifer and Hamlet and Dedalus —can only cry: *Non serviam!* And Nature, in the person of Molly—Ceres, Hera, eternal Mother Earth—must endlessly murmur: Yes I will Yes. Man, meanwhile, goes clowning his sentimental way into eternity, unable to reconcile himself completely to one or the other.

The two heroes of Joyce and of Dostoyevsky show that humility lies on the other side of spite. But the clown in man has many disguises. He is Bloom, "one lonely last sardine of summer."[33] He is also, as we shall see, an insect, a sentient tubercle, at best a shaggy wolf. The self in recoil cannot afford to be choosy.

Dostoyevsky's metaphor of man as an insect inevitably calls to mind Kafka's story, "Metamorphosis," in which the narrator is transformed into a huge, hideous, and pathetic vermin. This, too, is self-degradation, a form of the self in recoil. This, too, is protest. The theme is everywhere in Kafka, in *The Castle*, in *The Trial*, in "The Penal Colony" or "The Judgment." Man is always judged, and found invariably guilty. He is the victim of an unappeasable power, a horrible and recurrent outrage, and even in his most serene moments he can only exclaim, like the Hunter Gracchus: "I am here, more than that I do not know, further than that I cannot go. My ship has no rudder, and it is driven by the wind that blows in the undermost regions of death."[34] The vision of man is as grotesque as that of Dostoyevsky; but it goes farther, denying man freedom, the sheer horror of choice, and denying him grace. Indeed, of man Kafka can only say, "He found the Archimedean point, but he used it against himself; it seems that he was permitted to find it only under this condition."[35] The lever which gives man mastery over his universe, moving worlds at the touch of a finger tip, is still the inbred dagger of the soul. In Kafka as in Dostoyevsky, the sense of compounded guilt and absurdity defines the point at which victimization and rebellion meet.[36]

This view of the human predicament will no doubt seem to many both exigent and extreme. It borders, people argue, on disease. Exactly. In the panoramic view of Thomas Mann, whose sane vision did not prevent him from cultivating a life-long interest in Kafka and Dostoyevsky, disease and even death become an ultimate response to life. The idea informs at least two of his masterpieces, *The Magic Mountain* and *Death in Venice,* and it hovers about his latest work, *The Confessions of Felix Krull.* Hans Castorp reflects, as if prompted by the hero of Dostoyevsky's *Notes,* "Disease was a perverse, a dissolute form of life. And life? Life itself? Was it perhaps only an infection, a sickening of matter? . . . The first step toward evil, toward desire and death, was taken precisely then, when there took place that first increase in the density of the spiritual, that pathologically luxuriant morbid growth. . . ."[37] But the radical disease of consciousness, which the hero of Dostoyevsky resented to the end of his spite, and to which the Kafka hero finally submits in a lucid nightmare, is transmuted by Thomas Mann into a condition of spiritual refulgence. It is thus that Mann is able to claim, with Nietzsche and Dostoyevsky in mind, that "certain attainments of the soul and the intellect are impossible *without disease, without insanity, without spiritual crime,* and the *great invalids* are *crucified victims,* sacrificed to humanity

26

and its advancement, to the broadening of its feeling and knowledge—in short, to its more *sublime health* [italics mine]."[38] Man, we see, pitches himself at the terrible limit of experience, as Lucifer did.

Mann's statement reminds us that grace, if it is to be found at all, lies deep in the soft core of violence. The saint and the criminal stand back to back on either side of the demonic. Both are protestants, both victims. But pure violence, like the demonic, has no reality in the public realm, the domain of action. Pure violence, as we shall repeatedly observe in modern fiction, seems almost the ultimate form of introspection. That the saint and the criminal, the suppliant and psychopath—they are conjoined in the recent literature of hipsterism and in such enduring figures as Greene's Pinkie and Faulkner's Christmas—partake of violence compulsively is no surprise. For untrammelled violence is not an act, it is merely a state; it is the experience of world negation. As Miss Arendt saw, the saint and the criminal are both lonely figures: ". . . the one being for, the other against, all men; they, therefore, remain outside the pale of human intercourse and are, politically, marginal figures who usually enter the historical scene in times of corruption, disintegration, and political bankruptcy. Because of its inherent tendency to disclose the agent together with the act, action needs for its full appearance the shining brightness we once called glory, and which is possible only in the public realm."[39]

It is perhaps unnecessary to recover for our age the Corneillian idea of glory, but when the focus of moral energy moves so far from the center of human effort in the world, losing itself in the domain of holy silence or demonic violence, then it is time to give vent to our anxiety. The dissociation of action from intelligence, we remember, is manifest in Dostoyevsky's *Notes* whose hero openly contemns the active life. The consequences of this attitude are not limited to the cult of inactivity, living in a hole, like the man from underground, or in a jar like the hero of Beckett's *The Unnamable*, living, if you will, in the "packing-box shanty on the city dump" thoughtfully reserved by the editors of *Life* for our most promising novelists. The consequences also involve the alienation of the moral and artistic imagination from things of this world, often leading to a criminal state of autonomy.

The rebel-victim, we see, is also the outsider in search of truth.[40] Harry Haller, in Hermann Hesse's *Steppenwolf*, is still an isolate genius of suffering "whose fate it is to live the whole riddle of human destiny heightened to the pitch of a personal torture, a personal hell."[41] He is still grappling with the radical multiplicities of the human ego, oscillating not merely between the wolf and the man, not merely between two poles, such as the body and the spirit, the saint and the sinner, but between "thousands and thousands."[42] In the "Treatise on the Steppenwolf," however, the outsider is finally made to reckon with the fact that man may be nothing more than a temporary agreement between warring opposites, nothing more, in fact, than "a bourgeois compromise"—such as Bloom!

The idea of man as a transient compromise in the universe entails the acceptance of permanent outrage. Harry Haller could find some redemption of that condition in love or art, or even in humor which reconciles all opposites, and in whose "imaginary realm the intricate and many-faceted ideal of all Steppenwolves finds its realization."[43] Other writers—Mauriac, Bernanos, Graham Greene—sought for their characters a solution more commensurate with their religious faith; for, as Colin Wilson has loudly noted, the problems of modern man, rebel, victim, or outsider, lend themselves to an intense religious apprehension which need not be specifically Christian.[44] Yet even the Christian novelists, so Jansenist they seem in their insistence on human depravity, manage to convey only the terrible intricacies of damnation. Thus, for instance, is the pursuit of damnation conceived in *Brighton Rock* as an appalling manifestation of the mercy of God. The modern Christian martyr, it seems, can aspire only to perdition.

To the religious and the humanist solutions of man's plight in the universe must be added the Existentialist. The basic question here is still one of freedom, the search for identity under the aspects of violence or alienation. Freedom, we recall, is known to the hero of the *Notes* only as caprice; he understands that men, himself included, must seek freedom and must be repelled and horrified by it. The same ambivalence haunts the quest of Kafka's characters. Beginning with Gide, however, the ambivalence is seemingly resolved in favor of positive action. Man asserts his liberty in a gratuitous act of murder, as in Lafcadio's case, in acts of social repudiation, or ruthless heroism, as in the case of Michel and Theseus. Freedom consists of revolt, against morality, against the social order, against history. But the blood-curdling price is one that only heroes and supermen can afford. In this direction, the Existentialist novelists go farther than Gide was willing to go, and their view is correspondingly more special. Victory, in their novels, depends on the certainty of defeat, *is* the process of defeat. But unlike the heroes of classical tragedy, their protagonists act in full foreknowledge of their fatality, act *only* in *despite* of that fatality. And there is never any reconciliation.

It is thus that Sartre understands man—a creature *condemned* to be free. Antoine Roquentin, in *The Nausea*, suffers from metaphysical disgust. His consciousness is like a decayed trap door through which the sordid impressions of his world endlessly sift. Nothing happens in his life, nothing begins or ends; Phenomena merely change, and Things, grotesque, obdurate, and unnamable, simply exist. Roquentin thinks: "I have only my body: a man entirely alone, with his lonely body, cannot indulge in memories; they pass through him. I shouldn't complain: all I wanted was to be free."[45] Thinking is his game, the famous Cartesian proof of existence his plaything. In Kafka's work, as Erich Heller perceived, a cursed Intelligence asserts its omnipresence; the Cartesian formula becomes: "I think, and therefore I am not."[46] Such negation of being is inadmissible to

Sartre; the proper formula should read: "My thought is *me*.
. . . At this very moment—it's frightful—if I exist, it is because
I am horrified at existing."[47] The change is less of an improve-
ment than it may seem. For as Roquentin comes to believe,
existence is nothing if not superfluous. Everything is *de trop*,
everything is rooted in the Absurd, the irreducible condition of
all reality. Man, we see, is not only a clown or a transient compromise, he is a contingency of existence. The way to true being,
seldom realized, lies through Nausea.

Sartre's doctrine that existence precedes essence, carried to its
atheistic conclusion, defines no limit to the idea of freedom
and gives no value to the concept of being. Camus, a far more
accomplished artist if not a more systematic thinker, starts with
his "absurdist" philosophy of man and reaches, in *The Rebel*
and *The Fall*, a more complex awareness of freedom. In his
early novel, *The Stranger*, Meursault surrenders to the absurd,
the destructive element, and loses his life, it seems, without
ever finding it. In the following novel, *The Plague*, a small
light of hope, even of redemption, flickers through the night
of human victimization. Doctor Rieux says: "All I maintain
is that on this earth there are pestilences and there are victims,
and it's up to us, as far as possible, not to join forces with the
pestilences. . . . I decided to take, in every predicament, the
victim's side, so as to reduce the damage done. Among them,
I can at least try to understand how one attains to the third
category: in other words, to peace."[48] To join the victims is an
act of rebellion against and alienation from the prevalent norm.
But such an act is never purely nugatory. "Rebellion," Camus
wrote, "though apparently negative, since it creates nothing, is
profoundly positive in that it reveals the part of man which
must always be defended."[49] Rebellion is therefore an aspiration
to order, a means of lifting pain and evil from personal to
collective experience. For the rebel-victim, the Cartesian argument par excellence is: "I rebel—therefore *we* exist [italics
mine]."[50]

III

The problem of the anti-hero is essentially one of identity. His search is for existential fulfillment, that is, for freedom and self-definition. What he hopes to find is a position he can take within himself. Society may modulate his awareness of his situation, but only existence determines his stand. The recoil of the modern self is its way of taking a stand. The retreat weakens its involvement in the living world. It leads it in the ways of violence and alienation, augments its sense of guilt and absurdity, and affords it no objective standard for evaluating the worth of human action. But living in the world exclusively, living in what Ortega Y Gasset has called the Other, is also brutish and deadening. Complete immersion in the otherness of things is a ghastlier form of alienation: it is alienation from the self. "Without a strategic retreat into the self," Ortega rightly notes, "without vigilant thought, human life is impossible."[51] It is precisely in fear of the Other—total loss of selfhood—that the modern conscience has fallen back on its internal resources. The schizophrenic goes too far in that direction, the rebel-victim remains in the field of our vision.

Camus' statement, "I rebel—therefore we exist," brings to surface a dialectic that has been implicit in all the works we have viewed. In its naked form, the dialectic can be seen as an interplay between the essential Yes and the radical No, two piercing utterances beyond which the human voice cannot rise. Such utterances may sometimes blend. It is only silence they equally abhor. In the modern novel, man seems to overcome the contradictions of his experience, its destructive or demonic element, by assuming the role of the anti-hero, the rebel-victim. The rebel denies without saying No to life, the victim succumbs without saying Yes to oppression. Both acts are, in a sense, identical: they affirm the human against the nonhuman. The figure of modern man, when he chooses to assert his full manhood, always bears the brave indissoluble aspects of Prometheus and Sisyphus—the eternal rebel and the eternal victim. The paradox is resolved when man cries, in the ringing words of Jaspers, "Although I am an anvil, as a hammer I can consummate what I must suffer."[52] Sparks from the same anvil were struck when Christ said to his disciples, "For whosoever will save his life shall lose it; and whosoever will lose his life for my sake shall find it."[53]

The condition of modern life may not be more desperate, as relativists sapiently remind us, than those which prevailed in any earlier age. Men, as usual, like to exaggerate their predicament to convince themselves, if nothing else, that they are still alive. All this is beside the point. It is certainly not the wretchedness of modern existence that we have sought to illustrate in this chapter, but rather man's peculiar awareness of his own situation. This awareness is both critical and adverse. The spirit of recoil in modern literature continues to affirm itself despite all our bounties.

The figure of the rebel-victim, however, represents but a single incarnation of the eternal dialectic between the primary Yes and primary No. He is man's answer to the invitation that he abolish himself. But the world has traditionally extended another invitation to the self: the invitation to become an honorable part of it, to become *initiated*. The initiate is the second major incarnation of the dialectic between affirmation and denial. His response is the other major response to experience. And his chosen home is the land which was once full of promises: America.

It may have been possible to distinguish clearly between Europe and America in the time of Whitman and Emerson. Today we lack the confidence such clarity requires. Uncle Sam, never young, is hoary as ever. Europe, we think, has been in America from the beginning; and is not Europe being taken over by America in our days? (Mark Twain noted, more than half a century ago, how Europe was already beginning to emulate American social habits.) Offhand, it may seem right to consider the idea of victimization in the context of European experience, and natural to look for the idea of initiation in America. Such a view has more elegance than truth to recommend it.

America is not Europe and it is not the self-begotten country it once conceived itself to be. The contemporary American novel is part of the contemporary world, which is perhaps more uniform than any period since the Middle Ages. It is also the fruit of a flourishing native tradition. America has known *both* innocence and guilt, has evolved the patterns both of initiation and defeat in a unique ratio. The American novel comes to contemporary experience from a road Europe did not take, and its vision of the self in recoil is enriched by a vision Europe did not share. What we have observed in this chapter is a dominant image of the modern self. What remains to be seen is the American form of that image, personified by the *converging figures of the initiate and the victim.*

CHAPTER 2

THE DIALECTIC OF INITIATION
IN AMERICA

It was wonderful to find America, but it would have been more wonderful to miss it.—MARK TWAIN, *Pudd'nhead Wilson's Calendar*

I

IT IS nowadays proper to invoke the ideas of innocence and experience in any knowing discussion of American letters— as it is proper, say, to rise to the Stars and Stripes, hat clutched next to the heart. The received argument usually runs as follows: half a century ago, we used to say that the great and abiding theme of American literature was the theme innocence; now, after fifty full years of strange history, we recognize that America has at last come of age, that it has plucked the fruit of knowledge and that, in doing so, its writers have plainly risen to the assumptions of a world literature. The Song of Innocence, we are asked to believe, has finally given way to the Burden of Experience.

The fact, of course, is that innocence has *not* come to an end in America—it has become more radical—nor has guilt ever been absent from it. The relation between the two has been changing throughout our history, lending to each period its particular character. At present, the fact of guilt commands our interest and compels our allegiance. But it is important to perceive, as Leslie Fiedler did, that America is the only place where the encounter between innocence and guilt is still a meaningful reality.[1]

Our concern is the encounter between the self and the world in fiction, that confrontation of the "hero" with experience which may assume the form of initiation or victimization. Now initiation may be understood as a process leading through right action and consecrated knowledge to a *viable* mode of life *in the world*. Its end is *confirmation*. The result of victimization, however, is *renunciation*. Its characteristic mode is *estrangement from the world*, and its values are chiefly inward and transcendental. Whether the hero elects one or the other of these modes to fulfill his destiny largely depends on the particular world in which he finds himself. Though man is free to reject the image which culture has of him, his relation to the world must still be determined by that image. The context of the individual encounter between self and world is therefore defined, to a large extent, by the permissive or limiting dispositions of culture. In the American experience, these dispositions have appeared as a constant dialectic between innocence and guilt, hope and disenchantment, love and work, expansiveness and recoil. One side is the American Dream, the other, despite Henry Miller, not quite a Nightmare.

II

America was promises but paradox too. Discovered by a Genoese, pioneered by Saxon and Dutch, it was peopled by the brave, the humble, and the disaffected from the world over. Men as different as Calvin and Rousseau shaped its conscience, and the vast unconscionable wilderness of the continent shaped it more. Its experience was both prodigal and exigent, and it often remained at the poles.

Providence had brought God's Chosen People past a "sea of troubles" safely to Plymouth, but had omitted to provide them with the cornucopia of plenty: "They had now no friends to welcome them nor inns to entertain or refresh their weather-beaten bodies," wrote William Bradford. "And for the season it was winter. . . . Besides, what could they see but a hideous and desolate wilderness, full of wild beasts and wild men. . . .

Neither could they, as it were, go up to the top of Pisgah to view from this wilderness a more goodly country to feed their hopes. . . ."[2] But in the Puritan oligarchy which they established, the New England "saints" turned to "tithing men" watching jealously over the activities of their neighbors. Indians were exterminated; a prosperous fishing industry was started; the spiritual declension of the Chosen People began. The Old Adam had obviously crossed with the dark-browed Pilgrims to the New World. Untrammeled freedom could be practiced only at the outermost fringes of the frontier which often attracted the lawless, the desperate, and the improvident. "Thus are our first steps trod, thus are our first trees felled, in general, by the most vicious of our people," St. Jean de Crèvecoeur reported in his letters.[3] The forerunners of civilization were, like Leatherstocking, men who hated it—though seldom did they possess his probity. The worldly "saint" and visionary "anarchist" stand at the threshold of our history. It is as Loren Baritz, taking his cue from D. H. Lawrence, astutely perceived: "The fall of the People, the rape of the Land, the liquidation of the Indian— these were the formative sins of God's Country, the consciousness of which contributed to the birth of culture. Concretely, the fall contributed to secularism, the rape to materialism, and genocide to imperialism."[4]

America, we see, was not born blameless. It found ways from the start of thwarting the individual quest for an Eldorado that moved ever westward, always a step ahead, as man moved toward the setting sun. But if American Innocence means anything, it must mean just this: that every generation, native or foreign-born, began its task anew despite the secret betrayals of history. For them the frontiers of land or sea or space never seem to close. To this tendency, another, which we call Experience, has run counter; it is the urge to reflect on the past and redeem it. There is always the Territory Ahead to which Huck Finn can "light out." Evil could be left behind, and in the titanic struggle with Nature, man could still emerge victorious.

But there is always, too, the Eden we lost and which we persistently attempt to recapture by transforming the substance of our failure, *our passion*, into values for the conduct of life. The American dialectic, if so abstract a thing can take root in any soil, is thus seen as a running debate between Utopia and Eden, between the active will moving ever forward in time and space, unburdened by the memory of guilt, and the reflective or passional conscience moving toward the past in hope of knowledge or atonement. It is as if in our life, as in our history, the failures of the American Dream were constantly reenacted—and sporadically redeemed. So long as it was possible to start anew— to emigrate, to invent, plan or reform—the memory of guilt could be ignored. America remains, in dwindling measure, a persistent *escape toward freedom* which the American conscience perpetually qualifies. The power of that dialectic is richly attested by our history.

If we are to believe Crèvecoeur, the utopian transformation in the European immigrant began the moment he stepped down the gangplank: "He no sooner breathes our air than he forms schemes, and embarks in designs he never would have thought of in his own country."[5] Whitman utters his "barbaric yawp," now unfashionable; Emerson celebrates the "aboriginal self" for whose sake the perfection of the world solely exists; and Howells enjoins novelists to concern themselves with the "smiling aspects" of life as being the more American. And the obverse of the coin? "Doom! Doom! Doom! Something seems to whisper it in the very dark trees of America. Doom!" Lawrence intones in *Studies in Classic American Literature*, a dark, depth-dredging, and exasperating book into which every critic of American letters, it seems, must dip his fingers to cross himself.[6] Hawthorne, Melville, and Henry Adams, as everyone knows, bear Lawrence out. The "plain old Adam" of Emerson, standing against the whole world, stands really against Melville's Ahab who says, "I feel deadly faint, and bowed, and humped, as though I were Adam staggering beneath the piled centuries since Paradise. . . ."[7]

Events appear simpler in synoptic light than they are in the shadowy realms of experience. The lines of dialectic in American history are perhaps more fluid than the foregoing analysis might imply, the terms of the dialectic more capricious—no one who has read Whitman and Hawthorne alertly can deny them a common ground. Yet the function of dialectic is precisely to define the range of ambiguities which between every two poles must lie; it is a mode of grasping contradictions and transcending paradox.

The contradictions of experience in America have created the morality of the American novel and created its form. They constitute the obdurate stuff which the novel must compel into shape; and they comprise the stuff of which the life of the novelist, like that of his characters, is made. They are indeed themselves the provisions of culture which regulate the response of the self, limiting its hopes and pledging its safeguards. The specific nature of that response within the framework of our dialectic requires further elucidation.

At first glance, the utopian motive seems an affirmative projection of the self into the active life, and the Edenic a nostalgic withdrawal of the self from it. A more sober view, however, will discover in both motives, carried far enough, a mode of escape from that realm of uncertainty and compromise which *is* the world. Both, in a sense, are a form of radical innocence. Looking too far ahead or too far back amounts to the same thing: escape from the present, escape from time and death. For innocence may be located at either end of history, a little before or a little after, and, as we have noted, belief in primal innocence in no way contradicts belief in ultimate perfection. Americans who, it is said, live only on the wings of the future, are supremely conscious of youth and have developed the consciousness of it into a strict ceremonial of which the mandarins are swaddled infants. Childhood and youth satisfy

38

at once the demands of our past and the hopes of our future. This is our national neurosis, the form of *our recoil from an actual world* that brings Failure, Age, and Death.

But the dialectic of American culture supplies, besides the neurosis of innocence, a further impediment to initiation, a second motive for recoil. This, for lack of a better name, may be called the spirit of contradiction. Contradiction is always inherent in every *beginning*. History, in fact, knows no beginning, only development. The child is always father to the man. America, which began as a "contractual" society without a "prehistory," as F. G. Friedman would have it, began certainly as a contradiction.[8] The emblem of that contradiction is still the antithesis between Eden and Utopia based on an unresolved view of man's place in the world. Hence the manifold contrasts between nature and civilization, man and society, freedom and authority, instinct and mind, ideal and action, spirit and matter which Puritanism, Transcendentalism, and Naturalism all failed to reconcile in American culture.

The American, we saw, was both dreamer and rapist, builder of empires and misanthrope, Evangel and Faust—does not Ahab make Faust seem a sickly don? He envisaged a universal brotherhood, a love strong and wide and lasting as the land itself, yet he imposed his will ruthlessly on man and nature alike. To the individual he vouchsafed great liberties, and to the crowd he allowed oppressive powers. He was, therefore, at once lonely and gregarious, private and sociable. Loving freedom and equality, he seldom understood the proper limits of authority. He honored the "natural man," the generosity of instinct rather than of the mind, yet the symbols of status and wealth became his measure. Too often an idealist at heart, he permitted his democratic denial of consciousness, which Santayana saw as a form of "inverted idealism," to bolster a pragmatic and materialistic temper and to nourish anti-intellectualism.[9] Energy could be gauged by works, but inactivity is a terrible void. Who has not seen the void in the faces of Americans on a holiday?

Yet despite his frenzied will to conquer his environment, despite his sharp acquisitiveness and boyish delight in gadgetry, despite his eager conformity to a social norm, the American always put a high value on love, spirit, and the unconditioned self.[10] Anyone who has seen these angels of mercy in the garb of an airline hostess smile will understand Maritain when he says: "Deep beneath the anonymous American smile there is a feeling that is evangelical in origin—compassion for men, a desire to make life tolerable. This symbolic smile is a kind of anonymous reply of the human soul, which refuses to acknowledge itself vanquished by the pressure of the assembly line, or the big anonymous machinery of modern civilization."[11]

The neurosis of innocence, we found, is a regressive force that prevents the self from participating fully in the world. The spirit of contradiction disrupts the vital nexus of private will and public ordinance on which the life of man in society depends. As a result, the greatest values affirmed by the American conscience have often been affirmed *against* the ruling spirit of the land. "Where the voice of the majority is by definition affirmative," Harry Levin writes, "the spirit of independence is likeliest to manifest itself by employing the negative: by saying *no* in thunder—as Melville wrote to Hawthorne—though bidden by the devil himself to say *yes*."[12] Even so sanguine a pragmatist as William James advocated "the self-governing resistance of the ego to the world"; and as we might expect from his more somber brother, Henry chided America for being "a colossal recipe for the creation of arrears."[13] Resistance, rebellion, denial—these have been the ultimate defenses of the self in America as they have been in a continent America hoped to leave behind.

The step from resistance to victimization has always been short and easy to take. It is particularly easy when the resources of revolt are severely limited by the organization of society. As we have had occasion to observe in the last chapter, this is precisely the condition of the modern world. In America, the transition to victimization is witnessed, paradoxically, in the process of initiation.

One hardly needs to be an expert as Gesell is on the subject to realize that adolescence is an abrasive process of adjustment to conflicting claims. Indeed, the life of the adolescent or youth still in his teens mirrors clearly the ambiguities of rejection and affirmation, revolt and conformity, hope and disenchantment, observed in the culture at large. In his life as in our history, the fallacies of innocence and the new slate are exemplified. His predicament reflects the predicament of the self in America. The image he presents foreshadows the new image of man in contemporary fiction.

III

Initiation can be understood for our purpose as the first existential ordeal, crisis, or encounter with experience in the life of a youth. Its ideal aim is knowledge, recognition, and confirmation in the world, to which the actions of the initiate, however painful, must tend. It is, quite simply, the viable mode of confronting adult realities.

In the natural hierarchy of initiates in America, none, it seems, takes precedence over the irreverent Huck Finn. The comic, mordant lessons of Huck's experience lead him through the range of human corruption to a central ironic decision: Huck remains loyal to Jim, a runaway slave, at the risk of subverting his social conscience. The decision asserts the triumph of love and rejects the casuistries of society. In a famous passage, Huck reflects: "Then I thought a minute and says to myself, hold on; s'pose you'd 'a 'done right and give Jim up, would you felt better than what you do now? No, says I, I'd feel bad. . . . Well, then, says I, what's the use of you learning to do right when it's troublesome to do right and ain't no trouble to do wrong, and the wages is just the same?"[14] Instinct, we see, wins over logic as love does over "conscience." But the opposition between Nature—the river—and Civilization—the towns on the banks—is more simple than the facts of the novel warrant. The raft is a third estate. It is not, after all, a floating Eden; if anything, it is rather Noah's ark. The two people on it are locked in an anomalous situation; nor can they escape the guilt of a land which stays always within sight. The fact of slavery and the dream of the Open Road are thoroughly interfused in the novel.[15] Huck's initiation seems therefore a mixed and incomplete thing. It is true that Huck gains a first-hand knowledge of evil, and also true that he puts his knowledge to the test of a decision. But his final decision is to "light out for the territory ahead."[16] He does not become a part of the world—he's been there before, he claims. Indeed, Twain transforms the process of Huck's initiation into an extended criticism of the world itself, the implication being that while acceptance of the world is ultimately inescapable, the act of acceptance is a tragic one, as the Fall of Adam was both tragic and necessary. To preserve the comic character of the novel and elude the ambiguities of initiation to which we have just referred, Twain is forced to keep the structure of the novel open-ended, indeterminate. Yet the novel is undoubtedly an artistic triumph, for no one really cares to know what finally becomes of the Mississippi scamp.

Stephen Crane's *The Red Badge of Courage* probes a narrower area of moral significance—Henry Fleming is never allowed to gain as large an access to self-knowledge as Huck does. Fleming's panicky desertion under fire and voluntary return to the front is so punctuated by arrogance and humility, guilt and self-pity, that the novel may be considered a series of partial initiations. These cumulatively reveal to the reader the inadequacies of idealism, the subtleties of self-deception, and the vast, brutal anonymity of war, in which the private response and the public demand are so fiercely, so hopelessly, at odds. War—specifically the Civil War, that depthless shudder of American history, that tragic betrayal of blood and language brotherhood—provides the supreme test of man's relation to men in general. It is the occasion of murder and self-sacrifice, insane aggression and solidarity unto death. Running away from the battle scene for his life, Fleming finds some solace in the spectacle of a scampering squirrel, responding to the instinct of self-preservation. He decides to return, to re-integrate himself into the group, only when he beholds the hideous death of his friend, Jim Conklin, and experiences the full force of his guilt. Initiation takes the classic pattern of withdrawal and return; its context is the conflict between social and instinctive behavior, ideal choice and biological necessity. What the vivid, inflamed style of Crane marvelously creates is the ambience of individual passion and natural decay indissolubly mixed—the scene in which Fleming discovers a decomposing body in a chapel-like copse bathed in religious half-light comes to mind. Again, the tragic ambiguity of initiation is present. The plot of the novel indicates that the initiation of Henry Fleming, by his own choice, is finally successful; the style, in contradiction, questions the freedom of any choice and constantly refers to the radical antithesis between Man and Society, Nature and Spirit.

Daisy Miller is an "initiate" of a different kind. It is by conscious choice rather than necessity that she immolates herself to her own innocence. Huck and Henry pursue the process of initiation in fits and starts; James's heroine rejects it point blank. She will accept life only on her own terms, and will not compromise her innocence or ignorance or conscience—call it what you like—even for the sake of love. When she fails to win the unconditional trust of Winterbourne, she dies of Roman fever. It seems as simple as that. For Daisy takes pride in her American upbringing. Her most characteristic action in the novel is also the most crucial: she refuses the protective sanctions of Mrs. Walker's carriage, choosing rather to promenade in the Pincian Gardens, escorted by a shady suitor. In so doing she incurs the ruthless censure of a society based on strict assumptions. But in so doing she also affirms her faith in the autonomy of candor, in the rights of the individual against those of the group, in Protestant conscience against Catholic form. She is, in short, a rebel, and the price of her rebellion is death. But the splendid —or is it quixotic?—gesture does not escape the irony of James. As Dupee saw, the novel is "addressed critically to the *sentiment* of the American girl, and of American 'innocence' generally— the kind of sentiment which, as James was aware, frequently did duty for realism in the native mind."[17] The dialectic of innocence and experience is symbolized, on one level, by the contrasts between the bracing winter mornings of Schenectady and the miasmic spring evenings of the Colosseum, and rendered, on a deeper level, by the ambiguous point of view of Winterbourne, who is neither a "real" American, as Daisy suspected, nor a native European, but a resident of Geneva. The ambiguity is functional; for James knew that if initiation to the world was sometimes tragic, the refusal of initiation was more often pathetic. Indeed, his great heroines, from Catherine Sloper to Millie Theale, show that it is in sacrifice, and not merely in refusal, that the complex imperatives of self and world are finally reconciled.

The prototypes of initiation we have just considered all come from the late nineteenth century. In each case the opportunity for choice, for self-determining action, was present. Such action, we saw, led in varying degrees—greatest in the instance of Huck Finn, least in that of Daisy Miller—to a fuller confrontation of the self with reality. The hero retains something "heroic." But in each case, too, the contradictions of initiation were apparent. The tendency was already present to elude final confirmation, to transform initiation into renunciation. Innocence, we saw, had not so much come to an end as begun to lend itself to the uses of defeat.

It remained for the twentieth century to pick up the delicate reverberations of Daisy's defeat, which is also her apotheosis, and to counterpoint against them the pathos, whimsey, or despair of a more harried consciousness. At once more violent and more vulnerable, the adolescent in modern literature reflects in turbulent patterns that distinctive response of the modern self we have characterized by the strategy of recoil. The burden of initiation becomes increasingly heavier, its viability more painful and uncertain to achieve.

The growing burden of initiation can be understood with reference to the experience of disillusionment, revolt, and collapse of norms following the first world war which so many critics—Malcolm Cowley, Frederick Allen, Frederick Hoffman, John Aldridge—have already amplified.[18] It may be accounted for, in a more general view, by those assaults on the modern self we have expounded in the previous chapter, and which e. e. cummings hauntingly dramatized in *The Enormous Room*. It can be observed at closer range in the image of adolescent heroes, the creation of writers from Dreiser to William Faulkner, whose encounter with experience confers less value on worldly triumph than on defeat. That defeat creates its own peculiar values—they are the ruling values of recent fiction, as Aldridge failed to see—will be sufficiently clear in the following pages as it was in the case of the European novelists we have already viewed.

To the interest in the adolescent hero and the failure of his initiation, the influences of Naturalism, Primitivism or Freudianism, and Romanticism in the twentieth century, compounding their powers of dissent from the world to those of the American dialectic, all have made their contribution.

The Naturalists, invariably concerned with the conditioning role of society and the biological necessities of existence, found in the situation of youths like Maggie, Clyde Griffiths, or Studs Lonigan an exemplary subject. Joseph Wood Krutch's argument, in *The Modern Temper*, that man, faced with the destruction of his optimistic illusions about the world, and unable to retrieve his innocence, was doomed as an animal to an absurd fate, may have further encouraged novelists who shared his view to see in the ritual of adolescent initiation the representative dilemma of modern man in a scientific and valueless society.[19] One thing is certain: the Naturalists understood the discords of Spirit and Nature, free protest and iron-bound determinism, and though they could not always reconcile these conflicts in the forms of fiction, they went far toward clearing the air from fulsome or sentimental pieties.

"As I see him," Dreiser glumly said, "man is more led or pushed than he is leading or pushing."[20] This is the simple idea to which all apprehensions of victimization revert. The idea, of course, is central to *An American Tragedy*, the book which Dreiser first thought of entitling *Mirage*, after the American Dream, and which few others have equalled in probing the tenebrous relations of sex, success, and justice in our culture. The wages of Clyde Griffiths' ambitions in the world are crime, isolation, execution. Yet his ambitions were in accord with that bright hope of self-betterment America was never supposed to revoke. Clyde was weak: "perhaps too pliable and sensual and impractical and dreamy a mind."[21] Yet if the novel persuades us of anything, it is that Clyde's fate is *not* commensurate with his weakness. In a society reputed to be democratic, the cards are stacked against him, and they are all trumps: power, wealth, family. The operations of justice, seldom infallible this side of heaven, are not above discriminating between the humble and the mighty. More: the "chemic compulsions" of sexuality run counter to the social aspirations of man, leaving, for the poor, at least, no surcease from anguish. There is no question of initiation where Clyde is concerned, as there is none of choice.

It was on assumptions less stringent than these that Farrell based his Studs Lonigan trilogy. Farrell's view was less cosmic than Dreiser's and perhaps more social, and it lent itself to the urge for reform more readily. Between the youth of the two men much had intervened. Before 1924, when the quota system was imposed, the great influx of immigrants, first from Ireland,

and then from south and eastern Europe, was absorbed mainly by the big cities whose wretched labor force these immigrants constituted. Prohibition had come and gone, and the Depression lengthened a thousand bread lines the country over. An end to the flamboyant individualism of the Twenties was proclaimed; in the Thirties, intellectuals passionately felt, in the words of Arvin, "that to cooperate with an inhuman system is to be personally corrupted and demoralized."[22] Mencken, to be sure, still rasped about the superman, and Babbitt solemnly considered the creative possibilities of a leisure class, but for most writers the anger of Veblen and Ludwig Lewisohn was infinitely more pertinent. The quest for a socialized Utopia, dormant since Bellamy, was on again. For Farrell, anti-utopia was located in Chicago, South Side, on 58th Street.

Again, in anti-utopia there can be no initiation, only martyrdom. The world in which young Lonigan grows is one of pervasive spiritual poverty, without beauty, love, or hope. Boredom and violence are the order of each dismal day. One sees the Lonigan gang "shagging" Negroes and Jews, or indulging in sexual activity like some tireless machine; one never sees them at work or really at play. At school there is dogma; at home, hypocrisy; brutality is on the streets. For Studs, a normal lower-middle-class boy, as Farrell emphasizes in the preface to his trilogy, there is no forward movement at all. There is only a nostalgic awareness of the great moments in his life: a fist fight with Weary Reilly, a run on the football field, a tender moment with Lucy Scanlan up in a tree. On the dirty gray dawn of New Year's Day, 1929, a Negro finds an unconscious figure in the gutter, eyes puffed black, nose bent and swollen, coat odorous with vomit: "It was Studs Lonigan, who had once, as a boy, stood before Charles Bathcellar's poolroom thinking that, some day, he would grow up to be strong, and tough, and the real stuff."[23]

In Naturalism, we see, Society and Nature conspire against Man. Initiation is merely submission to forces man seldom can control. And the value bestowed on outrage is implicit in authorial protest: the call for a better social order, the definition of man's humanity within the bounds of necessity and defeat. Naturalism observes the human situation from an external vantage; Primitivism and Romanticism, from a point located within the self.

Primitivism proposes the candor of the naked emotion rather than the naked fact. Under its influence, the novel set itself to explore those instinctual gestures and primary sensations which adolescents have long favored before black leather jackets and tight jeans came into vogue, or Brando and James Dean scowled and muscled their way into our communal heart. The caged sensitivity, the lurid restraint often portrayed by these actors on the screen, find a more responsible antecedent in Hemingway's Nick Adams; and who knows but that they may ultimately derive from the frenzied image of Rimbaud's life? But more relevant than Rimbaud's brand of romantic primitivism is Bergson's subjectivist philosophy. As Justin O'Brien noted in his study, *The Novel of Adolescence in France*, the literary adherents of Bergson considered adolescent initiation a phase of human development in which society had not yet succeeded in separating the "real I" from its "symbolic representations."[24] To the evocation of this "real I" by the printed word, Gertrude Stein gave her most scrupulous attention. Some years later, when the impact of Freud began to be felt in America, Sherwood Anderson applied his awkward intuition to the same end.

Gertrude Stein's story "Melanctha," published in *Three Lives*, assigns to the instinctual life some of the values James's novella assigned to moral innocence—Daisy and Melanctha are sisters of light and dark, bound to one another by a chastity of heart for which the world has little use. As Daisy insisted on her idea of innocence, Melanctha, with her "break-neck" courage and boundless, formless capacity for love, insists on her view of freedom and experience. Yet the experience of Melanctha is

48

still a kind of radical innocence. It acknowledges no limit; it borders on wisdom without ever entering its tragic realm. Daisy refuses initiation and dies of Roman fever; Melanctha rushes headlong beyond initiation and dies of consumption. In either case no tragic recognition is achieved, and no viable mode of life in the world attained.

The intimate view of the human psyche allies itself naturally with Freudian psychology.[25] In the late Teens and early Twenties, the climate of Freudian thought proved congenial to the Primitivist writer on at least three grounds. It encouraged, first, his interest in prerational or subconscious motives, and in the subtle relations between dream and waking, fantasy and reality, normality and abnormality, wish and repression. Such interests, we now realize, extended the range of fiction to recesses of the soul which only the greatest writers had earlier explored. Freudian thought also provided, as we saw, new means of comprehending the stubborn resistance of the ego to the requirements of civilization. Freud believed that the tensions between the pleasure and reality principles, beginning in early childhood, continued through adolescence. These tensions reached their climax in the crisis of puberty when the Oedipal ambivalences of revolt and authority, guilt and gratification, entered their last formative phase. It was to be expected, therefore, that under the general influence of psychoanalysis novelists should take a deeper interest in the moment of initiation which reflects so clearly the ambiguities of American culture itself. Finally, the importance accorded to the power of sexuality in Freudian theory gave momentum to the crusade for sexual emancipation which had begun before Freud's impact reached America, and had invited in its sordid course Comstockery and the Mann Act.[26]

Labeled at one time by critics "the American Freudian," Sherwood Anderson denied repeatedly that he had ever read Freud.[27] He need not have. Novels like *Dark Laughter* and *Many Marriages*, stories like "I Want to Know Why," "Death in the Woods," and "The Man Who Became a Woman," with-

out owing a specific debt to Freudian theory, probe imaginatively
the same instinctual mysteries Freud kept at the center of his
system. This is apparent even in Anderson's earlier and perhaps
best work, *Winesburg, Ohio*. These stories, made up, as it were,
of the odds and ends of emotions that seldom see the light of
day, evoke loneliness, vague, sensual stirrings, crippled hopes.
The stories are studies of frustration and partial awakening in
the lives of inarticulate people caught between the stern Puritan
god and the bitch-goddess of success. Innocence is tucked away
in the past—when the land was still young and unblighted,
when the child ran freely in the cornfields—or else it is tucked
deep in the subconscious. The recurrent motif of *Winesburg* is
adolescence. "When in speaking of *Winesburg* you used the
word adolescence you struck more nearly than you thought,"
Anderson wrote to Van Wyck Brooks. "I am immature, will
live and die immature."[28] The immaturity of Anderson, which
his genius too eagerly confesses, derives from an obsession with
the *uncreated*: innocence lost, wasted desire, youth licked before
it starts, truth misshapen into a grotesque parody of itself. All
is arrest, as perpetual adolescence must be. All is arrest, as the
grotesque is frozen in its shapelessness. "It was his notion that
the moment one of the people took one of the truths to himself,
called it his truth," Anderson writes in "The Book of the
Grotesques," "and tried to live his life by it, he became a
grotesque and the truth he embraced became a falsehood."[29]
The grotesque, we see, is a product of elimination, the reduction
of all truths to one. It is a form of worldly *renunciation*, an
arrest of development, an *idée fixe* reality is not allowed to
modify. From a genetic point of view, grotesques have no viability. They are stillborn like the monstrous specimens of chicken,
kept in a jar by the restaurant owner in the story called "The
Egg." "Grotesques are born out of eggs as out of people . . . ,"
Anderson writes in that story. "The things do not live. They go
quickly back to the hand of their maker that has for a moment
trembled."[30] The grotesque is uncreated. But it is also, in people,

50

a kind of inwardness gone sour, a perverse insistence on *subjectivity*. It is innocence deformed and preying upon itself. The aim of the grotesque, in fact, *is to perpetuate the victim in the self*. No wonder that Doctor Parcival thinks all wisdom can be contained in a single idea (which all the grotesque characters of *Winesburg* exemplify): "It is this—that everyone in the world is Christ and they are all crucified."[31] No wonder that initiation seems quite beyond the capacity of youth. For David Harding, Seth Richmond, and Elmer Cowley, there is only the isolated moment of terror, shame, escape, the broken gesture trailing into silence. For George Willard, whose varied encounters in the book amount to something of an initiation, there is the retrospective glance. Here is the elegiac mood with which he leaves Winesburg for the great world: "The mood that had taken possession of him was a thing known to men and unknown to boys. He felt old and tired. Memories awoke in him. To his mind his new sense of maturity set him apart, made him a half-tragic figure. . . . There is a time in the life of everybody when he for the first time takes a backward view of life. Perhaps that is the moment he crosses the line into manhood. . . . The sadness of sophistication has come to the boy. With a little gasp he sees himself as merely a leaf blown by the wind through the streets of his village."[32] The passage is a milestone in the Edenic consciousness of American letters. When youth escapes the grotesque fate of the sufferer, it can only look backward in time and feel like "a leaf blown by the wind."

Primitivism, it seems, recognizes the validity of human instincts and seeks to defend their integrity against the encroachments of an order ruled by abstract social goals. But Primitivism seldom has the means of mediating successfully between the needs of the self and the demands of civilization. Man may submit to the aimless flow of experience, as did Melanctha, or clutch a single moment, like Anderson's characters, letting the world flow by. The result is either oblivion or immolation.

Primitivist regression and Romantic nostalgia put the self in the same defensive position vis-à-vis the world. Rousseau in his *Confessions* and Goethe in *The Sorrows of Young Werther* began, we know, that intimate exercise in self-revelation and disenchantment which may have made it possible, two centuries after, for Fitzgerald, Wolfe, and Salinger to strike their particular notes. The Romantic gifts of introspection and disillusionment, rebelliousness and heroic posturing, were the boons of adolescents in every age. The moment was particularly suited for them in the Twenties, rife as the decade was with cynicism and abandon, zest and despair. In his retrospective preface to *Three Soldiers*, first published in 1921, Dos Passos wrote some thirteen years later:

The memory of the spring of 1919 has not faded enough. Any spring is a time of overturn, but then Lenin was alive, the Seattle general strike had seemed a beginning of the flood instead of the beginning of the ebb, Americans in Paris were groggy with theatre and painting and music; Picasso was to rebuild the eye, Stravinsky was cramming the Russian steppes into our ears, currents of energy seemed breaking out everywhere as young guys climbed out of their uniforms, imperial America was all shiny with the new idea of Ritz. . . .[33]

It may be wise, for once, to let the Twenties rest in their tarnished glory. Dos Passos' statement stands for the feeling of many writers of his time who, after the initial bloody shock of World War I, after the craze and blaze which followed it, returned to their own youth in search of light, hope, or sanity, and reenacted in their fiction their own initiation.

No one spoke for "imperial America," all shiny with the new idea of Ritz, better than Scott Fitzgerald, and few wrote a more implausible first novel than *This Side of Paradise*. The book is dedicated to the simple proposition Fitzgerald called in "The Diamond Big as the Ritz" "the shabby gift of disillusion." Young Amory Blaine is the Romantic hero par excellence: aristocratic, imaginative, self-indulgent, and exquisitely modulated, a Celt to his finger tips. The decor is appropriate; there are the Gothic towers of Princeton bathed in moonlight, liturgical conversations with a cardinal, love affairs with a bevy of ineffable beauties. Despite all this, the novel possesses an underlying intuition into the pathos of a whole generation. Blaine, nurtured on the endless inexhaustibility of romance, gets to know in the course of the action something about death —the death of a friend, Humbird, or the death-wish of an entire generation—about the ruthlessness of the rich and the inequities of social life, about the subtleties of his own egotism and the lambent deceptions of his imagination. He perceives that the war had changed his world irrevocably, and wiped out the possibilities of heroic individualism: all the top-booted genera- tions of Burr and Light-Horse Harry Lee. Conscious, at the end of the novel, that his social, erotic, and artistic aspirations had failed him, he stands once again on the campus that had fostered so many illusions and stretching his arms out to "the crystalline sky," he cries out, "I know myself . . . but that is all."[34] We must take his word for it. Initiation in his case amounts to dis- enchantment, consent to the discrepancy between illusion and reality, recognition that a new generation had come into the world "dedicated more than the last to the fear of poverty and the worship of success; grown up to find all Gods dead, all wars fought, all faiths in man shaken. . . ."[35] But initiation to what end and for what use, we itch to ask? Blaine gives no answer. In his knowledge as in his actions, and least of all in that flurry of radical thought on which the book ends, Blaine implies no sustaining vision this side of paradise. It is quite as if Fitzgerald meant Amory to prove that there were no second acts in Ameri- can lives, all first acts having taken place in Eden.

In twentieth century America, the Romantic hero is a nostal- gic Faust. Blaine is the vague, idealistic rebel—there is more of Rupert Brooke than of Faust in him—who feigns a proud avidity for experience while glancing furtively over his shoulder at the cozy past. For the voracious and rebellious heroes of

Thomas Wolfe the recapitulation of the past is everything. Lost, lost, forever lost—that is the burden of their headlong maturity. Wolfe's quarrel with Time is a product of his Romantic conception of the self. In *Look Homeward, Angel*, the conflict between self and world is quite simply resolved: Eugene Gant is the world. He possesses what Freud called the "oceanic sense," a feeling of limitless extension prior to, and sometimes coexistent with, the perceptions of the mature ego.[36] Thus broods young Gant: "I am . . . a part of all that I have touched and that has touched me, which, having for me no existence save that which I gave to it, became other than itself by being mixed with what I then was. . . ."[37] The strategy of the self here is not one of recoil: it is of total inclusiveness. One is at first tempted to exclaim that here at last the vision of American adolescence has hit upon something grand and enduring. Second thoughts about the novel prove, unfortunately, less flattering. The flaw—and it is a serious one—lies in Wolfe's unresolved attitude toward experience, which the ambiguous use of his herculean memory betrays. Wolfe conceived, in *The Story of a Novel*, three dimensions of time: the actual present, the past, and "time immutable."[38] In *Look Homeward, Angel*, Eugene cultivates, on the one hand, a tragic consciousness of the *past*, "the sad waste of the irrevocable years"; and, on the other, he uses the great "forgotten language of memory" to capture the permanence of things under the aspect of *time immutable*.[39] Eugene, however, cannot bring one form of awareness into a meaningful relation to the other—he does not understand in what sense experience is wasted and in what sense it is permanent. Between innocence lost forever and experience preserved eternally there remains a large vacuum Wolfe can fill only with the omnivorous ego of his protagonist. Wolfe's heroes, in effect, spurn initiation, claiming nothing less than rebirth out of time. Yet the only purpose their rebirth serves is to unwind the reel of the past endlessly. You can't go home again, they all passionately say. And yet is not that *all* they say? Their ravenous search for experience brings them always back to the point from which they started—and to which they refuse to return.

It appears that even the Romantic hero in America cannot disentangle himself from the webs of Eden. Faustian he is in a tender way. The goal of his initiation, whose patterns conform more closely to the initiation of the artist than of the citizen, is self-exile and solitary self-knowledge. (It is no accident that both Wolfe and Fitzgerald gave us portraits of the artist as an adolescent.) Disenchanted and still defiant, Grail-bearer and fantasist of the ideal, the Romantic hero embodies all the proud ambitions of the self on whose farthest ramparts he stands militantly at guard. His inevitable defeat is the source of his greatest pride. The epigraph to Wolfe's last novel, *You Can't Go Home Again,* is his motto: "He knew his life was little and would be extinguished, and that only darkness was immense and everlasting. And he knew that he would die with defiance on his lips, and that the shout of his denial would ring with the last pulsing of his heart into the maw of all-engulfing night."[40]

Is the burden of initiation in America so crushing, then, that no confirmation of youth is possible? Has the dream of innocence ravaged the American soul, decreeing that its fate remain the fate of the victim forever? Or do the contradictions of American history still prevail against the self, forcing it into permanent alienation from the world? The images of initiation we have encountered suggest that though the answer to these questions tends to be fearfully affirmative, the best novelists have always created out of defeat values by which reality in America can be continually redeemed. But some have faced the burdens of initiation with greater valor, and gone farther than others in wresting from defeat the essence of human victory. Of these authors Hemingway and Faulkner must be accounted the foremost. Equally Primitivist, Naturalistic, and Romantic, they are none of these exclusively and are more besides.

The capacity for experience in Nick Adams is stronger than in any adolescent we have seen, as it is perhaps more sharply limited. Hemingway's style, hard, intact, and blameless, guarantees that Nick's experience remain just so. In the lucid stories of *In Our Time*—set against the vanishing innocence of the Michigan woods—young Nick confronts death, evil, love, and failure with courage. The code on which his lifemanship is based seems almost too simple: trust the senses, avoid cant, pare down your emotions, dispense with ideas, do well rather than good, and make sure you can take anything life has to dish out. The code stands him in good stead, and narrow though it may be, it is still viable. Nick almost starts life with a foretaste of its tragedy; his disillusionment is inborn, and always under control. In "The Three-Day Blow," Nick and Bill drink whiskey appreciatively—little water, no ice—and reflect on the failures of their sires. "It all evens up," Nick says, and both look into the fire "thinking of this profound truth."[41] The comment, to be sure, is qualified in the story by a good deal of authorial irony. It nevertheless shows what expectations of life the Hemingway adolescent carries, and it betrays the secret wound the Hemingway hero goes out of his way to hide. The end of initiation is always operational knowledge, the power of the *aficionado* to convert his tragic awareness of life into a highly skilled and ritualized mode of action—fishing, hunting, bull-fighting, etc. But the wound, the tragic awareness, is always there. It evokes, however distantly, an earlier state of innocence. "The End of Something," for instance, portrays not only the close of an adolescent love affair but also the end of a cultural era symbolized by the deserted lumber mill which haunts the backdrop of the story. Even in Hemingway's work, the image of initiation reflects a vanishing Arcadian glow. Nick is still the laconic brother of Huck Finn, though for him the Territory Ahead lies closer to Big Two-Hearted River.

The Arcadian dream meets the nightmare of guilt head on in the novels of William Faulkner; the encounter, so full of sound and fury, predicts the destiny of such youths as Quentin Compson, Charles Mallison, and Ike McCaslin. Against the innocence of the wilderness Faulkner recalls the rapine of the land, against the simple endurance of the Negro he revives the curse of slavery, and against the ceremony of aristocratic behavior he pits the terrors of miscegenation. The doom of inherited guilt, of tainted blood, acts like an inexorable force of retribution more Calvinist than Greek in its savagery.[42] To that glamorous fatality the suicide of Quentin Compson is dedicated. But there also persists in the Faulknerian youth, as Mizener has noted, a quixotic impulse which links him with Huck Finn in common pursuit of "the simple truth."[43] It is thus that we understand the actions of Mallison digging up the Gowrie grave with old Miss Haversham, and of Ike McCaslin renouncing his tainted patrimony. In every case innocence and guilt are both conjoined; the ritual of initiation fails or succeeds as the hero meets the claims of his unappeasable inheritance.

In *The Sound and the Fury* the shadow of fatality lies too heavily on young Quentin Compson; his pride and isolation are steeped in incestuous doom. When Quentin discovers that his sister Caddy is pregnant by some man, he chooses to take the blame upon himself. Immured in his selfhood and trapped by some precarious concept of Compson honor, he refuses the future and thinks to escape the past. But his fate, like the ancestral watch he tries to smash, ticks on relentlessly. The proud self retreats from the world into incest and from incest further into solipsism. Pride without courage or humility, Faulkner never tires of showing, is the brightest way to perdition. If the initiation of Charles Mallison, in *Intruder in the Dust*, is more successful than Quentin's, it is because Charles learns to give up his white-man's pride and accept his debt to the intractable Negro whom he tries to help in arrogant self-absolution.

It is through a voluntary act of renunciation, as Ike McCaslin learns in *The Bear*, that pride can be checked and guilt expiated.

Ike inherits from old Carothers McCaslin the guilt of incest, miscegenation, and brigandage. His initiation begins in the Big Woods with the ritualistic hunt of a huge bear, Old Ben, totemic symbol of a race of whom Sam Fathers with his blood of Indian kings and Negro slaves is the last remnant; and it ends with the repudiation of a bequest which was never really Ike's or Carothers' or even Ikkemotubbe's to hold or confer. In the wilderness he is witness to "the ancient and unremitting contest according to the ancient and immitigable rules which voided all regret and brooked no quarter."[44] He learns courage, humility, endurance, from a fyce attacking old Ben, from Katie, the brave mule, from ferocious Lion, and greedy, fearless Boon, and from the bear himself. Above all, he learns them from Sam Fathers, whose destiny is locked with a vanished order as Boon's destiny is linked with a rapacious new one. And he teaches himself renunciation early, giving up his gun to catch a glimpse of cunning Old Ben. At twenty-one Ike is ready to atone fully for his inheritance. Against the subtle arguments of his cousin, Cass, which are the arguments of the world, Ike affirms man's privilege "to hold the earth mutual and intact in the communal anonymity of brotherhood," and gives up his patrimony.[45] The statement —it is not without irony—crowns one of the most radical attempts of the American conscience to resolve the contradictions of the American past. It is the final reward of Ike's long and unwavering initiation to the estate of manhood. The reward is one of determined self-sacrifice. Ike McCaslin reveals that initiation in America appears most complete when its burden lies heaviest: youth takes upon itself the cumulative sins of God's country, and in the guise of a sacrificial victim redeems that act of Original Innocence which was the discovery of America.

IV

In the modern European novel the dialectic between the essential Yes and radical No found its incarnation in the figure of the rebel-victim. Controlled from the outside by an inflexible order that tended to reduce man to a function or simply an object, wracked inwardly by the sense of guilt, absurdity, and contradiction, the modern self took its stand both in defiance and affliction. Its search for an identity conceived in freedom led it through the dark undersides of experience from which it emerged still human only to find itself outlawed by the collective authority of men who had relinquished their full humanity. Like Dostoyevsky's hero, the modern self lived on underground, spiteful and isolate.

But Europe does not cease where America starts, nor has America stopped confronting Europe at every crossroad of their separate ways. By focusing on the characteristic process of initiation in America, which conveys the tensions of form in fiction and polarities of experience in history, we saw that confirmation of the adolescent in American society was seldom realized. Sacrifice, regression, defeat—these summed up the recurrent expense of initiation. The face of the initiate in modern America began early to shade into the face of the victim, less spiteful than vulnerable and elegiac perhaps, but still rebellious and still outraged. Initiation did not end with communion; it led to estrangement. Its stages were not broadly ritualized into viable modes of knowledge or action; each stage, rather, was attended by an acute sense of personal anxiety, a feeling of rage, loss, or despair. Compounding the ambiguities in our culture which *The Adventures of Huckleberry Finn* prefigured with the tortured self-awareness dramatized by *Notes from Underground*, the image of initiation in the modern American novel testified to the powers of denial which the beleaguered self summons to its aid.

Nor does the encounter of the mature hero with experience offer a more hopeful aspect in the modern American novel. Hemingway's Jake Barnes is emasculated by the war and victimized by the historical circumstances of the generation for which he stands. Frederick Henry and Catherine Barkley are trapped by organic death, in which all love is rooted; Henry learns that

59

the world "kills the very good and the very gentle and the very brave impartially."[46] Fitzgerald's Gatsby, though fed on "the incomparable milk of wonder," is sacrificed to Daisy's unattainable image, to a vision of "the fresh green breast of the new world," and to the Platonic conception of himself; he fails to see that his dream "was already behind him, somewhere back in the vast obscurity beyond the city, where the dark fields of the republic rolled on under the night."[47] Dos Passos' Charley Anderson is devoured by a cannibal society inflated by the author's technique of newsreel and biography into a monstrous gaping maw. And Faulkner's Joe Christmas, whose name refers us back ironically to the great symbol of sacrificial redemption, is violated before our eyes, murdered and castrated, the black and white blood in his veins gushing forth to haunt our dying moments with a memory of all the outrages we have helped to perpetuate.

The fate of the mature hero like that of the adolescent on the verge of initiation, we see, proves that the solitary individual in our epoch is on trial for nothing less than his *being*. This, and nothing else, defines the sense of existential crisis that novels in Europe and America now share. What continues to distinguish the American from the European novel is its critical awareness of *loss*, its ironic cultivation of human *vulnerability*, its bitter generosity toward all things *quixotic* and infrangible. The black stream of violence which flows through its pages wells from a turbid and extravagant hope, a radical innocence. The American myth and the American conscience, the dominant and the opposing images of man in America, continue to be at odds. The American novel, faced inevitably with the schizoid figure of the hero, seeks in his victimhood for the meaning of reconciliation, the meaning of being.

The form and values of being in the *contemporary* novel—limited arbitrarily to fiction since the last war, and viewed intentionally in the historical perspectives already defined—will remain our concern in the rest of this work.

CHAPTER 3

CONTEMPORARY SCENES: THE VICTIM
WITH A THOUSAND FACES

America is like a vast Sargasso Sea—a prodigious welter of unconscious life, swept by ground-swells of half-conscious emotion. All
manner of living things are drifting in it. . . .—VAN WYCK BROOKS,
America's Coming of Age

I

HISTORY in the West seems to be consumed before it is
made. The modern age belongs already to the past, the
contemporary period yields to the immediate present,
and the present in America fades in pursuit of an uncreated
future. Obsolescence is the tribute we pay to our faith in per-
fectibility. And yet we continue to wonder about the internal
logic, the unheard voice and impalpable fatality, of the moment
in which we live.

There are perhaps no answers commensurate with our yearning. Perhaps the best we can do is choose the way every good
novel chooses when it plunges into the underside of life and
comes up again for air with a grin or snarl. Standing, as it were,
in the depth of the contemporary scene—can America still be
called a vast Sargasso Sea?—we are naturally baffled by the flux
and seeming diversity which tease our sight. The capacity of the
novel to organize experience and to mediate between various
levels of perception in culture suggests a way out of our perplexity. Every society presents dominant and public images of man
as well as private and opposing images of him. These give each
period its singular character; they outline the motives and
regimen of society. The outline may provide no more than a

swift sketch in black and white, but a sketch may reveal sometimes as much as a portrait can. It will be to our advantage to glimpse three different levels of human responses in American culture of the last two decades before observing how the hero manages, in concrete instances, to distinguish between these levels while mediating their discrepancies.

II

The movement from the surface images to the hidden motives in our culture is subtle and continuous. There are no sudden gaps. But the distance is nevertheless great, and it is experienced every day by the individual in anguish or puzzled resentment.

When World War II came to an end soon after the holocausts at Hiroshima and Nagasaki, and millions of young men climbed out of uniform, a new age was ushered in. The men who went to war went, at best, with mixed idealism; they were not, it is often said, as innocent as their fathers who were sent from a Midwestern farm to a trench on the Marne. In retrospect, some of us may be inclined to feel as Edmund Wilson did in 1957 that "both Roosevelt and the country at large were moved mainly by the irresistible instinct of power to expand itself...."[1] Whatever the "real" motive may have been, the men who went to war finished what they or someone else had started, and they returned to put America in a position of unquestionable world eminence. The age of so-called comfort and conformity had begun. Other generations followed them—those who fought at Korea, those who are now entering colleges or have just graduated from them—and following their seniors, accelerated the established trend. A feeling of some intensity, an awareness of urgency and even power, was evident for a few years after 1945. But the feeling, which we sense in the best war novels, seems to have dissipated itself—with the possible exception of Norman Mailer, none of the "war novelists" commands our attention any longer. The new age often demanded another kind of novel and the image it projected began imperceptibly to bemuse the "veterans" whose youthful memories found their origin in the Depression.

"Ours is a society with more built-in tranquilizers of more different sorts than any that has ever existed," Russell Lynes recently said in his witty exposé, A *Surfeit of Honey*.[2] The statement might well serve as a standard keynote of contemporary culture. The diversity of works, flip or erudite, blithe or somber, on the subject of mass society betrays the extent to which we are fascinated by the aspect we offer to the world at the same time that we are made vaguely uneasy by its consequences. We cannot bring ourselves to believe that this is quite the way we are. And indeed the composite image of ourselves, made up of slogans and stock responses, seems more ludicrous than terrifying. It is the image of an organization man in gray flannel suit who foregoes the ulcerous rewards of executive suite, preferring to lead the good life in the suburbs (or, if his paycheck allows, in exurbia), pottering about a house with a cracked picture window looking into the crack of another picture window (or Doing-It-Himself, whatever it may be, in the backyard, with regulation brogans and blue jeans on), and viewing with a mixture of apathy and wise disaffiliation the coming caesars of our imperial state, the hidden persuaders and clowns of commerce on Madison Avenue, U.S.A., and the exploding metropolis on whose far fringes our Quiet American has found his corner of Shangri-La. Together with his family as with himself, he expects any day now Erma, the ambidextrous automaton, to fulfill all his physical needs at home; meanwhile, there is the astonished and astonishing muse of TV to provide his spiritual sustenance, and when the evening is done, he can sleep with an easy conscience, after the usual dose of Miltown, in the knowledge that when he wakes up at least one of the insolent chariots in his two-car garage will be ready to transport him to another appointment with a white-collar day. In this other-directed paradise, where everyone is another to someone else and nothing to himself, the American Adam can obviously have no knowledge of evil, except perhaps that which is vicariously rendered on his stereophonic set by Eartha Kitt: "I wanna be evil, I wanna be bad" (the awful daring of a moment's surrender to Mickey Spillane is no longer fashionable). Happy, adjusted, prosperous, without an enemy or thought in the world, the American Adam fulfills his manifest destiny in the republic of consumers united under God.

This is not a serious image of America. But ironic or preposterous as it may seem, it contains the partial and perverse truth every cliché contains. The portrait also supports Aldous Huxley when he says, in *Brave New World Revisited*, that the odds for us in America are now more in favor of a benevolent, dehumanized utopia such as Huxley described thirty years ago than of the totalitarian nightmare Orwell predicted by 1984.[3] One thing is certain: the septic surface image of our culture is far removed from anything we have traditionally considered, and still believe, to be crucial to our moral life, let alone to our instinctual needs. In this orgiastic technological fantasy in which our lives are led for us, it is all too easy to assume that basic human needs are altered or radically modified. Basic needs merely go underground; the distance between reality and illusion multiplies; and men brave heavier psychic and spiritual penalties as they try to reconcile the sharpening polarity of self and world. Obviously, all is not well in God's country. And however skillfully we disguise the fact from ourselves, we are even now improvising new defenses for our flattened egos. Culture itself retreats from the unreality of its surface image, allowing men to pursue their lives on various levels of uniformity and dissent. Where the first imaginary level of culture presents unrelieved homogeneity, the second evidences encouraging human discrepancies. The second level, one might say, harbors values still powerless to be born.

Since David Riesman gave currency in *The Lonely Crowd* to the term "other-directed," we have not ceased to wonder how well or ill our new slogan becomes us—Riesman himself, despite his lucid and critical intelligence, tends to be elusive on this score. Members of an older generation find it difficult to condone the accent on adjustment and security, the lack of ambition and independence, which the younger generation exhibits. They are not pleased that the aggressive Protestant Ethic of work and initiative on which the American Dream was predicated is giving way to the more unctuous Social Ethic defined by William S. Whyte, Jr., in *The Organization Man*, as "that contemporary body of thought which makes morally legitimate the pressures of society against the individual."[4] Whyte's definition is not without bias, but it serves to remind us that while we still pay lip service to the go-getter virtues embodied in the American Dream, we have in effect renounced these for the relaxed fringe benefits of communal existence. What has happened, in effect, is that the insatiable American Faust has gone epicurean. The situation has interesting implications, and it involves us in strange paradoxes. Worshippers of the bitch-goddess of success, whom the American conscience repeatedly censured, become worshippers of leisure and the small household gods. The decision to withdraw from the public realm, dramatized by *The Man in the Gray Flannel Suit*, leaves that realm open to the demonic and the obsessed. The Faustian spirit still finds its incarnation, as it always has, in science, about which the layman knows less and less, and finds its incarnation in the State, over which the layman has diminishing controls.

Obviously, what we are witnessing on this secondary level of culture is a double form of recoil: recoil from the compulsive materialism of the American tradition and also from the enforced homogeneity of contemporary life. The recoil manifests itself, ineffectually, as a search for privatism in the midst of conformity and for contentment in the midst of frenetic bustle —the old search for human innocence in the midst of a rat race. The other manifestation of recoil in contemporary America has gone by various names, disaffiliation, apathy, silence, coolness, and is supposedly common among youth of college age. An international study of youth in various cultures conducted by James Gillespie and Gordon Allport suggests that Americans now put a lower premium on such patent American values as ambition and competitiveness than some "backward" countries do.[5] A symposium in *The Nation*, entitled "The Careful Young Men," leaves us with the impression of a cautious, sane, and skeptical generation who will neither pluck the stars from their sockets nor yet detonate the cobalt bomb under our feet.[6] But despite the fact that our war with them is apt to be simply the old-fashioned war of generations rooted in different climes of childhood—the war of the generations and the battle of the sexes are perhaps the only wars we can still afford—despite the petulant accusations we level at them and the abject confessions we make of our own failures, we are finally bound to recognize that enlightened disengagement is complicit in moral apathy and therefore in guilt. The implications of this idea are recognized with a modest success in Richard Frede's recent novel of college life, *Entry E*. "Indifference. An inability to get emotionally involved in anything," as the Dean puts it, leads young Bogard to commit a crime by default of positive action.[7] Frede's novel is somewhat thin, and it is not entirely finished as a moral work of the imagination but, like *The Man in the Gray Flannel Suit*, it deftly isolates a popular dilemma of the times. Frede finally goes farther than Wilson when he intimates that beyond privatism lurks the shadow of indifference, and so the assumption of guilt for the very ills privatism seeks to escape. Clearly, the opportunities of commitment we ignore under the pretense of sophisticated realism are also the rights we abdicate in the name of disengagement. Recoil, on this level, becomes simply relaxation.

The resort to privatism and disengagement no doubt accrues to the benefit of the family which, despite its startling mobility, still remains one of the guiding influences in American society; so much so, that our mass media are forced to pay homage to the idea of familial bliss as they do to no other notion of success or power.[8] Privatism may also help us, among other things, to face more intelligently the problems of leisure which the uncouth billion-dollar spectacle of America at play yearly dramatizes.[9] But the response of privatism, on the whole, is not one calculated to crush the challenges of our time. It cannot help abate the global tensions in whose grip we writhe. It does not reckon with social facts: for instance, the vaunted statistics which claim that in 1950 a major crime was committed in the United States every 18 seconds, or that our rates of insanity, alcoholism, and suicide are among the highest in the world. More significant than these disembodied figures, perhaps, is the cultural climate which allows one of our most popular presidents to define an intellectual as "a man who takes more words than is necessary to say more than he knows"; and one of our greatest writers, Faulkner, to say, "America has not yet found any place for him who deals only in things of the human spirit except to use his notoriety to sell soap or cigarettes or fountain pens. . . ."[10] The failure of our intellectual life to invigorate our public realm of action is an old story now, and a story that is becoming, despite the joint efforts of the academy and market place— references to the Corning Glass Conference of industrialists and professors haunt any discussion of this subject—a story that is becoming a little sadder every day. How real can disengagement be, and what price ingloriousness?

Dissent from the ballyhoo and lunacies of mass society finds more compelling means of expression on a third, more fundamental level of human responses in culture. Beyond meek acquiescence to the dominant counters of the moment, beyond the reaction of disaffiliation and privatism, the search for *love* and for *freedom* continues with radical intensity. The search for love brings men to the threshold of religious experience— Zen or Buddhist thought, Christian mysticism, the I-Thou encounter so vividly explored by Martin Buber—and the uncompromising search for freedom sometimes ends in crime or anarchy—the hipster's burden. The two quests start from different points; they meet in the idea of the hipster-saint, the criminal-lover, the rebel-victim.

For the time being, suffice it to say that the current insistence on love may exceed anything the West has experienced since early Christianity. Love is sometimes felt to be the only safeguard against the total disaster we face, and it is sometimes seen, as in the works of Erich Fromm, as the only cohesive principle on which a sane society can be based.[11] In contrast with, in defiance of, the crass, depersonalized society in which men live, love in recent fiction is refined, desexualized, made the ultimate spiritual commitment, made, like anarchy, the last resource of revolt against organization and the last refuge of innocence. The minimal implication is that if love does not conquer all it must surely remain the belief which makes inevitable defeat *human*. But love penetrates the public realm with the greatest difficulty; in its more extreme and transcendent forms, love is indeed a reaction against that realm, infinitely more valid than disengagement but not infinitely more effective. From a crude collective point of view, love must seem a withdrawal into communion.

An even more radical course is pursued by existential man who defines freedom, like Sartre, and not unlike Thoreau, as the last-ditch, the inalienable, right to say No. His stance is not one of disengagement; it is one of downright refusal for which his comfort and sometimes his life are forfeited. More than an outsider, he is the typical rebel-victim. Like the lover, he distinguishes himself from the personalist and the disaffiliated not so much by the degree of his alienation as by the quality of his suffering. "It is on this bleak scene that a phenomenon has appeared: the American existentialist," Mailer writes in a crucial essay, "The White Negro": "To be an existentialist one must be able to feel oneself—one must know one's desires, one's rages, one's anguish, one must be aware of the character of one's frustration, and know what would satisfy it. The over-civilized man can be an existentialist only if it is chic. . . . To be a real existentialist . . . one must be religious, one must have one's sense of the 'purpose.' . . ."[12] To call existential man—existentialist is perhaps a more precise and therefore exclusive term—

to call him a nihilist is to allow words to frighten us from perceiving the acute plight of freedom in our time. His response is not un-American; the anarchic impulse he expresses is deeply rooted in the American tradition of self-fulfillment. But after conceding the integrity of his response, stripped from the glamor, bunk, and fanfare of San Francisco or Venice West, we must still ask how his inordinate vision may be interpreted for the uses of life and not merely those of destruction.

It is when we permit ourselves to probe still deeper into the organic life of culture, and there encounter stark irreducible instincts emboweled like sullen giants in the earth, that we recognize how far from the surface we have sunk, and how cheerless the fate of contemporary man must be, caught as he is between raging Titans and all-powerful Olympian gods. Solutions we patly require on more accessible levels of society may ultimately depend on the outcome of that epic conflict. But in our age, man seems to have become aware that his humanity rests precisely on the fact that he is an unredeemed and unredeemable creature. To his condition in the universe, he must always cry No even while conceding its inevitability. For him, tragic acceptance is no longer enough.

If the victim has a thousand faces in the contemporary novel, it is because human responses in culture do not manifest themselves on three levels, as our bare sketch seems to indicate, but on a thousand. That he attempts to reconcile so many levels of perception is not entirely surprising. Fools and holy victims rush in where angels fear to tread. And reconciliation, after all, is the business of art: reconciliation of nature and freedom, purpose and play, reality and pleasure, society and self.[18] But it is time we ceased to think of the victim as a cultural figure or archetype. It is time, that is, we allowed him to come forth as a character in fiction, engaged in the business not of abstract reconciliation but of concrete and dramatic living. Above all, we need to remember that if the victim, broadly conceived, is the representative hero of our time, he is by no means the only, or even principal, figure in current fiction. His condition is simply the test case of our moral and aesthetic life.

III

The end of adolescence is confirmation in the world, but childhood in America is its own place. Childhood stands for truth and Edenic innocence—it lacks the ambiguities of initiation—for the unconditioned in society, for the vulnerable moment in which our future is betrayed. The short story, which Frank O'Connor described as "a lyric cry in the face of destiny," lends itself more gracefully than the novel to this treatment of innocence.[14] We see, for instance, that the child who runs away to hide from the ugliness of racial prejudice in Salinger's story, "Down at the Dinghy," suddenly puts a recognized social fact in a new context of values. Likewise, the neglected little boy who kicks his detached father in the groin, in James Purdy's "Color of Darkness," protests in a patently symbolic gesture of aggression the loveless condition to which he has been subjected.

But there have also been longer works which portray the child as a suffering figure, commanding more pathos than tragedy perhaps, yet still capable of dramatizing sharply the unviable resistance to *growth* where growth entails surrender, isolation, and loss. This is the situation of Molly Fawcett in Jean Stafford's *The Mountain Lion*. Molly and her older brother Ralph are bound by a conspiracy of love intended to keep an insensitive world in abeyance. They present a front of common values against the rest of their family; and their allegiance to Grandfather Kenyon, who represents the uncouth integrity of the old Westerner, represents an age that knew Jesse James and lived freely on the land, is consciously held against the allegiance of the others to Grandfather Bonnie, a genteel manufacturer of buttons. The childhood of Ralph and Molly is thus caught between two orders, an idyllic past and an industrial reality, whose discordant values are still a part of the American consciousness. The death of Grandfather Kenyon at the beginning of the novel presages the death of the mountain lion at the end of it, and the latter event is conjunctive to the death of Molly during the hunt. As the last vestiges of a pristine nation are wiped out, so are the fanatic hopes of childhood brought to a violent end. Molly, we know, had wanted to marry Ralph, and had poured acid on her hand to punish him when in his superior wisdom he had rejected the idea as inadmissible. When Ralph grows up to discover the disturbing facts of his sexuality, Molly counters by savagely refusing any knowledge of birth or reproduction of mating animals on the ranch. And when Ralph suddenly whispers to his sister some obscene phrase in the gloom of a tunnel on a fateful train ride, Molly responds with the full force of her original fury. Now utterly alienated from her brother, who is more and more accepted by Uncle Claude, Kenyon's son, on equal footing, Molly can envisage no future in which her most passionate urges can be gratified. Her death —she is shot by Ralph—may be accidental, but it is also the logical outcome of human instincts refusing all compromise. If the mountain lion is nature perceived as the embodiment of some lost ideal, Molly is nature willfully conceived as an ideal that society can never allow.

Miss Stafford, a fine artist who has lately lapsed into silence, has written two other novels which deserve notice. *Boston Adventure*, her first and most impressive work, treated the initiation of a poor girl, Sonia Marburg, into the complex world of Beacon Hill. We first see Sonia as a sensitive child in her home town, a New England fishing village; and see her again develop into a young woman of moral responsibility, in many ways superior to the aristocratic world into which she had willed herself. A large and qualified acceptance, a certain tenderness, is all that Sonia can salvage from her Boston adventure. But in her case, at least, childhood evolves into sad maturity, though the emphasis of the novel is on the sadness.

In *The Catherine Wheel*, the focus is on the late maturity of Katherine Congreve. Her particular tragedy, however, is apprehended in relation to a boy, Andrew Shipley, the son of the only man she ever loved. The relation between the young boy and the aging empress of Congreve House is rich in moral and aesthetic overtones. But the central fact of the novel is that childhood is shown to be a condition which invites an ultimate sacrifice on the part of Katherine. Innocence, we see, can be preserved only at the price of adult renunciation. The child is saved, the aging woman is martyred—burned alive.

There is a superficial resemblance between Molly's relation to Ralph, in *The Mountain Lion*, and the relation of young Claire to his nineteen-year-old brother Fenton in Purdy's haunting novella, "63: Dream Palace," published in *Color of Darkness*. Purdy's work cultivates a dream-like literalness, a quiet, blood-chilling use of irrelevance, and a sense of human need so desperate and extreme that no cause is adequate to explain the agony we perceive. Bedridden and flea-bitten, haunted by a vision of God and possessed by the memory of a dead mother, little Claire asserts his presence—he is only a secondary character in the novelette—as the eternal victim. He is the innocent child murdered by Turkish soldiers for whom Ivan Karamazov cries out in metaphysical outrage. Only in this case it is Fenton, hopped up one evening on dope, who breaks Claire's neck like a small bird's, and conducts weeks later a harrowing service on his putrefying carcass.

The intolerable ambiguities of love, like the blistering experience of growth, can be dramatized more poignantly by the child because in his case self and society, fancy and fact, appear to be united when in reality they are still so far apart. Wrenched suddenly from the protective circle of love, fantasy, and play, the child reveals the nakedness of the human ego in its most piteous condition. He is the essential self, the vulnerable center of man. Growing toward the grave, we victimize the child within us without ever outgrowing his demands.

But the intricacies of love and pain do not end with unending childhood. They are played over and over again, in a wider sphere, by the adult lover. It is not strange that these intricacies should weave themselves into the weft of "modern marriage," or become knotted in adultery. Love and instinct, child and parent, money and morality are all bound together in this act of betrayal which gathers up so many flying ends in our chaos.

Howard Nemerov's *Federigo, Or, The Power of Love*, a brilliant novel that resolves itself in slapstick, examines married love with more complexity than we can intimate. The questions taken up are large, perennial, and difficult. What is love, sex, marriage? Who are we? And where is God? We see only the Devil, in the person of Federigo, who is Julian Ghent's Other Self, who is also the Doppelgänger everyone knows. We feel, in this novel, "the power streaming ceaselessly through all things, the violent fluidity which itself enabled the world to look relatively solid and stable," and we recognize it as the power of desire, not merely sex, but desire, wish, yearning, illusion, life itself, now masked as a ticking clock, now as an empty refrigerator—the wife has left for her assignation—and sometimes as the flesh of the beloved, devoured by the cannibal self and digested into subjective pulp.[15] But order is what God sees and God presupposes. In the absence of God, the first axiom of love becomes, as it is for Carson McCullers, "that whoever does not despise is despicable; love is, like chess, a contest in which tolerance is impossible, lucky accident unlikely and a draw very infrequent. . . ."[16]

Julian Ghent, who conceives himself to be "a victim of some fatally destructive irony deep in the nature of things," begins by sending himself an anonymous letter accusing his nearly innocent—no one is entirely so—wife of adultery.[17] The letter is Julian's way of committing himself to reality, the coward's way of finding himself out, which is also the way of finding who it is he *can* love. All the grotesque reversals that follow must persuade us that though love may still be earned, pain is the more ubiquitous. It is as Julian reflects: "If somewhere in this life tragedy existed, this perhaps was where it might be found, in the enduring pain of responsibility which provided no such symbolic escape—in duty, shame, guilt, fear, without the alleviation of sickness, madness, death."[18] A supple and fearless intelligence is felt everywhere in this novel which, nonetheless, manages in the end to shirk the formal logic of its rich implications.

The intentions of Robie Macauley's novel, *The Disguises of Love*, are more limited and its felt substance thinner though its technical accomplishments are sharper. The situation is deceptively banal: a college professor falls in love with one of his students with whom he carries on for a time an illicit affair. But Macauley uses so deftly the varied points of view of Gordon, the adolescent son, Howard, the father, Helen, the wife, Frances, the mistress, and the academic community at large that we behold as the action unfolds an ironic play of masks and identities refracted in diamond light. The transgressions of Howard disclose nothing new about the hoary institution of marriage or the operations of social sanctions, but they bring into cruel focus the relations of five people whose normal connections are suddenly wrenched from the matrix of habit and morality. When the Other Woman finally takes a plane out of Howard's life, Helen can only rage that the diabolic game she had begun to play with her husband had suddenly come to an end; Gordon is disappointed that his father must after all remain "the cold-in-the-head professor"; and Howard himself can only think: "If the dead are happy, I was happy. If the dead are satisfied, I was satisfied."[19] The tragi-comedy, presented throughout with a lively, witty sensuousness reminiscent here and there of Colette, comes grimly to a pause—of final retribution there can be none.

The condition of love in our time, however, is not exclusively defined by the tensions in modern marriage. We all know the facts on divorce in America, and if we have not read Kinsey, we have at least read of him and learned to deprecate his disturbing statistics with the elegance they lack. But the trouble, it seems, is more basic: it is that Eros himself has been maimed in our country. We see symptoms of the malady all about us and quarrel over the diagnosis. Momism and Sugar-daddyism, Puritanism and Materialism, Romantic Love and Misogyny, male Impotence and female Frigidity are trotted out of the cultural dispensary, sampled gingerly and put in smears under the microscope. We remain unsatisfied. We look again and observe the growing lack of differentiation between the role men and women play in society—those checkered shirts cut of the same cloth which husband and wife sport at the supermarket. We lament the absence of healthy friendships among men and deplore the rampant fear of homosexuality. We shake our heads in silence when someone mentions the increasing wealth, longevity, and political power of women in America—remembering the forecasts of Tocqueville, and the analysis of his countryman, Riencourt, a century later—and we put down with a sigh the wry comments of *The Decline of the American Male*, which treats the new feminine dispensation as *fait accompli.*[20] Meanwhile, fugitive magazines on the West Coast, born continually like phoenixes out of the ashes of sexual repression and state censorship, cry defiance at the oppressors of the national libido; and erotic advertisements, backed by the ethos of Protestant capitalism, continue to transform the scene into what Angry John Osborne has called "the biggest sexual nuthouse since the Middle Ages."[21]

There is, no doubt, some truth in all these charges and observations; the cumulative evidence of erotic distemper, though it does not point to a unique cause, betrays the malaise we feel about the relations of men and women in America, and betrays our disaffection with the way culture has put to use our sexual energies. But the lurid exploitation of sex in fiction, of which Tennessee Williams and Norman Mailer are so often accused, needs to be considered in the context they presuppose.[22] For it is the failure of human relations in contemporary life, and not the brutish interest in sexuality as such, that has led novelists to render their vision of disunity either by according to sex a reference it cannot bear alone—Williams, Mailer, McCarthy—or by desexualizing love into a mystic, gothic, or narcissistic ideal —Salinger, McCullers, Capote. The effect, in either case, is to enhance the split between self and world, instinct and society, lust and love. The promiscuous indulgence of the sexual will, like the abnegation of it, must be taken as an extreme form of reaction against the dead social center where love is known by its absence and compromise is dignified as the higher expediency.

But the rebel, as we have too often seen, ends by offering himself as victim; the hopeless victim of love, who neither indulges nor abnegates the sexual will but perverts it, is the homosexual. The subject of homosexuality, which so many contemporary novels force upon our attention, seriously involves clinical and legal issues hard to adjudicate. It is only as a manifestation of a particular attitude toward experience which reflects on the fictional imagination that we can approach the subject. The roots of homoeroticism, if not precisely of homosexuality, go back to the classic American novels of the nineteenth century, as Leslie Fiedler has perceived, in which the relation between man and man is often primary.[23] The urge to disengage love from domestic commitments and envision human relations under the aspect of a transcendent ideal, the urge, that is, to resist the socialization of love, is an American urge susceptible to corruption. Considering the background of "innocence" in America and the realities of our contemporary experience, it is not very strange that misogyny should be so apparent in some of the best novels to come out of the last war; nor is it shocking to hear from Malcolm Cowley that homosexuality is incipient in many unpublished manuscripts by young writers since the war for whom the central fictional situation is often an Oedipal conflict with an overpossessive mother.[24]

The situation in published novels treating the subject is usually more complex. The hero of Gore Vidal's *The City and* *the Pillar,* a novel as frank as it is pedestrian, bridles at the "personal and devouring look" of heterosexual desire: it means captivity.[25] Captivity without love is emptiness, yet love itself, as Jim Willard finds, must end either in affection, or for the pervert, in tragedy. Jim is willing to suffer ostracism, to be branded as a homosexual, which he is, even to drift from one perfunctory encounter to the next so long as he is sustained by the memory of his adolescent love for Bob Ford. But the modern Sodom, despite its concern for "freeing sexuality," cannot make love binding; the pillar of salt is its most lasting monument. Jim must, in the end, murder his boyhood friend when the latter grows up to normal sexuality.*

Pain erupts in violence, and violence consumes itself again. The hero of James Baldwin's tighter and more nervous novel, *Giovanni's Room,* also murders—and is beheaded—when his beloved abandons him to marry. Giovanni's shabby room is a cell, a lover's and fool's paradise; the key to the frightening disorder of that room is "punishment and grief"; and its acrid smell is "the stink of love."[26] But the world is not a shuttered room, we want to cry, and Giovanni would agree. As one of the characters puts it for him, no one dies of love in the world: it is simply that multitudes perish "every hour—and in the oddest places!—for the lack of it."[27] A dirty room, a loveless world—the choice must baffle flesh. The classic triangular drama which David, Hella, and Giovanni enact is finally concentrated in the novel at the point where man, woman, and child forever clash in Giovanni's soul. The privacy of love attains its most ambiguous limit.

In all these examples, we see the true heroes of love are its martyrs; the most secret quest of the soul ends in quiet or blazing defeat. And crime appears as the wage of a certain radical holiness.

Secrecy is the general condition of everything freakish, grotesque, or deformed, and grief the fate of any deviation from

* Gore Vidal has revised *The City and the Pillar,* which now ends with homosexual rape, not murder.

enforced orthodoxy. The pervert who allows himself to be massaged to death, every bone in his body broken, and literally devoured by a huge Negro masseur, in Tennessee Williams' story, "Desire and the Black Masseur," is a grotesque sacrificial victim to the cannibal gods of love—celebrated in more sardonic fashion by Wright Morris in *Love Among the Cannibals*. But the story also shows that the action of the pervert, like the suffering of the freak, denies the wider possibilities of communion which it seeks. Alienation is cultivated in the name of love and sacrifice in the interests of preserving the unique core of every individual.

It is in this perspective of estrangement and desire that the currency of grotesque figures in contemporary fiction must be viewed. Sherwood Anderson's grotesques hugged a single truth to themselves, made it private and freakish, a twisted badge of their inwardness. His idea of the grotesque may sanction the use of everything bizarre or deformed, as if Caliban were the only hero eligible to our affections. But the idea also proffers certain advantages to the serious novelist in our time. It allows him to extend the range of fiction to those tenebrous realms of which we have become reluctantly conscious. It permits him to question torpid habits and vapid norms, and to shock us through creative distortions into some recognition of truths we dare not face. The grotesque, as clown and scapegoat, is both comic and elegiac, revolting and pathetic. As hunchback or cripple, he is born an outsider, his very aspect an affront to appearances. His broken body testifies to the contradictions of the inner man, the impossible and infrangible dream, raging against his crooked frame and against the world in which flesh is housed.

We are determined to locate the grotesque in the South, though Anderson was no more a Southerner than such recent devotees of the genre as James Purdy or James Leo Herlihy, author of a crazy, searing collection of stories entitled *The Sleep of Baby Filbertson*: Baby Filbertson turns out to be a jumbo mamma's boy, weighing well over 200 pounds, whose main concern is to purloin his mother's phenobarbitals so that he may lay him down to sleep like "the corpse of some giant foetus."[28] The South, of course, is a place where the dialectic of innocence and guilt, communion and estrangement, primitivism and ceremony, can be clearly observed; it is a place where the Protestant mind and the folk spirit have not succumbed entirely to business ethics or urban impersonality. But Protestant in spirit, the grotesque appears in a different light when created by a writer who is both Southern and Catholic. With her own work particularly in mind, Flannery O'Connor has written: "But whatever Southern life may contribute to this impression of grotesquery, there is a more fundamental reason why these stories are the way they are. The reason is that the writer's vision is literal and not naturalistic. It is literal in the same sense that a child's drawing is literal. When a child draws he doesn't try to be grotesque but to set down exactly what he sees, and as his gaze is direct, he sees the lines that create motion. I am interested in the lines that create spiritual motion. It never occurred to me that my novel was grotesque until I read it in the papers."[29] The statement is lucid and penetrating, and it must challenge those tearful denunciations of Southern "degeneracy" and "gratuitous" violence which Miss O'Connor's novel, *Wise Blood*, has aroused.

Few writers command a sharper sense of evil, a greater degree of control in the face of demonic willfulness or baleful passions, than she does in the stories of *A Good Man Is Hard to Find*. Her first novel is no less taut, brutal, or ironic. Its hero, Haze Motes, is a young man with a curse in his heart; the descendant of revivalist preachers, he is himself a preacher of the Church Without Christ. The denial of God is his grotesque passion, and the form his denial takes is no less grotesque. Haze will brook no compromise with godliness or mortality; indeed, he murders a fake prophet used by a rival preacher to deceive the credulous. "No truth behind all truths is what I and this church preach!" he cries from the top of his jalopy to the few who gather in the street to hear him.[30] Is he demented? Or is the spectacle of sin, hypocrisy, indifference about him enough to convert the outrage of spiritual man into spite, his prayer into blasphemy? Enoch Emery, the innocent boy Haze meets in town, looks for love, companionship, simple recognition. But the world—Haze included—has little use for Enoch who must make the shrunken, embalmed figure of a savage his "jesus" or put on a gorilla suit to communicate with his fellow men.

If Enoch renounces his humanity, Haze gives up more. He gives up his very salvation though he blinds his eyes with quick lime, wears barbed wire next to his chest, and walks with broken glass in his shoes. Blasphemer, murderer, penitent without a god, Haze is at last found nearly dead in a ditch, and expires in the squad car which restores his mangled body, in lieu of payment, to his greedy landlady: "She sat staring with her eyes shut, into his eyes, and felt as if she had finally got to the beginning of something she couldn't begin, and she saw him moving farther and farther away, farther and farther into the darkness until he was the pinpoint of light."[31] Distortion, here, is moral judgment; perversity, criticism. The victim of a grotesque nihilism remains the pinpoint of light in a society too smug both in its skepticism and belief. When theology runs wild, as it so often does in the South, worship and heresy become indistinguishable. But negation, we are made to feel, may be the terrible, two-edged sword the Lord unsheathes against his Enemy. This is precisely the conclusion to which Miss O'Connor's second novel, *The Violent Bear It Away*, also arrives.

Unlike the grotesque, the Negro seems to present only a social or historical problem until we discover that the true question he presents is the old one of identity. "Who knows but that, on the lower frequencies, I speak for you?" asks the hero of Ellison's *Invisible Man*.[32] Victim, rebel, outsider, scapegoat, or trickster, the Negro finally confronts us, in the darkness of which no man can bleach himself, with the question: Who am I? "At the root of the American Negro problem," James Baldwin writes in *Notes of a Native Son*, "is the necessity of the American white man to find a way of living with the Negro in order to be able to live with himself."[33] This, at bottom, is a question of self-knowledge. But it is silly to assume that the predicament of the Negro can be finally identified with that of the white man in America—such an assumption may be just another prerogative white men exercise to their own moral advantage. And it is equally vain to suppose that the situation of the Negro is an isolated case, that his alienation from a usable past, his aching expressions of the instinctual life, his rages and pains, have not affected in some unspeakable way our image of the self in culture. Mailer's metaphor of the hipster as a "white Negro" is but a recent illustration of the point. The case of Joe Christmas is an older reminder of our unacknowledged passion for the violence of repudiation. Yet crime is only one form of negation; trickery, the play with masks, the disguises of identity, the jokes on reality, is another. Ellison's "Invisible Man" knows how to make his transparency count against the world so that he may become visible to himself. The trick is to say the "yes" which accomplishes the expressive "no."

We shall return to Ellison's rich book, which may be the best written by a Negro writer. James Baldwin's first novel, *Go Tell It On the Mountain*, is not very much less remarkable. The story does not focus on what social workers call "interracial tensions"—these merely crackle in the air everyone breathes, trickle unnoticed in the water they drink, are part of the gritty bread they eat. The story focuses, rather, on a Negro family, and particularly on the father, Gabriel Grimes, a proud, bitter, lust-driven preacher, and on his bastard stepson, Johnny. Baldwin depicts a world swollen with the power of God, howling with sin, in which good and evil clash with apocalyptic fury. Accursed and damned, the Negro characters are still God's black chosen people, as Gabriel believes, and he is the prophet to lead them out of Egypt. The prophet is tainted with the madness of sexual desire, but his terrible purpose remains steadfast. Every page thunders like a sermon, rolls in Biblical anger, shrieks as a Negro spiritual may shriek—and flashes forth in bursts of poetry.

The dark oppressive religious atmosphere of the novel, it finally dawns upon us, is itself a metaphor of an oppression nameless and dark. The white world is kept at a distance—we have only glimpses of a Negro soldier mutilated by the city riffraff, of Richard, Johnny's father, beaten up by policemen, of a white man spitting in front of Gabriel's feet. But the drama of black and white is transposed by the style into a wider setting in which guilt is incomprehensible and salvation hard. The first section of the novel ends with a scene in which the whole Grimes family attends a service at the Temple of the Fire Baptized. This remains the focal scene in the book to which the lengthy flashbacks of the second part—we are taken back to the Grimes family while they are still in the state of slavery—must return. The third part centers on the nightmarish experience of Johnny who grovels on the church floor and rises a "saved" man —here the images are as riotous, the vision as terrible and transcendent as in the Revelation to which another John testifies. Johnny traverses "the moment locked in darkness," sees himself in the moaning company of "the despised and the rejected, the wretched and the spat upon" who threaten to swallow up his soul, and finally emerges among the silent saints: "In the silence something died in John, and something came alive. It came to him that he must testify. . . ."[34] He can now testify on the mountaintop, "where the sun would cover him like a cloth of gold," or sing and dance before the Lord as David danced.[35] It is the pattern of spiritual rebirth. It is really the confrontation with the torment deep in every Negro's soul—the malediction on race, the curse on the father, the search for a human status —which must be faced and conquered on pain of eternal damnation: hate. The novel does not entirely succeed in uniting the fate of its two main characters, Gabriel and John, within a common dramatic structure, and it does not give sufficient play to its thematic power which it muffles in Biblical parables. But it is a wise novel, and it has that compassion which in the end makes the fate of the rebel-victim exemplary of the fate of man. It is as Baldwin put it in *Notes of a Native Son*: "It began to seem that one would have to hold in the mind forever two ideas which seemed to be in opposition. The first idea was acceptance, the acceptance, totally without rancor, of life as it is, and men as they are: in the light of this idea, it goes without saying that injustice is a commonplace. But this did not mean that one could be complacent, for the second idea was of equal power: that one must never, in one's own life, accept these injustices as commonplace but must fight them with all one's strength. This fight begins, however, in the heart and it now had been laid to my charge to keep my own heart free of hatred and despair."[36]

The predicament of the Negro is sometimes attributed to the simple fact that he is an alien in Western culture—his ancestors were not among the singing masons who raised up the spires of Chartres nor did they help Galileo invent the telescope. The condition of the Negro, however, is not irrelevant to the fate of modern man whose alienation from the proud tradition he once possessed has taken a more subtle and insidious character. This is clear, painfully so, in James Jones's first and best novel, *From Here to Eternity*.

If the whole of history, as Emerson thought, can be incarnated in the life of one man, then history can find its explanation only in the experience of each man. When the man is like Private Robert E. Lee Prewitt, son of Harlan County, Kentucky, coal miner, one-time hero on the bum turned into a U. S. Army thirty-year man, then history must be what he suffers in the Schofield Barracks Stockade. Prewitt is neither a Negro nor a

Jew—his Scotch-English ancestors swarmed the hills of Kentucky before the Revolution—but he is nonetheless the perennial collector of injustices, the consecrated underdog. His only code —the simple freedom to be a *man*, as Prewitt insists—is precisely what the Army he so desperately loves must crush until, still unbroken, he dies. The "tragedy" is familiar; it is the tragedy of the man who won't "play ball," who has no "angles" on life, who insists on his individuality in the barracks as in the whorehouse. "Men are killed by being always alike, always unremembered," Prew tells his beloved prostitute, Lorene.[37] But Prew has nothing to give that the world, let alone the Pineapple Army, can recognize as a valid token of social existence. (Proud and independent too, Warden has at least a Company to run, Stark his messhall, Malloy his quasi-mystical vision, and the inconquerable Wop, Maggio, ironic heir of the American Dream, has none of that loyalty for the Army which is Prewitt's nemesis.) A crack boxer who won't fight, an inspired bugler who won't barter his blues-drenched soul for stripes, and a prodigal lover who nevertheless can't renounce his peculiar idea of freedom, Prewitt in the last analysis is destined, is qualified, only to suffer. He suffers by a choice so free that it seems ineluctable, and he comes to know that there is a satisfaction in "having borne pain that nothing else could ever quite equal, even though the pain was philosophically pointless and never affected anything but the nervous system."[38] Unable to commit himself wholly to the philosophy of passive resistance which Jack Malloy, the jail-king messiah, tries to teach him in the stockade, and unable also to articulate, as Malloy can, an encompassing vision of love or justice, Prewitt remains locked within the all-too-human confines of his personal integrity. Malloy may be right in saying that men cannot be hated for what they do; it is only the "system" that must be hated. But for Prewitt justice, like history, is defined by that personal sense of outrage men feel in their bones; for him the killing of a sadist like Fatso is a necessary, self-appointed task, and violence sometimes the only means by which men regain the individuality of which they are despoiled. The best "soljer" in Company G, after Warden, turns out to be Prewitt who thinks of himself as "a sort of super arch-revolutionary . . . a sort of perfect criminal type, very dangerous, a mad dog that loves underdogs."[39] The life of our military hero is consummated in anarchy even more than protest.

It is not in the least difficult to deride in Jones's book that plainness of style of which the author seems almost proud (hardly an image, rhythm, or sentence, outside the dialogue, takes us with the surprise of discovery); or to deride the sub-literary psychology which constantly intrudes itself on the relation between men and women or the groin-clutching glorification of masculinity (men "step happily" to a fight, roar in their drinks, and bull their way past the madam); or again to deride the naïve exaltation of bum and tough as true rebels (the cream of American manhood, we are told with less irony than makes for comfort, reside in the No. 2 Ward for incorrigibles in the Schofield Stockade, patronized by the departed spirit of John Dillinger). Such offenses seem more like a parody of themselves than the result of any influence exerted by the infinitely more crafty Hemingway or more credible London.

But when all these faults have been dutifully noted in deference to our critical acumen, the novel, unlike its sequel, *Some Came Running*, remains to be reckoned with. Its anger and its compassion are not canceled by its misdeeds; its exposé of life in an army on the threshold of war discloses another war which is quietly ravaging—so well is it censored—the American soul. The social background of the action is awkwardly, unmistakably felt. There are frequent references to the Wobblies who exhausted their vision, to the "good" movies of the Thirties, starring Garfield and Cagney, which gradually yielded to the sentimental conceptions of Hollywood, and to the simple doctrine enunciated by General Slater at an army stag, that "social fear is the most tremendous single source of power in existence."[40] But Prewitt himself is never more than vaguely aware of those

85

"leftist" implications which the novel tries to engage. Consequently, the meanings of social and of individual protest jostle throughout the book without finding the theme or form to unite them. If the work has a focus, it is the nature of power or authority as defined by the responses of men to them—Jones's third novel, *The Pistol*, is not a very successful condensation of the same theme. In the unequal conflict between individual and society, Prewitt stands as an emblem of antipower. Recalcitrance is the badge of his heroism—and his victimization.

Prewitt may be eligible to the title of "White Negro" which Mailer bestowed on the "new American existentialists." He is certainly one of the dispossessed. Unlike the Negro, however, he does not lack a historical identity, though his identity is such that he must preserve it at the risk of anarchy. The true opposite number of the Negro forcibly transplanted from Africa to America is the white man transported in the novels of Paul Bowles from America to North Africa. Bowles's heroes are in flight from civilization. They are seekers of something they cannot name—the fullness of life, the graciousness of surrender, the meaning of identity—who frequently become victims when they suddenly immerse themselves in a primitive culture which deprives them of the few sanctions Western society still provides. They are drawn to the central, the destructive, element of experience in its most brutal aspect; but they are unequipped to survive the frightful encounter, and their disintegration follows the hypnotic pattern of inexorable violence. The sinister transformation from pilgrim into prey, from incipient decay to total regression, is unattended by regeneration or self-discovery—Bowles's last novel, *The Spider's House*, is the single exception.

The plot of *The Sheltering Sky* has the crescive intensity of a short story, its style the hardness and clarity of quartz. Three Americans, Kit and Port Moresby, and Tunner, have with various motives turned their back on the U.S. and plunged into the wildest parts of North Africa. The thematic focus of the novel is the love relation between Kit and Port, a relation complicated by Port's nihilism, Kit's passivity and superstitiousness, Tunner's presence, and the pitiless desert scene against which they all move. Port, in a sense, aspires to the state of consciousness symbolized by the vast, reciprocal blankness of the African desert and sky; his lone conclusion of a lifetime is this: "For in order to avoid to deal with relative values, he had long since come to deny all purpose to the phenomenon of existence—it was more expedient and more comforting."[41] The face of negation is revealed when civilization is stripped of its masks. But negation so deep allows for no love, and no life. After Port's senseless death of typhoid, Kit is permanently stunned into the world of childhood and, still a woman, of undifferentiating sensuality. There is a stark scene in which Kit bathes naked by moonlight and then walks like a somnambulist into the desert, to be found and raped by two nomads. She becomes the willing concubine of one of them, living in a mud-walled cubicle, yielding to nymphomania, the last affirmation of the senses, then drifting into madness, the ultimate negation of values.

Let It Come Down repeats the pattern. (In *Macbeth*, we remember, Banquo makes the innocent remark, "It will rain tonight," and his murderer replies, "Let it come down," while stabbing him to death.) The situation in the novel is equally stark, malevolent, and absurd. Nelson Dyar, a nice bank clerk whose unique distinction is the great void he carries about with him, suddenly decides to take off for Tangier. There, without passion or self-awareness, he tries his hand at smuggling, fornication, narcotics, espionage, and murder. Dyar is one of life's neutral children; he is like a man sealed within a dark bottle. When he acts, in pointless and lurid spasms, his actions reject all ideas of order or value. These actions seem to him, in a quasi-existentialist way, opportunities for involvement, a means of achieving "a place in the world, a definite status, a precise relationship with the rest of men. Even if it had to be one of open hostility, it was his, created by him."[42] Lying on the sand that covers the bottom of a ruined boat in the sun, Dyar reminds us for a moment of the hero of Camus' *The Stranger*, Meursault —the same dim consciousness, the same urge for gratuitous violence. And Dyar reflects as Meursault might have: "The whole of life does not equal the sum of its parts. It equals any one of the parts; there is no sum."[43]

A close reading of Bowles's earlier novels shows that what his characters seek to fulfill is an old paradox: discovery of self through loss of selfhood, recovery of identity through abnegation of the private will. They desire to return to the aboriginal night, to lose somehow the Western ego, to achieve freedom in unconditional surrender. Violence is the crucible in which their self is finally molten so that it may return to the fluid anonymity of existence. What distinguishes *The Spider's House* from the earlier two novels is a more complex awareness of the tension between East and West, of the revulsion against the ego and the horror of surrender—in effect, between fatalism and nihilism —which resolves itself in love. The true hero of the book is Amar, a sort of holy innocent, who finds himself caught between the Nationalist rebels and the French police, between progressive liberals and sentimental conservatives among the American tourists who befriend him. Amar, unlike Moresby or Dyar, is in touch with the spontaneous source of sympathy in human beings. He is attuned to his natural environment. Though he is finally deserted by all, his innocence is preserved because he refuses to yield either to dogma or despair. In his case, the tension between willfulness and surrender is admirably resolved.

The dialogue between East and West—witness Kerouac's *The Dharma Bums*—is at the heart of that movement to which literary conversation, nowadays, tends: the Beat Movement. It is after all, *our* movement—the glamorous fatality of the Twenties, the social earnestness of the Thirties, the formalism of the Forties are now enshrined in history—and whether we grunt our approval of its hipness or raise a supercilious eyebrow at its grubbiness, we are forced in the end to reckon with it as the cultural phenomenon of the moment. The improvised theology of Mailer, the inept prosody of Kerouac, the jazzy flapdoodle of the San Francisco cellars do not exhaust the meaning of Beat—indeed, some have been living quietly by that code for almost a century. Now the barbarians, as Lawrence Lipton asserts, are at our gates: Civilization, beware![44] However short the exponents of Beat may fall of their ideal, it is the ideal itself that must be scrutinized.

The ideal has a utopian aspect which Henry Miller—Papa Miller, as some beatniks call him—reveals. Arguing that the "human fundament" comes from the East, he foresees a new civilization that may take centuries or a few thousand years to usher in, and which "will not be another *civilization*—it will be the open stretch of realization which all the past civilizations have pointed to."[45] Man will not possess power; he will radiate it, will communicate with others. The "awakening of the love instinct will transform every domain of life"; neuters will vanish; ego worship, "the one and only cause of dissension" will vanish; the individual artist-genius will vanish.[46] "When men are at last united in darkness woman will once again illumine the way—by revealing the beauties and mysteries which enfold us," Miller concludes.[47] The appeal of the argument, as Miller saw, is particularly strong to that small band of seekers "roaming about in our midst like anonymous messengers from another planet," at once versed in the ways of rebellion and nonresistance, looking for another Walden at Big Sur or expecting to find some paradise for "Free Spirits" such as Hieronymus Bosch magically depicted in his painting, "The Millennium."[48] By denying the performance principle which has so long ruled our culture—in hipster language, ironically, the word for love-making is "work"—man can enter into a divine fraternity of love. What makes Miller's vision finally relevant to the Beat sensibility is its postulate of a future state in which the two warring elements of Beat, the saintly and the criminal, can be reconciled not only to one another but also to the human condition at large.

Both elements, we have repeatedly seen, are formed in violent reaction against civilization—that is, the great, flaccid life of middle-class America. One impulse moves toward nihilism, frenzied self-affirmation, psychopathy; the other toward surrender, love, holy silence. The first requires the intensification of the self, the second its diffusion. The practical embodiment of one attitude is rebellion; of the other, martyrdom. Both gestures, paradoxically, accomplish the same end: the preservation of a kind of radical innocence which has always been latent in the American tradition. The two gestures blend in the attitude expressed by Alan Watts, in *Beat Zen, Square Zen, and Zen*: "Odd as it may sound, the ego finds that its own center and nature is beyond itself. The more deeply I go into myself, the more I am not myself, and yet this is the very heart of me."[49] Such abysmal unity is not often granted to human beings.

The juvenile delinquent who commits a crime for "kicks" may be understood in several ways. He may be thought of as a poor man's existentialist who longs to do or feel "something meaningful" at a time when traditional forms of action have come to seem more pointless than a deeply-felt but gratuitous impulse. Such an attitude is not without moral implications; as John Clellon Holmes put it, "The only way to make the shocking juvenile murders coherent at all is to understand that they are specifically moral crimes."[50] To put it another way, the adolescent criminal judges the society which invites him to become a part of it by offering it the greatest affront he can invoke. This is even more applicable to the egomaniac or psychopath, the true rebel without a cause. Marginal as he is violently antisocial, the psychopath, according to Robert M. Lindner, was once attracted to the wild frontier of the West and is again flourishing in our great cities which generate, centrifugally, "behavior contrary to the best interests of the group."[51] Romanticizing his explosive energy, his sexuality, and his command of terror, hipsters see him as the new shaman, the radical visionary of an apocalyptic orgasm at the center of which all Being is fused.

The shaman loses his identity in frenzy; the holy trance follows. To be Beat is to be "hung up," to find the root of everything beatific.[52] It is to act the part of a Zen lunatic or Holy Fool, risking absurdity for the spirit's laughter. It is to reexperience the agony of God or to know him, in Mailer's words, "as a warring element in a divided universe. . . ."[53] It is to cultivate pacifism and denounce the "social lie."[54] It is to see the world as a *Haiku* poet does and feel it also as a jazz musician must feel it. In short, it is an attempt to recover that fabled state of innocence which saw the tiger and the lamb lie down together in perfect consort.

Needless to say, it is as easy to pounce on *some* of these motifs in Blake or Dostoyevsky as it is difficult to find them *all* impounded by a single writer of the Beat Generation. A good many recent novels, however, suggest that the interests of the movement are not as eccentric as they may seem nor its originality as signal as we are asked to believe. The following novels, for instance, all published in the Fifties, in some way reflect the attitude which Beat, Inc. has recently advertised on so grand a scale: Algren's *A Walk on the Wild Side*, J. P. Donleavy's *The Ginger Man*, Vance Bourjaily's *The Violated*, Willard Motley's *Knock On Any Door*, Chandler Brossard's *Who Walk in Darkness*, George Mandel's *Flee the Angry Strangers*, Norman Mailer's *The Deer Park*, R. V. Cassill's *The Eagle on the Coin*, Calder Willingham's *Reach for the Stars*. But in fiction the Grand Llama of the movement remains sweet Jack Kerouac,* and its most typical novelist, perhaps, John Clellon Holmes.

The tortured if childlike spiritual awareness of Holmes's *Go* is obvious from the Biblical epigraphs which preface the book —among the epigraphs is an utterance by Father Zossima on

* Jack Kerouac has died.

hell and love which is the key quotation in Salinger's story, "For Esmé, With Love and Squalor"—to the final scene in which the protagonist also ponders the meaning of modern damnation in a Hoboken diner. The characters of the novel are constantly on the go in their appointed orbits, "searching out a new degree of craziness . . . living by night, rushing around to 'make contact,' suddenly disappearing into jail or on the road only to turn up again and search one another out."[55] Their underground and mysterious vision, the cross or monster they carry around (usually a monkey on their back), are brought to each successive Wild Party in the wilder hope that by a ritual sharing of their guilt they may find surcease to their madness. Guilt is indeed what they eagerly take upon themselves, recognizing that the rest of us walk around furtive and guilty too but without wishing to confess our complicity. To madness, however, there is no surcease. "As if God were mad!" Stofsky exclaims. "It was as though the very pumping, physical heart of all humans was being remorsely atomized by the machine of a gigantic mind, over which hovered the sky, a dumb mushroom-head of smoke."[56] It is really no great jump from the nihilism contained in that statement to the holy attitude expressed by Kennedy. "It's just getting your kicks and digging everything that happens. Like everything was perfect. Because it really is, you know!"[57] Madness and bliss huddle in the same black cavern of the soul. Indeed, when God does appear to Stofsky in a dream—it happens in a rented house in Harlem—God says, "Being saved is like being damned. . . . You must go. . . . Go, and love without the help of any Thing on earth."[58]

The novel does not rise to the abiding issues it broaches, and there is no one in it who remotely approaches Raskolnikov, Dimitri Karamazov, Prince Myshkin. The powers of feeling and intelligence of its characters are not only limited by their limited articulations but further curtailed by weaknesses in the mind which dramatically conceived them. Go may strike some of us as a hobbling work; but the spiritual facts which it forces upon our attention must haunt our sleep. The greatest value of the book lies in its genuine effort to put Blake's soul-rending statement, "O rose, thou art sick!" in the urban perspective of our times.

The Beat Generation is a generation nurtured on the toxic secretions of the Big City. The hot spot and the wild party, jazz and marijuana provide the heightened context of crisis, purgation, and communion. But the compulsive quest for salvation must also put the hipster on the road, or start him on the "rucksack revolution." The highways peeled off furiously in the American night of Kerouac's novel, *On the Road,* are all, we are asked to believe, versions of Tao's way. "What's your road, man? —holy boy road, madman road, rainbow road, guppy road, any road. It's an anywhere road for anybody anyhow," the hero of the book, Dean Moriarty, intones.[59] Moriarty, like Holmes's Hart Kennedy, is the classic hipster whom the Beat writers, spurning art, keep invariably "true to life." He is described as a "burning shuddering frightful Angel," the "Holy Goof," whose criminality is a "wild yea-saying overburst of American joy."[60] Crazy, footloose, and uncommitted, he "guns" his cars, preferably stolen, across the continent in search of Kicks and Truth, as the blurbs put it, in search of an earthly parent and heavenly father. For him the first condition of salvation is not to care— holy unattachment!—to squeeze the present into the essence of pure being, to deny means and make every experience its own end. Violence and acceptance are the forms his charisma takes. With his amputated hand and boundless energy of suffering, he leaves on the land the pattern of an inglorious odyssey without origin or bourne.

What the novel glorifies is not a tough but a broken-hearted attitude—"sweet" and "sad" are among its most recurrent epithets. The ragged voyage to the end of the American night is, unlike Céline's, blurred in soft focus. Desperate without being despairing, *On the Road* trusts itself to experience in a manner that is sometimes childlike and more often thoughtless. Its unique combination of freshness and lassitude, American spontaneity and Oriental surrender, seems to confirm the wit who remarked that America has managed to pass from adolescence to decadence˙without ever reaching maturity. Yet its gospel, when it makes itself heard in the sweet beat of words, is a gospel of wonder and love, and its hero stands at the end of the line of American "innocents" who consume their vision in rebellion and are themselves consummated in affliction.

IV

The Beat Movement may seem no more than a bellicose exploitation of forces—holy renunciation and unholy denial—that have been long dormant in our culture. That these forces of the American psyche have been given free play in recent novels of the most diverse character must be now evident. The coincidence of radical dissent in a society known for its conformity with the most public and imperial moment in American history makes for a kind of irony we shall do well to recognize and redress. Ironic, too, is the fact that the *need* for dissent in the New World is most sharply felt by the American visiting Old Europe. Beat is unintelligible to Europeans because the privacies Europeans still enjoy are enjoyed without guilt or secrecy, whereas in our public lives the imperatives of freedom are pursued like a secret vice. Secret vices make public scapegoats, which is exactly what the new heroes of our fiction are.

But we shall find no redress for our ironies in elaborating the contrasts between Europe and America, and none in forcing continually the standards of the Lost Generation on the works of present writers. Suffice it to say that the ambiguities of initiation give way, in the recent novel, to the ambiguities of martyrdom. Stated baldly, the basic proposition which the American novel entertains at mid-century is this: that the nature of our civilization may be such that agony and outlawry, separate or conjoined, seem not merely inevitable; they further reveal the way by which man may affirm his deepest moral instincts. The courage to choose always ends in pain.

The context of fiction is ever changing, which is to say that its context is always the present. We have now observed the fading relation of the hero to his world in American fiction long enough to realize that a new type of hero is painfully emerging from the bedlam of history. To call him the victim with a thousand faces is but to evade the subtle task of definition. But definition is precisely what fiction abhors. Suffice it to say that our moment is discovering its hero, and that art, which is ever in the vanguard of culture, has already begun to limn his changing visage. His primary function is to liberate those values whose absence from our common experience is the cause of his predicament. The ethics he creates is inductive; it is defined existentially by his actions and even more by his passions. If he seems, at times, a throwback to pieties long honored by the American conscience, he is at least a radical in the proud or humble intensity of his vision. Radical, indeed, is that innocence which, drawing on the sacred anarchy of the soul both Twain and Dostoyevsky must have known, proposes to itself nothing less than the aboriginal freedom of man.

PART II

THE FORMS OF FICTION

There are many kinds of form in literature, and many theoretical concepts of it. There are didactic forms, mimetic forms, historical forms. But a genuine impulse, we may assume, always discovers its shape while it is being shaped. In the end, form is the way the mind acknowledges experience. It is a mode of awareness.

The novel derives its being from character, action, and milieu. Most often, it transforms these entities into a process. The process is complex, elusive, manifold. It can be described, nevertheless, as an encounter: the encounter of the self with the world, or the hero with experience. Form, we see, may be the pattern a concrete and existential encounter traces in the imagination.

In our age, the form of fiction tends to elude classic definitions. It conforms, more than anything else, to the spirit and shape of irony. The nine works discussed in this section show how the contemporary novel may be said to define an ironic pattern of its own; and how the pattern itself may vary as the fictional encounter, the experience of the hero, is molded by a grammar of freedom or of necessity.

CHAPTER 4

THE PATTERN OF FICTIONAL EXPERIENCE

The more we consider it the more we feel that the prose picture can never be at the end of its tether until it loses the sense of what it can do.—HENRY JAMES, *The Future of the Novel*

I

WHAT is the characteristic form of the recent novel in America? This is the question to be considered in successive stages.

The influence of formalist criticism is now such that no student of the novel, young or old, can afford to ignore its formal precepts even though he may choose to deprecate the "new" school. This is well; no one really likes to be identified with anything so obvious as a school, and the dogmatic wisdom of the "New Criticism" can benefit from heresy. For in our zeal to discover form, we have come to gauge the vitality of literary genres by the degree to which they may be judged "experimental." We challenge each novel as it appears hot off the press in the name of the innovations to which an older generation of writers gave glamor or authority. Is this zeal or merely nerves? Works such as *Moby Dick*, *The Scarlet Letter*, and *The Adventures of Huckleberry Finn* are not esteemed, after all, for exactly the same reasons we esteem the works of Kafka, Proust, or Joyce. "The real augmentations are not additions of technique, such as the writers of the last generation yielded," Van Wyck Brooks notes, "they are additions of . . . 'life-enhancement. . . .' "[1] One might add that fiction knows how to enhance and replenish life in more devious ways than we usually allow, and that some of these ways are more oblique than others.

In the last half century, to be sure, some of the farthest limits of language were attained in certain novels of which *Finnegans Wake* is the most notorious example. New possibilities for fiction were discovered, new styles created. But the changes in literary styles are functional, not simply continual. The most compelling authors of thirty years ago—Faulkner, Hemingway, Dos Passos, Farrell—do not continue to sustain themselves in an ever-changing tracery of new forms. These men, like European writers of their time, dramatized the shocking difference between their own values and those which their society still upheld by a violent breakup of accepted literary forms. But the revolt of one generation may be the orthodoxy of the next. For though no one may deny history with impunity, a novelist may deny a closer influence in favor of a more distant tradition. This is the impression we take from recent works which approach the business of fiction, the business of Twain or Dostoyevsky, from that peculiar angle, somewhat crazy and askew, which a new conception of the hero requires. Even those excessive refinements of language we find in the fiction of Capote, Buechner, or Stafford, and which we glibly take for evidence of an enfeebled sensibility, a decadence of form, even this verbal dandyism may represent, as Albert Guerard put it, "not merely a pose but poise," a mode of invoking reality, not of evading it.[2] And one must agree with Ralph Ellison when, speaking for the writers of his generation, he says, "Ours is a task which . . . was defined for us to a large extent by that which the novels of the twenties failed to confront, and implicit in their triumphs and follies were our complexity and our travail."[3]

Technique, we know, is seldom void of moral implications; it is often a strategy of the imagination against despair. But the contemporary novelist is death's quiet familiar. He is not as ready to snatch up the bright shield of form against the Medusa face of his time. He has looked into that face—and has not turned to stone. His ability to function owes much to the gallant efforts of his predecessors to subdue the intractable material of

American experience. For the bane of our writers, as Wright Morris has made sufficiently plain in *The Territory Ahead*, used to be that life constantly overwhelmed literature. This has been our artistic tragedy and also a source of our power. But we have worked our way through history to a new kind of *balance*—and are facing a new kind of danger. The contemporary novelist, despite the atomism, the discontinuities, of his world, no longer needs to fear the rawness of American experience; he no longer lacks the resources of technique. Barbaric frenzy and Alexandrian virtuosity constitute the extremes, not the alternatives, he faces. "Raw fact," and "processed fiction" are now equally within his reach. This is one of the factors affecting the pattern of contemporary fiction, and it is one that should persuade us to resist any simple correlation between experiment and vitality in the recent novel.

II

The image of the novel we have suggested may be one of poise and hover, a readiness to move in any number of ways. Critics have been at some pains to descry the present and future directions of the novel, and, as usual, their insights confirm their prejudices or give occasion to their wit. Yet the concerns of fiction may be reflected even in critical wit and prejudice.

Our prejudice nowadays runs against the smoothness of American writing. We think our fiction to be overprocessed. It is academic, distilled in the green alembic of summer workshops or constructed to the specifications of the formalist moguls who rule our universities. (There was a time, as Charles Fenton wittily observed, when our writers barely made the B.A. The following generation took an M.A., and now the Ph.D. seems almost *de rigueur*.)[4] Fiction is powerless to discover vital themes, incapable of giving itself to social generalizations. It is dedicated to the pursuit of private emotions and subtle or adolescent tremors. In short, the novel has renounced its lively and bastard heritage for the purity, the rigor, of death. It has abdicated to some Platonic or, more likely, Jamesian form.

That such abdication is less universal than we might suppose is made clear by novels like Jones's *From Here to Eternity*, Bellow's *Augie March*, and Ellison's *Invisible Man*; or, to cite the work of still younger writers, by Tom Berger's *Crazy in Berlin*, George Garrett's *The Finished Man*, and Philip Roth's *Goodbye, Columbus*. There is, indeed, something close to a renascence of the loose picaresque form. Nor has the Naturalistic novel lost completely the energy it gained, since Dreiser and Norris, from its intercourse with the newer symbolist modes —the vitality of Naturalism, however, is still plagued by sentimentality, as Willard Motley's *Knock on Any Door* and Ira Wolfert's *Act of Love* show.

Yet it is doubtless true that if a part of recent fiction has sprung its heroes loose upon the world in quixotic, rakish, or destructive fashion, another and equally important part has pushed the hero back on his most secret resources. The result may be described as a new *introversion of form*. It is the fictional correlative of the self in recoil. The rifeness of the novelette and short story form is thus seen not merely as evidence of our frenetic and accelerated mode of existence, and of all the distractions created by our mass media. That rifeness is evidence, on a more basic level, that our lives can take shape only in sudden epiphanies or isolated moments of crises, and that, indeed, since our world may come to end without notice, we lack those powers of anticipation and development which longer novels imply. Likewise, the current fashion of symbol, ritual, and archetype is not simply a compliment we pay to Sir James Frazer and all the anthropologists who have gilded the primitive past; it is rather an admission that we seek an order which reason and science have failed to provide, and look for verities which are not distorted by the conscious or sophisticated mind. Finally, the dandyism and refinements of style in some recent fiction do not only reflect our concern with, even our reliance on, sheer sensibility; they are also an attempt to preserve the integrity of language by removing it, perhaps too rashly, from the corruption of discursive speech in our age. As poetry aspired to the condition of music in the work of the French Symbolists, so does fiction now aspire, in certain instances, to the condition of poetry.[5] The lyrical cry is like love: it assumes a kind of exclusiveness. When the novel contracts into poetic form, it confesses its inability to share widely in the affairs of this world. But love must also call us to things of this world. The poetic novel is a paradoxical statement: it turns that failure of communication which is the shrill theme of our time into communicable form. In so doing, it cultivates the narrow metaphoric range of a novel like William Goyen's *House of Breath* or the autism of John Hawkes's surreal work, *The Cannibals*. The introversion of form, we see, guides the novel toward the inner processes of the psyche: epiphany, myth, poetry, dream. It has also required novelists to make large use—sometimes with dubious results—of the depth techniques of psychoanalysis.

What we are witnessing, therefore, is not simply a scattering of trends and unrelated fictional forms. These trends and forms find a common impulse in an attack on the accepted view of reality, an attack, in its quiet way, as radical as that which induced older writers to manipulate time and space in outrageous fashion. The decline in realistic techniques, the dearth of public themes, the aversion to ideology suggest a redefinition of the function of the novel which in the past has always tried to keep its vision centered on the highroads of life. The redefinition of function has now made some of our critical categories —symbolism and naturalism, tragedy and comedy—nearly obsolete. But it still allows for searching novels that retain the central vision of life, that treat, say, the hallowed family themes —Malamud's *The Assistant*, Agee's *Death in the Family*, Shirley Anne Grau's *The Hard Blue Sky*. And it has occasioned, as we saw, a recrudescence of the naturalistic and picaresque novel.

How, then, may that subtle redefinition of form be described? Or must the alleged variety and contradictions of the novel continue to elude our grasp? To say that the new novel while maintaining still the polarity of processed fiction and raw fact brings both to bear on its central problems is not to say enough. The sloshing writers and the finicky artists are not so far apart, nowadays, as they seemed in the time of Dreiser and James; but the fact itself does not make what they both share more clear. We still need to know how the new fusion of fable and fact, the ritual wedding "full of richness and ceremony, of black Iago and delicate Desdemona," as Hyman put it, takes place.[6] Nor is it quite enough to say that the poetic and the picaresque novels, the introverted and the extraverted forms, share a common denial of reality as we see it with our everyday eyes, the former conveying its vision through a grotesque or victim hero whose alienation defines the shape of the novel, the latter projecting its vision through a roguish or rebellious hero whose free actions upon the world still imply a private standard of conduct.

We shall probably come closer to an answer of our question by taking further account of the present and historic bias of American fiction as reflected in the perpetual tension between self and society in the novel. Our awareness of that tension has been colored by three views which are applied, with unequal success, to the criticism of fiction. These views concern the new ethos of mass society, the concept of manners, and the idea of romance.

III

Alienation of the self from society used to be, and in a sense remains, the basic assumption of the modern novel. But society has changed its contours—we now speak of it, inevitably, in terms of size and mass—and so is the novel presumed to have altered its shape.[7] In the postmodern world, society no longer lends itself to "assured definition," Irving Howe argues, and one can "no longer assume as quickly as in the recent past that a spiritual or moral difficulty could find a precise embodiment in a social conflict."[8] The breakdown of coherent, if not rigid, theories about society, in other words, breeds an agnosticism of fictional forms: the novel no longer finds in the vast spectacle of collective life a mirror to the pattern it seeks to create. Howe's argument is probably true as far as it goes. What we need to emphasize, however, is not the alleged disintegration of social categories in the novel but the creation of new categories of form which ultimately rest on the values of a hero confronted by a world intelligible in specific areas of experience, bewildering as a whole. A kind of aesthetic distance is thereby forced upon the contemporary novel, whether the latter takes the form of a psychological idyll or poetic pastoral. Even the naturalistic novel allies itself with the imagery of dreams—*Invisible Man*—and the picaresque with the assumptions of romance—*Henderson the Rain King*. The "as if" quality of so many recent novels, the fact that they are so candidly *contrived*, so clearly *abstracted* from quotidian life, does not necessarily vitiate their effectiveness as works of art; it merely enhances their distance from that brutishness of facts on which, say, *Moll Flanders* plumply rests.

The same conclusion about the novel is reached when the problems that mass society presents to the writer of fiction are viewed in a different light. For in a paradoxical way, the collapse of certain social norms has accelerated the collective trends of culture. Social manners, the distinctions they imply, have not entirely vanished; they have become either bureaucratized or reduced to the amorphous protocols of "other-direction." But if the traditional hero of drama and fiction has been, as Aldridge claims, the "inner-directed" man whose illusions or ideals were pitted against the world outside, then the rise of the "other-directed" personality "must cause us drastically to revise our conception of drama, just as it must drive the novel to extinction or to the discovery of new dramatic effects."[9]

Aldridge's point seems well taken, though his criticism does not go far enough toward envisioning a way out. We are still, and are quite likely to remain, heirs to the feud between reality and illusion. What has changed is merely the way we choose to define each. The uniform surface of society defines but one level on which illusion and reality may be seen at play. On this level, the given phenomena of human existence remain obdurate and discrete. On this level, too, the French "anti-novels" of Alain Robbe-Grillet and Nathalie Sarraulte seek, rather hopelessly, to dramatize their vision. In Sarraulte's novels, man, as Sartre observed, is "the incessant, shapeless oscillation from the particular to the general."[10] The flattened characters lead their lives without drama or dialectic, existing on a surface where the inner and outer worlds meet. For as Robbe-Grillet put it, "Le monde n'est ni signifiant ni absurde. Il *est*, tout simplement."[11] The hero of the anti-novel loses his inwardness, the analogical structure of fiction is denied, and language foregoes its powers of veiled suggestion. Vision is all a camera-eye may record.

But our world, even now, is not wholly defined by external phenomena. Flattened as the human ego may have become, it does not yet subsist on the surface of culture alone. It is doubtful that the sheer phenomenalism to which Robbe-Grillet has welded the novel can dictate the form of future fiction in America.[12] It is also doubtful that the human Self, whether it be directed from within or from without, can ever relinquish its dialectic relation to the Other. Furthermore, the heroes of contemporary fiction do not struggle only with the world: they still struggle for and against themselves. Their pressing concern with love—what sociologists might call interpersonal relations in an age of peer group dominance—does not obviate their regard for the perennial interests of the Self. Even Salinger's Holden Caulfield or Bellow's Augie March, who are perhaps among the heroes most sensitive to their environment, and in a special sense most obedient to it, even they derive their moral energy from an internal source of which their fellow travelers in life are somewhat ignorant. The central fact about fiction in a mass society may be this: that as the modes of behavior congeal into a hard, uniform crust, the hero attempts to discover alternate modes of life on levels beneath the frozen surface. The new hero is a diver, a subterranean, and this accounts for the aesthetic distance which the formal resources of the novel put between him and the standardized realm of social behavior. A diver, however, moves where light is seldom sharp, and the shadowy contours of things melt into the strange imaginings of the eye. Forced beneath the surface, the hero in a mass society lacks some measure of definition, lacks the basis to distinguish between illusion and reality which the traditional novel afforded. It is this, rather than the absence of conflict between inner dream and public fact, that prescribes the moral ambiguities of the recent novel, and determines the involutions of its form: the vague present or undated yesterdays of so many novels, their unworldly settings and symbolic actions, their submersed point of view, eccentric characters, and decorous structure.[13]

A mass society contributes to the formal ambiguities of fiction in still another way. It compels us to reconsider the role manners have in giving body and substance to the moral vision of the novel. Much has been said of manners in the last two decades, and some of it said in the peevish or unmannerly spirit which ironically befits its subject.[14] It may be unwise to reopen a discussion that has no issue but controversy. Yet Trilling's idea of manners as "a culture's hum and buzz of implication," and as "the indication of the direction of man's soul," involves too many concerns of fiction to be lightly dismissed.[15] We do not propose to lament that absence of manners in the American novel which James made famous in a passage from his life of Hawthorne—no sovereign, no court, no aristocracy, no church; no palaces or manors or ivied ruins, and so on down the line of distinguished things. Nor do we propose to predict the future of fiction as it reveals itself in the crystal ball of manners. A good look about us is work enough. A good look should convince us that the reality of hard cash is still tangible in our society, though it may be continually mediated by our current notions of power or leisure. Class distinctions are still perceptible, though these are often translated into the more elusive symbols of status. What Tocqueville called the hypocrisy of luxury in democratic cultures—the tendency to make every article conform in specious fashion to some ideal of opulence—persuades the designers of General Motors to make their cheapest and most expensive products look very nearly alike, yet the man in the street can still distinguish a Chevy from a Cadillac. The illusions created by snobbery, the clink and rustle of money, the gesture of tacit power—these are still alive in our midst, and the subtlety of their indirection challenges the fictional imagination as it was seldom challenged by a society more obviously structured. Which is to say that manners, in the widest and most serious sense, have not ceased to serve the novel by rendering the implicit life of culture into concrete and dramatic symbols. No one who has attuned himself to the Jewish ambience of Malamud's *The Assistant*, or the middle-class bohemianism of McCarthy's *A Charmed Life*, or the zany sense of kinship in Cheever's *The Wapshot Chronicle*, or the Southern community of Taylor's *A Woman of Means*, or the token of urban success—a particular kind of shirt or tie gives the man away—in Bellow's *Seize the Day*, or even to the mannerisms of the hipster world in Kerouac's *On the Road*, can say otherwise.

What these novels, picked almost at random, show is not the death of manners but the restriction of manners to particular subcultures which society furtively sponsors. This is the second paradox of mass culture: that enforced uniformity not only produces, in depth, levels of dissent beneath the surface; it also breeds pockets of heresy in the lateral direction. Thus the "society" of Malamud can be as incomprehensible to the characters of Peter Taylor as the "society" of Kerouac can be to the protagonists of John Cheever. The formal consequence of this cultural fact is that some contemporary novels are forced to create within the structure of their narrative a self-sufficient world of motives and manners that have little resemblance to the motives or manners a general reader may recognize. The structure of fiction, in other words, becomes more autotelic than the structure of the classic nineteenth-century novel. A fictional world created largely from *within* relies more heavily on the resources of organized form and universal symbols to attain dramatic objectivity; it is self-made, sometimes self-conscious, and not always self-evident. Its manners tend, therefore, to be self-reflexive. But this is not to say that its characters move in a vacuum—or that an American society does not really exist.

The peculiar disposition of manners in American life may induce the novelist to recover some ideology as a substitute for the social discriminations of character and action. This is a way out few contemporary writers have chosen—there is in our experience, as we know, much that repels any conscious application of dogma or even idea to the business of the imagination. The few "political novels" we still produce—William Manchester's *City of Anger* or Edwin O'Connor's *The Last Hurrah* —are sometimes executed with remarkable skill and authority. But they do not always succeed, as Conrad and Dostoyevsky do, in pushing through the precinct of local politics to a wider sphere of motive and idea.

It is because neither manners nor ideology can serve the full purpose of fiction that the American novelist, then as now, turns to romance. Trilling himself understood this when he saw that romance, the "operative reality of thought and desire, which, in the novel, exists side by side with the things 'we cannot possibly know'" contains the renovating power of fiction in America, and contains also, one might add, its chance to make a particular event universal.[16]

In recent years, the concept of romance has shone with even more luster and glamor than the idea of manners. Yet the concept is a serious one, and it has the advantage of making the characteristic form of the novel in America, its peculiar mastery and deficiency, seem all the more attractive. It is thus, for instance, that Marius Bewley can describe the life of the American writer as possessing "a distinctive quality and set of interests" which have "traditionally been determined and conditioned by the deprivations and confinements of the American condition. . . ."[17] The form of the American novel, the form of romance really, is an attempt to heal the split in American experience; or else to exploit, as Richard Chase claims in his influential view, the broken circuits of our history. Chase sees a line extending from Cooper, through Hawthorne, Melville, and Twain, and down to Faulkner, which suggests that "the American novel, in its most original and characteristic form, has worked out its destiny . . . by incorporating an element of romance." As it turns out, by romance Chase means a form less committed to the immediate rendition of reality than the novel, veering more freely toward "the mythic, allegorical, and symbolistic modes," toward idyll and melodrama, distinguished by some "formal abstractness" and a "tendency to plunge into the underside of consciousness," and prone, in its sharp and eccentric vision, "to abandon moral questions or to ignore the spectacle of man in society. . . ."[18] The freedom of action and the idealized context of the finest novels we have produced may help convince us that romance is a typical and native form, and that these works derive their shape from "the perception and acceptance not of unities but of radical disunities."[19]

This is an attractive view, perhaps even too attractive for the good of our own perceptions of disunities in criticism or history. The temptation to say that romance is the formal response of American writers to the insinuations of their radical innocence is a temptation we should both acknowledge and qualify. The liberation of experience in romance which Henry James extolled

—and Simms and Hawthorne extolled before him—may lead us by some direct or hidden path to understand such works as Capote's *Other Voices, Other Rooms* and Bellow's *Henderson the Rain King*. It may further account for the restriction on manners, the autonomy of story, the hidden energy, and poetic texture of some recent fiction. And it may explain why the contradictions still active in American culture find the disencumbered form of romance singularly congenial. All this is very much to the point. The matter, however, does not rest here. Romance, in the contemporary novel, has the knack of self-parody. We shall do well to push our inquiry a step farther by adopting still another view of fictional form.

IV

The view of form we propose is not meant to be definitive, but it has the advantage of a certain consistency with the broader outlook on our culture to which this study has committed itself. It seeks, that is, to recognize the discrepancies between the American myth and the American conscience, between hope (Utopia) and memory (Eden), nature and civilization, the energy of Faust and the passion of Christ. It is also a view of form that acknowledges the novel to be a judgment on *experience* rendered through fictional *characters*. Its main assumption is that a new type of character, a generic hero of mournful or roguish mien, fulfills his destiny by mediating the contradictions to which we are heir, and mediates them, particularly, in the process of his initiation, his discovery, which often leads him to the brink of defeat. The paradigm of form in contemporary fiction, it is suggested, may be the pattern of *encounter*: the shifting, straining encounter of the rebel-victim with destructive experience. What lies behind the hero's mask? And what shape does the process of his discovery assume?

Whatever else he may be, the new hero is not created like his classic predecessors, in a social image. To say, therefore, as

Sean O'Faolain does, that "the Hero is a purely social creation. He represents . . . a socially approved norm, for representing which to the satisfaction of society he is decorated with a title," is perhaps to grant society more ingenuity than it deserves.[20] It is the altered apprehension of the self, no less than the changed condition of society, that defines the character of the hero. His radical innocence, his deep and excessive awareness of the Self, makes him in many ways a postsocial creature, but makes him also a throwback to a presocial condition of mythic struggles and dreamlike aspirations. It is not surprising, therefore, that the new hero should rediscover for us some archaic or regressive qualities which remained in rich disguise while the novel enjoyed the sunny loyalties of bourgeois society. As we shall presently see, the rebel-victim of contemporary literature reveals some dark affinities with the heroes of a mythic past.

The ancient hero, it is usually conceded, is an epic character, a figure somewhere below the gods and above the common run of men. But the epic ideal of heroism is itself a modification of an older impulse that is given ample play in shamanistic poetry out of which the epic, according to C. M. Bowra, developed.[21] The Greeks recognized that impulse when they granted their heroes the right to be possessed by states of fearful madness, *menos* or *até*; in such states, Dodds writes, the heroes "can perform the most difficult feats with ease. . . . They can even, like Diomede, fight with impunity against the Gods."[22] It would appear, then, that the traditional hero, while insisting on the human freedom of will and action, betrayed an atavistic trait of divine fury which, paradoxically, bestowed on him power to the extent that it reduced his volition. Epic, we see, reverts to myth, and the God-born hero goes back to the divine king engaged in those primordial rites of fertility and rebirth of which he was the scapegoat.

Other lines of speculation confirm us in the belief that various degrees of rebellion or alienation attended the quest of the mythic hero. The mysterious circumstances which usually sur-

112

round his birth have led Otto Rank to propose that heroic myths have "sprung from two opposite motives, both of which are subordinate to the motive of vindication of the individual through the hero: on the one hand the motive of affection and gratitude towards the parents; and on the other hand, the motive of revolt against the father."[23] As might be expected, the true hero of these myths turns out to be the human ego itself, aspiring sometimes to childlike rebellion against omnipotent forces, sometimes crushed in the process of its revolt. Furthermore, in his birth as in his career the hero must know solitude. The essential pattern of his ritualized life has been isolated in the mythologies of various cultures. The pattern reveals the miraculous birth of the hero, his feats and ordeals culminating in accession to power, and his lonely death and displacement. Throughout his career, the actions of the hero are gauged by a standard of communal interests, of functional efficiency. But the ideal has another side apparent only to the hero. In all his ordeals, the hero is a man alone. He seldom fights with ordinary men or with ordinary animals. And his ending is equally solitary. "The hero of tradition," according to Lord Raglan, "unlike most heroes of history, normally ends his career by being driven from his kingdom and put to death in mysterious circumstances."[24] In a real sense, then, the ancient hero remains outside the very order he has helped found and maintain. To see both sides of the heroic avatar, therefore, is to recall that the archaic hero is both king and scapegoat, actor and sufferer, public symbol and private will.

"The essence of oneself and the essence of the world: these two are one," Joseph Campbell writes in his celebrated work, *The Hero With a Thousand Faces.* "Hence separateness, withdrawal, is no longer necessary. Wherever the hero may wander, whatever he may do, he is ever in the presence of his own essence. . . . Thus, just as the way of social participation may lead in the end to a realization of the All in the individual, so that of exile brings the hero to the Self in all."[25] This statement describes the ideal conditions of withdrawal and return, the innermost psychic action, of the mythic hero. It also describes the inescapable difference between the contemporary hero and the prototype he resembles.

The contemporary hero is a religious symbol without religion, a mythic image without benefit of a myth, a figure transcendent by virtue of its nakedness rather than its communal authority. For him the essence of the self and the essence of the world are *not* one and the same, and the broken pattern of all his actions recalls the futile courage of a Sisyphus toiling to unite one pole of experience to the other. No longer a representative of all the divine powers men want to propitiate, he is simply the mediator of forces that torment their existence. Insulted and injured, his strategy is more often subhuman than superhuman, though it is not the less heroic for that. A grotesque effigy to the rule of chaos, he still placates darkness with the light of human agony or human derision. Clowning his way to anarchy or immolation, his design is still to create a unity where none can obtain save in the momentary repose of artifice. Elements of the Greek *alazon*, impostor, compulsive rebel, or outsider, the *eiron*, the humble, self-deprecating man, and the *pharmakos*, scapegoat and random victim, unite to form the tarnished halo weighing on his head.[26] In the end, however, his character is simply what remains to a hero when self and world are thrown out of joint, and self-transcendence is sought though all the gods may be defunct.

Yet if the contemporary hero seems mythic in the sacrificial quality of his passion, his actions have the concrete self-definition of an existential encounter. The notion that fictional form may take the shape of an existential encounter should not prove unnerving to anyone save the most rabid of formalists. The forms of art cannot be exclusively aesthetic. As Kenneth Burke put it, "A form is a way of experiencing; and such a form is made available in art when, by the use of specific subject-matter, it enables us to experience in this way."[27] If Burke is right, then

114

the question of major interest to our inquiry must be this: In what form does contemporary experience lend itself to the dialectic of Self and World in Time? Or, put another way: Is there any recognizable pattern of encounter between the Hero and his Fate in contemporary fiction? No critic could hope to answer such questions precisely without making a display either of his arrogance or naiveté. The essential patterns of human experience, after all, are ageless, and the forms of fiction in any age are manifold.

Our hypothesis is that the pattern of experience in contemporary fiction is largely existential. There are those, no doubt, who still believe Existentialism to be a foreign and new-fangled philosophy, irrelevant to the concerns of American letters. This is not a point we wish to dispute. The apologists of Existentialism do not need our succor. The term *existential*, however, carries broader connotations. It is less exclusive. Just as Melville could be considered a symbolic writer without belonging to the group of French Symbolists who gathered around Mallarmé, so can an American novel be termed existential without benefiting from the dogmas of Sartre or Heidegger. The existential pattern implies a view of life which may be traced back to Job; but it is not, as the tragic form also is not, any less distinctive for that; nor is its peculiar relevance to our experience diminished by its historical reach. Serious writers, such as Ralph Ellison, Norman Mailer, William Styron, Paul Bowles, and perhaps Saul Bellow, have often placed the existential pattern of experience at the center of their work. The character of the American hero we have viewed, the piety, insolence, and contradictions of his life, emerges with some clarity in this pattern. Just what is the pattern, and how does it define a fictional form?

Probably the best we can do is suggest the main features of the "world," the "hero," and the corresponding "structure" of fiction in recent writing. This can be done in five interrelated points:

115

1. Chance and absurdity rule human actions. The hero recognizes this, and knows that reality is but another name for chaos. Intention and fulfillment, dream and fact, engage in a perpetual debate which can be both ludicrous and grinding.

The pattern of fiction is therefore one that recognizes disorder —gratuitous actions, demonic intrusions, obsessive motives. The form reflects the inward darkness of things. It is saturated with what Blackmur calls *moha*: "the basic, irremediable, irreplaceable, characteristic, and contemptuous stupidity of man confronted with choice or purpose. . . ."[28] The very idea of causality is carried to a depth of causelessness. In short, the novel becomes all metaphor, a metaphor of duplicity and unreason, and a high tension is maintained between the form of fiction and those turmoils of the modern psyche which psychoanalysis has raised to the level of consciousness.[29]

2. There are no accepted norms of feeling or conduct to which the hero may appeal. The eternal verities are either denied or affirmed in the spirit of irony. Courage, therefore, is the prime virtue because it is the virtue of self-sufficiency. It confers dignity on meaninglessness. The hero, as it is said, encounters nothingness, and his courage is the courage of simply being. For what is put on trial is the very existence of man, not his heritage or future, his property or beliefs.

The pattern of fiction is therefore contained and self-reflexive. It acknowledges the nakedness of man by a parody of manners, quests, social or religious absolutes. It is charged with scalding violence, comes to rest in extreme or archetypal situations. The metaphor of fiction is not simply one of disorder; it is also reductive. It creates meaning by referring to an autonomous dream, an arbitrary and personal truth.

3. Rebel or victim, the hero is at odds with his environment. He is at odds with himself. His energy is the energy of opposition, and his aggressions are either directed against himself (the victim) or against the world (the rebel). In either case, he remains an alien to society, a misfit.

Again, the imagery of fiction is dominated by cruelty and outrage, *sparagmos*, dismemberment, mutilation, and suffering. Dramatic conflict is ruthless, and characters prey upon one another.

Time itself is destructive; it serves to eventuate only defeat. But unlike the fiction of Naturalism, necessity in the contemporary novel is not defined externally. Necessity is an inner compulsion, purposeless and self-destructive. It is spiteful of itself. Frohock's distinction between the novel of "erosion"—the hero is simply eroded by time—and the novel of "destiny"—the hero meets time-bound defeat on his own terms—tends in this case to blur.[30] The legacies of Dreiser and Hemingway merge. In existential fiction, the illusion of choice is maintained though choice can bring no victory. The action of time is one of ironic and eternal recurrence—Sisyphus at his boulder—but the end is always the same: discomfiture. This is "demonic" time.

The process of initiation in time can take one of two forms. The initiation of the hero may coincide with his victimization. This is the tragic way to opposition. But there is another way, closer perhaps to the way of comedy. It is more roguish and sadistic than self-effacing and masochistic. In this case, the initiation of the hero, though it does not lead to defeat, results in his expulsion from the accepted order of society. The hero remains a clownish or marginal figure, a creature of the underground. In both cases, the process of encounter or discovery we have termed initiation denies its own purpose.

4. Human motives are forever mixed; irony and contradiction prevail. This is reflected in the situation of the protagonist who cuts across the lines of good and evil. There are no pure villains in fiction, no blameless heroes. The objects of our sympathy and the objects of our revulsion are often the same.

The form of fiction is correspondingly a form of ambiguities. Such ambiguities can be sustained only if the form maintains a kind of detachment. The function of form, therefore, is, first, to develop distance, and, second, to create conflicting levels

117

of meaning, a complex interplay of points of view. Even where the illusion of familiarity is intended—witness the neo-picaresque novel—a marked discrepancy may be found between the points of view of author and narrator. This kind of duplicity amounts to an inner ironic distance. Tragic catharsis (pity and awe) and comic relief (clarity and dissociation) are equally neutralized by this elusive point of view in which detachment and involvement ironically blend. Aesthetic distance in the contemporary novel is an ironic distance.

5. In a world dominated by error, even heroes do not possess the gift of complete knowledge. The hero acts or is acted upon, but his perception of the situation remains both limited and relative. (It is precisely the relativity of human actions that makes the discrete choices of the existential hero universal.) Because the hero seldom attains to full knowledge, he is seldom a tragic figure in the classic sense. And because his life is so rarely devoid of genuine pain, he is rarely a comic figure of harmless compromises.

The pattern of fiction is therefore neither tragic nor comic. It shows the hero to be a child of ironies, a mediator of polar claims. The pattern diffuses insight and fractures the whole truth. It is a parody of man's quest for fulfillment. The form provides the hero with more freedom of action than tragedy strictly allows, and less freedom than comedy permits. Form becomes, as it were, an ironic mask, weeping and leering in one concerted grimace at the proud fallibility of man. The grimace itself is the measure of man's dignity.

Our aim was not to offer a blueprint for the novel but merely to limn a certain kind of fiction. The value of literary principles is to dramatize for the discursive mind the liberties literature takes with itself. One thing is certain: the existential pattern does not conform to the traditional genres of comic or tragical fiction, and it exemplifies once again the fact that the contortions of literary form follow the distortions of function. Such contortions, however, are not quite so arbitrary as they may seem: the existential pattern, like the new anti-hero, has its origin in tradition. We can discover the ancestry of the form by viewing further some of its ambiguities.

The sapient thing to say nowadays is that contemporary fiction employs the resources of pathos rather than of comedy or tragedy. The observation is true within limits which it does not often acknowledge. Tragedy, we know, is an inevitable part of life since man's reach, the horizon of his awareness, so often exceeds his grasp. Tragedy means that there is no way out. This is what the contemporary hero knows. But as Jaspers put it, "Where there is no sense of the infinite vastness of what is beyond our grasp, all we finally succeed in conveying is misery—not tragedy."[31] This is the sense that the hero lacks. Hence the descent to pathos, the argument runs. Critics who adopt this view have a splendid time with American literature in particular, where the insistence on innocence, they claim, makes of everyone a worldly Christ.[32] But the American imagination is really more devious. It qualifies pathos with buffoonery and innocence with dark knowledge.

The hero of contemporary fiction is perhaps too much the victim to be considered tragic. But he is also too much the rebel to meet the requirements of comedy. Comedy is as equivocal nowadays as tragedy. It is a sign both of anger and desperation. It accepts the absurdities of our life in the same breath that it repudiates them. It leaves us face to face, as Wylie Sypher put it, "with the preposterous, the trivial, the monstrous, the inconceivable."[33] Laughter, in our time, is sickly, savage, demonic—or at least self-ironic. It feeds upon deformity, thrives upon unreason; it is fraught more than ever with peril. The barbs of frontier exaggeration have turned inward, and the zest of our trickster stories blends with the pathos of the long-suffering clown.

Thus may it seem at first glance that comedy and tragedy find their common ground, where the contemporary novel is concerned, in pathos which, as we are quick to assume, sums up the experience of the isolate and grotesque hero. This is but a partial truth. Thomas Mann was right to observe that "the striking feature of modern art is that it has ceased to recognize the categories of tragic and comic. . . . It sees life as a tragi-comedy, with the result that the grotesque is its most genuine style. . . ."[34] But as Mann himself goes on to say, the grotesque is also one guise in which the sublime appears, and its other guise is the ridiculous. Pathos, however, does not cover the range of emotions from the sublime to the ridiculous. Only irony may encompass that range. We shall be on firmer ground, therefore, if we base the equivocal existential pattern of fiction not on pathos but on *irony*. "This is the great irony of life," Cyrus Hay concludes in his attempt to discover the meeting place of tragedy and comedy, "that man can envision an ideal of good . . . and yet fails to achieve it. The failure can occasion either tears or laughter: tears in recognition of the fact this is the way life is; laughter at the folly of those who fail to recognize that this is the way life is."[35] At the root both of comedy and tragedy, we see, lies the perception that man is deficient in the knowledge of human limitations. The perception, insofar as it is a conscious insight, is ironic. Irony, we believe, is the traditional mode of which the existential form is but a modern variant.

Irony is a mode but also a form whose essential properties are cogently analyzed by Northrop Frye in *The Anatomy of Criticism*. Frye sees myth and naturalism as the two poles of literary design. Irony lies close to the second of these poles. The tendency of Western literature, and particularly of its fiction, has been to move steadily from the mythic toward the ironic modes. In modern literature, however, a regression from irony back to myth may be discerned.[36] Irony, which is a descendant of the "low mimetic" form of realism and dispassionate observation, returns to the mythic origin of all modes, "and dim outlines of sacrificial rituals and dying gods begin to reappear in it."[37] This mystic reversion, as we have seen, is exemplified by the ironic hero himself.

Frye characterizes, rather broadly, the ironic hero as "inferior in power or intelligence to ourselves, so that we have the sense of looking down on a scene of bondage, frustration, absurdity. . . ."[38] His characterization, however, gains in concreteness as the ironic hero becomes identified, on the one hand, with the ritual *alazon, eiron,* and *pharmakos,* and, on the other, with the *existential* hero. "The archetype of the inevitably ironic," Frye states, "is Adam, human nature under sentence of death. At the other pole is the incongruous irony of human life, in which all attempts to transfer guilt to a victim give that victim something of the dignity of innocence. The archetype of the incongruously ironic is Christ, the perfectly innocent victim excluded from human society."[39] Between Adam and Christ, between inevitable and incongruous irony, lies the figure of Job, a would-be rebel whose failure, unlike that of Prometheus, is more bitter or absurd than tragic. He it is, in his self-taught irony, who represents better than Adam or Christ the archetype of existential man.

The ironic hero emerges as the father of existential man; the ironic mode crystallizes the ambiguities we have already discovered in the existential pattern. For irony isolates from the tragic situation the element of arbitrariness, the sense of isolation, the demonic vision; from comedy, it takes the unlawful or quixotic motive of the *picaro,* say, the savagery which is the other face of play, as in the saturnalia, and the grotesque scapegoat rituals of comic expiation; and from romance it adopts the quest motif, turning it into a study of self-deception, and the dream of wish-fulfillment, transforming it into nightmare.[40] Indeed, Frye's penetrating study shows irony to be the form to which all other forms tend when disintegration overtakes them. It is nevertheless a distinctive mode, and its mythos is unique. As the mythos of comedy is spring, the mythos of romance is summer, and that of tragedy is autumn, so is winter the mythos of irony. All four *mythoi*, we see, contribute to the same unifying pattern. Yet each has its peculiar theme and form. "*Sparagmos*, or the sense that heroism and effective action are absent, disorganized or foredoomed to defeat, and that confusion and anarchy reign over the world, is the archetypal theme of irony and satire."[41] This is the principle of recoil or opposition on which the existential form is based. Its structural embodiment, as Frye suggests, is a *parody of romance*, "the application of romantic mythical forms to a more realistic content which fits them in unexpected ways."[42]

This, on the whole, is the pattern of fiction—call it ironic or existential—which we have tried to describe earlier in a five-point outline. We submit it as a useful hypothesis, useful, that is, because it may allow us to view the peculiar tensions of American culture and the formal bias of contemporary fiction in a single perspective.

V

We do not believe that archetypes can be invoked at a pinch in the hope that the dark gods may rise from the depths of prehistory to relieve us from our literary difficulties. Mythology, nowadays, is sometimes used as a kind of universal zipper, too hastily drawn to conceal our intellectual embarrassments. It is, however, as glib to assume that all change is recurrence as it is to believe that all phenomena are perpetually new. In literature, particularly, past and present, tradition and experiment, submit to the strange dialectic between a creative imagination and the constancies of the human heart. A radical form may sink its roots deep in archetypal forms. This justifies our mythical perspective of a modern development in literature.

Starting with the recognition that a "new" type of hero had put his bid for eminence in the novel, we saw him as a child both of doom and opposition, and saw his character defined by the ironic tensions between an ageless mythical function and a modern spirit of profound skepticism. The traditional rites of quest and initiation, with their existential ordeals, culminated, as we observed in recent fiction, either in the isolation of the hero or in his defeat. From this we postulated a distinctive pattern of fiction. The contemporary hero demanded a new language of experience, a different mold of expression. This mold we labeled, with some qualms, the existential pattern, and we perceived it to be a variant of an established ironic mode. But the argument, so far, has remained abstract and generic. Abstractions must also be submitted to the test of aesthetic experience.

In the next three chapters we shall try to discover how nine contemporary novels conform to this hypothetical form—how they question or modify it. These novels may be considered in three groups which correspond to three subclasses of the existential pattern, and define together its scope. The three subclasses can be described briefly as follows.

1. The hero appears primarily in the guise of a victim or scapegoat, *pharmakos*. He enjoys little or no freedom of action: he is ruled, that is, by necessity. The ironic mode borders here on tragedy. The form of fiction is *closed* to any real change in the life of the hero, any self-renewal.

2. The hero appears primarily in the guise of the self-deprecating *eiron*. He enjoys a limited degree of freedom, and makes an uneasy truce with necessity. The ironic mode, hovering between comedy and tragedy, may touch on romance. The form of fiction is, as it were, *suspended.*

3. The hero appears primarily in the guise of the rebel, rogue, or self-inflating *alazon*. He enjoys considerable freedom, and gives the illusion of escaping from necessity. The ironic mode veers toward comedy. The form of fiction is *open.*

CHAPTER 5

ENCOUNTER WITH NECESSITY:
THREE NOVELS BY
STYRON, SWADOS, AND MAILER

. . . we lie down in darkness, and have our light in ashes.—
SIR THOMAS BROWNE, *Urn Burial*

I

WILLIAM STYRON'S first novel, *Lie Down in Darkness*, 1951, remains one of the outstanding works of postwar fiction. This is not sly praise. *The Long March*, 1952, and *Set This House on Fire*, 1960, are in no way shoddy, and indeed the latest of Styron's novels is an exceptional work, as ambitious in meaning as his first may be deft in execution. The three books project very different types of heroes though each is preeminently a hero of our time. Captain Mannix, the protagonist of *The Long March*, is an awkward and unwilling rebel, a soft, scarred, bearlike man who defies the authority of his Marine commander. "Born into a generation of conformists, even Mannix . . . was aware that his gestures were not symbolic, but individual, therefore hopeless, maybe even absurd. . . ."[1] *Set This House on Fire* is a torrid, complex story of crime and punishment, the terror of guilt and the horror of freedom. Its hero, Cass Kinsolving, finally chooses being rather than nothingness because for him, "to choose between them was simply to choose being, not for the sake of being, or even for the love of being, much less the desire to be forever—but in the hope of being what I could be for a time."[2] In all three novels, Styron reveals a brooding imagination, sometimes obsessive, and a dark gift of poetry. The legacy of Faulkner is perhaps apparent in his earliest work; but it is a legacy that Styron has learned to put to his own service —one does not feel quite the same way about other talented writers, such as William Humphrey—and it is mainly recognizable in the intensity of the author's relation to a certain kind of material. For though Styron is a Virginian by birth, he has tried to shake loose from the local colorist's view of things without foregoing the advantages the Southern tradition provides. Thus, for instance, does he say of *Lie Down in Darkness*: "Only certain things in the book are particularly Southern. I used leit-motifs—the Negroes, for example—that run throughout the book, but I would like to believe that my people would have behaved the way they did anywhere."[3] Other motifs which we like to identify as Southern occur in his fiction: the Biblical rhetoric of story telling, the conflict between a tradition of religious fundamentalism and modern skepticism, racial contrasts, the industrialization of an agrarian society, etc. But his concern with some of these motifs, particularly the demonic power of guilt, the black oppressiveness of death or decay, the lurid ironies of Protestantism in the South—"a crazy colored preacher howling those tremendously moving verses from Isaiah 40, while riding around in a maroon Packard"—betrays an imagination nearly religious in intensity, a sensibility closer to the baroque tradition of John Donne and Sir Thomas Browne than to the gothic school of Poe and Company.[4]

The epigraph to *Lie Down in Darkness* contains the following statement from Sir Thomas Browne's *Urn Burial*: ". . . since our longest sun sets at right descencions, and makes but winter arches, and therefore it cannot be long before we lie down in darkness, and have our light in ashes." There is no single hero-victim in the novel. Milton Loftis, his wife Helen, and their daughter Peyton are all locked in a domestic tragedy in which love must wear the face of guilt, and the search for childhood innocence must acquaint the seeker with death. All lie down in darkness. But there is one character whose light is found in ashes: Peyton.

I pray but my prayer climbs up like a broken wisp of smoke: Oh my Lord, I am dying, is all I know, and *oh my father, oh my darling*, longingly, lonesomely, I fly into your arms! . . . Myself all shattered, this lovely shell? Perhaps I shall rise at another time, though I lie down in darkness and have my light in ashes.[5]

This is the stream of Peyton's doomed consciousness before she jumps from a washroom to her death. The two passages quoted, one lying at the outset of the novel, the other very near its close, form a kind of frame, a frame of two mirrors reflecting the darkness and the light of a single life, Peyton's, which in turn refracts the fate of all the others. For Peyton's darkness, however "clinical" it may seem—and there is no doubt that it is more dramatic than clinical—must still illumine the universal urge of human beings to clutch some impossible idea of eternal childhood or innocence, must illumine and expiate that urge. "The real point of *Lie Down in Darkness*," Geismar rightly perceives, "is that, dealing with the Electra complex itself, it has not only made it human and domestic but has returned it, so to speak, to its natural home of childhood feeling itself."[6] This is one aspect of a radical innocence to which Peyton, no simple innocent, is a perverse victim.

The drama of Peyton, however, is enacted within at least three circles of meaning: social, domestic, and private. First, there is the South of the tidewater in Virginia. The scene conveys, from the beginning, a feeling of something recently denatured and agelessly dissolute:

Riding down to Port Warwick from Richmond, the train begins to pick up speed on the outskirts of the city, past the tobacco factories with their ever-present haze of acrid, sweetish dust. . . .

. . . instead, you look out once more at the late summer landscape and the low, sorrowful beauty of tideland streams winding through marshes full of small, darting frightened noises and glistening and dead silent at noon. . . .

126

Halfway between the railroad station and Port Warwick proper
. . . the marshland, petering out in disconsolate, solitary clumps
of cattails, yields gradually to higher ground. Here, bordering the
road, an unsightly growth of weeds takes over, brambles and briars
of an uncertain dirty hue. . . . The area adjacent to this stretch
of weeds is bleakly municipal in appearance. . . . Here there are
great mounds of garbage; a sweet, vegetable odor rises perpetually
on the air and one can see—from the distance fairly iridescent—
whole swarms of carnivorous flies blackening the garbage and maybe
a couple of proprietary rats, propped erect like squirrels, and blink-
ing sluggishly, with mild, infected eyes, at some horror-stricken
Northern tourist.[7]

Nature may be deformed by factories and gas tanks squatting
on the landscape, but nature also knows its own forms of
corruption. In this, nature reflects Southern society—"The
ground is bloody and full of guilt where you were born and
you must tread a long narrow path towards your destiny,"
Milton's father says to him before sending him off to the
university.[8] There are scenes—the engagement dance of Loftis,
the wedding party for his daughter, the country club meetings
with Dolly, or the descriptions of the Cartwrights—which
reveal the manners of a society resistant to incursions and still
operant. But these ceremonial scenes should be balanced against
the glib wisdom of Berger, the New York invert who says to
Peyton, "It is symptomatic of that society from which you
emanate that it should produce the dissolving family: *ah, ah,*
patience, my pretty, I know you say symptomatic not of that
society, but of *our* society, the machine culture, yet so archetypal
is this South with its cancerous religiosity, its exhausting need
to put manners before morals, to negate all *ethos*—call it a
husk of a culture."[9]

Negation becomes gradually more emphatic in the three
generations which the novel encompasses: Milton's father with
his grandiloquent wisdom; the Loftises themselves, and the
minister, Carey Carr, still genteel in their impotence; and
Peyton or Berger for whom cynicism or self-destruction is the

127

measure of salvation. Milton's father says to Loftis, "My son . . . we stand at the back door of glory. Now in this setting part of time we are only relics of vanquished grandeur more sweet than God himself might have imagined: we are the driblet turds of angels, not men but a race of toads, vile mutations who have lost our lovewords. . ."; and Peyton says to Dick Cartwright, her contemporary, "Those people back in the Lost Generation. Daddy I guess. . . . They thought they were lost. They were crazy. There weren't lost. What they were doing was losing us."[10] And so the progress of negation leads to the historical event which casts a sinister shadow on the last pages of the novel: the explosion of the Bomb. For it is just as the war ends that Peyton commits suicide; and it is as she reaches out for the last time, reaches out in selfish desperation for her husband, Harry, that he retorts, "Do you realize what the world's come to? Do you realize that the great American commonwealth just snuffed out one hundred thousand innocent lives this week? There was a time, you know, when I thought for some reason . . . I could spend my life catering to your needs. . . ."[11] But does the insanity of the world overshadow Peyton's need or become merely the ghastly correlative of her disease?

Nor does the novel show religion to be a means of genuine social or spiritual salvation. The religiosity of Helen is an extension of her egotism, an inversion of her feminine possessiveness, a token of her revulsion against instinct and life. The gracious dialogues, so redolent with self-pity and theatrical despair, she conducts with Carey Carr are almost the perfect parody of a courtship. Yet Carr, though earnestly devoted to his Episcopal church, cannot raise his faith above the level of poetic compassion. He is good as chorus and preceptor, useless as comforter or savior. When in the final scene of Peyton's funeral Milton goes for Helen's throat in a rage, Carr can only stand by terrified and exclaim, "People! People."[12] Carr is indeed more impotent than Daddy Faith, the Negro revivalist whose baptismal rites fill the strange epilogue of the book. There is power and frenzy in this scene of Negroes ducked in the waters of life, cleansed and purified; there is also awe and joy and simplicity of faith, qualities that are absent from the lives of white people. Drowning is the controlling image of Peyton's last moments, but it is the element of rebirth for Ella and La Ruth. The white girl does not find the father and lover she so desperately needs, but the black congregation finds both: "You, Daddy! Daddy Faith! You loves us! You, Daddy!"[13] Yet what can the contrast do but sharpen our sense of incongruity? How can the tormenting events of the novel be explained in a scene of primitive religious fervor except ironically? The tragic tensions of civilized life, as Styron knows, are not so easily resolved; nor can we all worship at the altar erected on a raft which Styron thus describes: "On it had been erected a sort of stage, surrounded on four sides by a golden damask curtain; embroidered designs—dragons and crosses and crowns, Masonic emblems, shields, bizarre and unheard-of animals, an amalgam of myth and pagan ritual and Christian symbology—all these glowed against the curtain in green and red phosphorescent fabrics, literally hurting the eyes."[14] The depletion of religious symbols from their meaning parallels the depletion of manners from their content.

Domestic life in *Lie Down in Darkness* is equally corrupt. For this is a story of infidelity, of vengeful love, blocked, hurt, and perverted, of adults who can never escape their childhood. It is a story of a husband unfaithful to his wife, a mistress unfaithful to her husband, a girl unfaithful to the man she marries. It is the story of a woman, Helen, who can love only what she can control—her crippled daughter, Maudie, or the childish part of her husband, Milton; of a man whose sensuality is merely a form of dependence on Dolly, and whose love, for Peyton, can never become sensual; of a girl who frantically needs a husband, Harry, precisely because she loves her father, and who hates the mother who is viciously jealous of her. These

129

ambivalences of love are created by a man-child, girl-woman, and mother-neuter—the images of reversion in the novel are legion—who bind the family in a circle of guilt. Something, truly, is rotten in Denmark, as not Hamlet but the mortician, Mr. Casper, reflects, for it is the custodians of death who also hold, it seems, our conscience in custody. Yet the root of corruption may be a kind of innocence, an excess of love which, as Milton understands, always requires forgiveness. Where there is no forgiveness, vengeance takes over—and death. For the living, death is nothingness. It is what Milton feels when his efforts, after Peyton's suicide and Maudie's earlier death, fail to conciliate Helen: "With nothing left! Nothing! Nothing! Nothing!" It is also what Helen feels too late: "Peyton," she said, "Oh, God, Peyton. My child. Nothing! Nothing! Nothing! Nothing!"[15] Strangely enough, it is only Dolly, the outsider, the interloper, who is simple or stupid or forgiving enough to escape the final seal of negation.

And of course there is no surcease of terror as we move from the domestic to private experience where all terror begins, where it must end. The hell of love, the hell of purchasing one's happiness with another's pain, the hell, even, of failing to know the love one is supposed to know—these are dramatized in scene after scene. The gist of it all is that no one has a chance: "Oh Christ, have mercy on your Peyton this evening not because she hasn't believed but because she, no one, had a chance to ever."[16] Peyton must be locked in her destiny; locked in an interior monologue, the formal equivalent of her absolute isolation; locked in a nightmare of strutting pigeons and screeching katydids, those birds that haunt Peyton throughout the novel, symbolizing her sexual guilt and her childish yearnings for freedom, and rustling with their wings over her death; locked, again, in a stream of memories from which the sole escape is drowning in the airless void of time, so that at last her flightless birds may ascend, one by one, "through the suffocating night, toward paradise."[17] What paradise? That of a stricken mind, a heart dazed by its strange necessities? A paradise of childhood, never lost and yet never to be regained? A fool's or saint's paradise?

Obviously this is not the vision of an ancestral South which Styron described as "a land of prim pastoral fences, virgin lumber, grazing sheep and Anglo-Saxons: these, the last, spoke in slumbrous Elizabethan accents, rose at dawn, went to bed at dusk, and maintained, with Calvinist passion, their traditional intolerance of evil."[18] It is rather a vision of tragic ambiguities and ironic necessities, of human experience spanning the abyss. It is a vision which must create its own distinctive form.

Lie Down in Darkness is a brilliant formal accomplishment. Its focus is narrow in space and diffuse in time. Peyton's hearse is constantly in our view, and the story is quite literally its halting progress, from the Port Warwick railway station, where the remains of Peyton arrive, to the cemetery, where she is laid to rest. The physical fact of death is simple and immitigable. The complexity is temporal, for time, after all, is a function of man's urge to experience and to understand. Time is consciousness—and consciousness in our time has cracked and splintered. Time in the novel, consequently, is cracked, too; the story is revealed in flashbacks, and flashbacks within flashbacks. The fate of the Loftis family cannot be related by following the Aristotelian precepts of plot. The fate of the Loftises is, to be sure, settled before time began and, as Freudians know, time begins when we fall from childhood. This seems in accordance with the Aristotelian notion of a tragic necessity. But the dramatic emphasis of the novel is not on the end; it is rather on the beginning in which middle and end are swallowed. Nor is the logic of necessity clear; it is rather inscrutable as experience itself and demonic as guilt, the ruling principle of the book. Time, therefore, does not become merely the passive medium through which guilt is inherited and expiated. It is an active agent, not erosive in any predictable way—Dolly, Milton,

Helen, and Peyton come together and fall asunder several times in the course of the novel—but destructive in a mysterious fashion. None of the characters can fully penetrate his situation. Remembrance of things past guarantees no wisdom or control.

Fractured time makes for a fractured consciousness. Each of the seven sections of the novel is dominated by the point of view of one of the characters, though there are shifts within each section too. Together, these points of view constitute an ironic commentary on the limitations of each. Reality is larger than any of the characters can assess, and the novelist himself can assess it only by suspending his judgment in compassion for the helpless isolation of all. Or he can assess it, again, by deliberately creating various levels of narration in the same episode, creating, that is, an ambiguity which must stay unresolved. The crucial incident of Peyton, dressed in tight shorts, nuzzling up to her father is an example. We see the scene itself, as it must have occurred, through the jealous eyes of Helen who narrates the incident to Carey Carr and at the same time indulges her own vicious stream of secret thoughts; and we see it again, almost simultaneously, through the eyes of the novelist looking over Helen's shoulder. The incestuous interchange of feeling or gesture, whatever it was, thus appears in a haze of refracted light; reality is sicklied over with the cast of illusion; for the only power to assess facts may rest with fancy.

Retrospection in time leads to introspection in the stream of an isolated consciousness—thence the charged images welling up from the past, shards and splinters of experiences forgotten, repeated with hopeless urgency. Hence the involuted sentences, pressing and crowding the meaning of a whole life into one tortured, inexorable, poetic fragment: *"Helen, Helen,* he thought drowsily, my lost, *my lovely, why have I forsaken you?* Visions white as sunlight, perfect as one flower, a gardenia, once remembered from a dance that never stopped till dawn, they came to him briefly, vanished, and he believed he slipped off for a spell, thinking of Helen dressed like a cat, bearing down on him with a knife: only it wasn't a knife, it was something else, a flower or something, and they were in Charlottesville, and there was Peyton too, her lips pressed to his, saying Daddy Daddy Bunny dear, the globe revolving monstrously out of night into day again, turning and turning. . . ."[19]

Day merges into night, reality into dream. The counters of dreams are symbols, which seek, in their obscure way, to make the inalienable privacy of the soul public. These Styron uses with tact, though his obvious and awkward handling of Peyton's "birds" may be a greater concession to pathology than he usually permits himself. But the syntax of dreams is that of free associations, and it is these Styron employs to make vital connections between his characters. Thus, for instance, does Peyton begin by thinking of Harry and end, in the same movement of feeling, thinking of Milton: "How many times have I lain down to sin out of vengeance, to say *so he* [Harry] *doesn't love me, then there is one that will*, to sleep then and dream about the birds, and then to wake with one eye open to the sweltering, joyless dawn and think *my life has known no father, any road to any end may run*, to think of home. I would not pray to a polyp or a jellyfish, nor to Jesus Christ, but only to that part of me that was pure and lost now, when he [Milton] and I used to walk along the beach, toward Hampton, and pick up shells."[20]

This is deft transition. But no transition can establish the real connections in Peyton's life. Her "initiation" to adult recognitions ends in suicide. The pattern of her encounter with experience is finally a closed one, but it is not, for all its external neatness, intelligible. And in a strange way, a way undefinable by any dogma or creed but perhaps simply by the compassion art bestows, her ashes do give forth light. This is what *Lie Down in Darkness*, however overwritten it may be in parts, however elusive its resolution may seem, manages to dramatize for our minds. Stunned and horrified, the reader's mind is purified without recourse to a genuinely tragic catharsis.

133

II

Harvey Swados may not possess the intensity of Styron, but he has shown, in three novels to date, the kind of integrity, a quiet strength, which is fashionable to snub. More conscious than his coevals of the social climate in which his characters move, he has managed, nevertheless, to resist the encroachments of ideology on fiction, choosing, rather, to expose the apathy and abuses of mass culture in a scattering of lively essays. His fiction displays a variegated background of class, manners, and setting—there is little of the hieratic about it.

His first novel, *Out Went the Candle*, 1955, we shall presently discuss in some detail. His second book, *On the Line*, 1957, used the technique of conveyor-belt narrative, characters and episodes strung in space rather than in time, to describe the dramatic moment in the life of men bound to an assembly line. *False Coin*, 1959, probed the subtle pressures which, with the best of human and scientific intentions, subordinate the quality of individual excellence to the popular needs of mass communication. There is something faintly old-fashioned in these books, the sense of outrage or virtue we associate with Orwell more than Dos Passos; and the style, which can be fairly colorless at times, avoids the satin gloss of so much recent writing. The most compelling of Swados' novels—his first—brings to life an experience which we inevitably recognize as part of our own travail during the war and in the years to follow it. And it justifies Swados when he says, "Obviously the novelist has now to deal with the human heart pushed to such extremities as would have been beyond the most horrid imaginings of a Jane Austen or an Anthony Trollope, or even a Henry James."[21]

Out Went the Candle is also a novel about the family, its disintegration and final hope to resist chaos by an effort of love. The Feltons, Herman and Clara, and their two children, Betsy and Morrow, are Jewish, are, in fact, urgently conscious of their Jewishness; the action takes place, for the most part, in suburban New Jersey during the war years. The central relation, again, is between a false Cordelia, Betsy, with her haunted and defiant eyes, and a predatory Lear, Herman, who finally attains to some wisdom through sacrifice (the title of the book is taken from *King Lear*). Styron's and Swados' novels, we see, reveal remarkable parallels—the relation of a daughter to her father—and stand in obvious contrast—the Southern aristocratic family, the Jewish urban background.

As in Styron's novel, as in so many contemporary works of fiction, it is difficult to isolate the hero of *Out Went the Candle*. Joe Burley, from whose central point of view much of the action is observed, appears to be both a spectator and an interloper. The very fact that he is a Gentile excludes him from the innermost circle of the Feltons. (Yet as things turn out, Joe acquires the symbolic status of a son, and contributes to the salvation of that family. The symbolic or moral relation of Joe to the Feltons is reinforced by the suggestion that Joe's mother, Blanche, may have had, long ago, an affair with Herman Felton.) Morrow, who spends a lifetime denying his father— he denies him through college, an abortive business career, and two courts-martial—remains too far behind the scene to be considered a central character. It is the presence of Herman, of course, that dominates the book. A ruthless wartime profiteer and yet devoted family man, he is finally forced to choose between power and love, and choosing the latter—he travels to England at a dangerous moment, while a Senate committee is investigating his shady financial deals, in order to save his son from a court-martial—he gives his life, too late, the meaning it lacked. Yet the powerful presence of Herman is felt mainly through his impact on Betsy, the center of hope and focus of collapse in the novel. She it is who encounters destructive necessity, and all the charity of Swados cannot persuade us that she may escape it.

Betsy is a dreamer and realist both, a kind of girl Faust. Because she is so proud of her shrewd father, she glorifies ruthlessness in the world. She insists always on meeting life with arms outspread, and this is the weakness which Bunty Taylor, the cynical aristocrat, and all the men who follow him in Betsy's perverse affections, play upon—in her eyes these men are but feeble competitors of her strong Daddy. When she is finally unloosened from her home moorings, she finds herself drifting from one college to another, from a marriage with a naval officer she does not love to another smoldering marriage with a professional football player, from the arms of one lover to those of another. Academic life, the society of Navy wives, the parties of Communist intellectuals she attends, leave her with a sense of futility, the sense that the ambitions of all the people about her are still unworthy of her highest hopes. (It is only Herman, perhaps, namesake of her father, a refugee and brilliant mathematician who commits suicide, that escapes her contempt.) Obviously, it is because she desperately needs to shake off her Daddy that she invites men so easily into her life, and it is again for the same reason that she shakes all these men off, for they are easier to repudiate than her parent. As her brother Morrow puts it, "She believed he [Herman] was God. When she found out that he wasn't, that the world wasn't the way he'd said it was, she turned on him—not directly, but through those men."[22] Sex, we observe again, is utilized to avenge the love of a girl who cannot outgrow her childhood. The process of initiation is a process of blind and persistent self-immolation. Betsy expresses no understanding of her compulsion. She is a victim of a regressive attachment, incestuous love; but she is a victim, too, of a ragged and splendid vision for which, as befits a scapegoat, she must atone. This, Swados is careful to make Joe Burley reveal to us in the epilogue of the novel:

She [Betsy] had demanded—tantalized by the bitter knowledge that it was impossible—the right to see what he [Joe] had gone out and seen. . . . Of all the millions of dull, soft, and undemanding girls, she alone had the courage and the instinctive drive to hold out her hands for a man's share. Once denied what she had sought, she had to turn instead to the only avenues that women were allowed to enter, and then at the potential cost of ostracism and damnation.

With Betsy . . . every move that she made screamed of desperation. It was impossible for her to conceal from the world that she was swinging wildly, like a resin-blinded fighter threshing out of the bloody blackness against his maddening opponent. . . . With each successive attempt and each inevitable defeat, it would be less and less possible for her to try her hand at those pitiable compromises and time-gaining maneuvers. . . . The good ones . . . had every right . . . to regard Betsy as unstable, unbalanced, misdirected, neurotic, touched in the head, schizoid, maladjusted, cockeyed, bughouse, spoiled, warped, overprotected, underdeveloped, and just plain crazy. By their light they were right: in addition to all the phantastic, unachievable goals, she wanted some of the same things they did . . . but she took the lunatic's way of reaching for them, inventing nonexistent obstacles, overdramatizing those that did exist, and presenting herself as being completely unequipped to compromise or settle for anything less than everything.[23]

All of which does not prevent Betsy from ending in an orgon box in the Village, undergoing Reichian analysis, when Joe is dispatched to recall her to the side of Herman who is hiding out from the law in the Caribbean.

It is clear that Betsy conforms to the type of hero we have often described. For all her rage to experience, she lacks the power of self-understanding. Her furious quest is full of regressive turns. There are no values she can accept in the world about her, no anchors within or without. In her case, the call of freedom is the lure of necessity, and the image of her twirling with a Negro sailor on the dance floor, "spinning wildly yet feebly, like a helpless, dying leaf," is the image, in a real sense, of her undirected life.[24] Yet of all the characters in the novel, none shows the kind of headlong courage Betsy shows—not Blanche who plays it cagily, or Bunty who conceals his fears in a witty phrase—and none is more ready to pay the price of defiance. And pay she does.

Yet the structure of *Out Went the Candle* cannot be made to fit the ironic pattern without strain. For the novel deals with other characters—Joe Burley, Morrow and Herman Felton —who balance the fate of Betsy, and impose their more hopeful outlook on the shape of fiction. The crucial statement of the book is affirmative, and it is pronounced by Joe Burley: "There are times when you have to do things that you know are useless," he says to Morrow after buying some obscene trinkets from a Neapolitan urchin, a quixotic gesture of charity. "There are times when you can't pass by, even though everybody else is, even though you know that it makes no difference whether you do or not. It isn't just conscience-salving. It's a way of proving to yourself that you're still a person. And that's something you have to prove over and over again. It never ends."[25] (Affirmative as it may seem, does not the argument bring to mind Sisyphus and his existential courage, the courage merely to be *human*?) And it is Joe, of course, who gets Morrow to suspend his Zionist activities after the war—running Jewish refugees through the blockade in Palestine—and return to the father who is now stripped of his power, bereaved of his wife, lost to his daughter, and hiding out in a Caribbean island. Filial revolt has its limits, as Morrow finally concedes to Joe, and Herman's act of love—when he leaves Washington, inviting self-ruin, to rescue his son in London—is recognized for what it is by young Felton. The false Edmund turns out at last to be the true Edgar, his father's son in need. Even Herman, proud and stubborn and driven as he is, comes to knowledge. He learns that money cannot purchase the happiness of his children; that his own private failings cannot be blamed on "Hitler"; that business ethics—"dog eat dog"—and personal morality cannot be separated. Herman even learns to humiliate himself before a *goyem*, Joe, begging him to retrieve Betsy from her degradation so that he may surrender to the authorities in peace. All three men, we note, arrive at some form of recognition while Betsy, the central character of the novel, does not. Hence the structure of the book which wavers between conventional tragedy and the ironic form.

For one thing, the management of time in the novel is largely conventional. Three sections—"The Short Summer," "The Long Winter," and "The Aftermath"—reveal the gradual dissolution of Betsy's life. There are flashbacks, of course, but these do not unsettle our notion of temporal flow. The action, as we have noted, is unified by the point of view of Joe Burley who tries to make experience intelligible both to the reader and himself. Yet Joe's consciousness of time is by no means simple or wholly intelligible; it does not explain the developments of his life, much less the development of others. The existential ambiguity of time is present.

It seemed to him now that, while the Joe Burley who had spent the summer at Benedict so long ago, who had studied physics with Betsy and half fallen in love with her, who had gone so reluctantly into the Army, was as sharp and clear in his mind as any of the men and women with whom he had become entangled at home and in Europe, it was impossible for him to establish an identity between the someone else he had been then and the person he was now. At what point had he shed the old personality. . . ? Or was there no specific point, but only a gradual metamorphosis, so that in another decade he would again look back in wonder at what he was now, marveling once more at the stranger who had inhabited his skin?[26]

Then, too, no matter how hard Swados tries to place Betsy in a framework of actions or ideas that would make her life observable, the ironic duplicity of experience intrudes itself, shielding subjective truth from objective scrutiny. "You had to be able to hide and muffle what seemed to you to be most true if you wanted to be counted on the right side of the nuthouse walls," Joe reflects.[27] The whole truth, in fact, is even concealed from the individual himself. Hence the ambiguity of motivation in some of the most crucial actions of the novel —Bunty sleeping with a waitress while Joe and Betsy sit next door, Morrow performing an act of heroism under fire, Herman going to the rescue of his son in England. Neither Joe nor the characters themselves can fathom these deeds; "truth" is scattered out wide on the vast undersurface of many lives; and the "mad" actions of Betsy are interpreted and reinterpreted again by husband, brother, or lover almost—were it not for Joe—in vain. When the candle goes out, we are "left darkling." Perhaps only Lear's fool could make sense of it all.

Swados' novel is a fine work, which is not to say that it is faultless. Morrow, we feel, is actually dramatized too late in the book for the role he eventually plays in its resolution. And the two burning motives of Betsy's life—her incestuous love and its wider correlative, the urge to know and experience everything—are precariously balanced, and, too late, too summarily, unified by Joe's final statement, a choruslike effort to round off the play. And yet *Out Went the Candle* manages to hold up an urban milieu as a powerful reflector of the relentless warfare waged within a Jewish family and within its individual members. It demonstrates, in scenes and manners which epitomize the times, that the diseased soul cannot insulate itself from the world, nor can the sickness of the world be kept from blighting the self. And it engenders the sense of life felt in pain or amazement—the scene of the London blitz is one among many such—the sense that even if the characters may be hindered, confined, or betrayed, there is still a chance that men may some day learn to make society a worthier thing. There is no reality for Betsy, however, other than that which she creates in anguish or solitude, and there is little hope. Her encounter with experience is disastrous; the pattern of her life is closed.

III

Norman Mailer is a novelist of undeniable power. He is unpredictable, extreme, edgy, and disturbing in the genuine sense that his aim is always to get at the root of things, to impart the radical view of life. His stance, from the beginning, has been one of opposition. In a symposium sponsored by the *Partisan Review* on "Our Country and Our Culture," a chorus of deferential praise and criticism, Mailer spoke out: "Is there nothing to remind us that the writer does not need to be integrated into his society, and often works best in opposition to it? . . . I wonder if there has been a time in the last fifty years when the American artist has felt more alienated."[28]

We know Mailer in many guises: the young liberal who wrote a baleful novel on war, *The Naked and the Dead*, 1948; the revolutionary socialist of *Barbary Shore*, 1951; the hierophant of sexual mysteries and existential nihilism, in *The Deer Park*, 1955; and the new spokesman for Hipsterism, *Advertisements for Myself*, 1959. It is a serious critical error to identify his achievement with his first novel. His earlier interest in socialism has not prevented him from developing the more anarchic point of view of "The White Negro." For Mailer is a novelist of passionate and shifting ideologies, and his shifts are induced by a "capacity for seeing himself," in the words of Podhoretz, "as a battleground of history."[29] The shift from liberalism to radical socialism, and from the latter to anarchic existentialism also shows a determined effort to resist the call of *illusion* in America. This ruthless aversion to illusion, the false promise of hope, piety, and fashion, may be, as Geismar pretends, a central flaw in Mailer's artistic character.[30] More likely, it is the product of Mailer's peculiar demon which Geismar calls "juvenile malice," and which is juvenile only in the sense that it is perpetually protestant. Mailer's demon is obsessed, as all his novels in some way or other testify, with the meaning of *power*: the condition of vitality itself in the personal, social, and historical realms. Ideologies are merely the political foil of this radical awareness of life, as sex is its personal expression. This, in crude outline, is the logic of Mailer's development. It is what prompts him to write a novel—still unfinished— which is a "dissection of the extreme, the obscene and the unsayable," a tale of "heroes and villains, murderers and suicide, orgy-masters, perverts, and passionate lovers," aimed to "destroy innocence."[31] It is also what persuades him to open the novel itself, as a form, to "new moral complexities which I feel are more interesting than anything the novel has gotten into yet." Why not? God himself, as Mailer conceives him, is still on the make, still exists as a "warring element in a divided universe, and we are part of . . . His great expression, His enormous destiny."[32] Men still share God's battle for eventual omnipotence, and their fate is not a mean one. This heroic view of human destiny, however, is subverted by a conviction deep as it is implicit that men can do no more than hurl themselves against the iron walls of necessity. Rebellion and victimization, we see once again, go hand in hand in an apocalyptic battle for ultimate power. The demon-hero and the victim-hero are two personae of man caught in the process of realizing his *being*. Yet the inescapable fact about the process remains the fact of human frustration.

The Naked and the Dead presents a terrifying view of men at war, specifically the invasion of the Japanese-held island of Anopopei which the novel follows from the landing operations to the final mopping-up details. But the war, as we see it in this grinding, blundering campaign, is used as a mirror of vaster social and historical issues, issues that pertain to the kind of world men must live in when the battles are finally won or lost. The dramatic link between these areas of meaning in the novel are Cummings, the brilliant, power-crazed general who directs the campaign, and his staff officer, Lieutenant Hearn, a disillusioned and misanthropic liberal. The war itself is seen in a double focus. It is first observed from the impersonal vantage of staff officers playing a military chess game. This is the vantage of General Cummings and his servile, inept aid, Major Dalleson. But it is also observed from the individual point of view of the men who constitute a reconnaissance platoon headed by the ruthless and efficient Sergeant Croft. (The sole connection between these two areas of meaning—an unbridgeable gulf of prejudice and authority separates enlisted men from the officers —is Lieutenant Hearn who assumes command of the platoon on its final, fateful, and futile mission.) The discrete, personal view of the action, however, is linked again with the broader cultural implications of the novel by means of the "Time Machine," terse and highly suggestive portraits of the men involved, their dreams and background. The thematic structure of the novel is thus seen to be a series of points of view running full circle. At the dead center: an image of man, broken and harried.

The philosophy of history Cummings reveals to Hearn, in conversations charged with irony and silent antagonism, is one in which power looms dominant and unabashed. The future belongs to those exceptional members of the ruling class who can translate the potential of America into "kinetic energy"; the true aim of the war is to supplant the decadent fascism of the Old World by an authority more vigorous and cunning. Our century, as Cummings believes, belongs to the reactionaries; Hitler is our interpreter. The highest value men can achieve is not ethical or religious, as liberals think; it is rather to make men, oneself included, the instrument of one's policy. Men, therefore, must be controlled by hate and fear. And so Cummings lectures Hearn: "I can tell you, Robert, that to make an Army work you have to have every man in it fitted into a fear ladder."[33] This theory Cummings is ready to extend to society at large. The machine age requires the consolidation of power—and for that fear is required. Hence the inexorable conclusion of Cummings: "The natural role of twentieth-century man is anxiety." And again: "Only the innocent are healthy, and the innocent man is a vanishing breed. I tell you nearly all of humanity is dead, merely waiting to be disinterred."[34] This, indeed, is the impression readers take from the novel, though they may be hard put to reconcile Cummings' view with his statement: "There's that popular misconception of man as something between a brute and an angel. Actually man is in transit between brute and God."[35] What is puzzling here is not the apparent contradiction of the General's thought; it is rather the ambiguity in Mailer's vision. For sickness and anxiety are the historical facts which the novel dramatizes; the aspiration to omnipotence—in Croft, in Cummings—though dramatized too, is merely shown to be futile. Thus we sense that even if the divine ambition of the two men may have the illicit endorsement of the author, the explicit statement of the novel asserts defeat. Croft does not climb his mountain, and the General wins the campaign despite himself. Omnipotence, as private motive or historical destiny, gives way to impotence.

The campaign itself is successful. But in the over-all view of the war, absurdity prevails. It is the bungling Major Dalleson who mounts the decisive offensive while Cummings is away; the brilliant maneuver of the latter turns out to be quite pointless. Cummings, who likes to think the whole island is an ocarina on which he plays his tune, is driven to despair by the sudden, irrational lethargy which descends upon his troops. Entrenched in their foxholes and duck-walked bivouacs, they refuse to respond to his will—it is no wonder that the main section of the novel is entitled "Argil and Mold." The image of the invasion army, "like a nest of ants wrestling and tugging at a handful of bread crumbs in a field of grass," describes it all.[36]

The picture is not infinitely more promising when we move from the division to platoon level of action. Croft's platoon is one of the best in the invasion force; it responds to his efficient commands invariably. But there is no real community between the men, no love lost or friendship acknowledged—the relations between Croft and Martinez or Red and Wyman are really no exception. Racial prejudice and misogyny, self-interest and self-pity, and lust seem to be the only feelings most of the men share. The unvarying obscenities, stock attitudes, hair-triggered aggressions, weariness, resentment, and perpetual discontent of the soldiers define their emotional range. The platoon snarls or moans its way to boredom or death. The two men who come out best, in their human and bungling way, are Ridges and Goldstein—they carry Wilson on a stretcher through the jungle, though they could have easily abandoned him. Yet the two, a devout farm boy and a mildly paranoiac Jew, also carry the lowest prestige among their comrades.

Nor is the portrait of the men, taken individually, much brighter. They are all, in some way or other, caught, vexed, or defeated. Thus from Gallagher: "Everything turned out lousy for him sooner or later"; from Croft: "I HATE EVERY-THING WHICH IS NOT IN MYSELF"; from Red: "You keep rolling along and you never know what the hell the score is."[37] The few hopes and illusions they retain after the Depression are shattered by their war experience. And they have little to look forward to: "The months and years ahead were very palpable to them. They were still on the treadmill; the misery, the ennui, the dislocated horror. . . . Things would happen and time would pass, but there was no hope, no anticipation."[38]

The world of *The Naked and the Dead*, on all levels, is a dying world. Instinct rules it, power and fear; idealism makes but a weak, transitory show of itself in the person of Hearn or Goldstein. In the background is American society, the eternal betrayals of the American Dream. Mexicans, like Martinez, "breathe the American fables," but they can never become "white Protestant, firm and aloof"; Jews dedicate themselves to accept injury; and Swedes spend their puberty in coal dust.[39] Even the rich, like Hearn, must pay for their awareness in self-banishment: "A bunch of dispossessed . . . from the raucous stricken bosom of America."[40] In the foreground is the war. The stench of a Japanese corpse fills our nostrils, as it does Red's, and questions the meaning of human endeavor. "Is there really anything special about man?" Red cynically asks. The novel does not allow us to wonder much.

This is the world of the novel. Who, then, are its heroes? Excepting Hearn and Cummings, surely none of the officers. Or is it the enlisted men? Some of these, like Red Valsen, are eternal nay-sayers; some, like Roth, eternal victims; and a few, like Wilson, just average and sensual men. None manages to understand his experience or bring life to account. But it is Cummings, Croft, and Hearn who possess the richest personalities, and it is in their actions that the novel reveals itself.

General Cummings, we have already seen, nurses a vision of his manifest destiny. It is fed on sheer intelligence and power, sheer, that is, because it recognizes no human categories foreign to its aims. His character, nevertheless, is complex and contradictory, is compelling precisely because ruthlessness and sensitivity mingle in it. His consciousness of power is very nearly demonic; a mighty hunger chokes him. In trying to become God, his vision is constantly blunted by the resistance of men, and is constantly thwarted by its own peculiar form of corruption. The trajectory of an artillery shell, the curve of sexual excitation, the pattern cultures trace in their growth and decline—all manifest, as the General broods, the same sudden, sharp death. Against the harsh necessities of gravity or death, Faust can only rage. But Cummings' rage subsides into a shudder. The campaign he wins defeats his most exalted ambition.

Sergeant Croft is Cummings' earthy double. The General wants to mold the curve of human destiny, the Sergeant must climb Mount Anaka, highest peak on the island. Faust here assumes the shape of a Texan hunter—and criminal. For Croft shoots a man dead, though he is merely ordered to fire above the head of the rioters, and he murders a Japanese prisoner, after giving him a cigarette, simply for the sinister excitement of the thing. Croft's sense of his omnipotence, compared to Cummings', is primitive, almost feral. The mountain comes to represent for him everything he must know and conquer, the way to his own immortality. He is repelled and fascinated by it, views it with "awe and hunger and the peculiar unique ecstasy he had felt after Hennessey was dead, or when he had killed the Japanese prisoner."[41] The purity, the austerity, of its peak beckons him, and he contributes to the death of Hearn and goads his men to the breaking point so that he may plant his feet on its crest. But a nest of hornets explodes his purpose; in a scene of sheer horror, the hornets riddle Croft and his men in the last stage of their ascent, following them down the wild slopes like an avalanche of fire. Croft's hunger finds its limit:

Croft kept looking at the mountain. He had lost it, had missed some tantalizing revelation of himself.
Of himself and much more. Of life.
Everything.[42]

Croft and Cummings, the two "demonic" heroes, are balked. Lieutenant Hearn stands between them, the natural enemy of both. But his defeat, though more final, has greater value. And his position in the novel is central from a dramatic as well as thematic standpoint. For Hearn is the dramatic link between the two other men who never meet. His humiliation by Cummings sends him to Croft's platoon, and it is Croft who plots the death of Hearn at the hand of the Japanese before the latter can fully redeem his earlier failure. Furthermore, Hearn shows a secret affinity with the Faustian impulse of the two men he must oppose. He, too, wanted to make the world in his own image and impose his will upon it: "Not a phony but a Faust."[43] But he does not have the passion or confidence or ruthlessness it takes; his intelligence is too skeptical, his disenchantment, like Red's, too thorough. Aloof and somewhat cold, he rebels first against his father and the affluent Chicago society his parents represent. He drifts through the literary circles of Harvard and, later, of New York, drifts away from the inadequacies of a liberal ideology, though Communist intellectuals reject him as a quixotic bourgeois. Faust, we see, is chained to Quixote in the person of Hearn who thinks of himself as an indolent seeker but finds nothing worthy of his acceptance.

147

A rebel first, he becomes a drifter, an outsider, a spectator—till the war. But his contest with Cummings, and with Croft afterward, rescues Hearn from hollow disengagement—one of his mistresses calls him a mere shell. Defeated by the General, who forces Hearn in a symbolic gesture of subjugation to pick up a cigarette butt, and destroyed by Croft, Hearn, nevertheless, finds some dignity in the role of victim. He comes to understand why "it is better to be the hunted than the hunter."[44] The statement is a product of his crisis, the end of his encounter with adversity. It expresses the typical insight of the rebel-victim. In the case of Hearn, it is an advance over the philosophy which so far had shaped his life: " 'The only thing to do is to get by on style.' He had said that once, lived by it in the absence of anything else, and it had been a working guide, almost satisfactory until now."[45]

Hearn's belief in *style* stands in contrast with the belief of Cummings and Croft in *effectiveness*—the form of an action as against its results, the means versus the ends. But in all cases, the characters appeal to no standard outside of themselves, no objective ideal. They have in common the courage of meaninglessness. The demonic hero creates meaning by blindly asserting his will. The victim hero finds meaning in carrying his rebellion to the point of self-destruction. None of the "heroes" in the novel really succeeds in his search, though Hearn, the typical scapegoat—his brother officers think of him as the kind of man they *like* to see humiliated—Hearn comes closer than any other to redeeming the wasteland of Anopopei.

Given its kind of world and its type of heroes, it is not surprising to find that the structure of *The Naked and the Dead* exhibits most properties of the ironic form. The structure, in fact, can be construed as an ironic edifice to the nakedness and mortality of man.

For one thing, its vast sweep over the battlefield, and back in time into the lives of men, creates an image of controlled disorder. Chance, the very form of the book seems to say, is the necessity which controls men. The last section of the novel, and perhaps its weakest, focuses on the ineffectual Major Dalleson, and removes us from all the characters we have got to know intimately, from their trials and tribulations, as if they had all been lost in an absurd cosmic shuffle. From the first movement of the invasion, "Wave," to the last, "Wake," effort is wasted and purpose lost. The ending brings no resolution; the camera simply fades off leaving bubbles on a scarcely rippled surface.

The shifts of point of view, back and forth, from staff headquarters to platoon foxholes impress upon us not only the enormous distance between officers and men, but also the discrepancy between public policy and individual motive. The men are not simply lost in the great erratic shuffles of a military campaign; they are dwarfed by a grand design no one seems fully to comprehend. In the end, some men die and others live, but there is no real change in their outlook and no recognition. Even Hearn dies before he can restore himself in his own eyes or resign his commission. And the episodes Mailer calls "Chorus," a chorus of dissident, rueful, and sometimes bantering voices, manifest an ironic lack of awareness of what the total action means.

Again, the action of time is largely destructive. The "Time Machine" sections, which remind us less of H. G. Wells's science fiction than the vivid "Biographies" of Dos Passos' *U.S.A.*, reveal to us in clipped, poetic form how each character came to be what he is. Mailer's selection of crucial details or actions in these grim histories betrays his deterministic view of the American environment. The Time Machine is a machine indeed, an engine grinding men's hopes. Compassionate as Mailer wants to be, his tone strikes us with a secret sardonic note, as if the author were jeering at the stupid delusions of his characters. The ambiguity is there because the true sympathies of Mailer are divided between victims and oppressors alike. The "humility" of the author of which he speaks in the following confession is incomplete: "It took all of me to be at best a fair rifleman. No surprise then if I was a modest young man when it was all over. I knew I was not much better and I was conceivably a little less than most of the men I had come to know. At least a large part of me felt that way, and it was the part in command while I was writing *The Naked and the Dead*."[46]

The style of the novel reflects the same ambiguity. Cold and dispassionate, it pretends to be objective, naturalistic. Human agony is simply another phenomenon in the universe, mortality a fact of existence. The style brutalizes what it seeks to describe; it reduces the scope of our apprehension to the most common denominator. Yet it allows, despite all this, the straining quality of human life to come through. Here is a characteristic image of soldiers pulling guns through the jungle:

Once or twice a flare filtered a wan and delicate bluish light over them, the light almost lost in the dense foliage through which it had to pass. In the brief moment it lasted, they were caught at their guns in classic straining motions that had the form and beauty of a frieze. Their uniforms were twice blackened, by the water and the dark slime of the trail. And for the instant the light shone on them their faces stood out, white and contorted.[47]

Rigid, even static, the surface of *The Naked and the Dead* conceals violent life underneath. It is the kind of life hard to disclose, difficult to dramatize, for it is blind and impulsive. At best, it can be felt in moments of symbolic intensity— Croft killing the Japanese prisoner or brooding over his unattainable peak, Cummings thrilled by the fire of artillery, and musing over the trajectory of human destiny. (The very fact that sexual imagery is often used, in both cases, to evoke the latent content of their aspiration betrays the depth, the incoherence, of their motives.) Sometimes the pent-up life of the novel reveals itself, less successfully, in perverse gestures—Hearn bumping the General or dropping a map board on his feet, Croft squashing melodramatically a bird in his fist—gestures whose intentions far exceed their occasion. Even the monotonous exploitation of erotic fantasies in the novel may be seen as a clumsy attempt to bring into the open the unspeakable yearnings and frustrations, not exclusively sexual, of the men. It is as if Mailer, knowing that the spectacle of death is not drama enough, were constantly seeking to redeem it with tokens of life, a life he cannot quite define and which he can only express in clandestine ways.

The classic redeemers of death are scapegoats—people like Hearn, perhaps Goldstein. It is they who give to life some form. The form they give to fiction is ironic. If the structure of the novel does not highlight the sole fact of Hearn's victimization, it is because Hearn is sandwiched between two "demonic" characters, as Betsy was flanked by two "tragic" protagonists. Yet the book adapts itself, on the whole, to the existential pattern. Necessity rules the encounter of all. For Hearn there is no self-renewal.

IV

The three novels we have examined are long and heavy works. They may owe something, perhaps, to the ethos of Naturalism. But the world they depict is not merely harsh and brutal; it leaves us with no sense of how injustice may be rectified. The characters do not simply submit to some external necessity; they are their own executioners. And the technique is not only socially descriptive; it tries to convey all that it cannot define. Naturalism in these works seems to merge ironically into myth.

The protagonist, in all three novels, is finally crushed. He begins with vast ambitions of knowledge, goodness, or love; like Faust, he takes his chances with life. At first, he appears to us almost an impostor, a prideful *alazon*. But the process of his encounter with experience serves to chastise him. Initiation leads to alienation or defeat. His goal is never attained, nor is tragic reconciliation achieved. The hero, carrying his hopeless, shining vision with him, succumbs. From his defeat, however, a kind of victory is snatched. The victory belongs not to him but to those who may recognize it: to the readers. This is the function of *pharmakos*: to do for us what he cannot do for himself. For the scapegoat himself is neither innocent nor guilty, as Northrop Frye saw. "He is innocent in the sense that what happens to him is far greater than anything he has done provokes. . . . He is guilty in the sense that he is a member of a guilty society, or living in a world where such injustices are an inescapable part of existence. The two facts do not come together; they remain ironically apart."[48] The light of the scapegoat burns in his ashes.

Likewise, in all three novels the pattern of action is closed to change or escape. Demonic imagery prevails. Time destroys but destroys in no predictable way. Yet there is no final synthesis, for the form is a parody of tragic resolution, a denial of ultimate insights. There is, in the structure of fiction, no guaranty against the ironic recurrence of the same defeat. Pity and awe are wholly muffled by ambiguities. And no single protagonist emerges clearly as the anti-hero—no single eminence is accorded even to failure. The same pattern of tragic irony may be discovered in Flannery O'Connor's *The Violent Bear It Away*, Paul Bowles's *The Sheltering Sky*, Carson McCullers' *The Heart is a Lonely Hunter*, and Saul Bellow's *Dangling Man*.

CHAPTER 6

THE QUALIFIED ENCOUNTER:
THREE NOVELS BY
BUECHNER, MALAMUD, AND ELLISON

> Please, a definition: A hibernation is a covert
> preparation for a more overt action.
> RALPH ELLISON, *Invisible Man*

I

IT IS a common presumption that Frederick Buechner is the
delight of the more precious academic critics. His novels, it is
said, honor their stately edicts on the art of fiction, and his
exquisite sensibility—hushed comparisons are made with Henry
James, Elizabeth Bowen, Truman Capote—offends no canons
of taste. True, Buechner is sometimes the willing victim of his
most elegant vices, but he is also the victim of a larger controversy in which the word academic has become a shibboleth.
Buechner has taught in preparatory schools; he is also an or-
dained Presbyterian minister, and a novelist who has tried, with
uneven success, to harmonize a world of subtle human feelings
and complex religious ideas. Steeped, by his own admission, in
the great prose writers of the seventeenth century—Jeremy
Taylor, Sir Thomas Browne—he has also schooled himself in
the theology of Buber and Tillich, and he has lately shown
unexpected interest in the broils of American politics. After
A Long Day's Dying, 1949, a novel written when the author
was 23 years old—its aura still hangs about his name—Buechner
produced two others. *The Season's Difference*, 1952, is an over-
refined account of a mystical experience, the way it infiltrates
the consciousness of children and adults in a narrow circle of

people. In *The Return of Ansel Gibbs*, 1958, Buechner makes a more decisive departure from his earlier manner. The book is reasonably forthright; its material, though rich in moral ambiguities, is topical rather than mythic, dramatic more than allusive. But though it calls for the resolution of complexities in action, it fails to unify the political, moral, and ideological questions which distend the framework of its story. All in all, and hackneyed as it may seem to say so, Buechner remains a writer of distinct promise rather than incontrovertible achievement. His failures are not the product of a trivial imagination. They happen, in fact, to reflect some chronic difficulties of fiction in our time, and are, therefore, instructive to follow.

A Long Day's Dying is not the small masterpiece which the dust-jacket blurbs claim it to be. The book promises far more than it actually delivers, asserts more than it renders. It does not bring its characters to life. The euphonious style modulates itself with moral and sensuous perceptions of high order, but it fails, in the end, to create dramatic or moral significance. The central action of the novel—a sexual act between two unmarried people—refuses to carry the burden which the author places upon it, even though he may bolster it with a mythical structure. Furthermore, some episodes never become integrated in the narrative. Despite all this, the intention of the author is serious enough, his tact so fine, that we are compelled to give the novel our grudging acquiescence.

The world of *A Long Day's Dying* is the world of love betrayed. Two myths frame the action: one is Christian and implicit, the other pagan and rather more explicit. The title, taken from Milton's *Paradise Lost*, refers us to the Christian story of the Fall. It refers us, more specifically, to a passage Buechner chose as his epigraph in which Adam bids Eve, after their expulsion from Paradise, to

> . . . rise, let us no more contend, nor blame
> Each other, blamed enough elsewhere, but strive

In offices of love how we may lighten
Each other's burden in our share of woe. . . .

In the novel, however, the offices of love serve to aggravate
the woes of everyone concerned. The altruistic Christian resolution of Adam leads ironically to a fate of lust and vengeance
which Tireus, Procne, and Philomela enact in Greek myth, and
the various characters reenact in the novel. Charity or love,
without awareness of man's radical limitation, defeats its
ends; guilt is universal. This, if any, seems to be the orthodox
moral of the book.

The moral, however, does not come through quite so simply.
In fact, the ambiguities of the plot, the absence of any background of felt beliefs, preclude the definition of any moral.
The plot is something as follows. Elizabeth Poor is an attractive
widow, a lady of some wealth and breeding. She has the sleepy
charm of feminine as well as social self-centeredness. She is
admired by Motley, a rather greedy, witty writer who is anxious
to claim part of her—any physical relation with the birdlike
Motley would be, as he says, grotesque—for the purposes of his
own intellectual vanity. She is also loved, in a silent and fragile
way, by Tristram Bone, Motley's friend. Tristram's great hulk
dominates the novel, and so does his vast, vague, spiritual
presence. When Elizabeth goes to hear a lecture by Motley at
a university which her son, Lee, attends, she meets Lee's best
friend, a clever instructor of English called Paul Steitler.
Elizabeth ends by spending the night in Steitler's bed. Motley
infers the fact, and with motives of mixed loyalty and jealousy,
tells Bone about it. Tristram, in turn, attempts to ascertain the
facts from Elizabeth in a blundering, painful way. She denies
everything, and to protect herself further, implies a homosexual
relation between Steitler and Lee. Bone writes a note to Steitler
and arranges a meeting with him at the Cloisters. During their
interview, it becomes evident to both men that Elizabeth had
implicated her son to save herself. With a shock, Steitler realizes

that he may have loved Lee, and Tristram realizes that his beloved Elizabeth may not be all she seems. The finale—it is not really a resolution—takes place in the death chamber of Maroo, Elizabeth's mother, a splendid old lady who rushes to the aid of her family, leaving their ancestral home in the South, only to die of pneumonia in Elizabeth's apartment.

Bare as this plot summary may be, it allows us to recognize some moral and dramatic qualities of the book. The "sin" is committed by Elizabeth; "retribution" overtakes all. Lee, who is the most innocent of the group, suffers the corruption of his friendship with Steitler. And Maroo, the distant goddess whose moral aegis hangs over the actors, expires without doing anything more than protect her grandson, leaving the crisis itself in suspension. The innocence of Lee, though mysteriously preserved for the world later to sully—Steitler's dark or subversive vision of existence seems to have no effect on the young god —becomes the agent which precipitates the crisis. And the knowledge of Maroo, laden with ceremonial wisdom, the firmness of a vanished way of life, sustains no one really but herself. Even the hazy sanctity of Tristram does not prevent him from undertaking meddlesome queries which in turn set the wheels of vengeance churning. All relations, except perhaps that of Maroo to her grandson, are disrupted; each character returns to his primal solitude. Innocence, ceremony, and humility, exemplified by Lee, Maroo, and Tristram, guarantee no salvation from the slow-paced evil of love which masquerades in the frayed coat of human egoism.

These various strands of the novel are gathered in the person of Tristram Bone who is undoubtedly its main protagonist. Tristram is the self-deprecating *eiron*, with shades of the scapegoat about him. His power, insofar as we become aware of it, is the power of self-abnegation and tragic knowledge. The images which describe him, in the barbershop, cloisters, or aviary scenes, are priestly, saintly, and sacrificial. His true and secret purpose, we are asked to believe, is to lighten the pains of the world. Thus he discourses on love to a manicurist and, like Milton's Adam, prescribes: "Let there be no sacrifice of the happiness of three for the possible ecstasy of two, let morality dictate as it choose."[1] (The doctrine, of course, is one which he unwittingly betrays while hoping to enforce.) The spiritual investiture of Tristram takes place before our eyes in the earlier of the two Cloisters scenes in which he jams his hand in the cavity of a wooden effigy, that of a medieval saint, and then kneels impulsively before it. The stance is one which he figuratively preserves throughout the novel: his actions and speeches express the inarticulate depths of his humility.

This in itself is sufficient guarantee for his isolation. Even his doctrine of love, we are not surprised to discover, is predicated on the kind of self-punishment which can only intensify this isolation. In this respect, Bone's idea of love is very much like the one Carson McCullers expresses in *The Ballad of the Sad Café*. "The entire question of whom one loved," Bone pontificates, ". . . seemed to him of relative unimportance. It was whether one loved at all, and how much that love cost, and what was its reception then, that mattered."[2] Nor are we surprised to find that the only confessor Tristram has is Simon, his devoted monkey. When, toward the end, the little creature slits its throat with a razor, in mimicry of the desperation his master had just exhibited, we realize that part of Tristram has also perished. Love is defeated even where altruism reigns. The death of the monkey is the symbolic suicide of Tristram. Nothing remains for him except the memory of one rare quixotic gesture as Tristram gracefully stoops to retrieve a silver coin for a stranger:

Never in all eternity could he have repeated it, but never, he felt, would that be necessary. It was only once, perfect, a unit, and it had happened in full view of the statues behind him. As he crossed to the garage there came, to augment his exultation, a sense that if everything else went wrong and failed there would still, triumphantly, be that; that all his life was perhaps a progression towards that moment and could descend now easily from it; that he had been created perhaps for no reason more obscure than he might one day pick up that silver coin and return it to the young woman who had let it fall as he passed.[3]

Since Tristram Bone cannot suffer the passion of Christ, the hero of humility can only redeem Adam's day, "death denounc'd," in a quixotic moment of charity.

The world of A Long Day's Dying is strained by unresolved ambiguities. Its hero is a mock saint, quixotic and self-derisive. And its form shows numerous affinities with the ironic mode. For one thing, moral judgments are almost wholly suspended. Christian beliefs may be remotely implied in the narrative, but they are never dramatized, nor is any action criticized by the standard they establish. Images of religious observances abound without referring to a particular religion. And the most overt devotional act in the novel—Tristram kneeling before the wooden saint—is performed impulsively, almost accidentally, "with a quick flood of self-consciousness and fatigue."[4] The Christian motif is concealed in a Greek myth, and it is the latter which Buechner intends as a moral correlative to his tale. Yet his use of the Tireus myth remains oblique, contrived, and fragmentary. It would be tedious to work out in detail the parallels between the ancient myth and the modern narrative. The parallels, contained in the elusive parable Tristram gives to Elizabeth and in Motley's speech at the university, have been noted by critics.[5] They do not enrich the dramatic structure of the book, nor do they carry its moral to any new depths of perception. The symbolic identifications between Elizabeth and the seducer Tireus, Philomela and Steitler, Motley and the tapestry Philomela weaves to convey her rape to Procne, who is Tristram, between Lee and Itys, Maroo and the god who turns all into birds—a hawk, a sparrow, and a nightingale —these identifications disclose to us no fresh insight into the nature of love and vengeance. They merely offer an ironic contrast of motives, a parody of myth, a way, really, of avoiding moral statement. Christian dogma, we see, is not only dissolved into the dark complexities of mythology, but myth itself is further neutralized by parody. This may not have been the author's intention; it is, nevertheless, the effect his product conveys.

One product of irony is ambiguity in point of view. Between the two allegedly fixed points marked by the innocence of Lee (Itys) and knowledge of Maroo (Zeus), all is relative. Guilt is shared and motives are mixed. There is no way of ascertaining the facts, as Tristram hopes, which would grant absolution, distinguish the hunter from the hunted, the seducer from the seduced. The "quest for a kind of accuracy, a true recording of all that went on" fails because no vantage is provided in the book from which a complete account of human actions may be rendered.[6] When all the characters meet at Maroo's death-bed, as people in a detective story do to discover the culprit, no supersleuth emerges to point a finger and end the search. Each person stays within the bounds of his ignorance or culpability; each repeats to himself, like a prayer or malediction, the broken judgment of his existence. "Everything now will be different," Tristram murmurs, taking his phrase from Emma's comment on the death of his monkey; "There's nothing to do but wait," Motley drones; "You're all making too much of a fuss," Lee keeps insisting; and Maroo hopes her grandson will never realize, "Because of this old lady I am in some way safe now."[7] The orchestra of voices is as dissident as the hubbub to which Tristram listens in Grand Central—and it adds up to as little meaning.

This, the final scene, also betrays the essential function of time in the novel. Time confounds, rather than destroys, the seeker in his love quest. The encounter with experience brings symbolic, not actual, death: the monkey kills itself leaving its master suspended in a state of bewildered agony. Tristram, Elizabeth, and Steitler are all transformed into birds in Maroo's consciousness: "Three now were gone, or almost gone, flown up and off it seemed, yet circling still, wings spread, around, around, through what appeared a sky high, high and blue above."[8] Only Lee remains, unchanged and unchanging. Time, which in its literal development had brought nothing but doubt and betrayal to the three major characters, perpetuates the pattern of vengeance in the mythic image of a hawk pursuing a sparrow and nightingale. Ironic time repeats itself.

The quality of the novel is finally incarnated in its style. The style, like the structure, is a metaphor of spiritual death. Mannerly as the style may seem—the book could be termed an ironic melodrama of manners—it confesses to the absence of meaningful ceremonies. It persists in transforming reality, intimating that every action or scene may be rife with hidden meaning; yet its symbolic virtuosity operates in a void. The literal and the symbolic levels of the novel are interchangeable, for neither corresponds to anything outside the other. The metaphor is almost entirely self-created. The opening paragraph of the novel—Tristram in the barbershop!—sets its tone:

The mirror reflected what seemed at first a priest. A white robe, which fell from his thick shoulders in crescent folds, circumscribed with diminishing accuracy the ponderous art of his great head, and gave to his obesity the suggestion of vulnerability rather than strength as he sat face to face with the fact of himself. This effect was intensified by the resignation with which he suffered what might have been his acolyte, also dressed in white, either to anoint his flourishing, gray-brown hair as if in preparation for some imminent solemnity or to give it a tonsure.[9]

The style, we see, attempts to mythicize Tristram by establishing symbolic connections between the sacred and profane, the priestly and lay qualities of existence. Yet the sacred world turns out to be no more sacred than the profane is profane. (Other scenes in the novel—one in an aviary, between Tristram and Elizabeth, another in Central Park, between Tristram and Emma—show dream and reality to be equally indistinguishable.) Irony, which is the sole link between the two worlds, also envelops everything. This is the existential form of a quest suspended in a vacuum more terrifying than interstellar spaces. For all its baroque richness, *A Long Day's Dying* is a novel about the experience of nothingness.

II

In Bernard Malamud we find further testimony that the urban Jewish writer, like the Southern novelist, has emerged from the tragic underground of culture as a true spokesman of mid-century America. It may be difficult to classify Malamud in the scheme which Fiedler devised for Jewish authors of the last two decades: Bellow (highbrow), Salinger (upper middle-brow), Shaw (middle middlebrow), and Wouk (low middle-brow).[10] If Malamud does not possess the intellectual vitality of Bellow, his finest work shows an order of excellence no critic —however beetling or elevated his brow—can justly deny. The first and most obvious quality of his fiction is its "goodness." This is a complex quality, compounded of irony, trust, and craft—a touch of Dostoyevsky and Chagall, someone observed. It is the product of a sensitive yet enduring heart, vulnerable where it counts, and deeply responsible to its feeling of what transforms a man into *mensch*. Behind it is a wry vision of pain, and also of hope. We are not surprised, therefore, to hear Malamud say that "Jews are absolutely the very *stuff* of drama," or that the purpose of the writer is "to keep civilization from destroying itself"; or that much of current fiction is "under-selling Man."[11] But these pronouncements, which may express the natural bent of a man reared virtuously among immigrants in Brooklyn, do not explain the subtleties of his craft. Malamud's vision is preeminently moral, yet his form is sly. It owes something to the wile of Yiddish folklore, the ambiguous irony of the Jewish joke. Pain twisted into humor twists humor back into pain. The starkness of suffering, the leaden weight of ignorance or poverty, the alienation of the Jew in a land of

161

jostling Gentiles—all these become transmuted, in luminous metaphors and strange rhythms, into forms a little quaint or ludicrous, a bittersweet irony of life, into something, finally, elusive.

His first novel, *The Natural*, 1952, is a bizarre, authentic, troubled work about a thirty-three-year-old baseball player who suddenly emerges from painful oblivion into the crazy light of fame and big league corruption. The snappy slang of sport and gloomy language of the soul are fused in an allegorical tale which probes deep into the meaning of personal integrity but fails ultimately to make itself comprehensible. His collection of short stories, *The Magic Barrel*, 1958, includes some of his worst and best fiction. The poorer pieces are usually set abroad; the best deal with native Jewish material and have in common with his second novel, *The Assistant*, 1957, a blazing poetic insight into the daily aches and indignities of man which add up, somehow, to a kind of nobility, a form of aspiration.

The Assistant, presumably, is a love story, a domestic romance, a grocery store idyll of unwarranted poverty and harsh spiritual deprivation. It is a tale of loneliness, of lifelong frustrations and delicate, budding hopes. It is a "human" story albeit deeply ironic. For irony is indeed the key to Malamud's attitude toward man, to his estimate of him. The irony is not "dry," not scathing; it is best described by Earl Rovit when he says, "The affectionate insult and the wry self-deprecation are parts of the same ironic vision which values one's self and mankind as both less and more than they seem to be worth, at one and the same time."[12] This is the ambivalence of vision which qualifies, sometimes even undercuts, the affirmative power of Malamud's fiction.

The world revealed by *The Assistant* is, materially speaking, bleak; morally, it glows with a faint, constant light. Morris Bober and his wife, Ida, toil sixteen hours a day in a grocery store, barely eking out a living. They are well past middle age, and have given up their lives, their illusions, even the promise of a richer future which comes with education for their single daughter, Helen. The store, as we are told many times, is an open tomb. Twenty-one years are spent in it, and in the end Bober dies of double pneumonia, leaving his family penniless; he has to be buried in one of those huge anonymous cemeteries in Queens. America! "He had hoped for much in America and got little. And because of him Helen and Ida had less. He had defrauded them, he and the blood-sucking store."[13] This is what Bober thinks as one of two men who hold up his store slugs him on the head, because he is a Jew, and Bober falls to the ground without a cry. An appropriate ending to his weary, profitless day. Others may have luck, like the affluent Karp who owns a liquor store across the street, or the Earls whose son, Nat, attends law school—and takes Helen's virginity. But the Bobers live on stolidly, honestly, in squalor and sickening destitution. They are, like the grocery "assistant," Frank Alpine, victims of circumstance. What, then, gives these characters the measure of spiritual freedom they still possess?

The nature of the characters themselves holds the answer. Morris Bober, to be sure, is another example of the *eiron*, the humble man. He is more. He has endurance, the power to accept suffering without yielding to the hebetude which years of pain induce. He is acquainted with the tragic qualities of life—"The world suffers. *He* felt every schmerz"—and he defines the Jew as a suffering man with a good heart, one who reconciles himself to agony, not because he wants to be agonized, as Frank suggests, but for the sake of the Law—the Hebraic ideal of virtue.[14] Yet this is only one source of Bober's strength. His other source is charity, which in his case becomes nearly quixotic. Bober, though close to starvation himself, extends credit to his poor customers. He wakes up every day before dawn so that he may sell a three-cent roll to a Polish woman on her way to work. He takes in Frank Alpine, feeds him, and gives him an opportunity to redeem himself, though Frank

163

begins by stealing the grocer's bread and milk. Nor can he bring himself, in the extremity of despair, to burn down his property in order to collect insurance. Inured to failure, Bober still strives to give suffering the dignity of men who may trust one another in their common woe. But Karp calls him a "schlimozel."

The central action of the novel, however, develops from Bober's relation to Frank Alpine, and from the latter's relation to Helen. Frank, as the title suggests, is probably the hero of the book. He, too, is an *eiron*, a collector of injustices—with a difference. The regeneration of Frank—his literal and symbolic conversion to the Jewish faith—is the true theme of the book. His regeneration, at best, is a strange and mixed thing. When Frank first appears, he is a wanderer, an anti-Semite, even a thief. Yet one of his idols is St. Francis, and his hardened face conceals a hungry soul. "With me one wrong thing leads to another and it ends in a trap. I want the moon so all I get is cheese," he tells Bober.[15] The grocery store, which is Bober's grave, becomes a cave or haven for Alpine. It also becomes the dreary locus of his painful rebirth. Impelled by his gratitude to the grocer, and motivated by his guilt at having robbed him, with the aid of tough Ward Minogue, Frank puts all his energies into the store and ends by pumping some of his own obstinate life into the dying business. Meanwhile, he falls in love with Helen Bober.

From here on, ambiguities prevail. The racial prejudices of Frank are matched by those of Ida Bober, and to some extent, of her daughter Helen, against Gentiles. (The store improves, it is suggested, precisely because Frank is not a Jew.) Frank's gratitude to Morris does not prevent him from continuing to steal petty cash from the register—which he keeps account of and intends to return. Yet when Bober is incapacitated by sickness, Frank takes a night job, in addition to his grocery chores, and secretly puts his pay in the cash box. And his gnawing love for Helen, which she is slow to return, finally ends, ironically, with an act of near-rape as he rescues her from the clutches

164

of Ward Minogue, only to force her himself, right there and then in the park, at the very moment in their relationship when she is at last ready to surrender herself freely to him. "Dog," she cries "—uncircumcised dog!"[16] Guilt, gratitude, love —perhaps even the hope of a life he could glimpse but never attain—combine to sustain Frank Alpine, Bober's strange, saintly, pilfering assistant, in his impossible struggle against poverty, against hopelessness itself.

He wanted her but the facts made a terrible construction. They were Jews and he was not. If he started going out with Helen her mother would throw a double fit and Morris another. And Helen made him feel, from the way she carried herself, even when she seemed most lonely, that she had plans for something big in her life —nobody like F. Alpine. He had nothing, a backbreaking past, had committed a crime against her old man, and in spite of his touchy conscience, was stealing from him too. How complicated could impossible get?

He saw only one way of squeezing through the stone knot; start by shoveling out the load he was carrying around in his mind. . . .

So the confession had to come first. . . . He felt he had known this, in some frightful way, a long time before he went into the store, before he had met Minogue, or even come east; that he had really known all his life he would sometime, through throat blistered with shame, his eyes in the dirt, have to tell some poor son of a bitch that he was the one who had hurt or betrayed him. This thought had lived in him with claws; or like a thirst he could never spit out, a repulsive need to get out of his system all that had happened—for whatever had happened had happened wrong; to clean it out of his self and bring in a little peace, a little order; to change the beginning, beginning with the past that always stupendously stank up the now—to change his life before the smell of it suffocated him.[17]

Purgation in humility, rebirth through love—this is Frank's inchoate purpose, the reason for his willing acceptance of a backbreaking burden others—Minogue, Karp—find easy to reject. Yet it is in consonance with the character of the novel that purgation and rebirth both should appear ironic, awkward, and inconclusive. Frank tells Bober about his complicity in the robbery only to discover that the latter already knows. Bober catches his assistant rifling his till just when Frank had resolved never to steal again. And Frank's attempt to make a clean breast of it all to Helen merely serves to confirm her revulsion. His dogged and desperate love expresses itself in the form of a physical outrage. The savior of the Bobers is, in a sense, their archenemy. (The symbolic inversion of this relation may be discovered in the burial scene in which Frank topples accidentally into Bober's open grave.) But enemies suffer too, according to their conscience. Frank Alpine, it seems, can only expend the last vestige of his money, energy, or hope in agonized silence, a prey to the ironies which rip and twist his purpose. In the end, the value of confession is to the soul that makes it. And even love is a kind of realized solitude. Like Frank, Helen goes her lonely way, carrying the broken dreams of the Bobers to some distant and uncompromising end.

It is obvious that if the world of *The Assistant* is not drained of values, it is nevertheless saturated with pain, flooded with contradictions. Its two major characters find their identity in humiliation, an extreme and quixotic sense of obligation. They are not tragic heroes but merely heroes of irony. They retreat before the ultimate tragic ordeal: the fullness of tragic awareness itself. This is a fact the form of the novel supports.

Time, we know, leaves the characters suspended in the void which their failures create; the hints of regeneration are barely audible. Morris Bober dies in bankruptcy; Helen continues at her dreary job, dreaming of a better life; Frank slaves at the store, trying to provide for the Bobers, send Helen to college, and win back her love. The fate of each remains less than what it could be in heroic tragedy, less even than what it usually amounts to in realistic fiction. Thus, for instance, does Helen evaluate the life of her father: "People liked him, but who can admire a man passing his life in such a store? He buried himself in it; he didn't have the imagination to know what he was missing. He made himself a victim. He could, with a little more courage, have been more than he was."[18] And thus does Frank reflect upon his incessant labors: " 'Jesus,' he said 'why am I killing myself so? He gave himself many unhappy answers, the best being that while he was doing this he was doing nothing worse.' "[19] Whatever awareness time brings to the characters, whatever qualified dignity it confers upon their failures, every act in the novel is whittled by irony, every motive is mixed with its opposite.

Because time cannot unravel the knotted relations of the characters—what could be more gnarled than the relation of Gentile to Jew, of savior, seducer, and thief to those upon whom he preys, those from whom he gains an identity—the point of view of *The Assistant* dissociates itself from the protagonists, veering toward one then the other in friendly detachment. The characters are simply there, and they criticize each other's behavior; the point of view encourages us to perceive how ludicrous pain can be, and how unhappy virtue. The subtle, incredible twists of the plot, the reversals and accidents which affect the fortunes of the Bobers, are finally envisioned in a moral as well as dramatic perspective which acknowledges no certainties except the fact of suffering. (It is appropriate that Morris Bober should be an unorthodox Jew, and that at his funeral the rabbi should say, "Yes, Morris Bober was to me a true Jew because he lived in the Jewish experience, and with the Jewish heart. . . . He suffered, he endured, but with hope.")[20]

The achievement of Malamud's style, which survives his ironic play, lies in the author's capacity to convey both hope and agony in the rhythms of Yiddish speech.

> "I think I will shovel the snow," he told Ida at lunch-time.
> "Go better to sleep."
> "It ain't nice for the customers."
> "What customers—who needs them?"
> "People can't walk in such high snow," he argued.
> "Wait, tomorrow it will be melted."

"It's Sunday, it don't look so nice for the goyim that they go to church."

Her voice had an edge in it. "You want to catch pneumonia, Morris?"

"It's spring," he murmured.[21]

There is a Hemingway cleanness in this dialogue, a kind of humility and courage, but also a softness Hemingway never strove to communicate.

Morris, however, does catch pneumonia and die. Nor can the poetry of the style persuade us to forget that the search of Frank Alpine for an identity ends, in the last, brief paragraph of the novel, with the ritual of circumcision. The act is one of self-purification, of initiation too, in Frank's case, but it is also an act of self-repudiation, if not, as some may be tempted to say, of symbolic castration.

III

Ralph Ellison has written but a single novel to date. *Invisible Man*, 1952—he is known to be at work on another—yet his position seems to be even more secure than Richard Wright's who blazed the way some decades ago with *Native Son*, giving voice to such outrage and perplexity as the American Negro inherits, giving to anger the complex dignity of art. Anger and art: these are also the poles which define Ellison's pursuit of the old question of an American Negro identity, masks black or white shimmering in a vortex of light. For there is nothing simple, nothing that does not reek of violence and betrayal, in this question of identity; nothing that can be resolved in the spirit of liberal generosity or romantic primitivism.

To understand the form of Ellison's—and Wright's—work it is important to know something of the destructive attitude from which the best Negro novelists *begin*. "What are the ways by which Negroes confront their destiny?" Ellison inquires. "In the South of Wright's childhood there were three general ways: They could accept the role created for them by the whites. . . ; they could repress their dislike of Jimcrow social relations while striving for a middle way of respectability. . . ; or they could reject the situation, adopt a criminal attitude, and carry on an unceasing psychological scrimmage with the whites, which often flared forth into physical violence."[22] The Negro hero must shed his identity to find his skin, and he can only do so in painful and successive stages, as the hero of *Invisible Man* is there to testify. The only difference between the South of Wright's and Ellison's childhoods may be that in the latter acceptance of the Jimcrow mask has become increasingly difficult, and "the unceasing psychological scrimmage" with society has grown to be a necessity which white and black feel alike. But the "criminal attitude" is merely the beginning of a road that has no end. Crime abhors itself, and chaos, because the human mind is what it is, seeks to define itself in multitudinous patterns. Ellison, who has the formal sense of a jazz musician and the instinct of a singer of blues, understands that anger or agony is transient without art. Turbulence, in private or political life, amounts to a denial of the dignity of man. To acknowledge the innate dignity of mankind is also to reconcile the idea of freedom prescribed in the founding political documents of America with the violence of a Harlem race riot. The act of reconciliation is an action of what Ellison calls Mind, a fact of *form*. The "Negro question" becomes a question of determining the essence of the human in a way that the questioning and tormented Mind can grasp. This, if any, is the artistic credo of Ellison. The credo is one that requires him to exploit the resources of irony. And it prompts him, as will become evident, to draw upon the healing powers of the American joke and Negro blues.

The world of *Invisible Man* is vividly real and surreal, charged with insane violence and crazy humor. It is a world of magic transformations, for nothing in it is exactly what it seems. The contours of objects melt and vanish, ebony black paint is transmuted before our eyes into a shiny white, Sambo paper dolls dance madly on the curb without obvious support, and the invisible hero sits in a forgotten coal cellar illuminated by 1,369 electric bulbs. Acceptance, humiliation, and rebellion—these are the emotions we sometimes associate with the various characters. But in this phantasmagoria of fact and fiction, no character is solid or stable enough—they are sleepwalkers all, captives of their particular illusion, hence grotesques in the sense Sherwood Anderson gave to that word—no character is "real" enough to make his emotions hold more than a fragment of reality. For the simple and astounding fact of the novel is this: no one is more visible than the invisible hero; no one is visible to another. "Behold, a walking zombie!" the mad Negro doctor expostulates for the benefit of the wealthy New England philanthropist, Mr. Norton. "Already he's learned to repress not only his emotions but his humanity. He's invisible, a walking personification of the Negative, the most perfect achievement of your dreams, sir! The mechanical man!"[23] Does not this definition of invisibility apply equally to Norton, Dr. Bledsoe, Brother Jack, Ras the Destroyer, and Rinehart? "Humanity" may be discovered in a hole underground, but the way to a coal cellar is long and hard, full of monstrous illusions. It is in the process of acquiring vision and visibility, the process of the hero's initiation, that the various dragons of illusion are slain —and the world of the novel is defined.

The hero, who remains nameless, begins as a docile Southern Negro anxious to please the white masters, and eager to do honor to his people within the rigid limits set for them. A gifted boy orator, he is compelled to perform, in a smoker, in front of the leading white citizens of his community, battle it out half-naked and blindfolded with other Negro boys, and pick up coins from an electrified blanket. The scene is a twitching nightmare, but the boy earns a scholarship to a Negro college, and goes on, still full of his meek illusions, determined to make a place for himself in the world. At college, his dream of "social responsibility" under the dispensation of white men comes to a shattering end. He chauffeurs the influential Norton around, allows him to hear from a Negro sharecropper the story of his incest, and steers him finally into a bedlam of Negro veterans. This is not what the Northern philanthropist, despite all his protests, *wants* to see. Incest, for Norton, comes too close to home, and the rantings of the "deranged" Negro doctor make too sharp a sense. The Northern white man, like the Southern white man, has his own image of the Negro which he cannot allow anyone to challenge. The boy is dismissed from college by Dr. Bledsoe, a black Machiavel who knows how to wield and retain power by working underground, knows how to betray ruthlessly white and black alike. Bledsoe gives the boy a devastating lesson in cynicism, duplicity, the pragmatic way to survival—still another way of distorting the human thing in man. He sends him North with a sealed letter of recommendation that insures his continued unemployment. This is the Southern part of the story, the end of the obsequious persona of the hero. Acquiescence does not teach the virtues of acceptance. The Negro who "knows his place" finds that he has none.

In New York, the hero develops a new surliness. He becomes caustic, cantankerous, belligerent, as the occasion requires. Rebellion begins. And it begins, appropriately enough, in the boiler room of a factory which puts out paint—*white* paint. The factory scene is as insane as any we had witnessed in the South—and as ludicrous. The paranoiac suspicions of the pro- and anti-union factions make for grim comedy. The industrial North offers the hero no better way of realizing his identity than the slave-conscious South. (In a Kafkaesque scene, he is shown held by the metal tentacles of some electric machine while the doctors at the factory hospital, who try to force back upon him some awareness of his identity, treat him as the object of a "scientific" experiment.) It is only Mary, his Harlem landlady, who recognizes him for what he may be: an individual seeking to make himself recognized. But the pendulum now swings the other way. The hero begins to repudiate his Negro persona—he savagely breaks Mary's iron figurine which represents the very idea of the Negro in parody, concealing it in his briefcase for the rest of the novel because he cannot, literally and symbolically, dispose of it in any manner. He is drawn into the circle of the Communist Brotherhood which is willing to sacrifice the interests of the colored people to its expedient interpretation of history. He is seduced by a wealthy white woman, a sympathizer of the Brotherhood, who confuses "the class struggle with the ass struggle"; and is cast by another woman into the role of a rapist. He is pursued by Ras the Destroyer, rabid prophet from the heart of darkness, who rides the streets of Harlem on a charger, brandishing shield and spear, and crying the annihilation of everyone in a skin whiter than his own. And he is finally mistaken for Rinehart, the faceless man of many faces, lover, hipster, number man, and revivalist preacher, who moves through the undergrowth of the Harlem jungle on his pointed toes, incarnating crime, imagination, a life of stealthy guises and possibilities. But none of these ways leads to the discovery of self, none is commensurate with full, ergo human, rebellion. The way of the hero, we know, lies underground. With this ends the second and final part of the book, and begins the true life of its protagonist.

The external developments of the narrator reflect the values which Ellison affirms or denies in *Invisible Man*. From the very start, we are told that men are sleepwalkers, invisible shadows flitting across one another's paths. Culture moves forth by contradictions: "Not like an arrow, but a boomerang."[24] Ideologies, whether radical, liberal, or reactionary, betray the human quest for self-definition. Ellison, to be sure, exhibits a restless, perhaps even irate, political consciousness in the long middle section of the novel, which, incidentally, is not its most convincing part. But in the end, all ideologies must be rejected. The central issue is existential, not political. The hero learns a crucial lesson from Clifton who deserts the Brotherhood to sell dolls on the streets of New York—and is shot to death by a policeman. Clifton seems to revert, atavistically, to all that the narrator has been indoctrinated to suppress in himself. Clifton plunges, hoping to fall outside of history. "All things, it is said, are duly recorded—all things of importance, that is," the narrator muses after Clifton's death. "But not quite, for actually it is only the known, the seen, the heard and only those events that the recorder regards as important that are put down, those lies his keepers keep their power by." But what happens to "the transitory ones," "birds of passage who were too obscure for learned classification, too silent for the most sensitive recorders of sound; of natures too ambiguous for the most ambiguous words, and too distant from the centers of historical decision to sign or even to applaud the signers of historical documents?"[25] Invisibility is historical too, not merely personal. And ambiguity, such as a Rinehart may practice, is perhaps the true badge of the hero in our time. It is winner take nothing that is the truth of America as of every country. The disintegration of the public realm, which finds dramatic expression in the terror, violence, freedom, and exultation of the Harlem race riot, precedes the reconstitution of the individual in the privacy of his illuminated cellar. Morality, nowadays, *begins* with irresponsibility.

But the question still remains: what kind of hero is the narrator of *Invisible Man*? And what is the precise quality, the *internal* logic, of his encounter with experience? To say that the process of his initiation is a process of disillusionment is merely to state the obvious character of initiation in America.

In the beginning, in order to avoid the role of scapegoat, the hero tries to assume the guise of the modest *eiron*. He is not ready yet to accept the subversive doctrine of his grandfather, a freed slave: "Live with your head in the lion's mouth. I want you to overcome 'em with yeses, undermine 'em with grins, agree 'em to death and destruction, let 'em swoller you till they vomit or bust wide open."[26] It is only gradually that he brings himself to reject the feeling, so deeply inculcated in him, that "white is right." It is only later that he begins to understand what the mad doctor tells him, when the hero is about to leave town, that there is always an element of crime in freedom. "Play the game, but play it your own way . . . ," the doctor advises him. "Be your own father, young man. And remember, the world is possibility if only you'll discover it."[27] The *eiron* has to become first a rebel, and the rebel a dupe of utopian visions, before he can realize that the possibilities inherent in crime, which the *alazon* always exploits, point the way to invisibility, and hence to a kind of salvation. But the narrator is not satisfied to remain a Rinehart, the underground man lurking and skulking above ground. He goes literally underground, cutting himself off resolutely from a world in which he could live only at the price of anarchy or skullduggery. The movement underground is occasioned by necessity—the hero falls into the coal cellar while fleeing from some of Ras's henchmen—but it is maintained by choice. Only thus could he escape the more serious threat to himself which every faction of society poses as it tries to impose upon him its biased image of reality. For by *pretending* to agree to these images he had indeed *agreed*. (In this perception, the hero goes farther toward the truth than his grandfather would have ever foreseen.) After a time in the cellar, however, the narrator feels compelled to come up again. After the fall, the journey through the heart of darkness, comes the return, the ascent. The hero of *Invisible Man*, though his movements have geographical, social, and intellectual scope, though he encounters crosswise and crabwise and in circular fashion all the absurd selves he discarded, can still be known as a rebel-victim whose initiation leads but to invisibility, a state of existential illumination and suspended action. And yet, is it not better to play out one's own absurdity than to die for the absurdity of another, this hero asks?

The form of initiation of this anonymous hero, who may

speak for all of us on the lower frequencies, is the form irony takes—the novel is neither comic nor tragic—when outrage is turned into art. For one thing, the effect of time is to keep all the acts of the narrator in a state of suspension, a kind of perpetual self-qualification. This is evident in several ways. A great number of images in the novel, which sustains its high pitch over long stretches of the story, serve to freeze time, to stop its flow. The consciousness of the hero is inflated in crisis after crisis till it fills the whole of time and space, dissociating itself from both; the sense of continuity is shattered by intense metaphors reminiscent of Rimbaud. Here is a typical statement: "I leaped aside, into the street, and there was a sudden and brilliant suspension of time, like the interval between the last ax stroke and the felling of a tall tree, in which there had been a loud noise followed by a loud silence."[28] There are also passages, jazz-like improvisations in italics, in which the narrator removes himself from the action, extending his consciousness back and forth over the whole sweep of his life, standing, as it were, in disembodied fashion outside of it all. Here is a reflection of the mature hero, interjected in a scene from his youth. The scene is a college chapel:

Hey! old connoisseur of voice sounds, of voices without messages, of newsless winds, listen to the vowel sounds and the crackling dentals, to the low harsh gutturals of empty anguish, now riding the curve of a preacher's rhythm I heard long ago in a Baptist church, stripped now of its imagery. No suns having hemorrhages, no moons weeping tears, no earthworms refusing the sacred flesh and dancing in the earth on Easter morn!

Then we have to recall, too, that the very ending of the novel is inconclusive. The hero is driven underground because he becomes "ill of affirmation, of saying 'yes' against the nay-saying of my stomach—not to mention my brain."[29] There he loses all sense of time. Is it days or weeks or months since he has been in the cellar? Soon, however, the narrator gains his primary insight. "And here's the cream of the joke: Weren't we *part of them* as well as apart from them and subject to die when they died?"[30] In the end, one can only blame oneself, and stand shivering and naked before a million unseeing eyes. One can also overstay one's hibernation, and that, as the hero knows, is perhaps the arch social crime, even for an invisible man schooled in the difficult morality of irresponsibility. The stench in the air, outside the cellar, may be the stench of death— or spring. Who knows? The total action of time leads to a paradox: "So it is that now I denounce and defend. . . . I condemn and affirm, say no and say yes, say yes and say no."[31]

Contradiction is also inherent in the point of view of the novel. The narrator speaks in the first person, and he must be actor and chorus, defendant and judge. The framework provided by the Prologue and Epilogue places the events in this double perspective. So do the snatches of blues and italicized fragments of commentary which Ellison employs to lift his hero out of his own story so that he may interpret its meaning for us. For the simple fact is that the narrator cannot swear to "the whole truth" of his life: he cannot be entirely "honest." "Let me be honest with you—a fact which, by the way, I find of the utmost difficulty," he says not without some self-irony. "When one is invisible he finds such problems as good and evil, honesty and dishonesty, of such shifting shapes that he confuses one with the other, depending upon who happens to be looking through him at the time."[32] It is not only that the narrator has many masks, or rather many levels of consciousness organized like musical themes through which he travels to the heart of music:

And beneath the swiftness of the hot tempo there was a slower tempo and a cave and I entered it and looked around and heard an old woman singing a spiritual as full of Weltschmerz as flamenco, and beneath that lay a still lower level on which I saw a beautiful girl the color of ivory pleading in a voice like my mother's as she stood before a group of slave owners who bid for her naked body, and below that I found a lower level and a more rapid tempo and I heard someone shout:

176

"Brothers and sisters, my text this morning is the 'Blackness of Blackness.'"[33]

No, it is also that the very nature of the point of view adopted forces Ellison and the autobiographical narrator to engage one another in a game of mirrors, mutual exposure and concealment, endorsement and ironic dissociation.

The final, indeterminate quality of the work, a tragi-comedy of people whom now we see and now we don't, depends as much on this point of view as on the nature of the material used. There is hysteria, violence, nightmare, and pain syncopated throughout in the form of a performance by Louis Armstrong. And there is slapstick, absurdity, grotesque laughter, and even puns—the paint slogan, "If it's the Optic White, It's the Right White," referring to the white-is-right theme; or the hero's statement while guzzling yams. "I yam what I am!" referring to the identity theme.[34] The feeling of the blues and the idea of the joke merge. This is to be expected. "The Blues is an impulse to keep the painful details and episodes of a brutal experience alive in one's aching consciousness, to finger its jagged grain, and to transcend it, not by the consolation of philosophy, but by squeezing from it a near-tragic, near-comic lyricism," Ellison writes.[35] And the joke? The American joke, as Ellison perceives, is born of cultural contradictions; it is a child of diversity. The joke and the blues, we see, find their common ground in the attempt to reconcile opposites: "There is a mystery in the whiteness of blackness, the innocence of evil, and the evil of innocence, though, being initiates, Negroes express the joke of it in the blues."[36] One might also say that the pain of it is in the joke. And this is what is meant by irony, the mediation between poles of awareness, the final, modest triumph of the invisible man, not because he decides to emerge from his burrow but because prompted by intelligence—"In going underground, I whipped it all except the mind, the *mind*" —he gives to his life the *form* which only imagination can give

177

to chaos.[37] In the qualified encounter of the hero with experience, the most affirmative act is the ironic expression of art itself.

IV

One fact about the three novels considered in this chapter is clear: their forms sustain ambiguity as the fate and future of their respective heroes. The resolution is neither comic nor tragic. A certain freedom of action is allowed to the protagonist, but it is not the kind of freedom which permits him to control his destiny or integrate himself back into society. The degree of freedom, of choice and regeneration, is smallest in A *Long Day's Dying*, greatest in *Invisible Man*.

The shift from the first of these novels to the last is continuous in other respects too. Tristram Bone comes closest to the figure of the saintly or quixotic victim, Ellison's Negro approaches at times the figure of the roguish or criminal rebel, while Frank Alpine stands somewhere in between. Yet all three are projected, generally speaking, in the image of the self-deprecating *eiron* whose main function is to appear less than what he is, thereby implying, like Socrates, more than his words or deeds communicate. The *eiron*, in other words, employs irony to expand our consciousness of his situation, evoking possibilities where none but limitations exist. He does not, like the victim or scapegoat, derive his being from martyrdom and defeat. Rather does he assert his humanity, and ours, by accepting the dissolution of heroism, by maintaining, not without dignity, the dialectic between how things are and how they could be. This is the basic morality of the *eiron*.

The aesthetic of the *eiron* is usually one of parody: specifically the parody of myth, of idyll, and of a quest romance in the three works discussed earlier. The formal purpose of parody in each case is to create an objective and complex point of view. "When we try to isolate the ironic as such," Northrop

Frye writes, "we find that it seems to be simply the attitude of the poet as such, a dispassionate construction of a literary form, with all assertive elements, implied or expressed, eliminated."[38] This is precisely what we found to be the objective of *Invisible Man*. In Mailer's *Barbary Shore*, Bellow's *The Victim*, McCullers' *The Member of the Wedding*, and Styron's *Set This House on Fire*, the hero's encounter with experience is qualified, in much the same way, by irony which dominates the existential pattern of fiction.

CHAPTER 7

ENCOUNTER WITH POSSIBILITY:
THREE NOVELS BY
GOLD, CHEEVER, AND DONLEAVY

If you make mistakes, undo them the best you can.
HERBERT GOLD, *The Optimist*

I

W ITTY, vital, and prolific—he can be slick too—
Herbert Gold has published five novels to date, and
written a large number of stories and essays. The
latter, crowded as they are with insight and prejudice, jubilantly
express his views on fiction. "What the novelist seems to be
doing at his philosophical best is to explore possibility," Gold
states. The art of possibility is the art of comedy which, nowadays, requires every man to be his own Don Quixote, and every
writer to "stare into the sun of alternatives."[1] The need to bounce
with life, to take risks with its incompleteness, to celebrate the
"tin and hope" of human existence, knowing all the while that
reality may be its own end (the mode of comedy) or, less frequently, that ambition contains its own death (the manner of
tragedy)—these are the primary concerns of Herbert Gold when
craft and vision meet in the felicity of a fictional moment. When
craft and vision fall asunder, the style of Gold crackles with
forced gaiety, and his wisdom degenerates into a knowing wink,
a mere knack for poetic sapience. The writing, it then seems,
gets ahead of itself; the author strives to attain his goal too
easily or too fast.

After his first two novels, *Birth of a Hero*, 1951, and *The
Prospect Before Us*, 1954, Gold turned out, in *The Man Who*

180

Was Not With It, 1956, a tangy tale of carnival life, portraying with fine understanding the makings of love and betrayals of friendship. *The Optimist,* 1959, came next; it was followed by *Therefore Be Bold,* 1960, a joyous, truncated novel about the adolescent intimations of power and sexuality.

The Optimist is a parable of man refusing to accept less than his full share of life. The limit is death, and death, as everyone knows, throbs in the heart and courses in the blood. For the time being, however, why not ask for more of everything? This is the question which Burr Fuller must constantly answer— and learn to ask.

The Optimist is a parable but it is also a novel. It is set in Detroit. It covers the years before and after the last war, moving with the fortunes of Burr from his late adolescence at college to his candidacy for Congress at the age of thirty-five. And it penetrates those areas of American life in our century where love and politics may mingle under the aspect of a romantic ideal. The novel, that is, has a world of its own which is more richly specified in the later sections than in the sketchy college or war scenes.

The power of illusions dominates the book in overt or insidious ways. From the very beginning, the tension between romantic idealism and an equally romantic realism is made evident in the dialogues Mike and Burr conduct as youths attending the University of Michigan. Mike is the man of principles to which reality is forced to conform. Burr is the opportunist whose sense of reality excludes darkness, difficulty, defeat. Thus, discussing the role of fraternities with Mike, Burr says, "Belonging is the way to success in America. It's part of doing things. It's the generous and sociable part."[2] Allen Turner, the local Chapter president, refines conformity to a ludicrous mystique. And young Laura, whom Burr subsequently marries, turns her beauty into some vague ideal of success, and dreams of a love she is powerless to sustain. But obedience to romance is merely the obverse of obedience to authority. Hence the suicide of Private Weinstein whom Burr meets in the army. Weinstein is viciously persecuted by Sergeant Stamp; his suicide is motivated by tact, a sensitivity, beyond appeal, to the judgment of others. Only Cal Janus, a preacher who lost his call, silent, mournful, and incorruptible—"He was excellent but both saintly and as wild as a criminal"—can stand outside the framework of military authority or romantic idealism and defend a position, unlike Mike's, based on his own impersonal agony.[3] For other veterans, there is a life in the suburbs, which reaches back, somehow, to the stale hopes of adolescence, and enshrines the pieties of love, politics, or Natural Childbirth, "one of the several religions not born on the shores of the Mediterranean," promising "shapely heads, undrugged spirits, and a rosy intercommunication for those women who will train themselves and their husbands for the climactic procreative experience."[4] Eternal youth, America, land of eternal desire. But is not romance, where loneliness is absolute and sociability is compulsive, where women are raised to question the prerogatives of men, and men are given the conscience of their mothers, better defined by the parable of the praying mantis which placidly chews on the head of its dancing mate in order to consummate the act of love? Sex and happiness are promises our culture makes but seldom keeps. For Laura, happiness is a right, a statement made in order to fill the void of loneliness. For Burr, happiness must be captured, grabbed, ravished. For both, love and happiness are a consumer's product, consuming itself. Burr conducts his campaign, and commits adultery with Barbara, the daughter of his political boss. Laura raises her two children, takes sleeping pills and nurses her headaches, and commits adultery with Mike, Burr's childhood friend. "What of me, what of me?" everyone asks. And what of Love and the American Dream? A man who gives up adult love or responsive privacy becomes the clever hunk of meat men call a public man, the leader who is no longer the principle of organization in a society but rather the principle which expresses its disorganization most eloquently. Encased in our loneliness, we cannot love. Immersed in others, we cannot act or lead. The death of love and the disease of politics both stem from the same kind of excess, the desperate blandness which is the other face of isolation. This is the major insight of Herbert Gold in *The Optimist*. It is the destructive principle in the world he has chosen to depict. Destructive and yet somehow vital too, the principle presupposes the aching solitude of Americans and their indestructible optimism: that quality of hope or vision which makes free with reality, turning facts into dreams.

Irony qualifies the values which the novel shows to be in conflict, and irony attends the developments of the hero's fate. Burr Fuller, as a boy, thinks that a man may attain anything he wants by rinsing his socks and obeying his dreams. He enters his resolutions for self-improvement into a diary, and waits his day. At college, he bends easily with the wind, lives on his self-esteem, uses Laura or Lucille, the "townie" with whom he carries on his first affair. The time will come. "The camel lives off its hump in the desert. The politician, the actor, the artist lives off the abstract love of an audience."[5] Is there more? The world he creates stands without girders high in the air; the childhood hunger for love which his thoughtless mother could not assuage turns on itself. Yet Burr would not become Congressman Fuller if he were powerless to take a stand. He punches Allen Turner on the nose when the latter humiliates him in a barbaric rite of fraternal expiation, exposing him naked before Lucille. The act comes late, but not too late. We are not witnessing a tragedy.

During the war, Burr makes the rank of sergeant, performs under fire, almost accidentally, like a hero. He fights with the Maquis in France, and carries on an affair with Fillette. Endowed with too much life, he cannot follow the suicidal example of Weinstein; and undermined by a love for expediency, he cannot emulate the example of Cal Janus. Cal dies of a brain tumor, but perhaps that's what idealism is, Burr Fuller broods. Cal haunts Burr even more than the rumor of Mike's death, reported missing in action. Meanwhile, back home on a furlough, Burr uses a girl in the darkened parlor of the Fuller residence to avenge himself on his mother. The griefs of childhood never end. Which does not prevent Burr from admitting: "My trouble, apart from dandruff and the fear that I am the shyest person in a room, is that I have a passion for Excellence, what Aristotle called Virtue. I can see myself growing old, bald, and scruffy in it. How can I justify this desire which may have the same results as a passion for power, money, love, saintliness—all good things which also make trouble?"[6] Excellence is a quality of intensity, of *life*. But the first thing Burr really learns, at the end of the war, is the possibility of *death*. At twenty-two, his advice to himself is: "Dead men look worst when they look alive"; and, "If you make mistakes, undo them the best you can."[7]

The logic of error is the grammar of possibility. Errors also beget responsibility. Ten years later, Burr is married to Laura and living in the suburbs of Detroit. He is a rising lawyer, the Democratic Party's hard choice to run for Congress against Mrs. Theophile Grant, a timeless and indefeasible Republican institution. Laura is anxious, bored, withdrawn; Mike is aging, still idealistic, and querulous. But Burr is ambitious. And there is the lovely Barbara McKinley to comfort him when Laura fails to provide that nourishment for self-esteem which goes by the name of love. Burr must test himself—against the best and the worst in himself. "Is there a time when a man has the right and the power to do anything?" Burr asks. Might is not right, but neither does right guarantee the power needed to go with it. Burr must find out. You are running for yourself, Mike says to him in a dying echo of their old argument. And of course Burr is—up to a point, as he insists. "Should a man answer his ambition and talents, defined by himself, or should he put himself to useful work, letting the sense of duty give shape to talent and ambition?"[8] Can a man be a natural law unto himself, and therefore an outlaw to all others? The questions are explicit; the answers are not forthcoming. Burr works, breaks the sacrament of marriage, succumbs to the nightmare of a protracted fever. The body rebels at last. The whole man learns one other thing besides the possibility of death: he learns that he must *earn*. He learns what other heroes of contemporary fiction have learned before him: that even for a promoter, an entrepreneur, a manipulator of men, earning is suffering. Burr returns to Laura, not out of love or hope, nor out of his rabid optimism. He returns because he knows now that with Laura he must try to defeat her or be defeated; that his marriage never had the chance to play itself out; that to reach out for Barbara, whom he does not really love, is merely to encourage his tendency to slip and slither through life. Burr, once again, takes his stand. Once again, as it were, he punches Allen Turner on the nose. It is late, but once again, not too late.

Our hero, we see, is a hero of errors. The optimist begins as an impostor, an *alazon*. There is a touch of the *miles gloriosus* in him. But he is also the child. His optimism is another disguise of American radical innocence. Such innocence, we saw, brings destruction. It can also give life. "Yes! Yes!" Burr exclaims. "If there weren't some childishness in me I'd be dead by now!"[9] And like a child, Burr ends by saying to life, "More." Burr begins as an impostor, remains, in a sense, a child, but ends with a kind of knowledge. The knowledge is an insight into the paradoxical nature of his ambition, which is also the paradox of American reality. "He had entered the law, politics, and marriage with a lust for shifting experience; yet he had hope for permanent value in this American faith in never-permanent event. He believed in himself with no evidence for belief but himself."[10] A change is possible for Burr Fuller, though the change is enunciated in the ironic inflections which admit futility: "If we cannot change ourselves, we can try anyway. If we cannot change ourselves, we can try anyway, and perhaps change ourselves and the world before we destroy it."[11] The proposition, obviously, can be put only in the negative. Why not try anyway? There is nothing to lose.

Is this, then, the form of comedy or of tragedy? A child of possibility, the hero nevertheless comes to a knowledge of himself which is neither comic—the heroes of comedy seldom change at all—nor yet tragic—the heroes of tragedy accept their limitation—but ironic. How does *The Optimist* end?

"Burr Fuller was now thirty-five years old and had two sons. Eyes clouded by longing, he reached out to take a cloud in his arms. "More. More. More! More!"[12]

The encounter is open. Yet will not Burr's life repeat its failures? Can he use or keep what he learned? The novel predicts no finality; it sustains the ambiguities of the future as of the past. The quest for romantic perfection in all things has no terminus. Ironic time, in the novel, is the temporal dimension of recurrence. More, Burr says. More begets more. Initiation in America is endless.

The progress of the novel from Burr's adolescence, 1941, to the middle of his journey through life, 1959, is conveyed in six stages, each constituting a formal division of the book. These stages, particularly toward the end, are composed of broken and disconnected scenes, reveries, moments of crisis. The point of view often shifts from one isolated character to another, and changes from first person to third person narration, and again to the view of an omniscient author. These shifts seem a little haphazard, and the design of the novel may strike us at times as arbitrary. But such arbitrariness is itself functional. "We should expect the fragmentation of self in the modern novel," Gold writes, "just as we expect it in the man bound to a factory or office, within a social structure which cannot use the largest capacities of millions of individuals."[13] Arbitrariness, when it is not the product of faulty design, is one of the forms fragmentation takes. It is also the form of a life shaped by accident or error. Thus Burr reflects on his past: "Floating, open to anything that can define him, he risks being defined by accidents."[14] This is the essential and ironic fact that the structure of *The Optimist* must dramatize.

A final, and uneasy, ironic qualification may be sensed in the style of the book. Gold's style tends to possess verve, color, pace. It has its mannerisms too: a facile, aphoristic turn of expression, an elliptic trick of striking off-key rhythms, a touch of false glamor, even where genuine sentiment is called for. But these are quirks of sensibility. The real difficulty is more subtle. It is that the style tries to give hope and humor to dramatic material weighed down by genuine desperation. The bounce of words cannot conceal a fairly bleak spectacle of loneliness and frustration. Hence the glibness of Burr's affirmative editorials on life. His rapt comment on Frank, the sergeant who sells obscene pictures and traffics in the black markets of Paris, is one of numerous examples. (The comment reminds us of the more convincing statement of Bellow's Augie March on laughing Jacqueline, the Norman maid.) Frank may have "a paltry and unprotected heart," as Burr thinks, but the wonder or gaiety of life cannot be caught and dismissed in an elegant phrase. What joy the events and actions of the novel lack, the style seeks to create unaided. *The Optimist* remains, in this sense, a self-created metaphor of hope, and an ironic act of dissection. A severely diminished man, the hero still wants more of everything. Metaphor and action, we see, suffer from the disunity of the age; nor can illusion and reality be entertained in a common perspective. Irony, which endeavors to reconcile opposites, also assumes that things, at bottom, are irreconcilable. But perhaps this is the way things really are.

II

Humor, in our world, averts its face in pathos or whimsey. As everyone knows, *The New Yorker* has sponsored a breed of writers whose arcane formula compounds tenderness and irony in cunning measures. These writers often find the poignant form of the short story more suitable to their ends than the novel, though some manage, at least once in their lifetime, to expand the wry insight of the story into a sustained dramatic performance. Salinger comes easily to mind as a distinguished example of this group, and Salinger's *New Yorker* rival, John Cheever, who is less spiritually exclusive.

Like Salinger, Cheever has also written only a single novel to date, *The Wapshot Chronicle*, 1957. He is perhaps better known for his short stories, collected in a first and tentative volume, *The Way Some People Live*, 1943, and in two fine works, *The Enormous Radio*, 1953, and *The Housebreaker of Shady Hill*, 1958. There is a good deal of variety in Cheever's fiction, though its steady concern is with the manners, urban and suburban, which express or conceal the hearty contradictions, perhaps even the absurdities, of human beings. Cheever's emphasis, however, is on the heartiness, the gaminess, of it all; so much so that his characters, like the deft and lively caricatures they are, often move in a cartoonist's world where the explosion of a sawed-off shotgun at point-blank range leaves the victim a little singed or blackened perhaps but essentially unharmed. This is fantasy, the fulfillment of a dream of immortality. But in dreams also begin responsibilities, and in fantasy men find a meaning or hope to live by. All of which does not prevent Cheever from saying, in the recent *Esquire* symposium on "Writing in America Today," that "having determined the nightmare symbols of our existence, the characters [of fiction] have become debased and life in the United States in 1960 is Hell."[15]

In *The Wapshot Chronicle*, the Wapshots of St. Botolph show life to be at worst a kind of whimsical Puritan purgatory, a preparation for a fine action which, though never quite completed, is transmitted to the next generation in a spirit of pride and joy. St. Botolph, as its memorials prove, was an aggressive village in the Civil War days, and an important inland port in the great days of Massachusetts. On Independence Day, the town musters its past under the elm trees and cheers the parade. The town, we are told, is an image of permanence in the middle of decay. The first Wapshots came to it, on the "Arbella," in 1630, but their genealogy may be traced to a Norman ancestor, Vaincre-Chaud. The Wapshots have the green sap of life in their Yankee veins. The men are erotic, their soul touched by romance; the women are formidable, iron ladies in their delicate summer dresses. All incarnate the New England virtues of thrift, cleanliness, individualism to the point of eccentricity, and a kind of stubbornness that combines the qualities of rock and sea. They have no need of the honors the world bestows, choosing to decline decorations even from the hands of General Washington himself. One ancestor, shipwrecked in the Java Sea, rode a wooden spar for three days, kicking at sharks with bare heels. Another played the piano in dime stores, married the merchant prince who owns them all, and grew old, in fierce widowhood, to import whole castles from Italy or France, annexing them to her imperial residence at Clear Haven. Yet the smell of orange rinds and wood smoke hangs over the exuberance of the Wapshots, and a note of melancholy creeps upon them on land and sea.

It is important that we give ourselves to the flavor of the book since its dramatic structure remains dubious and its collection of quaint episodes is far from unified. The spectacle of history and nature, the panorama of people, towns, seascapes, and countryside, finds a kind of unity in the marvelous state of mind the author wishes to impress upon us. But character and action seem always to fall short of the fabulous evocation of time, place, and archetype. The Wapshot legend, the New England myth, overreach the dramatic resources of Cheever. This is to say that the world of the novel is a metaphor which the plot cannot adequately sustain. It is a world created by style.

The central action of the plot, insofar as it can be ascertained, is the initiation of two young brothers, Moses and Coverly Wapshot, into the estate of marriage. The central metaphor is erotic; for love, where the men are concerned, expresses the Wapshot spirit and nourishes the myth which they reenact. The connection between action and metaphor is tenuous, perhaps artificial: Cousin Honora is determined to will her fortune to the two boys only when they have fathered male heirs. Cousin Honora is one of the iron and eccentric women of the family. Born in Polynesia, she is raised by an uncle at St. Botolph who bequeathes to her his estate. A brief marriage to a Spaniard does not mollify her tough and virginal spirit. Back in St. Botolph, she rules the family with ruthless benevolence. She never opens her mail, nor does she pay fare on public buses, preferring to send the company a check at Christmas. She eats her cookies with ants on. Alone, she climbs to her seat in the baseball stadium, and sits there in the clear light of harmlessness, "the image of an old pilgrim walking by her lights all over the world as she was meant to do and who sees in her mind a noble and puissant nation, rising like a strong man after sleep."[16] She suffers Leander Wapshot, the father of Moses and Coverly, to live his fine, indolent, and erratic life on the farm she owns, or to steer the old *Topaze*, full of summer tourists, into the bay. But when Moses carries on an illicit affair with a girl stranded accidentally·on the Wapshot farm—Honora is caught in the bedroom closet while Moses and Rosalie make love on the bed—she cracks down on Leander, threatening to sell the boat and rent the house, thus forcing Leander to send Moses out into the world.

Moses goes out into the world, and Coverly—the pact between the two brothers is one of love—joins him, a runaway from home, on the train. The adventures that befall them are zany, improbable, poignant, and disconnected. Moses goes to

Washington, joins the Civil Service, is kicked out as a security risk when his affair with the wife of a local bandleader flares up in his face, stumbles into the good favors of a wealthy businessman who enrolls him in the Fiduciary Trust Company Bond School. Then he meets Melissa, a golden-skinned beauty who is the ward of the formidable Justine Wapshot Molesworth Scaddon, widow of the multimillionaire dime store "merchant," who owns the lugubrious castle at Clear Haven. Moses becomes engaged to Melissa, pays his courtship to her by crawling naked across the rooftops of Clear Haven to her room—Justine orders a servant to fire at him with a shot gun—and finally marries her. Later, of course, they have a son.

Coverly goes to New York, tries to join the carpet business of a rich relative, and is flunked out by a battery of psychologists and personnel managers—this is one of the most hilarious scenes of the book, and one of the most devastating fictional satires of mass society—as utterly unemployable. But the innocence of the Wapshots, a quality of wholesome self-reliance, a radical trust in life, cannot be violated by the modern techniques of quantitative measurements, which trust in norms of behavior because the realities of behavior have become indefinable. Coverly meets a pretty waitress, Betsey, lives with her, marries her. He joins a military school of rocket engineering, passes his exam, and is qualified as a Taper. He is sent to Island 93 in the Pacific, is reassigned to a rocket-launching base at Remsen Park. Betsey joins him, then leaves him. Coverly becomes embroiled with his homosexual superior. Temptation is resisted. Betsey returns to him. And, of course, they have a son.

Evidently, Fortune rather than Fate rules the Wapshot house, and Fortune, moreover, in her more antic disposition. This fact qualifies the values which the novel proffers—it does not negate them—and modifies our awareness of the characters as representatives of a plausible action. The values of courage and honor and clean living are upheld by the Wapshot women, particularly Honora, and Sarah, Leander's gentle and civic-minded wife, who turns his beloved *Topaze* into a floating gift shop. But there are also the values of Leander who wanted his sons to grasp that "the unobserved ceremoniousness of his life was a gesture or sacrament toward the excellence and continuousness of things."[17] Hence the pithy, childlike wisdom Leander passes on to his children: "Never make love with pants on. Beer on whisky, very risky. Whisky on beer, never fear. . . . Never sleep in moonlight. . . . Never hold cigar at right-angles to fingers. . . . Ecclesiastical dampness causes prematurely gray hair. . . . Courage tastes of blood. Stand up straight. Admire the world. Relish the love of a gentle woman. Trust in the Lord."[18] The values of the novel, we see, are the simple and essential values of life itself, and they come to focus in the pervasive metaphor of love. But unlike the original mysteries of Dionysus, which Coverly is made to experience in a burlesque tent, with sawdust on the floor, the sacraments of life are constantly rendered in whimsical terms by the novel, as if the Great God Pan, in our age, could masquerade only in the dress of Peter Pan. Similarly, the initiation of Moses and Coverly Wapshot into the estate of matrimony, and of fatherhood, makes of every ordeal a source of merriment, and of every setback a display of ingenuity or ingenuousness. The reality of pain is evaded by adopting the conventions of whimsey, and the sharp discriminations of New England manners dissolve into the haze of a legendary town where a bell from Antwerp tolls sweetly from the spires, and old four-posters creak to the rhythms of young lovers.

A single, and small, episode will serve as illustration of Cheever's method. Rosalie is taken to the Wapshot farm after an automobile accident from which she barely escapes alive. Her lover is killed. Rosalie is in bed recovering from the shock, and Sarah Wapshot has brought her some eggs for breakfast. Rosalie bursts out crying, tears rolling down her cheek:

"Oh, I'm sorry," Mrs. Wapshot said. "I'm very sorry. I suppose you were engaged to him. I suppose. . . ."

"It isn't that," the girl sobbed. "It's just about the eggs. I can't *bear* eggs. When I lived at home they made me eat eggs for breakfast and if I didn't eat my eggs for breakfast well then I had to eat them for dinner."[19]

Now there is nothing particularly false in this scene. It is entertaining enough. But the tragedy is deftly averted, dismissed, relegated to the background of humor in a single twist of dialogue. Likewise, the mythical touch, turned to whimsey, is employed to introduce a character for the first time. This is Betsey, Coverly's future wife: "All things of the sea belong to Venus; pearls and shells and alchemists' gold and kelp and the riggish smell of neap tides, the inshore water green, and purple further out and the joy of distances and the roar of falling masonry, all these are hers, but she doesn't come out of the sea for all of us. She came for Coverly through the swinging door of a sandwich shop in the Forties where he had gone to get something to eat after classes at the MacIlhenney Institute."[20] Similarly, Melissa, caught in a womanly reverie, is conceived by Moses to be "recollecting some distaff voyage over distaff waters to a walled island where they [women] were committed by the nature of their minds and their organs to some secret rites that would refresh their charming and creative stores of sadness."[21] And when the *Topaze* hits a rock and sinks, derelict and forsaken, the boat seems to Leander, "like those inextinguishable legends of underwater civilizations and buried gold, to pierce the darkest side of his mind with an image of man's inestimable loneliness."[22]

Cheever's style in *The Wapshot Chronicle* has wondrous powers of sensuous evocation and light-hearted mummery. It seeks to capture the reflections of eternity in the eyes of Harlequin. But the preceding examples show that, in this novel, myth tends to assume the guise of romance, and comedy borrows the spirit of fantasy. It is not unfair to say that

Cheever's affirmative statement is a whimsical statement. But does not whimsey imply an ironic stance, a denial of, or at least detachment from, the disagreeable aspects of reality in order to *create* a metaphor of the excellence and continuity of things? Irony, which stands behind whimsey, acknowledges what the latter is forced to exclude. If *The Wapshot Chronicle* is a testament of life, it is one that the style contrives. The most memorable incidents of the book have no direct bearing on its plot or structure; and even its characters, in their studied eccentricity, conform too readily to the vision, hearty and fleeting as laughter, which the author frankly imposes on them. Still, the novel permits the American hero to be confirmed, at long last, in his initiation, even though his confirmation may take place in a whimsical society. And there is always the coaxing, ironic smile of the author to temper our disbelief.

III

A New Yorker of Irish extraction, now living abroad, J. P. Donleavy has earned a measure of notoriety with his first novel, *The Ginger Man*, 1958. Comparisons have been shyly made between Donleavy, James Joyce, and Henry Miller, calling attention to the roguish Dublin setting of *The Ginger Man*, its experiments with the stream of consciousness, and its ribald, off-beat poetry. Like Samuel Beckett, however, Donleavy really belongs to a post-Joycean world. The particular quality of nihilism exhibited in his book refers us to the postwar, existential era. Traditional values are not in the process of dying; they have ceased entirely to operate, and their stark absence leaves men to shift for themselves as best they can. Donleavy, therefore, cannot be placed in the camp of the Angry Young Men of England, whose rebellion is ultimately a social gesture; nor can he be assimilated to the Beat writers of America, whose search, at bottom, is a religious quest. Donleavy is perhaps the new expatriate American, exploring the fictional resources of a scruffy and criminal life, but finding both sides of the Atlantic equally desolate, hence uproarious. The revulsions of the expatriate in our time take the form of a metaphysical, or at least international, leer.

The world of *The Ginger Man* confirms the ancient bond between cruelty and humor. It is full of gusto, seething with life, but its energy may be the energy of negation, and its vitality has a nasty edge. The adjectives applied most often to it are "riotous" and "wild." But do not the same adjectives apply to chaos itself? Even the exuberance which attends the old ceremonies of food, drink, and sex appears touched by morbid desperation; even a prank may become a criminal act. In *The Ginger Man*, the catharsis of comedy depends on a recognition of human absurdity, the futility of all social endeavors. The primary value which the novel asserts is the value of courage, the ability to stare into the void.

The novel depicts the adventures of one Sebastian Dangerfield—known as Danger to the small, rowdy clique of initiates into nothingness—an ex-G.I. living in Dublin and waiting, quite frankly, for his father to die so that he may inherit his fortune. Dangerfield is married to a genteel English girl, Marion, and has a baby daughter. His favorite game is to bait Marion, smear her pieties with sadistic relish—Osborne's Jimmy Porter comes to mind—and steal the milk money for his daughter— she develops a severe case of rickets—to carouse with his friends. He beats up his wife, tries to smother the child when she screams, cheats the butcher and the landlord, drives nails into the plumbing till the ceiling is drenched with excrement, and hacks a blanket to make "Trinity rowing pinks." Presumably, he is studying law at Trinity. In reality, however, he leads the life of a rogue on the loose, brawling in saloons, conning creditors, and seducing working girls in the four corners of Dublin. And his friends do likewise: Malarkey who barricades himself in his bare rooms, sleeping in an ingenious hammock, to escape creditors; O'Keefe, the expatriate American, Harvard-bred, who wanders all over Europe, trying desperately to end his virginity; Percy Clocklan, reputed to have committed suicide, but turning up from nowhere with a Rolls Royce; and red-bearded MacDoon, a shadowy Leprechaun of the London underworld, to whose house we are admitted by pulling on the tongue of a lion statue. All are quite zany and bizarre. All are denizens of what Dangerfield calls the Catacombs, where cats and honest men hide, the secret underground of the twentieth century, pitch-dark save for a few pinpoints of light given by sensual stirrings or Celtic horseplay.

The mood of the novel alternates between the mood of a "day on which all things are born, like uncovered stars," and that of the song:

> In this sad room
> In this dark gloom
> We live like beasts[23]

Ruthless honesty, carried to the point where the joy and negation of being meet, shows a twisted, clownish face. Life "starts and ends in antiseptic smell," but it also offers "good things and pints of the best and pineapples too and fields and guts and lust, soil and bull."[24] There is no final purpose to things, no social aim worth the effort. "Get on where? Where to?" Sebastian asks his wife when she urges him to make something of himself.[25] Religion is spoofed—there is as much blasphemy as there is obscenity in the book—and God, of course, is nowhere to be seen, though he may still be loved, despite all his faults, as Dangerfield caustically remarks. (The seduction of a devout Catholic girl, like Miss Frost, seems to him both "safe and sad" because "I guess I pull her into my own pit.")[26] In the end, the perfect union of sheer joy and radical denial, the crackling laughter of nihilism, is achieved in a gratuitous act or absurd gag: Dangerfield poisoning a potted plant with an eye dropper or masquerading in the streets of

London in a kangaroo's skin, Dangerfield reflecting how French letters floating out to sea on the Thames may be salvaged and sold in Dublin as waterproof socks to be hung on a line.

Indeed, the plot of the novel amounts to nothing more than a series of such gratuitous moments. The reader, following the bare thread of the action, witnesses the separation of Sebastian and Marion, the various shenanigans, including three affairs, of Dangerfield in Dublin, and his final departure to London where he lives in style with a buxom, green-eyed Irish maid called Mary. His father, at long last, expires, leaving his fortune as a trust fund which Dangerfield cannot spend before twenty years have fully elapsed. The penury of Sebastian, however, is suddenly ended by the resurrection of Percy Clocklan from the dead, and his arrival on the scene with more money than all the Catacomb dwellers could waste. Obviously, the plot itself, in good picaresque fashion, is a gag, and the attainment of wealth is an absurd accident because money itself, in a world without social or even moral goals, is the ultimate absurdity.

What kind of hero, then, is Sebastian Dangerfield? He is, of course, the *alazon*, the impostor, the scoundrel, cheat, and perfect cad. Playful and exuberant, he is also devoid of any scruples and capable of frightening brutalities. Violence lurks close beneath the surface of his skullduggery. Mockery and self-mockery inform all his speeches, and the zest with which he sometimes humiliates himself betrays the ferocity of his vision. The vision can be full of poetry and hope. Dangerfield, in a certain sense, can never hold enough of life; the sun—a recurrent symbol for him—will always rise again. Like Joyce's Bloom, he feeds on kidneys and brains, and the sight of a pretty ankle sends the blood trilling in his veins. But Dangerfield is no Rabelaisian sensualist. He is essentially an outsider, "a straight dark figure and stranger" whose final vision is of wild horses "running out to death which is with some soul and their eyes are mad and teeth out."[27] His grip on life, as he says, is cloacal; the sense of the abyss—sinking is one of his favorite metaphors—is always with him. In his moments of desperation, he crumples up, as he does on Miss Frost's bed: "Dreaming out this sunset. Tacked up on a cross and looking down. A cradle of passive, mystifying sorrow. Flooded in tears. Never be too wise to cry. Or not take these things. Take them. Keep them safely. Out of them comes love."[28] Dangerfield, we see, is a sufferer too, a victim no less than a rebel, a man condemned to live as if there is no reality behind illusions, and hence to live his illusions with an absurd flourish. The Gingerbread Man, we remember from our nursery days, is the roguish figure who escapes all his pursuers—only to be swallowed up, in the end, by the fox. The Gingerbread Man is the new American, not James's Newman confronting decadent Europe with his frontier innocence, or perhaps ignorance, but Sebastian Dangerfield, living by his wits in the underground of Dublin and London, a charming and thorough knave whose innocence is a kind of radical intransigence, the determination to be himself though the old fox, absurd death, will munch his bones at last.

The vision of absurdity is incorporated into the form of the novel. Its happy ending, as we have seen, is adventitious, a product of pure chance. The plot denies purpose, and denies any real connections between desert and reward. The action of time seems a mockery of order in human lives. When Dangerfield suddenly finds himself rich, he says to MacDoon, "And I've something to tell you in strict confidence so spread it everywhere. I know that my redeemer liveth."[29] Redemption, we see, is entirely a matter of irony.

More striking than the plot is the use of point of view in the novel. Much of the book is written in the stream of consciousness method, abrupt transitions from past memories to current scenes, disconnected or fragmentary sentences and dangling present participles intended to convey with some immediacy the states of Dangerfield's mind, his acute isolation. The point of view shifts, within the same paragraph, from the first to the third person, as if Dangerfield could find no way to acknowledge the objective existence of other human beings, as if reality were entirely subjective, to be rendered only in elliptic reflections or fleeting sensations, and all action were illusory, to be rendered in perfunctory fashion by a third person. The following passage will serve as well as another for illustration:

"Mary, I may not be black but I'm not bad."
Under the train trestle went the horse cab. Past the monument makers. And a shop where I used to keep my rations. A milky, cold smell. I often bought two eggs and one slice of bacon. From a bowl-breasted girl. She eyed me. And once I bought oatmeal and went out and got dreadfully drunk across the street. Invited the pensioners in for a pint. They all told me stories. About men and their daughters. I heard them before but once is never enough—got to have them again. Later I spilled my bag of oatmeal all over.
Sebastian kissed Mary. She put her elbow over her breasts. But she's opening her mouth. And she's got a hard, little back and thick thighs but I can't get my hand to her bosom.[30]

The impression of disorder is further emphasized by the grotesque poetry of the style, its harsh mixture of elation and disgust: "Dublin looming a Swiss Cheese of streets and running through them screaming in tears. Children shrinking in the doorways. Gutters running pig's blood. Cold and winter."[31] And to round off each chapter in the appropriate manner, Donleavy allows his hero to sing a nasty or twaddling little song, usually a sardonic commentary on the futility of whatever action may have preceded it:

> *There was a man*
> *Who made a boat*
> *To sail away*
> *And it sank.*[32]

The Ginger Man is neither a profound nor a happy work. The insights of its hero are elusive; his self-awareness is so entirely ironic that it permits no explicit statement of values on his part. In fact, one is never quite sure whether Dangerfield is a supreme humbug—so expert he is in mimicry—or a bitter, questing soul. The episodic structure of the novel, its style, rich and spontaneous but also chaotic and contrived, imply no ideas of order, only the acrid sense of life. It is as if the very spirit of comedy could only find its affirmation in a mad, nugatory snarl.

IV

The three novels discussed in this chapter deal with the art of human possibility. They are, as it were, the equivalents of comedy in an age of anxiety. Their primary commitment is to an ironic view of life.

The hero of Gold is full of illusions; the hero of Donleavy has none. Both are impostors of some kind. The first, a manipulator of dreams and men, is an insider who discovers that worldly success is not quite enough. The latter, a roguish nihilist, is an outsider who finds that a man cannot really escape pain by going underground. The future of both men seems open to the possibilities of change; but the change, as we come to realize, is merely external. Fortune intervenes on behalf of the hero, though his character remains, quite ironically, the same. The aching consciousness of being is the one constant in their lives. Thus the romantic entrepreneur, Burr Fuller, and the nihilist sensualist, Sebastian Dangerfield, share a denial of complex social realities in favor of the realities of the self. Cheever's heroes remain somewhere in between. The Wapshots are not so much impostors as quixotic scamps. They are finally confirmed into their special world. But for them confirmation is possible precisely because their world is so eccentric. St. Botolph, we saw, stands as a whimsical anachronism in the midst of twentieth-century America. It is Prospero's island tinged in a fading Yankee light. The heroes of all these "comic" novels fail to reconcile themselves to the realities which, for better or worse, we come to accept. This is the source of their appeal, and also of their radical innocence. Burr strains to attain a guarded victory over himself; the Wapshots enact a dreamlike fable; and Sebastian Dangerfield grubs in the depths to sustain the semblance of human life. Obviously, in their case the art of possibility is a troubled art.

Comedy, therefore, is not the true form of their existence. In comedy, as Frye has noted, there is a social judgment *against* the absurd.[33] The novels we have witnessed, however, either judge by implication *for* the absurd or else suspend their judgment in irony. In comedy, a new order of society crystallizes around the hero. The hero, in the novels under consideration, neither creates nor accepts society. Comedy predicts the ritual expulsion of death and disorder; the *alazon*, the interloper, is confuted and repulsed. But the presence of death is as strongly felt in these novels as is the presence of disorder, and the traditional comic redemption of society is markedly absent. Where fantasy does not openly reign, vestiges of the demonic world, of conflict and pain, intrude upon our attention. The area which the three novels engage is obviously the area where the mythos of vernal comedy dissolves into that of frosty irony.

This is perhaps why the voice of affirmation finds itself in such grave difficulties in our time. The glibness of Gold, the coyness of Cheever, and the jaunty malevolence of Donleavy are symptomatic. Our joys are caged, our hopes marginal. We look out on life between prison bars. How then can the imagination free laughter from our throats in forms that we can value and recognize? Regeneration in a real world is not, after all, an act of will; nor is it a fiat of the fictional imagination. It is an experience quite foreign, it seems, to most sensitive men of the age. The novelist's problem is still to express the exuberance of life in comic forms which do not lend themselves to shrill optimism or unwarranted affirmation, do not lend themselves to unreality. The "solutions" of the problem in the three works we have observed must be judged as partial. It is perhaps Saul Bellow who came closest to writing a genuinely comic novel in *The Adventures of Augie March*. Other versions of the human encounter with possibility may be found in Bellow's *Henderson the Rain King*, Capote's *Breakfast at Tiffany's*, Roth's *Goodbye, Columbus*. These books echo our hollow or wistful laughter.

PART III

THE INDIVIDUAL TALENT

A writer's work does not take its being from critical generalities. Its life, if it has any at all, is its own. The schemes we have entertained of the hero, the designs we have observed in the novel, find their justification in the serious efforts of contemporary novelists. But they also find there a kind of refutation. In the four writers to follow—McCullers, Capote, Salinger, and Bellow—manifestations of the ironic pattern and the self in recoil are evident. But progressively evident too, as we move from McCullers to Bellow, is the need to overcome the condition of recoil and seek a reconciliation between self and world. This is the kind of affirmation which makes denial a human possibility.

The four writers chosen in this section are not presented as the final vindication of the fictional imagination in our time. Their collective work, nevertheless, defines a certain character of achievement which typifies the age. The backgrounds of the rural South and the industrial city, the recollections of an American past and intimations of its future, the motives of radical assent and radical denial, the techniques of realism and surrealism, are present on the unique terms each individual talent prescribes for himself. And they are present on a high level of artistic performance.

CHAPTER 8

CARSON McCULLERS:

THE AESTHETICS OF LOVE AND PAIN

Un Ange, imprudent voyageur
Qu'a tenté l'amour du difforme,
Au fond d'un cauchemar énorme
Se débattant comme un nageur.

BAUDELAIRE

I

IT is no longer in doubt that Southern literature has under-
gone a brilliant renascence in the first part of our century.
Nor has the renascence run itself out. It is only the critics,
both Rebel and Yankee, who have run themselves dry trying
to account for the movement and explain its power. Their
speculations usually come to rest in the notion that the South
possesses a culture and a distinct tradition congenial to the
production of literature. This is true. But it would also be true
to say that part of the vitality of Southern fiction derives its
energy from the energy of opposition, which is but another way
of saying that the Southern novel, insofar as it has a regional
identity, is more openly hostile to those popular assumptions
the country entertains at large. This is most evident in the
novels of Carson McCullers where opposition informs the
eccentric design of her form.

Since the publication of *The Heart Is a Lonely Hunter* in
1940, when its author was only twenty-three years old, Carson
McCullers has been recognized as one of the most likely talents
in the South, one who brought strange and artful gifts of
sensibility to the contemporary novel. The strangeness, however, reminded some readers of Poe's artifices, and it persuaded

them to discredit her fiction as simply gothic. The judgment is aberrant and at best specious. It is true that Mrs. McCullers lacks the scope, strength, and fury of Faulkner, lacks his dark apprehension of the Southern past and his profound insight into the American wilderness, symbols both of our guilt and innocence. And it is also true that Mrs. McCullers, hypnotized as she seems to be by the burning point where love and pain secretly meet, foregoes a certain richness of surface which, let us say, Eudora Welty seldom foregoes. Still, the gothic element, the personal principle in Mrs. McCullers' work, excludes none of the larger aspects of the Southern tradition to which it belongs. In his recent introduction to *Great Tales of the Deep South*, Malcolm Cowley has summarized well these aspects of the Southern literary mind: a mind preeminently aware of custom and ceremony yet deeply responsive to the elemental nature of existence, a mind anxious to preserve the sense of place and time, of family and community, of folk life and, above all, of oral discourse. Its basic assumption seems to be, as Robert B. Heilman has noted, that "the concrete evidence of the human being is that he does not change much, that he may actually be harmed by the material phenomena usually implied by *progress*, and that in any case his liability to moral difficulty remains constant.[1] Formal and conservative, oriented at once toward the personal and the mythic, therefore symbolic, the Southern imagination seems determined to capture man in his very essence. Hence its marked anti-pragmatic bias: "In the *ethos* of Jefferson and Yoknapatawpha, the essence of man lies in being, not in having or doing," John Maclachlan has remarked of Faulkner's country.[2] It is precisely the being of man that modern civilization has put on trial, and the Southern novel has sought the means, wayward sometimes and excessive, to redefine.

Within the framework of these general assumptions the

gothic imagination of Carson McCullers is put to play. Yet being gothic, which is to say Protestant—for the gothic may be conceived as a latent reaction to the Catholic hierarchy under God—being both Protestant and gothic, her imagination derives its peculiar force from a transcendental idea of spiritual loneliness. Our business will be to consider the spectacle of love and pain which constitutes her fiction, and in which the idea of spiritual isolation comes repeatedly to focus. For so broad a view, some provisional clarification of terms is necessary.

To say that Mrs. McCullers has a gothic penchant is but to note, and note superficially, her interest in the grotesque, the freakish, and the incongruous. Such qualities, to be sure, exert a large influence on the contemporary imagination; and they stand in a necessary and paradoxical relation to the facts of Southern life which emphasize the power of tradition and pull of community. For alienation, like monstrousness, can become a dramatic condition only when viewed against those special norms—however vestigial—which make divergences from them meaningful. There is another sense, however, in which the gothic element may be defined more pertinently. The gothic insists on *spiritualization*, the spiritualization of matter itself, and it insists on *subjectivism*. We have it from Erwin Panofsky that "late Gothic art broke up into a variety of styles" reflecting the ideological developments of the Middle Ages; these developments were "unified by a subjectivism" which extended from the visual arts to the political sphere.[3] The gothic impulse is also transcendental: it reaches out in a piercing line to the sky. The distinction Allen Tate has made, in *The Forlorn Demon*, between the symbolic and the angelic imagination is apposite. The first, like Dante's, is Catholic: "It never begins at the top; it carries the bottom along with it, however high it may climb." The second, like Poe's, is both gothic and Protestant: in a transcendental effort of the will, "It declares itself independent of the human situation in the quest of essential knowledge."[4] It should not be difficult to see how the mysticism of Suso and Eckhart, the idea of prayer in Luther, the experience of spiritual horror without sensible correlative in Poe, and the gothic nightmare of alienation in the fiction of Carson McCullers fall into a somber sequence. But Protestant as the fundamentalist tradition of the South may be, and gothic as its experience of guilt and tragedy is likely to appear, it is the peculiar stamp of subjectivism, wistful and bizarre, that emerges like a watermark on every page Mrs. McCullers has written. Such introversion, we know, is a result of the disjunction between self and world which contemporary life has magnified. The disjunction is formalized into a cross to which the characters of Carson McCullers are bound, and often bound without hope of remission.

Yet it is only fair to add that her attitude is more complex than we imply. There is, of course, one sense in which Mrs. McCullers can be said to celebrate the lonely and the outcast, the frail children of the earth, those, like Singer in her first novel, who have in their face "something gentle and Jewish, the knowledge of one who belongs to a race that is oppressed."[5] Adolescents and freaks are her rueful heroes because the first are as yet uninitiated and the latter are forever unacceptable; both do not belong, and in both physical incompleteness is the source of a qualitative, a spiritual difference. And lonely as her characters are, encased as they are in their dreams, most private of human expressions, their actions usually serve only to intensify their solitude. Their situation is, as Oliver Evans has noted, "not so much a comment on the futility of communication as it is on the undesirability of it."[6] But there is still another sense, deeper and more significant, in which Carson McCullers can be said to underscore the inadequacy of subjectivism, of silence. Indeed, the integrity of her vision depends on her guiding insight into the tensions of our situation, caught as we are between immersion of the self in a mass society and

dissipation of the world leading to madness, crime, or hermeti-
cism.

The challenge of form is the measure of insight; the formal
tension between the self and the world in the novel corresponds
to the thematic juxtaposition of the power of love and the
presence of pain in the vision of Carson McCullers. It is in
The Ballad of the Sad Café that the doctrine of love, implicit
in all her fiction, is most clearly enunciated. The passage deserves extensive quotation:

First of all, love is a joint experience between two persons—but
the fact that it is a joint experience does not mean that it is a
similar experience to the two people involved. There are the lover
and the beloved, but these two come from different countries. Often
the beloved is only a stimulus for all the stored up love which has
lain quiet within the lover for a long time hitherto. And somehow
every lover knows this. He feels in his soul that his love is a solitary
thing. He comes to know a new strange loneliness and it is this
knowledge that makes him suffer. . . . Let it be added that this
lover . . . can be man, woman, child, or indeed any human creature
on this earth.

Now, the beloved can also be of any description. The most outlandish people can be the stimulus of love. . . . Therefore, the value
and quality of any love is determined solely by the lover himself.

It is for this reason that most of us would rather love than be
loved. . . . And the curt truth is that, in a deep secret way, the
state of being beloved is intolerable to many. The beloved fears and
hates the lover. . . .[7]

Here are some consequences of this remarkable statement:
to love is to suffer, to intensify one's loneliness. Love needs no
reciprocation; its quality is determined solely by the lover; and
its object can be as "outlandish" as the world may offer. Hence
the grotesque nature of the objects of love in Carson McCullers'
fiction: hunchbacks, deaf mutes, weddings, clouds. Hence also
the desexualization of love since the love relation, often incongruous, does not admit of sexual communion. "By nature
all people are both sexes," Mrs. McCullers says. "So that

marriage and the bed is not all by any means."[8] Singer, Brannon, Penderton, Amelia, and the men-women freaks who appear in her fiction are all bisexual, which is to say asexual. Then, too, without reciprocity, love becomes a crazy whirligig, the object of one love becoming the subject of another—witness Macy, Amelia, Lymon, in *The Ballad of the Sad Café*. Finally, love as a pure attitude of the lover toward *any* object seems to arrogate to itself the powers of God. As Tate put it with regard to Poe, man as "angelic delegate of God" is empowered to perform His functions: "Not only is every man his own God, every man *is* God."[9]

As a strategy of the deeper self, love is often expected both to protect man against his own inadequacies and redeem the inescapable fact of pain in the world. But the idea of love Mrs. McCullers proposes is not so palliative. By far the most startling consequence of her notion is love's avowal of pain, of *death* itself. Love, in intensifying the lover's pain, in precluding communion, and in electing outlandish recipients, seeks its own impediments. A revealing parallel is suggested by Denis de Rougemont in his book, *Love in the Western World*. De Rougemont argues that certain types of love which seek continually to defeat their end mask the fearful powers of the death wish. Boundless Eros, or transcendental Love, "despises Venus even when in the throes of sensuality," and whether it manifests itself in Courtly Love or Manichaean mysticism, it "intensifies our desires only to offer them up in sacrifice."[10] Its real end is death. The omnipresence of pain in the work of Carson McCullers, the spectacle of a love forever seeking its own denial, leads us to a similar conclusion. Love, to be sure, redeems, but only provisionally. The critical limit imposed on the privacy of love—death, sacrifice, withdrawal—is exceeded again in the greater privacy of pain. The failure of communion ends in individual immolation, but the presence of pain makes of all men martyrs. Pain, we see, binds men in a universal brotherhood—like a chain gang—even more than love can.

No longer an external threat to the self, pain, as psychoanalysts say, becomes introjected: it acts internally in the higher interests of the self. Thus the single affirmative note in Mrs. McCullers' work, sounded almost accidentally, is sounded by those who simply suffer and endure: by Portia and Brannon in her first novel, by members of the chain gang in her last story. "Radiance" and "darkness," "ecstasy" and "fright"—these are the words with which the two works end, words that predict no resolution to the human condition. They are interchangeable!

II

The Heart Is a Lonely Hunter, 1940, the first of Mrs. McCullers' books and the longest, anticipates in many ways the power and ambiguities of her achievement. Despite its disconsolate title, the novel finds a way of acknowledging the social realities of its time. Its events hark back to the economic distress of the Thirties and reverberate with the distant echoes of Nazi tyranny, and its spirit shudders with the "strangled South." But it is from the singular relation of the characters to one another that the book takes its shape. What makes the relations singular, literally, is that they are all centripetal: all the characters are singly drawn toward one man, the deaf-mute Singer, who stands bewilderedly at the center. The novel's structure is broken up to convey the sense of "mutual isolation"; each person remains in a padded cubicle, victimized by the very dreams which nourish his dignity.

There is Biff Brannon, quietly observing the scene from behind his restaurant counter, a lonely man capable of strange, ambivalent feelings of tenderness—toward his dead wife, Alice, toward the adolescent girl, Mick Kelly, toward the revolutionary, Jake Blount. Brannon, forever waiting, forever asking the impossible question: Why? There is Jake Blount, the uncouth Marxist, violent and rootless, forever crying out "you dumb bastards" to all the world, forever dreaming of himself as a wanderer among crowds, carrying on his shoulders a great burden which he can never put down. There is Benedict Copeland, the Negro doctor, forever smoldering with the fire of the oppressed, and bound by a harsh concept of dignity to a life of labor. He is proud, like Faulkner's Lucas Beauchamp and as intransigent, but less wise in his attachment to an abstract idea of justice. Alienated even from his family, he can assent to but never allow himself to understand his daughter, Portia, when she says: "Us talk like our own Mama and her peoples and their peoples before them. You think out everything in your brain. While us rather talk from something in our hearts that has been there for a long time."[11] Through Copeland and Blount, the novel gains its force of social reference; the idea of fascism abroad is constantly played off against that of racism at home. Yet it is only fair to add that neither Copeland nor Blount is permitted to present his simplistic view of social evil unqualified—in their rare meetings, reformers both, they can only testify to their discord. But it is probably Mick's story of negative initiation to the world that imparts to the book its ironic pathos. Searching at once for privacy and recognition, she moves outward from a musical core in the "quiet, secret night" of her being. We see her revert momentarily to childhood in a decorously adolescent party; grope toward an adult understanding of her broken father; suddenly confront the experience of sexual knowledge; and finally, assuming too early a financial duty incommensurate with her dream of fulfillment, we see her settle down to a life of drudgery in a Woolworth store. Her "initiation," which leads to a dead end, is complete, and it is attended by the bitter feeling that she has been somehow cheated. "Only nobody had cheated her. So there was nobody to take it out on."[12]

Singer, of course, appears as the focus of repose in a circle of sad, tormented, and lonely people. He becomes the town legend, its hero, confessor, and enigma. "Each man described the mute as he wished him to be."[13] He asks nothing, listens endlessly to what he cannot hear. To him flock all who would unburden themselves: their desperation requires no fuller response than a mute can offer, and their Protestant confessions need only a deaf confessor. He is sought, as Brannon puts it, "Because in some men it is in them to give up everything personal at some time, before it ferments and poisons—throw it to some human being or some idea. They have to. In some men it is in them—The text is 'All men seek for Thee.' "[14] At times he appears to take upon himself the mystery of things, playing the role of an unwilling Christ for men whom, in the end, he is powerless to redeem. In the spiritual hierarchy of the novel, Singer's position is clearly defined in his own dream:

> Out of the blackness of sleep a dream formed. There were dull yellow lanterns lighting up a dark flight of stone steps. Antonapoulos knelt at the top of these steps. He was naked and he fumbled with something that he held above his head and gazed at it as though in prayer. He himself knelt halfway down the steps. He was naked and cold and he could not take his eyes from Antonapoulos and the thing he held above him. Behind him on the ground he felt the one with the moustache [Blount] and the girl [Mick] and the black man [Copeland] and the last one [Brannon]. They knelt naked and he felt their eyes on him. And behind them there were the uncounted crowds of kneeling people in the darkness. His own hands were huge windmills and he stared fascinated at the unknown thing that Antonapoulos held.[15]

What the novel makes abundantly clear is that the charisma of Singer does not derive simply from his receptivity to the sorrows of others, nor from his own affliction and forbearance, but mainly from the fact that he alone in the novel is a *lover*, he alone loves. The object of his love is a cretin, a deaf-mute, Antonapoulos, who appears in the preceding passage sanctified, and who elsewhere appears sitting motionless in his bright, rich garments like some wise king from a legend, but who is in the end simply Man, the Unlovable Creature, redeemable only by an impossible Lover.

The meeting of the various characters in Singer's room, late in the novel, is a focal point in its development. Hitherto, each character had been impelled to seek the mute by a sense of his own desperation; when they all meet together at last, their jarring interests—each is ridden by a master passion, a sort of modernized "Humor"—their spite and suspicion, fling them further apart. Together at last, they represent a society, not of communion, but of collective isolation. The ironic void, of love as of authority, at the center of the novel is made evident when Singer, after the death of his Greek friend, commits suicide, precipitating a debacle in the lives which surround him. (Only in this sense can the novel be seen as "an ironic parable of fascism," a phrase which seems to have encrusted itself like a barnacle on all the standard reference works on contemporary novelists.)

It is at this point that our attention is drawn back to Biff Brannon, with whom the novel opens and also closes. In Brannon we are asked to behold an image of clumsy endurance, a will for right action which no excess of hate or suffering or disenchantment can wholly suspend. And we recognize that his final vision, though its promise falls short of redemption, is somehow more central than Singer's and more viable:

> For in a swift radiance of illumination he saw a glimpse of human struggle and of valor. Of the endless fluid passage of humanity through endless time. And of those who—one word—love. His soul expanded. But for a moment only. For in him he felt a warning, a shaft of terror. Between the two worlds he was suspended . . . he was suspended between radiance and darkness. Between bitter irony and faith. Sharply he turned away.[16]

The action, which extends from the winter of one year to the summer of the next, is adroitly punctuated by events that give a sense both of finality and progression to the novel. The wretched meeting of the protagonists in Singer's room is one such event, and the suicide of the mute is another. Thus the first part of the book, ending with Singer's sudden departure to visit Antonapoulos in the asylum, establishes the false dependency of the different characters upon him, and the second part, of which the meeting is a climax and the suicide is a terminal point, explores the consequences of this dependency. The final section covers but a single day, August 21, 1939. It is an epilogue of defeat. The center, as Yeats would say, can no longer hold and things fall apart in four distinct scenes, Morning, Afternoon, Evening, and Night, focused respectively on Copeland, Blount, Mick Kelly, and Biff Brannon. But no Second Coming is foreseen in the novel, nor do the characters hope to resolve their predicament by resorting, like the characters of Capote, Salinger, or Bellow, to fantasy, ironic disaffiliation, or vitality born of knowledge.

The presence of pain, the failure of initiation, the betrayal of love, and the horror of solitude—these somehow define the confrontation with reality which Mrs. McCullers chooses for her characters. But the tragic confrontation, in this novel much more than in the later works, retains a certain ambiguity, a kind of elusiveness, which the form is incapable of bringing to account. *The Heart Is a Lonely Hunter* is addressed to some wide social and religious issues, and it is at the same time deeply concerned with the secret issues of the soul—symbols of the latter are the inner music of Mick, the shy hands of Singer (reminiscent of the hands of Anderson's Wing Biddlebaum), the lips of Blount, etc. Yet the nexus between the soft private thing and the world of pogroms and economic exploitation is never firmly established, just as the nexus between Singer's love for the Greek and the Christian idea of redemption is never made convincing. The metaphor of the freak as sacrificial hero cannot hold the novel together, and neither can the style, which vacillates between a perception of things as they are and a feeling of things as they are hoped to be. It is as if the theme of gothic isolation really demanded something less novel-like than this, the most novelistic of Mrs. McCullers' works, could afford.

215

III

Reflections in a Golden Eye, 1941, is a starker tale. It shares
with Mrs. McCullers' best work, *The Ballad of the Sad Café*,
the atmosphere of primitive terror, "that Sense of The Awful
which is the desperate black root of nearly all significant modern
art, from the *Guernica* of Picasso to the cartoons of Charles
Addams," as Tennessee Williams, who ought to know, has put
it in his Introduction to the book.[17] It also shares with the
Ballad the laconic form of a fable, just as her earlier novel
shares with *The Member of the Wedding* a certain density of
social specification and an underlying mood of ineffable sadness.
The novelette renders a world of stealthy, chaotic feelings in a
lapidary style, poetic through the precision of its implications;
the grotesque aberrations of the characters involved are reflected
in a cold and steady mirror of which the disquieting symbol
is a peacock's eye. "A peacock of ghastly green. With one immense golden eye. And in it these reflections of something
tiny and . . . grotesque"—in these words, Anacleto, the Filipino
servant, playfully describes a sinister vision to his ailing mistress.[18] But the Golden Eye only reflects; it does not see. The
various personages move toward an inexorable fate, which is
itself a product of their instinctual necessities, in a manner
reminiscent of Paul Bowles's somnambulist creations.

The novelette is set in a Southern army camp. The action,
which contrasts in its growing violence with the monotony of
the camp, covers little more than a month. In the austere
words of the author, the participants are two officers, a soldier,
two women, a Filipino, and a horse. A savage, improbable
relation soon develops between Private Ellgee Williams and
Captain Weldon Penderton, and in developing it energizes
the whole story. Williams is a silent twenty-year-old animal
who remains to the end an enigma. His sudden actions—
whether he buys a cow, declares his faith in the Lord, kills a
man, enlists in the army, rides a horse naked in the sun, or

216

steals in every night to watch the Captain's voluptuous wife, Leonora, sleep in her bed, unconscious of his feral presence— all remain equally unaccountable in logical, moral, and, perhaps even dramatic terms. But the motives of Williams' antagonist take on a more subtle color. Captain Penderton—who, incidentally, wears a truss, and is at once a savant and a kleptomaniac—shows a penchant for becoming enamored of his wife's lovers; and he is also both a coward and a masochist. The polarity of the two men is obvious. It is further magnified, or rather distorted, by a network of unstable relations. Leonora, sensual and obtuse, takes Major Morris Langdon for her lover, a bluff, thoughtless man whom the Captain greatly admires— till Williams comes on the scene. The Major's wife, Alison, is a suffering, neurotic woman. Ever since the death of her malformed baby—it *would* be malformed!—she can attach herself to no one except the festive Anacleto, an Ariel to Williams' Caliban, who shares with his mistress a world of tender fantasies. And in the middle stands the brilliant, powerful horse of Leonora, Firebird.

The horse may stand as an embodiment of instincts and the military camp as an image of social regimentation. Between the two, men must somehow mediate. This is the predicament on which Captain Penderton reflects: "You mean . . . that any fulfillment obtained at the expense of normalcy is wrong, and should not be allowed to bring happiness. In short, it is better, because it is morally honorable, for the square peg to keep scraping about the round hole rather than to discover and use the unorthodox square that would fit it?"[19] The unorthodox square! This is one way of mediation. But Mrs. McCullers implies that there is another, the way of love, of *relation*. In the book all relations fail: the relation of man to man and man to woman, of man to environment and woman to child. All communication is blocked, vitiated, or restricted to the inarticulate moment which witnesses Private Williams riding a horse naked in the sun or watching Leonora sleep in a dark room. Love, dispensing with its object, reaches the dead end of protestant isolation.

Technically, of course, the book has more firmness than its predecessor. The style can light on a fraction of huge time, while the mind is both shocked and sensitized beyond speech. The skillful structure makes good use of flashbacks, developing the action without halts, and maintaining a certain overlapping in the narrative—hints dropped and picked up again—so that suspense and revelation keep in step. And Mrs. McCullers finds the right if lurid gesture for each character—the Captain abandoning himself voluptuously to a mad ride on Firebird, Alison cutting off her nipples with garden shears, etc. Yet the novel remains somehow inert, brutish. In the peacock's golden eye, the dreadful existence of each person remains unintelligible. As the novel shifts its focus from one character to another—it is a portrait gallery—no "lucid consciousness" emerges to interpret or qualify the whole. Only Alison, who has the gift of partial insight, can do so, though she is herself blind to what touches her most closely. And the violent denouement of the novella, which neither she nor Anacleto is present to interpret, confirms our prevailing sense of barrenness. Yet it is not the presence of underlying dreadfulness to which one objects; it is rather the absence of life. A comparison with D. H. Lawrence's "St. Mawr" and "The Prussian Officer," or even Faulkner's *Sanctuary*, makes it clear that Carson McCullers is no Primitivist. She can recognize the forms which primitive impulses take, but she cannot, on the one hand, render the sense of joy and defiance that the best Primitivists irradiate, nor, on the other, qualify passion by the moral intelligence. Her novelette, haunted by the need to suffer, lacks the energy that redeems suffering, and lacks also the kind of commitment which makes suffering meaningful. It is, that is to say, arrested on the level of incongruousness its title proclaims. But the absurdity it reflects goes far to show how much our desires outstrip the particular reality of our day—and how much we pay.

IV

In *The Member of the Wedding*, 1946, Carson McCullers exhibits the kind of formal unity which her first novel lacks. There is also a smarting sense of life in the work, a profound sense of change, and a quality of intense groping which the behavior of the central characters seeks continually to incarnate. The story is primarily that of Frankie Addams, a motherless, twelve-year-old girl engaged in a romance with the world. The agonies of growth, the search for identity, the paradoxical desire to escape, to experience, to belong, suddenly converge on Frankie on the occasion of her brother's wedding which becomes the intolerable symbol of all her longings and the focus of her perverse misunderstanding of the adult world.

Like Mick Kelly, Frankie is first of all animated by the desire to escape: escape boredom, escape her adolescent self, escape the South itself. Her life, like the dream she relates to a fortune teller, is a door slowly opening on nowhere. "You going, but you don't know where. That don't make no sense to me," Berenice, the Negro cook, expostulates.[20] Yet Frankie dimly knows what she is escaping *from*. It is partly the familiar scene of lazy buzzards, rotten gray shacks, and lonesome cotton fields she watches on her bitter return from the wedding. (Snow throughout the story acquires the romantic reference of the Far Away—and it may be of interest to note here that Mrs. McCullers has confessed she never saw snow until she came to New York at the age of seventeen.) It is also the accident of her identity that Berenice recognizes as inescapable: "We all of us somehow caught," Berenice says. "We born this way or that way and don't know why. But we caught anyway. . . . And maybe we wants to widen and bust free. But no matter what we do we still caught." And when John Henry, Frankie's six-year-old cousin, asks in his child's voice, "Why?" Berenice can only answer, "Because I am black. . . . Because I am colored. Everybody is caught one way or another."[21] Frankie, however,

cannot reconcile herself to the condition of "being caught."
She is still propelled *toward* experience, still obsessed by images
of the "spinning world" which riddle the novel in response to
her romantic imagination, to her need of giving substance to
her dreams. Images of the "world," the same that in *Antony
and Cleopatra* betrayed the expense of love, betoken here the
promise of initiation. Yet it is characteristic of initiation in the
contemporary world that its course must be oblique and its
rewards ambivalent. Mrs. McCullers' treatment of the traditional theme of sexual initiation is to the point. The sexual
impulse, as we might expect, is diffused through the novel; it
acts as a faint, persistent scratching on Frankie's consciousness;
and it is never really understood. Nowhere do we perceive
Frankie's insight into sexual experience or confront the action
which gives form to that insight. This is not to say that sexual
initiation is the central theme of the novel. It is not. The point
is simply that initiation no longer requires the commitment
of action, the definition of choice, or the confirmation of self-
knowledge. Frankie's dominant mode of coming to terms with
the world is *feeling*, and her prime mode of acquiring experience is *dreaming*. She dreams of participating in the war as a
Marine, of traveling round the world with the bridal pair; she
likes to pretend that she is a Mexican or a Hollywood star.
Against the wiles of her fantasies, even earthy Berenice is powerless. But the animating center of the novel, the unifying force
in Frankie's character, is of course her wish to *belong*. "She
belonged to no club and was a member of nothing in the
world."[22] If she dreams inordinately, it is because her dreams
confirm her in the illusion that she is enlarging her experience
at the same time that she is communing with the world at large.
Thus, the blood she wants to donate to the Red Cross is not
simply a modest token of heroism; it would flow "in the veins
of Australians and Fighting French and Chinese, all over the
world, and it would be as though she were close kin to all
these people."[23] The urgent need to belong comes to focus in

the ritual of the wedding. Frankie, in search of "we-hood," says of her brother and his bride, "they are the we of me"; and Berenice, with her customary shrewdness, quickly sees that Frankie has "fallen in love" with the wedding, that in fact, she is determined to walk down the aisle between the bridal pair.[24] But after the wedding, what then? "We will have thousands of friends, thousands and thousands and thousands of friends. We will belong to so many clubs that we can't even keep track of all of them," Frankie gloats.[25] If the novel accords to the idea of the wedding so much significance, it is because the ceremony happens to satisfy all of Frankie's needs in that particular August of her life.

Formally the novel is divided into three parts, each taking its character from the role Frankie assumes. We see her first as Frankie Addams, the tomboy, bored and restive. "Until the April of that year, and all the years of her life before, she had been like other people." Her actual world is defined by the kitchen which she shares with Berenice and John Henry. "The three of them sat at the kitchen table, saying the same things over and over, so that by August the words began to rhyme with each other and sound strange."[26] The transformations begin when Frankie suddenly decides to become a member of the wedding: her heart divides like two wings. In the next section of the novel we see Frankie as the new, exotic personality, F. Jasmine, who is all pride and anticipation. Her flirtation with a soldier, her lengthy conversations with Berenice on the subject of love, her lone wanderings through the town, reflect the mood of willfulness which is the prelude to disenchantment. It is in the last part of the novel that disenchantment—what else?—sets in. Mrs. McCullers beautifully disposes of the wedding itself in a few lines and devotes the rest of the book to convert the initial bitterness of, not Frankie or F. Jasmine, but Frances now, to a final affirmation of youth's resilience. Frances, entitled at last to her full name, outgrows the humiliation of her first defeat. Unlike Mick Kelly, she moves beyond the acrid feeling that the world has cheated her. And with the heedlessness of youth she takes up new friends and other illusions, remotely conscious of the death of John Henry and the separation from Berenice. There is change; there is really no knowledge or confirmation. Guilt and anxiety are equally forgotten, only pathos remains. As the identity of Frankie changes from part to part, so do her images of "the spinning world," now fractured, now whole; and the seasons, keeping richly in step, change from spring to fall. The mode is often the mode of poetry as is the mood:

After the plain gray winter the March winds banged on the windows, and clouds were shirred and white on the blue sky. April that year came sudden and still, and the green of the trees was a wild bright green.

In June the trees were bright dizzy green, but late the leaves darkened, and the town turned black and shrunken under the glare of the sun. . . . At last the summer was like a green sick dream, or like a silent crazy jungle under glass.

It was the time of golden weather and Shasta daisies and the butterflies. The air was chilled, and day after day the sky was a clearer green blue, but filled with light, the color of a shallow wave.[27]

The style of the novel presents the blossoming of human feelings no less aptly than it presents the varying moods of nature. But it is a style of confession, or rather manifestation, sensitive to the sudden epiphanies of daily life. It is not dramatic despite the inimitable tang and humor of its dialogue, and despite the plasticity of character which allowed the novel to be made into a successful play.

What drama the novel contains, it draws from the juxtaposition of three characters to one another—not from their interactions. Thus is Frankie caught between the violated innocence of John Henry and the viable experience of Berenice. Berenice is indeed the rock on which the novel rests. She calls to mind both Portia and Brannon, and calls forth a quality of existence

222

as wholesome as our daily bread and as enduring. To all of Frankie's wild dreams, she stands as a silent modifier—for she is too wise to rebuke. With three husbands behind her and a fourth in the offing, she speaks as one who has known love and experienced loneliness. Her understanding of life is as tragic as Frankie's misunderstanding is pathetic. Without her, the tortured sensitivity of Frankie—a sensitivity, after all, which has no correlative but the wistfulness of puberty—would seem pointless and contrived. But between innocence and experience only illusions can lie. And the illusions of Frankie disguise the hopes of all mankind even if her destiny falls short of what our moment fully requires.

V

It is interesting that the least and the most successful of Mrs. McCullers' works, *Reflections in a Golden Eye* and *The Ballad of the Sad Café*, 1951—the story was published in magazine form in 1943—should strike us as a variation on the same fictional genre. There is a statement by Frank O'Connor which serves to clarify the genre, and serves also to put both works in a nice relation to the tradition of the novel. "If Jane Austen were writing *Pride and Prejudice* in the modern way," O'Connor says in *The Mirror in the Roadway*, "the hero would never need to reveal his arrogance by all those subtle touches which Jane Austen analyzed. He would have been satisfied with a peacock on the lawn, and Elizabeth Bennett would have ultimately wrung its neck. . . . The main thing is that the character would be represented by an image corresponding to the author's view of his principal obsession or the author's view of his part in a poetic phantasmagoria. Either way, his character and role are determined, and his part in the story is more metaphorical than real."[28] The characters of *The Ballad of the Sad Café* are both metaphors and grotesques (grotesques almost in Anderson's sense); the plot moves in the familiar pattern of a whirligig spinning out the impossible intricacies of love and pain; and the style, unconscious of its power, transforms this eccentric tale into something as universal as the old ballads about love and dread, madness and revenge.

The decayed house of Miss Amelia, its porch half-painted, its shuttered windows boarded, appears in the first scene of the story and in its last. The house, edifice to love betrayed, to loneliness irrevocable, stands in a small, dreary Southern town. The winters are short and raw, the summers white with glare and fiery hot. From behind its shutters, the strange face of Miss Amelia occasionally peers, a face "sexless and white, with two gray crossed eyes which are turned inward so sharply that they seem to be exchanging with each other one long secret gaze of grief."[29] Firmly and with a sense of finality the narrative unfolds in retrospect before it comes to pause once again, at the end, on the same scene; the gothic touches never seem out of place, so strong is the feeling of mystery and doom. The story itself is simple. Miss Amelia, a powerful blunderbuss of a person, more than six feet tall, owns the only store in town. At the age of nineteen, she is courted by a strong, darkly handsome loom-fixer, Marvin Macy, with an "evil reputation"—he is supposed to carry around the dried, salted ear of a man he killed in a razor fight. Under the spell of love, Macy reforms temporarily, and Miss Amelia marries him in her slow, absent way. But the marriage, which is never consummated, lasts only a few days; Miss Amelia, despite all of Macy's pitiful protestations, beats him out of bed, and subsequently out of the house, after despoiling him of his possessions. Macy vanishes to lead a violent criminal life in other counties. Some years after, Lymon, the hunchback, appears at the doorstep of Miss Amelia, a tired and forlorn figure, seeking shelter, timidly claiming the rights of a dubious kinship. Lymon touches a hidden chord in Miss Amelia's character, touches in her a formless instinct, neither wholly feminine nor altogether maternal. She takes him in; he becomes Cousin Lymon; and the miraculous transformation in her life, of which the new café is evidence, induces a comparable transformation in the town. For Miss Amelia had ceased to be alone and ceased to find herself the beloved: she has suddenly become the lover, with all the pain, perplexity, and uncertain joy which attend that condition. Cousin Lymon thrives on her affections; alternately sour and saucy, mischievous and coy, he soon becomes the natural center of the café. But quick as Lymon is to respond in his egocentric fashion to any external interest, and much though he may be pampered by Amelia, he must secretly wilt, as Mrs. McCullers would have it, until *he* can find an object for *his* love.

The object is ironically provided by the sinister return of Macy, recently out of the penitentiary and bent on vengeance. The hunchback becomes immediately, outrageously, attached to Macy; he follows him around like a crippled mongrel, wiggling his ears, a figure of humble and obscene subjugation. And so the wheel has come full circle. Macy can torture Miss Amelia through the hunchback almost at will. The tension rises to an intolerable pitch, the showdown is preordained. The showdown is a marvelous and frightening scene, a grim wrestling match between the tigerish Macy and the virginal Amazon, Miss Amelia. It takes place by tacit consent on Ground Hog Day in the café, is witnessed by the whole town, and presided over by Lymon who stands watch on the counter, an unholy trophy of man's eternal struggle with Evil, with Death itself, which is the negation of Love. And just as Amelia is about to win the day, Lymon alights screaming and clawing on her back, to give the victory, after all, to Macy. The intruding *alazon* is not confuted or expelled: he triumphs. Lymon and Macy go off together after wrecking the café, wrecking the town really, and wrecking Amelia. Miss Amelia immures herself, the town resumes its sleep of death. "There is absolutely nothing to do in the town. Walk around the millpond, stand kicking at a rotten stump, figure out what you can do with the old wagon wheel by the side of the road near the church. The soul rots with boredom. You might as well go down to the Forks Falls Highway and listen to the chain gang." Yes, the chain gang. It is the envoy of the ballad, its hidden refrain: "The voices are dark in the golden glare, the music intricately blended, both somber and joyful. . . . It is music that causes the heart to broaden and the listener to grow cold with ecstasy and fright. . . ."[30] Unlike Pascal who saw in the image of a chain gang looking at each other sorrowfully and without hope a parable of the human condition, Mrs. McCullers manages to summon for once, in the song of "twelve mortal men," the indestructible joy of endurance and transcendent pain.

The novelette sets a standard of performance for Mrs. McCullers and gives authority to a certain gothic vision, at once quaint and elemental, stark and involuted, which writers like Truman Capote and Tennessee Williams have been inclined to explore. What the novelette does not set forth is a new conception of the irrefragable conflict between the selfhood of man and the otherness of reality, between private need and communal fulfillment. Hints of man's buried life, here as elsewhere in Mrs. McCullers' work, flash darkly to the surface. There is Miss Amelia's whiskey, for instance, which has the power to reveal the secret truth in a man's heart, and which goes a long way toward creating the convivial fellowship of the café, creating the sense of pride and openness and ceremony: "There, for a few hours at least, the deep bitter knowing that you are not worth much in this world could be laid low."[31] But good whiskey alone is not enough; the broad sense of community in the café springs from a more personal source—Miss Amelia's love for the hunchback. It is a love, of course, that remains wholly desexualized; as the town puts it, there is no "conjunction of the flesh" between Amelia and Lymon. For love, it seems, must remain beyond sexual reach, untainted by casual gratification or instinctive need.

Few readers will insist that Mrs. McCullers' image of love should be touched by the Corneillian attributes of reasonableness and high-soulfulness—the age requires another image, less

226

rational, perhaps, and more grotesque. But many readers will regret that no one in the novelette seems to have full access to his experience, to have any ultimate or even provisional understanding of it. In a sense, the work denies the possibility of *recognition*, and avoids, therefore, the fictional equivalent of tragedy, a feature symptomatic of an age in which experience seems, more than ever, unyielding to human intelligence. Moreover, when love specifies the only contact between the hero and his world, heroism itself becomes not merely a call to isolation as in tragedy, but also an inducement to surrender all volition. Without volition no external field for our interests or our actions can ever be defined. The wages of alienation are always compounded. Irony prevails. It is the envoy, the style of anonymous celebration and immitigable sadness, that raises the work to the condition of a haunting performance. The style of pretended ballad reticence and naïveté, of folk motifs and stark tragedy, of augurs and foreshadowing, of incremental repetition and telescoped action—the enfabled style seems to incarnate the very spirit of story-telling whose medium is language in and for itself.

VI

Since 1951 Carson McCullers has been publishing short stories only. (She is known, however, to be at work on a novel, entitled *Clock Without Hands*,* "about good and evil," as the author puts it, "prejudice and the affirmation of the dignity of life."[32]) The themes of Mrs. McCullers' stories are not likely to surprise the readers of her novels and their manner is far less distinguished—with the exception of "A Tree, A Rock, A Cloud," which contains the germ of her doctrine of love, the stories seem by comparison both nerveless and contrived. But the deficiencies of Carson McCullers in the short form only serve to enhance her mastery of the intermediate form. And her mastery of that form in turn underscores the limitations of her sensibility.

* *Clock Without Hands* has been finished, and Carson McCullers has died.

Against "the beautiful and blest *nouvelle*," as Henry James called it, no American need cavil. It is a genre as congenial to the pace of the American mind, the quick, nervous apprehension of our experience, as it is eminently suited to the intense lyrical gifts of so many contemporary writers. But "intense" and "lyrical" are words often used to denote a literary fruit growing out of slightly morbid soil. We are quick to sense that the subjective bias of Mrs. McCullers' imagination is but an artful response to the forces that have driven the self into recoil, and that the scope of her novelettes, unlike that of the novel, permits her characters to elude the repeated assaults of reality, permits them, that is, to leave their wishes unconverted into dramatic action.

It is upon the unconverted, and even inconvertible, wish as it seeks embodiment in love and suffering that the art of Carson McCullers has fastened. In so doing, her fiction, in good Southern style, declares itself opposed to the general aspects of our culture. The quality of that resistance, however, is passive, and it suggests a limit this side of quietism which the literary imagination may not safely transgress. For though love is the great opposing principle which Mrs. McCullers embraces in her fictional critique of our civilization, the failure of love—and love seems always to fail—leaves man encapsulated in a state not very distinguishable from anguished solipsism. The aesthetic and social consequences of this predilection are not hard to recognize. Mrs. McCullers is not only forced to do with the slighter form of the novelette but also to invoke that tone of writing whose affinities with the "buried life" are closest: the tone of romance, poetry, and dream fantasy. The fate of her lowly heroes, however—always chosen among the innocent, the grotesque, and the sacrificial—shows that her work falls somewhere between the realm of tragic experience, where defeat acquires a meaning that transcends the fact of defeat, and the province of irony, where absurdity qualifies the intelligibility of all human suffering. In this perspective, as we saw, the typical proud hero of tragedy merges into the lineaments of a self-deprecating hero of irony to appear again in the guise of a scapegoat. Since the characters of Carson McCullers are granted a more limited freedom than the hypothetical audience in our society may be thought to enjoy, it is the need for freedom, conceived in the broadest sense consonant with our humanity, that her sacrificial victims most urgently express in the very instant of their immolation. Beyond love and beyond pain, striking through the closing circle of their consciousness, the heroes of Carson McCullers evoke a secret idea, some elusive imperative or dream, which by its very absence from their lives must haunt our own. It is this idea, delimited so implicitly, so shyly, by her fiction, that Capote, Salinger, and Bellow seek to make progressively more explicit in theirs.

CHAPTER 9

TRUMAN CAPOTE:
THE VANISHING IMAGE OF NARCISSUS

The terror of which I write is not of Germany, but of the soul.

POE

I

THE name of Truman Capote is already legend, and the picture of his boyish face—the famous bangs, the wide, mysterious eyes—is on the cover of all his books to give the legend credence. To some, Capote is the sprite with a monstrous imagination, the lonely child—"I had the most insecure childhood I know of. I felt isolated from all people" —living with his aunts in Alabama, painting flowers on glass, and tap-dancing on the Mississippi boats. To others he is simply the ephebic purveyor of gothic extravaganzas, the fashionable opportunist of a mid-century madness. Whatever the faults of Capote may be, it is certain that his work possesses more range and energy than his detractors allow—witness the clear ring of *The Muses Are Heard*, the crackling impressions of *Local Color*, the crazy humor of his filmscript, "Beat the Devil"—and it is equally certain that no faddish estimate of his work can suggest his real hold on the contemporary imagination.

Yet it is, of course, as a Southern and gothic writer that we insist on knowing Capote. Southern he is by accident of birth more than natural affinity; he once said, "I have lived in many places besides the South and I don't like to be called a Southern writer."[1] He is right. We are quick to sense that the elemental quality in the fiction of Faulkner, Warren, or McCullers is consciously poeticized in his fiction, and that their loving adherence to the manners of Southern life often vanishes before the surrealist appearance of his reveries. Nor can his work be called gothic in the same sense that makes the idea of spiritual isolation in the novels of Carson McCullers functional and intelligible. Of protest and isolation, as we shall see, Capote has much to say. His broader intentions, however, are more nearly defined by that native tradition of romance we discussed in an earlier chapter. Romance, as practiced with ironic intentions by Capote and defined by Henry James, is "experience liberated . . . experience disengaged, disembroiled, disencumbered," and as such it remains open to the gothic impulse which is but one of its elements.[2]

The idea of romance, informed by the modern techniques of dream symbolism and analysis, suggests the general quality of Capote's work. We begin to perceive the specific concerns of Capote's fiction when we note the division between his "daylight" and "nocturnal" styles, and when we understand both as developments of a central, unifying, and self-regarding impulse which Narcissus has traditionally embodied. The impulse brings together dread and humor, dream and reality, "in-sight" and "ex-perience." The differences between "Miriam," 1945, and "House of Flowers," 1951, between *Other Voices, Other Rooms*, 1948, and *The Grass Harp*, 1951, distinguish the two styles of Capote; the chronological development suggests a deepening awareness of the tensions between self and world, a redistribution of love between ego and object, a movement toward light which retains the knowledge of darkness. *Breakfast at Tiffany's*, 1958, carries these developments a step farther, and, though it appears to elude some of the distinctions we make, confirms the emergent pattern of Capote's work.

The nocturnal style of Truman Capote—and it is the style we are likely to identify with his achievement—makes the greater use of uncanny trappings and surreal decors. The sense of underlying dreadfulness compels the style to discover "the

231

instant of petrified violence," the revelation which only the moment of terror can yield. In stories like "Miriam," "The Headless Hawk," "A Tree of Night," or "Shut a Final Door," fear seems to take the characters by their entrails and reduce them to that curious condition of insight and paralysis which is the best expression of their predicament. "All our acts are acts of fear," Capote writes in the last story, and so man is consigned to perpetual solitude, not so much because he cannot love or be loved—these are merely the symptoms—but because his dreams must remain unsharable and his night world must rise continually against his daily actions.[3] It is this recognition of the unconscious, and all that it holds of wish and terror, that specifies the nocturnal mode of Capote's writing. The recognition is impelled by a force which D. H. Lawrence noted in Poe's work: the disintegration of the modern psyche. Like Poe, like Carson McCullers, Truman Capote shows, in his nocturnal mood, that his image of the modern psyche is preeminently isolate and Protestant. Hence Capote's interest in the theme of self-discovery—Narcissus may have been the first Protestant—and in the technique of character doubles or alter egoes—"Miriam," "Shut a Final Door," etc. Hence also the omnipresence of dreams in Capote's fiction. Dreams in the earlier stories do not only constitute a private and self-sufficient world, and do not only contain the destructive element of our psyche ("It is easy to escape daylight," Randolph says in *Other Voices, Other Rooms*, "but night is inevitable, and dreams are the giant 'cage"); dreams also reveal, in the later stories, the creative element of the unconscious, and permit that release of the imagination which, as Capote implies, is the prerequisite of love.[4] "But a man who doesn't dream is like a man who doesn't sweat: he stores up a lot of poison," Judge Cool tells Verena in *The Grass Harp* when the latter derisively calls his marriage proposal to Dolly, his confession of love, a dream.[5] If Capote's darker style seems uncanny, it is because uncanny effects are produced, as Freud knew, "by effacing the distinc-

tions between imagination and reality . . ," by seeing, as
Rimbaud did, a mosque at the bottom of a lake.[6]

But in effacing the distinctions between reality and imagination, the nocturnal style not only evokes the shapeless world
of our dreams; it evokes, no less, the fabulous world of myth
and fairy tale. In our age, alas, dream, myth, and fairy tale are
no longer allowed to drowse in their separate corners. Freud
has noted the occurrence of material from fairy tales in dreams,
and Geza Roheim has argued that myth, animistic thought,
and in fact culture itself, find a common source in oneiric
fantasies. In Capote's work, the familiar figure of the Wizard
Man partakes both of dream and archetype, and it is there to
remind us that our archaic fears must be forever conquered,
our childish past reenacted. Such fabulous evocations must
reclaim the universal symbols of human experience. Yet it is
wise to remember that Capote once said, "All I want to do is
to tell a story and sometimes it is best to choose a symbol. I
would not know a Freudian symbol as such if you put it to
me."[7] In the end, the nocturnal style of Truman Capote appeals
to the qualities which Henry James found essential to all fiction
of the supernatural, appeals, that is, "to wonder and terror and
curiosity and pity and to the delight of fine recognitions, as
well as to the joy, perhaps sharper still, of the mystified state.
. . ."[8] Of these qualities, and of the human failings which these
qualities silently criticize, the supernatural element in Capote's
fiction is a metaphor.

But if the supernatural defines the nocturnal mode of Capote,
humor defines his daylight style. The style, evident in "My
Side of the Matter," "Jug of Silver," "Children on Their Birthdays," *The Grass Harp*, and *Breakfast at Tiffany's*, assumes
the chatty, first-person informality of anecdotes. It also specifies
character and admits the busyness of social relations more than
its darker counterpart. And the scene which it lights upon is
usually the small Southern town—not the big city which witnesses in abstract horror the so-called alienation of man from

his environment. (The one notable exception, of course, is *Breakfast at Tiffany's*.) Now it is true that humor, like the supernatural, must finally rise to universal implications. But if one may judge from the differences between Twain and Poe, between the American tall tale and the native ghost story, humor is always more of this earth; it is apt to individualize rather than generalize; and it can rise to universal meanings but gradually. Humor has also a social reference. Humor—which may be called a Catholic if the supernatural can be called a Protestant impulse—binds rather than separates: it is as much a mode of communion as the gothic is a mode of self-isolation.

We have suggested that *humor* and the *supernatural*, metaphors of the daylight and nocturnal styles of Capote, reflect the central motive of his fiction. The motive will be understood when the relation between the two elements which express it is further clarified. In his essays "Humor" and "The Uncanny," Freud has some interesting things to say on the subject. The uncanny, Freud believes, derives from an animistic conception of the universe occasioned by a narcissistic overestimation of the self. Freud also characterizes humor as a triumph of the pleasure principle, and of "narcissism, the ego's victorious assertion of its own invulnerability."[9] His essays make it evident, however, that a humorous comment, while it begins by recognizing the threat of reality—and to that extent we are justified in seeing humor as a movement toward objectivity—ends by refusing to meet the threat. Humor, therefore, is like the uncanny in that both suggest a reactionary or "regressive" impulse toward the security of the narcissistic state.

This may sound more simple than art should be allowed to sound. A more sensitive observation is made by Wylie Sypher when, taking his cue from Bergson as well as Freud, he says that "the comic gesture reaches down toward the Unconscious, that dim world usually assigned to tragedy, the midnight terrain where Macbeth met the witches. The joke and the dream

incongruously distort the logic of our rational life."[10] The bulk
of Capote's work persuades us, in the same way, that both
humor and the supernatural are acts of the imagination intended to question our surface evaluations of reality, and indeed
to affirm the counterreality of fantasy. The prevalence of dreams,
the interest in childhood, the negative conception of adolescent
initiation, the concern with self-discovery, the emphasis on
homoeroticism, and the general stasis of the mythic world of
Truman Capote—all these, though they are often presented in
ironic terms, must confirm the central narcissistic impulse of
his fiction, an impulse which serves both as a critique and a
crooked image of American reality. Ancient paradigm of the
Artist, the Lover, and the Dreamer, Narcissus must also reconcile
appearance and reality within the scope of romance, that
"neutral territory," as Hawthorne said, "somewhere between
the real world and fairy-land, where the Actual and the Imaginary may meet, and each imbue itself with the nature of
the other."[11] This is the aesthetic burden of Narcissus. His
moral burden in the contemporary world, which Tate's "Ode
to the Confederate Dead" presaged some decades ago, is still
self-transcendence in the moment of action or love. The former
seems to us now irrecoverable, the latter, it appears, our only
hope. But there is always Holly Golightly to reckon with, and
the peculiar image of freedom she invokes.

II

The contrast between the two styles of Capote can be rapidly
observed in his short stories, of which the best are collected
in A *Tree of Night and Other Stories*, 1949, a selection that
excludes such premature efforts as "The Walls Are Cold" and
"The Shape of Things."

With "My Side of the Matter" and "Miriam" the divided
mood of Capote can already be distinguished. The first is a
chatty, whacky story, or rather anecdote, of a youthful bride-

groom persecuted by two colorful harridans, his wife's aunts, in a tiny Alabama town. The racy narrative, told in the first person by the bridegroom with yarnlike exaggeration and naïveté, remains nevertheless episodic. "Miriam" is a different matter. Set in New York, it is a sinister and surrealistic tale of a child, Miriam, who haunts an elderly widow, Mrs. Miller. But what appears in one perspective as a chilling tale of the supernatural —Miriam can vanish at will—appears in another as the hallucination of a lonely old woman obsessed by a guilty image of her other self, a self bold and adventurous as her own is timid and weary. The theme of the double is not new to literature. Conrad and Dostoyevsky made rich use of it, and both Rank and Freud, acknowledging its uncanny effects, understood it as a stratagem of the ego to preserve itself against the intolerable fact of death, a stratagem, in fact, reverting to an early mental stage in which the narcissistic state of the child protects it against the foreign reality of death and corruption.

The regressive quest for identity, revealed in a moment of terror, is also present in Kay's story, "A Tree of Night," in which a college girl on her way back from her uncle's funeral finds herself cornered, robbed, and even mesmerized, by two grotesque show people on a train whose act it is to perform the macabre story of Lazarus in every tank-town. Taken together, the traveling show-couple summon a force of unspeakable tawdriness and evil which awakens in Kay "a childish memory of terrors that once, long ago, had hovered above her like haunted limbs on a tree of night." It is a memory of black omens and death, and of "the unfailing threat of the wizard man."[12] Kay, under the spell of past and present, slips into the dreadful anonymity of night, finally relaxing into that sublunary sleep for which no identity is requisite. In the story called "Master Misery," it is dreams that define our identity. Hence the agony of Sylvia, the solitary girl who sells her dreams to a mysterious figure, Master Misery, who lives in a great marble mansion off Fifth Avenue. It is as the clown, Sylvia's only friend, says, "Dreams are the mind of the soul and the secret truth about us. Now Master Misery, maybe he hasn't got a soul, so bit by bit he borrows yours, steals it. . . ."[13] We understand Master Misery for what he is when we recognize him not only as a wry image of the psychoanalyst or simply an aspect of the "dehumanized" society in which we live—where Santa Claus is a robot and plaster girls pedal mechanical bicycles in shop windows—but also an extension of the self on which he preys. What saves the symbol—the Wizard Man is not a "character"—from sentimentality is precisely what endows the story with the feeling of improbability: the transposition of myth and actuality. For it is in fabulous, and hence generic, terms that Master Misery is described: "All mothers tell their kids about him; he lives in hollows of trees, he comes down chimmeys late at night, he lurks in graveyards and you can hear his step in the attic."[14] The Wizard Man appears again as Mr. Destronelli in Capote's densest story, "The Headless Hawk." Considered merely as an account of the demented girl, D. J., the story loses much of its significance; considered as the record of Vincent's relation to D. J., of sanity criticized by madness and love betrayed by self-betrayal, the story expands in reference. Already, we see Capote's running interest in the connection between the inability to love and the fear of self-knowledge.

D. J., we find, is a young Southern girl, escaped from an asylum, and now running loose in New York. Vincent himself, the art gallery clerk who cohabits with her for a time and is literally haunted by her thereafter, is described as "never quite in contact." As a child, Vincent had a weakness for carnival freaks, and when he sees D. J. in her eccentric attire, something from his past responds to the girl. The picture she comes to sell, lurid with color and heavy with symbolism, the picture of a headless trunk and a headless hawk, compels him to an "inward recognition," "a private inexpressible perception," which is really the perception of his own fractured life.[15] Used to find in his lovers only the broken image of himself, he turns to D. J. for wholeness or surcease. But D. J. can bestow her tenderness only on violets and the homosexual memory of a music teacher. For her the evil of the world is concentrated in the figure of a certain Mr. Destronelli—the Wizard Man, Master Misery—who also assumes the shape of her alienist, and later of Vincent himself. Strangely enough, the mad equation is borne out in a nightmare Vincent dreams: "Before him is an old man rocking in a rocking chair, an old man with yellow-dyed hair, powdered cheeks, kewpie-doll lips: Vincent recognizes Vincent." The old man, avatar, perhaps, of all wizard men, becomes a fixture on Vincent's back as are the other figures in his dream—"saddled with malevolent semblances of themselves."[16] Vincent also recognizes a massive headless hawk which wheels above him and swoops down, claws foremost—there is to be no freedom. All the tenderness and beauty that D. J. can summon are shredded by the Wizard Man, the Darker Self, whom, in knowing fully, we risk D. J.'s madness, and in ignoring we accept the cowardice and debility of Vincent.

But the unconscious, the hidden self, of which the supernatural is a metaphor, has another reference: it is also the source of our uniqueness, our insight and creativity. This positive aspect emerges in the "daylight" stories of Capote. In "Jug of Silver," for instance, told in the half-credulous, half-humorous note Capote can strike at will, the strange unlettered boy, Appleseed, born supposedly with a caul over his head, "counts" the exact amount of dimes and nickels in a huge, sealed glass jar to win the drugstore prize and procure a "lovely set of white false teeth" for his gawky sister. Wish and fulfillment become one here, and the dream incarnates its reality; for Appleseed, unlike Kay, Mrs. Miller, or Sylvia, retains the wholeness of his being and the quickness of his intuitions. He is still unspoiled by the world; his original powers are unimpaired; and what he lacks in moral intelligence, Capote would have us believe, he fully makes up by the special circumstance of his birth. Like his namesake, Appleseed simply has *mana*. And so has Miss Bobbit in "Children on Their Birthdays," a story narrated very much in the same manner, and one of the best Capote has told. Not at all a Witch-Child in the sense that Miriam is, Miss Bobbit appeals to the most lively and quixotic impulses in the lumpish, sleepy town in which she arrives, and succeeds, before she is run over by a bus, in transmuting its lead into fine particles of gold. Little Miss Bobbit, though a victim of an untoward fate, is rather a good fairy and redeemer, and her strange powers of releasing the charitable impulse in the townspeople stems, once again, from the inner harmony of her being. She is, in Capote's theodicy, like Appleseed among the saved and saviors, as Vincent and Walter in "Shut A Final Door," are among the damned.

III

The bald dichotomy set up by these stories is more amply elaborated by Capote's two earlier novels, *Other Voices, Other Rooms*, 1948, and *The Grass Harp*, 1951.

The peculiar mixture of fantasy and reality in Capote's first novel begs for allegorical interpretation. Carvel Collins has suggested the quest of the Holy Grail as a possible framework for the action, pointing out numerous parallels between the details of Joel Knox's story and those to be found in Jessie Weston's account of the Grail myth. John Aldridge, on the other hand, has seen Joel's story essentially as an archetype of the Boy in Search of a Father.[17] Both views correspond to genuine analogues of the narrative. But Joel Knox is not only a miniature Dedalus-Telemachus in Dublin-Ithaca, or Parsifal-Galahad at the Chapel Perilous. He is also a smaller model of Castorp-Tannhäuser at Davos-Venusberg, and Narcissus sitting by his pool. Above all, he is simply Joel Knox who, no matter how much or little he may resemble Capote, is still a character in a work of fiction.

Joel is in search of an image which reflects darkly his own identity, his inner reality, which becomes available to him, ironically, only when reality is dispelled in the palace of pleasure, the secret house of dreams. (To call *Other Voices, Other Rooms* a story of initiation is to recall how shrunken the range of initiation has become since Huck Finn bounced down the Mississippi on his raft.) What Joel elects is what the enchanted world of Skully's Landing forces upon him, and what he finally accepts is beyond good and evil, as dreams are, which alone are real. Love, which used to be an anchor of reality, is set adrift in the darkness of the human heart—"The heart is deceitful above all things, and desperately wicked. Who can know it?" is the epigraph of the novel, taken from Jeremiah. Love returns upon itself as the mirror image turns to the beholder and absents itself with his absence. The search for the Other, who may be god, sweetheart, or father, ends in the discovery of the Self, and initiation to the world amounts to regression to the world of infantile fantasy in which the father is also a lover. Such is the apotheosis of the love between Joel and Randolph at the spectral Cloud Hotel towards the end of the novel.

The novel begins with Joel's arrival at Noon City, an oasis in the busy world, less pre-Civil War than legendary, near which is the even more legendary mansion of Skully's Landing, where he expects to meet his father for the first time. He is glad to leave Aunt Ellen's house behind: "It was as if he lived those months wearing a pair of spectacles with green, cracked lenses, and had wax-plugging in his ears, for everything seemed to be something it wasn't, and the days melted into a constant dream."[18] But Joel does not see his father, Mr. Samson, for a long time. He roams the wild, incredible garden of the Landing which, like some lost ruin, is haunted by the enfabled past; and, true to Capote's vision, he perceives in an "instant of petrified violence," the apparition of a strange lady in a window. This is his first glimpse of Randolph, of his own fate. Randolph, prototype of the Evil Magician, of the artist, the teacher, and the criminal, whose eloquence and learning are like echoes of a spectral chorus, is the genius who dominates the Landing. Exquisite in his cultivation and irrelevance, at once languid and sinister, lucid and depraved, Randolph has all the unpredictability and perverted innocence which qualify him for becoming the mentor and lover of Joel. Whether he is exposed to the half-pagan Sabbath ceremonies of Jesus Fever and his daughter Zoo, or the primitive magic of Little Sunshine, the wizened Negro hermit who haunts the Cloud Hotel, or the talcumed world of invalids, lunatics, and perverts who inhabit the Landing, Joel's sense of reality is constantly subverted by his environment. Like Little Sunshine, who acts, together with Randolph, as father-substitute, Joel is drawn to the terrible Cloud Hotel: "For if he [Little Sunshine] went away, as he had once upon a time, other voices, other rooms, voices lost and clouded, strummed his dreams."[19] The progressive attenuation of external reality is evident as Joel moves from Aunt Ellen's to Skully's Landing to the Cloud Hotel; the movement is indeed a descent into Hades, a journey, in various stages, toward the darkest unconscious, or perhaps toward the womb of death. Dreaming of the Cloud Hotel, Joel realizes that it was not and never had been a real hotel: "This was the place folks came when they went off the face of the earth, when they died but were not dead." And dreaming of his journey through its rooms, he sees himself "in the dust of thorns listening for a name, his own, but even here no father claimed him."[20]

The second part of the novel, of the "journey," opens with a climactic incident. Joel finally meets his father, and finds him a paralytic with two glinting eyes, who can only communicate with the world by dropping red tennis balls. Meanwhile, we are apprised in a grotesque tale of love and violence that Randolph is responsible for Samson's condition. Joel's resistance to Randolph, and to all that he stands for, receives its first check when Joel discovers that his real father is nearly a zombie.

His resistance is further weakened when his relation to Idabel Tompkins fails to confirm his groping manhood. When Joel attempts to kiss Idabel on a fishing trip, she fights him off viciously and overpowers him; and on their excursion to a decayed mill, it is she who kills the water moccasin with Jesus Fever's old Civil War sword. The snake has the eyes of Joel's father, and the boy fails equally in asserting his manhood with Idabel as in conquering the phantom of his father with the ceremonial symbol of the past. Thus it is in *failing* the traditional ordeals, in overcoming which he might have earned his manhood, that Joel makes himself eligible to the insidious knowledge of the Cloud Hotel. Three further incidents clinch Joel's failure, and therefore clinch his regression, the form that his initiation takes. An appeal he sends to Aunt Ellen in the form of a letter is intercepted by Randolph. When Idabel and Joel decide to run away, they encounter in the woods two Negroes making passionate love. The scene reawakens Idabel's hostility toward Joel; it is a firm intimation that between them no stable relation can obtain. A little later, both find themselves at a fair, and they strike up an excited companionship with a wistful midget, Miss Wisteria. They all ride a ferris wheel. Then Miss Wisteria begins to take a special interest in Joel:

> She placed her hand on his thigh, and then, as though she had no control over them whatsoever, her fingers crept up inside his legs . . . and Joel, disturbed but knowing now he wanted never to hurt anyone, not Miss Wisteria, nor Idabel . . . wished so much he could say: it doesn't matter. I love you, I love your hand. The world was a frightening place, yes, he knew: unlasting, what could be forever? or only what it seemed? rock corrodes, rivers freeze, fruit rots; stabbed, blood of black and white bleeds alike; trained parrots tell more truth than most, and who is lonelier: the hawk or the worm?[21]

On the ferris wheel the vision of love, loneliness, and mutability is suddenly illuminated in Joel's mind, and it is in the name of love that he renounces the willfulness of sexual possession. At the same instant he glimpses Randolph staring fixedly at him from the ground underneath.

The discovery of reality and the search for fulfillment in heterosexual terms fail. Zoo, who dreams all her life of journeying to Washington after her father dies, does not get very far. She is raped by three white men and a Negro driving a truck and returns to the Landing crushed, her dream desecrated, Even Idabel, who makes good her escape, winds up with Miss Wisteria as companion. With Idabel away—she and Randolph, like images of day and night, are never seen together in the novel—Joel can only turn to Randolph.

Part Three opens with the return of Joel to the Landing. He returns in a coma, his world contracted, appearance and reality altogether fused, and when he recovers from his illness, he is finally at peace, fully attuned to the enchantments which await him: "Lo, he was where he's never imagined to find himself again: the secret hideaway room in which, on hot New Orleans afternoons, he'd sat watching snow sift through scorched August trees. . . ."[22] It is with Randolph, not Idabel, that he finally visits the Cloud Hotel, while Aunt Ellen looks for him in vain. But for Joel there is no going back to the old realities; like Randolph, like Little Sunshine, he finds at last his Other Room in the Hotel—with a hanged mule in it for effect. And strangely enough, the last acts of Joel indicate not surrender but liberation. Faithful to the Jungian archetype of the Descent into Hades, Joel reemerges somewhat healed, possessed of a dangerous and ambiguous knowledge. " 'I am me,' Joel whooped. 'I am Joel, we are the same people,' " he shouts exuberantly on his way back from the Cloud Hotel. And he is suddenly wise enough to see "how helpless Randolph was: more paralyzed than Mr. Samson, more childlike than Miss Wisteria, what else could he do, once outside and alone, but describe a circle, the zero of his nothingness?"[23] At the end of the novel, when Zoo overturns the cracked, moss-covered bell with which the old plantation owners used to summon their slaves, ancient symbol of a vanished order, and when Randolph appears in a window, beckoning in his female attire to Joel, we are not sure whether it is in triumph or defeat that Joel responds to this mute appeal. We can only sense that the traditional modes of behavior are no longer in command of life.

Mr. Aldridge has objected to the self-contained quality of evil and guilt in the novel, to the failure of the book to "stand in some meaningful relation to recognizable life," and to the feeling that Capote's world "seems to be a concoction rather than a synthesis," its purity "not the purity of experience forced under pressure into shape" but rather the "sort that can be attained only in the isolation of a mind which life has never really violated. . . ."[24] The objections appear serious; but as usual, the impatience of Mr. Aldridge is not entirely justified. We need to remember that Capote's work is, in its intentions, at least, a novel-romance, and that it attempts to engage reality without being realistic. Evil and guilt in it are self-contained only in the sense that they are defined by the individual consciousness without reference to an accepted social or moral order. Evil, in other words, is mainly poetic and archetypal; its moral issue is confined to the predicament of the victim without visible oppressor, and of the beloved almost without a lover. The result is a sharp focus, a reflexive vision seeking constantly to penetrate the arcana of personality. As Randolph puts it to Joel:

They can romanticize us so, mirrors, and that is their secret: what a subtle torture it would be to destroy all the mirrors in the world: where then could we look for reassurance of our identities? I tell you, my dear, Narcissus was no egotist . . . he was merely another of us who, in our unshatterable isolation, recognized, on seeing his reflection, the one beautiful comrade, the only inseparable love. . . .[25]

Experience is limited to what a mirror reveals of the beholder, and if the novel sometimes appears to be a "concoction" rather than a "synthesis," it is perhaps because the job of dramatic resolution is surrendered to ambience and verbal magic. Here is the context of Joel's final revelation at the Cloud Hotel:

(He looked into the fire, longing to see their faces as well, and the flames erupted an embryo; a veined, vacillating shape, its features formed slowly, and even when complete stayed veiled in dazzle; his eyes burned tar-hot as he brought them nearer: tell me, tell me, who are you? are you someone I know? are you dead? are you my friend? do you love me? But the painted disembodied head remained unborn beyond its mask, and gave no clue. Are you someone I am looking for? he asked, not knowing whom he meant, but certain that for him there must be such a person, just as there was for everybody else: Randolph with his almanac, Miss Wisteria and her search by flashlight, Little Sunshine remembering other voices, other rooms, all of them remembering, or never having known. And Joel drew back. If he recognized the figure in the fire, then what ever would he find to take its place? It was easier not to know, better holding heaven in your hand like a butterfly that is not there at all.)[26]

The recognition of Joel is, to a large extent, the event upon which the dramatic unity of the novel depends. It is characteristic of Capote's nocturnal mode that the event should be presented in the guise of a trance or hallucination, a verbal *tour de force*, and that its moral effect should be muffled by "atmosphere." Though other novels seem to us greater, it is otiose to take their more realistic mode as a judgment of Capote's fiction.

IV

Of his first novel Capote has recently said, in *Writers at Work*, "I am a stranger to that book; the person who wrote it seems to have little in common with my present self. Our mentalities, our interior temperatures are entirely different."[27] The remark accentuates our transition to Capote's second novel, *The Grass Harp*, which is indeed a different story. That the book contains much autobiography is evident from a later story

Capote wrote, "A Christmas Memory," in which the prototypes of Collin and Dolly are shown to be, in words *and* picture, young Capote (then an urchin with a happy, toothless grin) and his elderly female cousin. The narrative, written in the "daylight" style, is told in the first person by young Collin Fenwick. The story is not "strummed in dreams," as in *Other Voices, Other Rooms*; it is strummed by the wind on a field of Indian grass adjoining a cemetery—the Grass Harp. To be sure, the contrast between the two novels is not as striking as if Poe had taken up residence at Walden Pond, but it suggests, nevertheless, a welcome restoration of reality to the surface of things, and an expansion in social awareness. *The Grass Harp*, at any rate, sings the story of all people, as Dolly Talbo says, people alive and dead, and to sing one needs more space than the Cloud Hotel affords.

The "initiation" of Collin Fenwick results less in a regression to the oneiric fastness of childhood than in a nostalgic awareness of past innocence and lost love. Collin is an eleven-year-old orphan when he comes to live with Verena and Dolly Talbo, two elderly cousins of his father. The two women are as dissimilar as cactus and violet. Verena, who represents the ruthless, practical world, is shrewd, grasping, and masterful. Her single weakness, the memory of a liaison with a certain Maudie who leaves Verena to get married, enhances her apparent toughness. Dolly, on the other hand, is shy and retiring—her presence is a delicate happening. She lives in a tender, wistful world, gathering herbs for her dropsy cures, feeding only on sweets, and extending her sympathy to all created things. Her devout friend, Catherine, an old Negro who claims to be of Indian descent, calls her Dollyheart, and calls Verena, That One—the Heart, the Self, versus the Other, the World. With Dolly and Catherine, Collin enters into a spiritual sisterhood dedicated to preserve everything frail, lovely, and unique.

But the trouble comes when Collin is sixteen. The world, in the person of Verena, decides to ask the unworldly trio to

246

account for itself. Verena bullies Dolly to obtain from her the formula of the dropsy cure which has commercial possibilities. When force and persuasion fail, Verena humiliates Dolly by reminding her of her uselessness and dependency. The trio takes to the road, finding refuge in a tree house, a raft floating in the sea of leaves, up an old chinaberry tree.

The tree house, of course, is the last refuge of innocents abroad. But though it is unlike Huck's raft in that it offers limited opportunities of experience, it is not so much a vehicle of escape, Capote would have us believe, as a harbor of lost values. For Dolly teaches Collin that the tree house is a ship, "that to sit there was to sail along the cloudy coastline of every dream." At peace in the tree, the two women and the boy feel at one with their surroundings: "We belonged there, as the sun-silvered leaves belonged, the dwelling whippoorwills."[28] But most important, they feel at one with one another, and with the two "outcasts" from town whom they attract, Riley Henderson and Judge Cool.

Inspired by the enraged Verena, and led by a brutal sheriff, the representatives of Church and State attack the tree and are repulsed time and again in hilarious scenes of impotent fury and gentle mockery. The spirit of the chinaberry tree, the presence of Dolly, the insight into their separate predicaments, unite our five refugees as the sheriff's posse can never be united. "I sometimes imagine all those whom I've called guilty have passed the real guilt on to me: it's partly that that makes me want once before I die to be right on the right side," the Judge, who is the voice as Dolly is the heart of the group, says. He continues: "But here we are, identified: five fools in a tree. A great piece of luck provided we know how to use it: no longer any need to worry about the picture we present—free to find out who we truly are."[29] As usual, the search for identity in Capote's work precedes the discovery of love. But here, for the first time, both the reflexive and the outgoing impulse are caught in a single vision.

247

The outgoing impulse, the burden of love, is defined when Judge Cool says to Riley—and his message is identical with that of the hobo in Carson McCullers' "A Tree, A Rock, A Cloud"—"We are speaking of love. A leaf, a handful of seed —begin with these, learn a little what it is to love. . . . No easy process, understand; it could take a lifetime. . . ." At which Dolly with a sharp intake of breath cries, "Then . . . I've been in love all my life."[30] Yet Dolly is not so out of touch with reality that she can accept the world, like Pollyana, on silly faith. The persecutions of Verena, the fact that her friend Catherine is "captured" and thrown into jail, force her to ask Collin—and how ironic that an old woman should ask an adolescent questions about the world—force her to ask him in pain and perplexity, "Collin, what do you think: is it that after all the world is a bad place?" Collin is wise enough (almost too wise) to reflect: "No matter what passions compose them, all private worlds are good, they are never vulgar places: Dolly had been made too civilized by her own, the one she shared with Catherine and me, to feel the winds of wickedness that circulate elsewhere. . . ."[31]

We are never quite sure whether the novel portrays the disenchantment of an elderly woman or the initiation of a young man. But of this we can be more certain, that Dolly in renewing her powers of universal sympathy by drawing constantly on the resources of her inner world strikes a parable of the artist who, secure in the freedom of his imagination, reaches out to free ours. In this sense, the healing powers of Dolly can be said to extend, through the medium of the Grass Harp, not only to the fictive community of tree-dwellers but also to the real community of book-readers. The idea of the artist as healer is, of course, quite ancient. What makes the idea interesting in the works of such contemporary authors as Salinger and Capote is the particular form it acquires. In both writers the concern with lovelessness seems to have allied itself with a criticism of the new Philistinism, the implication being that the poet and lover, to leave out the lunatic, are of one imagination compact. Hence Salinger's interest in Zen and Haiku poetry, which bring the aesthetic and spiritual to meet at a still point, and Capote's interest in Narcissus whose adoration of beauty may be considered an act both of love and cognition.

The reaction against a grim and unlovely world, which insists that all private worlds are good *and* beautiful, tends to perpetrate the myth of the Noble Unconscious. It may also lead to the myth of the Noble Freak. Of this Dolly is an example, and Sister Ida, with her revivalist tribe of fifteen children all sired by different fathers, is another. Ida's wandering brood, whose slogan is Let Little Homer Honey Lasso Your Soul For the Lord, brings into the novel a good deal of bustle and folksy humor. They also reveal a certain outgoingness, an attitude which, in its vigor and acceptance, qualifies the pathos of Dolly. But the impression remains that though Dolly and Ida have suffered much, their idea of freedom is undoubtedly romantic and the form of their rebellion extravagant.

Nothing is very extravagant about the denouement of the novel. Verena, robbed and deserted by the infamous Dr. Ritz, is utterly broken. In a candle-lit, tree-house scene, while rain pours and thunder rages, Verena, who had actually climbed the chinaberry tree, confesses to Dolly: "Envied you, Dolly. Your pink room. I've only knocked at the doors of such rooms, not often—enough to know that now there is no one but you to let me in."[32]

Dolly's "pink room" is a place for Collin to start from; Joel's "other room" at the Cloud Hotel is a place to which he can and must return. When Dolly dies, it is as if a ceremony of innocence and beauty had come to an end, and behind each character the Garden of Eden had clanged its gates shut. But life continues. Riley Henderson goes on to become a public figure, and Collin journeys North to study law. Reality does not surrender to the dream; it is merely redeemed by it. The childish self-absorption of a Joel yields to the wider horizon of a Collin. Seen in retrospect from Collin's point of view, the novel still appears as a pastoral elegy to irrevocable innocence. But the elegy is also mythicized; it is sung by the field of Indian grass, "a grass harp, gathering, telling, a harp of voices remembering a story."[33] The elegy is present and continuous; it may even affect the future. Yet Collin confesses, as Huck would never confess, that "my own life has seemed to me more a series of closed circles, rings that do not evolve with the freedom of the spiral. . . ."[34]

V

With *Breakfast at Tiffany's*, 1958, the closed rings begin to evolve into a spiral, some open and continuous motion of the hero's spirit, or rather of the heroine's, the amazing Miss Holiday Golightly, Traveling, as her Tiffany cards insist. But whether the driving motion of a spiral, so endless and implacable, possesses more freedom than a circle affords is a conundrum only Euclid may solve.

Holly, like Capote's other protagonists, is not yet out of her teens: "It was a face beyond childhood, yet this side of belonging to a woman."[35] But her initiation began long ago, before she became the child-bride, at fourteen, of Doc Golightly, a horse doctor in Tulip, Texas; began, probably when she lost father and mother and was dumped with her brother Fred, half-starved, on "various mean people." The process of that initiation remains secret—there are intimations of outrage and misery beyond the limits of a child's endurance—for Holly behaves as if past and future were no more tangible than the air she breathes; but its result is nonetheless permanent: a wild and homeless love of freedom. When we see her during the war years in that New York brownstone of the East Seventies, she is fully nineteen, and she strikes us as an improbable combination of the *picaro*, the courtesan, and the *poète maudit*.

Improbability is indeed the quality she uses to criticize a dreary and truthless round of existence, and artifice—she is an inspired liar—to transform it. "I'll never get used to anything. Anybody who does, they might as well be dead," she cries at one point, and we realize that her rebellion against the *given* in life, the useful and prudential, is one of the sources of her vitality.[36] It is as her dwarfish friend and Hollywood agent puts it, the "kid" is a *"real* phony," and her specialty is presenting "horseshit on a platter." Screwball, phony, or saint—some will find it more convenient simply to say "sick, sick, sick"—it does not take us very long to recognize, to admire, Holly's hold on experience. Her philosophy is quite elementary—and hopelessly at odds with our times. "I don't mean I'd mind being rich and famous," she tells the narrator. "That's very much on my schedule, and someday I'll try to get around to it; but if it happens, I'd like to have my ego tagging along. I want to still be me when I wake up one fine morning and have breakfast at Tiffany's."[37] When Holly's dream comes true—the vision symbolized by the *"ordre, luxe, et volupté"* of Tiffany's which she uses to cure her spells of *angst,* "the mean reds"—she wants to be no other than herself. Implied here is no revulsion against one's identity, no holy surrender or unattachment. Holly is in fact very much attached to this world, and therefore to herself. In this respect, she seems the opposite of Salinger's Holden Caulfield with whom she shares the quixotic gift of truth, and shares the ability to gamble everything on a wayward love for, say, Man O'War—Holden's ducks in Central Park—or her brother Fred—Holden's sister Phoebe. But also unlike Holden, whose stringent idealism limits the scope of his commitments, his joy, Holly's truth refers to no self-transcending concept. As she candidly admits: "Good? Honest is more what I mean. Not low-type honest—I'd rob a grave, I'd steal two-bits off a dead man's eyes if I thought it would contribute to the day's enjoyment—but unto-thyself-type honest. Be anything but a coward, a pretender, an emotional crook, a whore: I'd rather have cancer than a dishonest heart."[38] Her loyalty to others—

the inmate Sally Tomato, for instance—is a loyalty to her own feelings for which she is willing to risk all.

Morality, we see, is still defined in the privacy of the passing moment. But privacy has many shades that we cannot afford to ignore. As the phantasmal vision of young Knox at the Cloud Hotel was followed by the elegiac insight of a more mature Fenwick, so does the latter give way to Holly's sustaining faith, belligerent almost, in the honesty of the heart. The last allows Capote's heroine to implicate herself in a wider range of experience than her predecessors could encompass; it permits her to check her code against the play of reality in a manner Knox and Fenwick would have been powerless to command. But the crazy valor of Holly does not prevent her from carrying the customary burden of pain; the price of unorthodoxy, the intensity of her involvement with life, is fully paid. In this she is not unlike the hipsters whose badge, the dark glasses, she constantly wears. Holly has no possessions other than the moment requires—she is "camping out" in New York. Like the ugly tomcat she picks up by the river one day, her existence is thoroughly improvised: "I don't want to own anything until I know I've found the place where me and things belong together." And like a wild thing she lives in the open sky; but she knows, too, that "it's better to look at the sky than live there. Such an empty place; so vague. Just a country where the thunder goes and things disappear."[39] When her beloved brother, Fred, dies in the war (at which time her brave soul goes berserk, the jaunty dark glasses are shattered, and her true piteous human nakedness is revealed), when her Brazilian lover abandons her, pregnant, when she becomes involved in a narcotics scandal and the friends who fed on her emotional bounty desert her, when she jumps bail and takes off for Latin America, and thence to darkest Africa, the defiant spiral of her life, swirling into the unknown, leaves us breathless and afraid that so much light can diffuse itself into darkness, that such brave exuberance could be the product of greater desperation. And indeed Holly herself becomes afraid. On her way to the airport she stops in Spanish Harlem to let "her" cat off, admonishing it in a scene frankly sentimental to find a proper home for itself. Then she breaks down: "I'm very scared, Buster. Yes, at last. Because it could go on forever. Not knowing what's yours until you've thrown it away."[40]

Holly Golightly may be what we should all like to become if we could deposit comfort and respectability to an insured bank account; and her breezy excesses of fancy as of intuition may be, again, just what our stuffy age most requires. In her case the misfit hero certainly shows a fitting genius for *living*—rebellion here is secondary, spontaneous. But Capote himself is not entirely taken in by Holly's verve and piercing glitter. His tale, though lovingly told, has wit and sharp precision. As Holly sweeps through her zany adventures, one becomes conscious of a groundswell of gentle criticism. Mildred Grossman, the grind whom the narrator recalls from his schooldays, may be a "top-heavy realist," but Holly by the same token must be considered a "lop-sided romantic"; and antithetical as the two girls seem, both "walk through life and out of it with the same determined step that took small notice of those cliffs at the left."[41] Even Holly's incorrigible tomcat finds at last a home with potted palms and lace curtains, a home and a name; but for Holly the narrator can only pray that she may be granted, sometime, somewhere, the grace of knowledge and repose. Narcissus found both in a reflected image; Holly, whimsical child of old Faust, looks for them beyond a vanishing horizon. For Holly—sooner or later we must say it—is a child too. She is premature in ways both delightful and regressive. (The latest avatar of Capote's Wizard Man is the "fat woman" who haunts Holly's "red nightmares," threatening to inflict punishment, withhold love, or destroy everything high and rare. But does not childhood itself, to which adults wend such tortuous ways, present a criticism of maturity for which we seldom have a ready answer?)

Criticism, the interplay of views, is sustained by right form. The form of *Breakfast at Tiffany's* approaches perfection. It has pace, narrative excitement, a firm and subtle hold on the sequence of events from the first backward glance to the final salutation. A novelette in scope, it still manages to treat a subject usually accorded the fuller scope of the picaresque novel with marvelous selectivity. The point of view, the tone, the style herald no technical discoveries in the field of fiction: they simply blend to make the subject spring to life. Capote allows the story to be told in the first person by a struggling young writer whose vantage of perception, now in the shadow, now in the light, captures the elusive figure of Holly with the aid of such minor figures as Joe Bell and O. J. Berman. The device is both revealing and discreet, for there is, no doubt, something about Holly's complexion that cannot bear too sharp a light. By establishing the right relation between his narrator and subject, Capote also strikes the right tone. For though the whole story is unfolded backward in one sweeping flashback, the tone is not, like *The Grass Harp's*, elegiac. Elegy, where so much hope is called to question, is out of place. The tone comes closer to that of an invocation, a blessing: hail, Holly, and farewell. Criticism, as we have noted, is implied, patronage never. What keeps the tone from becoming patronizing—look at that wonderful spoiled child!—is the style. The style matches the exotic quality of the subject with its clear-headedness, matches whimsey with wit, though here and there, as in the description of the cat, Capote indulges himself in a superfluous flourish of imagery. Holly's lack of self-criticism is balanced by the searching temper of the narrator. Tension and control are maintained. This is evident in the most casual bit of description. Here is one of Holly:

She was still on the stairs, now she reached the landing, and the ragbag colors of her boy's hair, tawny streaks, strands of albino-blond and yellow, caught the hall light. It was a warm evening, nearly summer, and she wore a slim cool black dress, black sandals, a pearl choker. For all her chic thinness, she had an almost breakfast-cereal air of health, a soap and lemon cleanness, a rough pink darkening in the cheeks. Her mouth was large, her nose upturned. A pair of dark glasses blotted out her eyes.[42]

Holly Golightly will remind a good many readers of Isherwood's Sally Bowles, and remind the greater community of movie-goers of Julie Harris' fine rendition of that role. But it is not chauvinism, we hope, that compels us to recognize her peculiarly American quality: the quixotic ideas of hope, sincerity, truth. (Sally might or might not have stood up for the gangster Tomato, while Holly could not have done otherwise.) Though Holly's life is completely open-ended, and her "initiation," once again, brings with it no confirmation or knowledge—neither does it bring nostalgia—it is a life, like Verena's, that leaves behind it a trail of love and affection. Secret doors, which might have remained forever closed, are unlocked when she passes, and even savages commemorate her presence in carved images. She is in this, we see, like other heroes of contemporary fiction, scapegoats and liberators all, and if we refuse to emulate them or accept their painful destiny, noting in our wisdom its shortcomings, we cannot in good conscience ignore the truth their proud fate so urgently implies.

VI

The nocturnal style of Capote revealed a sea-green world of silence and sudden violence; characters vanished and appeared in mystery; things happened, as it were, intransitively; connectives of motive as of syntax were omitted; time was suspended; and the liquid, dreamy density of sentences absorbed the shock of action and thrust of sense. Against the former mode, the daylight style commits itself to the autobiographical stance; it feigns literalness, personal authenticity; it seeks to clarify temporal and spatial relations; and it acknowledges the external claims of reality by yielding to a kind of humorous naïveté. Here is Collin's moment of illumination to stand against the witchery of Joel's vision at the Cloud Hotel:

> Sister Ida chose a place on the bank from which she could supervise the bathing. "No cheating now—I want to see a lot of commotion." We did. Suddenly girls old enough to be married were trotting around and not a stitch on; boys, too, big and little all in there together naked as jaybirds. It was well that Dolly had stayed behind with the Judge; and I wished Riley had not come either, for he was embarrassing in his embarrassment. . . .

> Those famous landscapes of youth and woodland water—in after years how often, trailing through the cold rooms of museums, I stopped before such a picture, stood long haunted moments having it recall that gone scene, not as it was, a band of goose-fleshed children dabbling in an autumn creek, but as the painting presented it, husky youths and wading water-diamonded girls; and I wondered then, wonder now, how they fared, where they went in this world, that extraordinary family.[43]

The contrasts between the two passages, style and context, are obvious. Joel is led to his insight by departed spirits, once the guests of the Cloud Hotel; Collin is led to his meditation by naked children bathing in the sunlight. Joel ends by choosing "a butterfly that is not there at all," by embracing a qualified autism; Collin ends on a note of "objective sympathy," wondering about the fate of "that extraordinary family." In short, the earlier passage looks inward, the latter outward. Narcissus, having plumbed his shallowness, harks once again to Echo. Holly's parallel insight into her situation—these are all flashes of self-knowledge—takes us even farther toward finding a dramatic correlative to private intuitions. In the crucial passage already quoted, Holly confesses her fear of perpetual homelessness in a rented car speeding toward an airport, and confesses all to a *real* listener. The bounds of autism, of pure self-reflexiveness or even reflection, are finally broken. Holly's voice answers both Knox and Fenwick: that beyond the imperatives of self-discovery, beyond love itself, lie the wider horizons, shimmering and undefinable, of *freedom*.

The development of Capote's adolescent heroes from Joel Knox to Holly Golightly has both an internal logic and a public interest relevant to the prejudices of literature in our time. Joel's urge for self-definition, pursued under its peculiar circumstances, dreamily evokes the idea of Narcissus. But the essence of narcissism, as Theodore Reik maintains, "lies in seeing oneself with the loving eyes of another. The phenomenon does not mean the expression of self-love but the desire of the self to be loved."[44] That same desire presages the broader view Collin Fenwick takes; for the love of all created things that Verena teaches him presupposes some security in the identity we discover to ourselves, presupposes, that is, an ability to turn the need for love outward. Holly Golightly, though she impresses us by her self-sufficiency—indeed, one is sometimes led to wonder how "permanent" any of her attachments can be—converts her restless love for the world into an active and existential pursuit. The movement, we see, is toward greater involvement, a breaking out.

The three heroes, standing for knowledge through dream, love, and free action, represent also three typical attitudes of recent fiction. Joel Knox reflects the current feeling that our world is now discovered, our life organized, our vision confined to some private room of lost childhood. The only freedom we still possess is the freedom to dream, and to the extent that reality becomes more intractable our dreams become compulsive. Collin Fenwick expresses the need to redeem reality through love, a need to which a great part of contemporary fiction is so intensely dedicated. Holly Golightly approaches the ideal of the new picaresque, the free-wheeling hero who insists on the freedom to experience and to denounce precisely because that freedom is no longer granted with immunity by our society. In all cases, the American hero, equally so much more innocent *and* experienced than of yore, remains an outsider, a fugitive from the central concerns of American life, hiding in secret rooms or up a chinaberry tree, or still "lighting

257

out" for the "territory ahead" which is now situated in Africa. Given our burden of bitter and inexhaustible illusions, our hopeless nostalgias and secret regressions, it is no wonder that romancers of Capote's gifts should speak keenly to our condition. But the growth of his vision and the evolution of his more dramatic style also promise, without foregoing the advantages of romance, to discover a form commensurate with the maturity to which we have so long aspired.

CHAPTER 10

J. D. SALINGER:
RARE QUIXOTIC GESTURE

Through our own recovered innocence we
discern the innocence of our neighbors.

THOREAU

We know the sound of two hands clapping.
But what is the sound of one hand clapping?

A ZEN KOAN

I

THE worried hush with which each Salinger story is now
anticipated in the pages of the *New Yorker* has become
almost audible. Rumors seek the author in his stern
retirement from the public glare and dwell on his silences with
the insistence criticism reserves to his speech. The satiric author
of American adolescence in revolt already commands the authority of a prophet, the sanctity of a guru, and the teasing
charm of a Zen Master. And yet it was only in 1951 that the
apotheosis of *The Catcher in the Rye* as a Book-of-the-Month
selection took place. Since then American youth has learned to
speak of Salinger and Dostoyevsky in the same breath, and to
read them in the same measure, as a recent survey in *The Nation*
claimed. This is all very well. James Dean and Elvis Presley
have also had their moments. But we do Salinger ill-service to
base his reputation on anything less enduring than his art.

Salinger, of course, has written some of the best fiction of our
time. His voice is genuine, new, and startlingly uneven. In his
work we find no showy or covert gesture in the direction of
Symbolism or Naturalism, Gothic design or Freudian chiaros-
curo; and indeed there was a time when we were unsure whether

his intentions came closer to those of Fielding or Firbank, Twain or Chekov. If close to anything, Salinger's intentions are probably more in keeping with Fitzgerald's idea of self-created innocence and Lardner's biting renderings of corruption, with the spiritual assumptions of Martin Buber, and, more recently, with those of primitive Christianity and Zen. Yet to speak of his uniqueness in these terms is simply to indulge in the small talk of criticism. We are more anxious, nowadays, to discover the opportunities of literary significance, the conditions of heresy, and protocols of formal excellence. We question *Kitch* and middle-brow art to the extent that we consume it in prodigious quantities, and are adversely disposed to any serious work that carries the aura of either. It is in response to this line of criticism that the work of Salinger proves itself to be seriously engaged by a current and a traditional aspect of reality in America.

The traditional aspect wears no elaborate disguise. It is the new look of the American Dream, specifically dramatized by the encounter between a vision of innocence and the reality of guilt, between the forms love and power have tended to assume in America. The natural locus of that conflict in the work of Salinger is childhood and adolescence. In them the counterplay of hope and despair, truth and mendacity, participation and withdrawal, commands a full range of comic, that is ambivalent, reference: it is the old story of the self against the world in outlines blurred by a mass society. To say as Fiedler does that the "images of childhood and adolescence haunt our greatest works as an unintended symbolic confession of the inadequacy we sense but cannot remedy" is to view a profound truth in a partial perspective.[1] Nostalgia, as we saw, is the result of our compulsion to reenact the story of the American fall. We do not always resist it well. But nostalgia, when it is known to itself, has its ironic and artistic uses. The retreat to childhood is not simply an escape; it is also a criticism, an affirmation of values which, for better or worse, we still cherish;

260

and the need for adolescent disaffiliation, the refusal of initiation, expresses the need to reconceive American reality.

Yet it is hard for some critics to recognize that no act of denial in Salinger's work is without some dramatic and social correlative, which is more than we can generally say of equally serious novelists writing today. The urban, suburban, and ex-urban society which circumscribes Salinger's child and adolescent characters—the white dinner, not black leather, jacket circle—is usually well specified. About that society we have recently learned a good deal. We know that it exhibits a sad decay of genuine sensibility and even of simple truth. There are, no doubt, many opportunities of significant action still left in it, and we are justified in requesting our best writers to discover them. But the nature of action is such that its results are seldom commensurate with its motives. And the reverse is no less true. The anger of a child confronted for the first time with the force of anti-Semitism, the spirit of an adolescent who dons a red hunting cap in New York City, the tender cruelty of a woman, who is bereaved of her lover, toward her child, even the suicide of a misfit genius, can suggest possibilities of action which we hastily reject in favor of a mechanical gesture at the polling booth. Social realities are no doubt repressed in the work of Salinger—note how gingerly he handles his Jews—and this puts a limit on the total significance we can accord to it. Yet it is by what an author manages to *dramatize* that we must finally judge him.

The dramatic conflict which so many of Salinger's stories present obviously does not lend itself to sociological classification. It is more loving and particular, and it partakes of situations that have been traditionally available to literature. The conflict, however, suggests a certain polarity between what might be called, with all due exaggeration, the Assertive Vulgarian and the Responsive Outsider. Both types recur with sufficient frequency to warrant the distinction, and their interplay defines much that is most central to Salinger's fiction. The

Vulgarian, who carries the burden of squalor, stands for all that is crude, venal, self-absorbed, and sequacious in our culture. He has no access to knowledge or feeling or beauty, which makes him all the more invulnerable, and his relationship to the world is largely predicated by Buber's I-It dyad. He or she can be rich or poor: Evelyn Cooney in "Elaine," Mrs. Ford and the Croftses in "The Inverted Forest," Sandra and Mrs. Snell in "Down at the Dinghy," Joanie in "Pretty Mouth and Green My Eyes," The Matron of Honor in "Raise High the Roof Beam, Carpenter," Maurice, Stradlater, or any number of others in *The Catcher in the Rye*. These, in a sense, are Spiritual Tramps, as Seymour called his wife in "A Perfect Day for Banana Fish," though he might have better said it of her mother. The Outsider, on the other hand, carries the burden of love. The burden makes of him sometimes a victim, and sometimes a scapegoat saint. His life is like "a great inverted forest/with all foliage underground."[2] It is a quick, generous, and responsive life, somehow preserved against hardness and corruption, and always attempting to reach out from its isolation in accordance with Buber's I-Thou dyad. Often there is something in the situation of the Outsider to isolate him, to set him off, however slightly, from the rest of mankind. He might be a child or an adolescent, might wear glasses or appear disfigured, might be Jewish, though seldom is he as crippled or exotic as the characters of Capote and McCullers often are. His ultimate defense, as Rilke, to whom Salinger refers, put it, is defenselessness. Raymond Ford, Boo Boo Tannenbaum (Glass) and her son, Lionel, Seymour and other members of the Glass family, Holden and Phoebe, in the previous stories, are examples of that type.

The response of these outsiders and victims to the dull or angry world about them is not simply one of withdrawal: it often takes the form of a strange, quixotic gesture. The gesture, one feels sure, is the bright metaphor of Salinger's sensibility, the center from which meaning drives, and ultimately the reach of his commitment to past innocence and current guilt. It is a gesture at once of pure expression and of expectation, of protest and prayer, of aesthetic form and spiritual content—as Blackmur would say, it is behavior that sings. There is often something prodigal and spontaneous about it, something humorous or whimsical, something that disrupts our habits of gray acquiescence and revives our faith in the willingness of the human spirit. But above all, it gives of itself as only a *religious* gesture can. In another age, Cervantes endowed Don Quixote with the capacity to perform it, and so did Twain and Fitzgerald endow their best creations. For the gesture, after all, has an unmistakably American flourish. The quest of American adolescents, as we saw, has always been for an idea of truth. It is this very idea of truth that the quixotic gesture is constantly seeking to embody. The embodiment is style in action: the twist and tang, the stammering and improvisations, the glint and humor of Salinger's language. Hence the examples of the deserted husband who memorizes his wife's farewell note backwards, the woman who, out of pity, starts smacking her husband at the sight of any dead animal, the man about to commit suicide who makes up a story about banana fish for a little girl, the lover who calls the sprained ankle of his sweetheart Uncle Wiggily, the young man who insists on giving half a chicken sandwich to a stranger, the college girl who trains herself to pray incessantly and does so in the toilet of a restaurant, and the bridegroom who is too happy to appear at his wedding. Out of context these may well sound trite or crazy; in their proper place they are nodes of dramatic significance.

But gesture is language too. The quixotic gesture, the central dramatic metaphor, to which Salinger has committed himself defines the limits of his language and the forms his fiction takes. When the gesture aspires to pure religious expression—this is one pole—language reaches into silence. To a writer of

263

fiction, this is a holy dead end, much as the experiments of Mallarmé, say, impose a profane—that is, aesthetic—limit on the language of poetry. (One of "The Four Statements" of Zen, we recall, is: "No dependence upon words and letters.") When, on the other hand, the gesture reveals its purely satiric content—this is the other pole—language begins to lapse into sentimentality. This is the most persistent charge leveled against Salinger. Salinger's "sentimentality," however, is not obedient to the *New Yorker* doctrine of sardonic tenderness, which is really a way of grudging life emotions that the writer feigns to indulge. But if sentimentality means a response more generous than the situation seems objectively to warrant, then Salinger may choose to plead guilty. And he would be right to do so, for the spiritual facts of our situation invite us to reconceive our notions of dramatic objectivity, and the right kind of emotional excess, nowadays, can be as effective as the sharpest irony.

Between the poles of silence and sentiment, language reels and totters. Salinger's cumbersome experiments with character, tense, and point of view in his most recent stories betray his efforts to discover a language which can reconcile the worldless impulse of love to the discursive irony of squalor. In the past, while the quixotic gesture could still convey the force of his vision, reconciliation took the shape of the short story, that genre so richly exploited by the single lyric impulse seeking embodiment in dramatic form. But the quixotic motif seems no longer commensurate with the complex spiritual states by which Salinger has lately been possessed. Language must be refracted into its components—speech, letters, diaries, etc.— and the form of the short story itself must be broken and expanded into something that is neither a short story proper nor yet a novelette. In this development, the risks Salinger has taken with his art are contained in the risks he must take with his religious view of things.

II

In the two decades which constitute Salinger's professional career, he has published one novel, three novelettes, and some thirty short stories. This fair-sized body of work—fair-sized by contemporary standards but slim in comparison with the output of many earlier writers—may be classified into four "periods": the early tentative efforts, up to "The Inverted Forest," 1947; the fine stories which appeared in the *New Yorker* and were later included in the collection *Nine Stories*, 1953; *The Catcher in the Rye*, 1951; and finally the more recent narratives, beginning with "De Daumier-Smith's Blue Period," 1953, which express a new religious bent. Since the focus of our inquiry is the American novel, it is natural that the longer works of Salinger must receive our greatest attention. Salinger, however, is the kind of writer who returns to favored themes and characters with some consistency. *The Catcher in the Rye* was in fact developed from six earlier stories in which the two Caulfield brothers, Vincent and Holden, appear; and the central sibling relation between Holden and Phoebe is prefigured by the relation of Babe Gladwaller to his sister, Mattie. There is also the hope some critics entertain that the Glass family stories—all seven of them and perhaps more to come—will be some day transmuted by a miracle of chance or art into a novel. Finally, one must defer to the opinion Salinger expressed of himself, even though it was expressed in 1945: "I've been writing short stories since I was fifteen. I have trouble writing simply and naturally. . . . I am a dash man and not a miler, and it is probable that I will never write a novel."[3] It seems therefore an act of necessity rather than piety to consider Salinger's longer works in the light of his shorter pieces.

The earliest stories of Salinger appeared, for the most part, in magazines to which we refer as slicks, though four of these were also published in the now defunct *Story*. The majority of these pieces makes an uneasy lot, and some are downright embarrassing—it is gratifying to find that Salinger has excluded them all from his collection. One recalls Matthiessen's comment: "In the years just before, and now after, the war, there has been a special importance in the little magazine for the experimental writer who found that what he had to say did not fit in the mode of the slick magazines. . . . It was often an acute conflict between the outer and the inner, which came to expression not in a sustained form but in a short story."[4] Narratives like "Elaine" and "The Long Debut of Lois Taggett," which center on female protagonists and possess a certain quickness of perception which other stories of Salinger's early period lack, reflect the conflict of which Matthiessen speaks. More often the conflict is translated into the situation of wartime America—"The Last Day of the Last Furlough," "A Boy in France," "The Stranger," "The Hang of It," etc. But the war is treated blandly—there is nothing here comparable, say, to the urgency of John Horne Burns—and the form which the stories assume is only remotely experimental. What we do sense, however, is Salinger's awareness of *craft*, of a structure that owes much less to Kipling than to Lardner, who may have directed Salinger's interest in the first person point of view, the diary and letter devices, the uses of irony and slang. And we sense, too, the gradual assertion of a dramatic theme—the quixotic gesture, in "Soft-Boiled Sergeant," the predicament of the sensitive outsider in "The Varioni Brothers."

It is, of course, the outsider theme which figures largely in "The Inverted Forest," tagged by *Cosmopolitan* as a short novel. The piece is at best terrifying, at worst awkward, and its style vacillates between glamor and doom. The story unfolds ponderously; the introduction, midway, of a narrator who sees the action both in the first and third person seems like the intrusion of a Nick Carraway gone slightly schizophrenic. Yet the piece strikes with the impact of an old theme given a new

Freudian wrench. Raymond Ford, the poet genius, once under the domination of his unspeakably coarse mother, grows up only to throw over marital love and self-respect for a woman every bit as offensive as his parent. The Oedipal surrender is complete, the regression almost savage. But what Thomas Mann presented, in *Tonio Kröger*, as the metaphysical attraction of health and normality for the artist is here rendered as the pathological submission of the outsider to the vulgarian. The symbols of submission are Ford's renunciation of his glasses, the result of long, devoted study, and his practice of eye exercises to suit the taste of his mistress. Without love or irony, Ford bows to squalor.

The second phase of Salinger's career includes at least three stories which are among the very best he has written: "Uncle Wiggily in Connecticut," "Down at the Dinghy," and "For Esmé—With Love and Squalor." This phase also marks the level of his most sustained achievement. The cellophane transparency and geometric outlines of the earlier pieces give way to a constant energy of perception and irritation of the moral sense. Here, in a world which has forfeited its access to the simple truth, we are put on to the primary fact of mendacity. Here, where the sources of love are frozen and responsiveness can only survive in clownish attire, we are jolted by the Zen epigraph: "We know the sound of two hands clapping. But what is the sound of one hand clapping?" (Buber, who did much to introduce Zen to the West, suggests another parable of love: "There is no *I* taken in itself, but only the *I* of the primary word *I-Thou* and the *I* of the primary word *I-It*.")[5] Here, too, are three of the Glass stories.

In "A Perfect Day for Banana Fish," the taste of life's corruption is so strong in the mouth of Seymour Glass, and the burden of self-alienation, even from his wife, Muriel, is so heavy, that suicide seems to him the only cleansing act possible. While Muriel is engaged in a drab and vindictive long-distance conversation with her mother, for whom the mere name of a fashionable analyst is insurance against all the ills and mysteries of the universe, Seymour entertains a little girl at their hotel beach, whose foot he has just kissed:

> Sybil released her foot. "Did you read *Little Black Sambo?*" she said.
> "It's very funny you ask me that," he said. "It so happens I just finished reading it last night." He reached down and took Sybil's hands. "What did you think of it?" he asked her.
> "Did the tigers run all around that tree?"
> "I thought they'd never stop. I never saw so many tigers."
> "There were only six," Sybil said.
> "*Only* six!" said the young man. "Do you call that *only?*"
> "Do you like wax?" Sybil asked.
> "Do I like what?" asked the young man.
> "Wax."
> "Very much. Don't you?"
> Sybil nodded. "Do you like olives?" she asked.[6]

The contrast between the monstrous and psychotic Seymour, as seen by his mother-in-law—she is genuinely worried about her daughter—in the first half of the story, and Seymour with Sybil at the beach makes the silent ironic statement of the piece. Yet even Sybil cannot prevent the world, ruthless as it is with the power of spiritual vulgarity, from collecting its toll. One feels, however, that the story needs the background of the later Glass family narratives to give Seymour's suicide its full reference.

If Seymour Glass, like Raymond Ford, concedes the victory to the world much too easily, Walt Glass and Eloise, in "Uncle Wiggily . . . ," do not. The plight of Eloise, who survived the tender and imaginative Walt to lead a conventional married life in Connecticut, is clear. The hysteria of Eloise focuses on her lonely and sensitive daughter, Ramona, who *could* be the illegitimate child of Walt, and is certainly the living reminder of the vision Eloise has compromised and the innocence she has lost. Again the contrasts between the embittered and knowing Eloise and her inane visitor, Mary Jane, between Walt, the dead lover, and Lou, the oafish husband, serve to heighten the inability of the self to reveal itself to another. All that is left to Eloise by way of recognition is the spontaneous and quixotic gesture of kissing the glasses of Ramona, whom she has bullied into conformity and disillusionment. In another story, "The Laughing Man," the end of Innocence is more obviously compounded with the end to Romance, and the pressure of adult on boyhood disenchantment is rendered particularly effective by the use of a narrator who, like Lardner's narrators, serves to elicit from the situation more irony than they intend. The narrator recollects a crucial experience of his childhood in which the primary figures are John Gedsulski, nicknamed the Chief by the admiring boys who are his charges in the Commanche Club, and Mary Hudson, a girl from a more sophisticated background. The Chief tells the boys of the Commanche Club a serial and fantastic story about the Laughing Man, who is really an idealized projection of himself. When the love affair between John and Mary fails, the Laughing Man dies. Here the story of the fabulous Laughing Man is itself the quixotic gesture which has the power to influence the youthful audience of boys, including the narrator of Salinger's story, but is powerless to save Gedsulski himself.

Wistful as these stories may appear, Salinger's ideas of innocence and romance, of the urgency of truth and readiness of imagination, take on a broad social meaning. The stories present in poignant, ironic, and roundabout ways the radical absence of communion; they define the scope of our guilt. (It is this helpless sense of *shame* that pieces like "Just Before the War with the Eskimos" and "Pretty Mouth and Green My Eyes" dramatize so fastidiously.)

The easy efficient gestures of social amenities, which usually conceal an abyss of human failure, are not even present in "Down at the Dinghy." Quite simply, the story is that of sensitive, four-year-old Lionel Tannenbaum who hears the

269

housemaid, Sandra, denounce his father as a "big sloppy kike."
Lionel does not fully understand the opprobrium of the term,
but the tones and inflections of hate are unmistakable. He
runs away to hide his shame and fear in a dinghy, from which
his wise mother, née Boo Boo Glass, attempts to rescue him
back to a troubled world:

> "Well, that isn't too terrible," Boo Boo said, holding him
> between the two vises of her arms and legs. "That isn't the *worst*
> that could happen." She gently bit the rim of the boy's ear. "Do
> you know what a kike is, baby?"
> Lionel was either unwilling or unable to speak up at once. At
> any rate, he waited till the hiccupping aftermath of his tears had
> subsided a little. Then his answer was delivered, muffled but in-
> telligible, into the warmth of Boo Boo's neck. "It's one of those
> things that go up in the *air*," he said. "With *string* you hold."[7]

The ignorance of Lionel is as consonant with the immediate
requirements of the story as it is with Salinger's larger intentions. Here as elsewhere, what Salinger has undertaken to discover is that old, ironic discrepancy between illusion and reality.
But in an age of mass reactions and semantic instability, the
distance between illusion and reality must increase to the extent
that the opportunities of self-deception are multiplied. In these
circumstances, the child becomes both the dramatic analogue
and corrective to our modes of awareness, both the victim and
savior of our squalor. His lack of experience is at once parallel
and antithetical to our blind immersion in experience and his
natural sagacity is the corrective to our practiced insensibility.
It is much as if Salinger meant innocence to be, in our particular situation, the redemption of our ignorance. And it is
perhaps only by the grace of something like the tender play-
fulness which Boo Boo exhibits toward her outraged son that
we can recapture the sense of reality, beyond ignorance, beyond
innocence. We concede this ungrudgingly, and in conceding
still ask: is this all that so gifted an author can do with the
deep-down complexity of a Jew's fate in our culture?

The mode of irony, shield of Perseus against the Medusa face of our time, qualifies the elegiac motive of Salinger's stories. But even irony must exhaust its resources, and a time must come for love to show its face in the noonday light. To the unabashed lyricism of "For Esmé—With Love and Squalor," one can only respond joyously. The story is a modern epithalamium, written on the occasion of Esmé's wedding. The narrator, who carries his autobiographical burden sprightly and high, recollects the time he was a sergeant stationed with the invasion forces in England. On a rainy afternoon he wanders into a church, and is struck by the angelic voice of Esmé, a girl singing in a choir. Later he meets her, escorted by a governess and a younger brother, in a tearoom. She rescues him from boredom and loneliness by her wonderful gifts of pertness and sensibility —precocity, which is the concession adults make to the understanding of children, is not the point of the story. The young lady—for she has a title—promises to write him, and in return asks him to write for her a story of squalor. Sometime afterward, we see him at the front, in the third person, suffering from an acute case of battle fatigue. The intolerable Clay, an eternal vulgarian, is his only companion. Squalor, real and tangible like the dust of death, has settled all about him— until he finds a battered package from Esmé, in which she has quixotically enclosed her dead father's watch. The narrator can finally fall asleep, for he knows that hell, which Dostoyevsky defined as the suffering of being unable to love, has been kept in abeyance for another day. The inscription a German Nazi woman had scrawled on Goebbels' *Die Zeit ohne Beispiel*, "Dear God, life is hell," is superseded by the statement of Father Zossima which the narrator appends to it.[8] The horrendous social fact of our century and the outstanding spiritual motive of the age—genocide and love—are united in the history of a single American soldier, Staff Sergeant X. Thus the style of personal encounter in the first half of the story redeems the waste and anonymity of the second half. Thus may love overreach squalor as only love can, and the sound of two hands clapping may be heard the world around.

III

The Catcher in the Rye inevitably stands out as Salinger's only novel to date. As a "neo-picaresque," the book shows itself to be concerned far less with the education or initiation of an adolescent than with a dramatic exposure of the manner in which ideals are denied access to our lives and of the modes which mendacity assumes in our urban culture. The moving, even stabbing, qualities of the novel derive, to some extent, from Salinger's refusal to adopt a satirical stance. The work, instead, confirms the saving grace of vulnerability; its protest, debunking, and indictments presuppose a willing responsiveness on the part of its hero.

On the surface, Holden Caulfield is Salinger's typical quixotic hero in search, once again, of the simple truth. Actually, Holden is in flight from mendacity rather than in search of truth, and his sensitivity to the failures of the world is compounded with his self-disgust. In comparison with his dear, dead brother, Allie, a kind of redheaded saint who united intelligence and compassion as no other member of the family could, setting for all a standard of performance which they try to recapture, Holden seems intolerant, perhaps even harsh. The controlling mood of the novel—and it is so consistent as to be a principle of unity—is one of acute depression always on the point of breaking loose. But despair and depression are kept, throughout, in check by Holden's remarkable lack of self-interest, a quality of self-heedlessness which is nearly saintly, and by his capacity to invoke his adolescent imagination, to "horse around," when he is most likely to go to pot. These contrary pressures keep the actions of the novel in tension and keep the theme of sentimental disenchantment on the stretch; and they are sustained by a style of versatile humor.

272

The action begins at a prep school from which Holden has flunked out, and continues in various parts of Manhattan; it covers some three days of the Christmas season. The big city, decked out in holiday splendor and gaudiness, is nevertheless unprepared for Holden's naked vision, and it seldom yields any occasions of peace, charity, or even genuine merriment. From the moment Holden leaves Pencey behind, leaves its Stradlaters and Ackleys, its oafs, creeps, and hypocrites, and dons his red hunting cap—why not, it's a mad world, isn't it? —we know that we are on to an adventure of pure self-expression, if not self-discovery.

In New York, it is once again the same story of creeps and hypocrites revealed in larger perspective. We hardly need to recapitulate the crowded incidents of the novel to see that Holden is motivated by a compelling desire to commune and communicate, a desire constantly thwarted by the phoniness, indifference, and vulgarity that surround him. He resents the conditions which force upon him the burden of rejection. In protest against these conditions, he has devised a curious game of play-acting, of harmless and gratuitous lying, which is his way of coming to terms with a blistered sensibility, and of affirming his values of truth and imagination. But above all, he is continually performing the quixotic gesture. Thus he socks Stradlater, who is twice his weight, because he suspects the latter of having seduced Jean Gallagher, without any consideration of the fact that she is the kind of girl to keep all her kings, at checkers, in the back row. He gives money away to nuns. He can read a child's notebook all day and night. He furiously rubs out obscenities from the walls of schools. And when Phoebe asks him very seriously what he would like to be, he muses on Robert Burns's song, "If a body meet a body coming through the rye," which he had heard a kid hum in the street, and answers back: ". . . I keep picturing all these kids playing some game in this big field of rye and all. Thousands of little kids, and nobody's around—nobody big, I mean

273

—except me. And I'm standing on the edge of some crazy cliff. . . . That's all I'd do all day. I'd just be the catcher in the rye and all. I know it's crazy. . . ."⁹

A closer look at *The Catcher in the Rye* might allow us to separate its real from imaginary failings. Mr. Aldridge, for instance, taking his cue perhaps from Phoebe's comment to her brother, "You don't like *any*thing that's happening," has recently observed—Maxwell Geismar makes exactly the same point—that Holden "has objects for his contempt but no objects other than his sister for his love."¹⁰ It is true that Holden has *more* objects for his contempt than his love—this is the expense of his idealism and the price of his rebellion. But it is impossible to overlook his various degrees of affection for Allie, his dead brother, for James Castle, the boy who was killed because he wouldn't retract a statement he thought true, for the kettle drummer at Radio City, the nuns at the lunch counter, the kid humming the title song, or even the ducks in the park, without missing something of Holden's principal commitments. And his answer to Phoebe, "People never think anything is anything *really*. I'm getting goddam sick of it," may do for those who find these commitments rather slim.¹¹ Nor can we disallow the feeling of pity which often modifies Holden's scorn, his pity for Ackley and the girls in the Lavender Room, or his confession to Antolini that he can hate people only part of the time, and that he quickly misses those whom he may have once hated. Holden, of course, is not in the least cynical; nor is he blind except to part of the truth which he can otherwise entertain so steadily. Still, there are those who feel that the novel accords no recognition to its hero, and that it fails to enlist our sense of tragedy. The lack of recognition, the avoidance of conversion and initiation, is almost as inherent in the structure of the novel as it is consonant with the bias of the American novel of adolescence. The action of the book is recollected by Holden who is out West recuperating from his illness, and Holden only chooses to tell us "about this

madman stuff that happened to me around last Christmas"—
nothing more.[12] He refuses to relate incidents to his past or
to his character, and he refuses to draw any conclusions from
his experience: "If you want to know the truth, I don't *know*
what I think about it. . . . About all I know is, I sort of *miss*
everybody I told about. Even old Stradlater and Ackley, for
instance. . . . Don't ever tell anybody anything. If you do, you
start missing everybody."[13] This is an embarrassed testament
of love, full of unresolved ambiguities, the only lyrical and
undramatic recognition the novel can afford. The partial blind-
ness of Holden, which has been correctly attributed to Holden's
juvenile impatience with the reality of compromise, is made
more serious by Salinger's failure to modify Holden's point of
view by any other. In *Joseph Andrews*, for instance, the innocence of Adams is constantly criticized by the tone of the book
and the nature of its comic incidents. There is also some danger
that we may be too easily disarmed by the confessional candor
of Salinger's novel. When Holden says time and time again,
"I swear to God I'm crazy," the danger is equally great in taking
Holden at his word as in totally discounting his claim. Holden
does succeed in making us perceive that the world is crazy, but
his vision is also a function of his own adolescent instability,
and the vision, we must admit, is more narrow and biased than
that of Huck Finn, Parson Adams, or Don Quixote. It is this
narrowness that limits the comic effects of the work. Funny it
is without any doubt, and in a fashion that has been long
absent from American fiction. But we must recall that true
comedy is informed by the spirit of compromise, not intransigence. Huck Finn and Augie March are both, in this sense,
closer to the assumptions of comedy than Holden Caulfield.
This once understood, we can see how *The Catcher in the Rye*
is *both* a funny and terrifying work—traditional distinctions of
modes have broken down in our time—a work full of pathos
in the original sense of the word. But suffering is a subjective
thing, and the novel's sly insistence on suffering makes it a

more subjective work than the two novels which relate the adventures of Huck Finn and Augie March. Adventure is precisely what Holden does not endure; his sallies into the world are feigned; his sacrificial burden, carried with whimsey and sardonic defiance, determines his fate. The fate is that of the American rebel-victim.

IV

The view that Salinger's most recent work predicts something of a new trend is vaguely supported by the troubled, spiritualistic bent which the latest six narratives share. The content of these stories invites some comparison with the ideals of Mahayana Buddhism and primitive Christianity, and also invites the condemnation of those who feel that "mysticism" is out of place in literature. The trend, nevertheless, is a natural outcome of Salinger's earlier interests. For it is not difficult to imagine how protestant disaffiliation may lead to holy unattachment, and how mysticism may appear, beyond childhood or adolescence, the last resort of innocence. If love is to survive in a world where personal communication has signally failed, then it can at least survive in universal compassion: love betrayed into dumbness may still speak in silence. Such an argument, however, makes the best of a dubious case. All writers may not succeed, like Carlyle, in extolling the virtue of silence through twenty volumes. And one suspects that Chekhov spoke for all artists when he said that he who doesn't desire anything, doesn't hope for anything, and isn't afraid of anything cannot be an artist.

It is perhaps as impertinent to inquire into Salinger's personal convictions as it is profitless to reconsider, at this time, the relation between literature and beliefs. The pointed references to Buddhism which he has recently made are best viewed in a more general way. Two of the cardinal assumptions in Salinger's work find expression in the Buddhist ideas of *tanha*, or blind self-demandingness, and of *moksha*, a state of liberation achieved by the kind of impersonal compassion which "The Parable of the Mustard Seed" exemplifies. In Mahayana Buddhism particularly, a religion of the Middle Way which avoids the excesses of worldliness and asceticism, the characters of Salinger seem to find a gentle and practical ideal against which their actions may be gauged. The ideal is matter-of-fact rather than mystical, and its emphasis in the Zen Buddhist variant, to which Salinger refers most directly, is on effortless and continuous love, on the superrational insights of the Koan exercises, on the poetic concreteness of Haiku, on the virtues of silence, and on the unmediated vision of nature. For Zen is essentially a condition of being in which, without losing our identity, we are at one with the universe, and it requires, as does Haiku poetry, a certain harmony between our imaginative and spiritual responsiveness to all things. It becomes evident that these qualities of Zen define some of the interests which Salinger has constantly kept at heart, and that Zen itself, in Salinger's work, makes up to an odd way of criticizing contemporary failures. As William Barrett has observed in his introduction to the writings of D. T. Suzuki, the Radical Intuitionism of Zen may allow the West to experience its own opposite at a critical stage of its moral, scientific, and historical development. "In this new climate," Barrett continues, "a concern with something like Zen Buddhism can no longer be taxed as idle exoticism, for it has to do with the practical daily bread of the spirit."[14]

Art, unfortunately, sometimes falls short of the best spiritual intentions. This is evident in the two narratives which usher Salinger's "religious phase" in. "Teddy," the story of the strange boy who believes in Vedantic incarnation and detachment, and who vaguely foresees his death, is much less satisfactory because it draws on notions that are alien to the West than because it fails to relate, within the dramatic structure of its narrative, the egoism of Teddy's parents and the ambiguous malice of his sister to the peculiar source of his own repose. There is also in "Teddy," and much more in "De Daumier-Smith's Blue Period," an uneasy juxtaposition of aesthetic and spiritual motives which are sometimes blurred and sometimes too simply resolved. In the latter story, the central character recollects, in manhood, the guiding revelation of his adolescence. On the surface, the revelation takes a quasi-mystical form. De Daumier-Smith discovers that art is less important than the sacramental view of life, which can itself transform, better than the creative imagination, the objects of ugliness and misery—the enameled urinals and bedpans of an orthopedic appliance shop—into "a shimmering field of exquisite, twice-blessed enamel flowers."[15] But as Gwynn and Blotner have argued in their pamphlet on Salinger, a sexual element enters into the story—witness the imagery —and brings to a religious situation the Oedipal complications of a young art instructor in love with a nun whose drawings— and only the drawings—he has seen.[16] The piece serves to remind us that the power of sexuality is never directly acknowledged in Salinger's work, and that love, when it is not refined into a transcendent or artistic ideal, centers on relations from which sex is notably absent: the love of a woman for a dead sweetheart or a boy for his little sister, or the Glasses for one another.

The exasperating Glass family does indeed provide Salinger with the means to exploit the nonsexual forms of love. One is never quite sure whether the intensely spiritual web of relations they weave around one another betokens an incestuous or narcissistic motive—it is as if the same tortured ego were seeking to express itself in seven fractured Glass images. Of this we can be more sure: that in their separateness and cunning identity the Glasses tell us far more about the darkness of love and self-hate than about the conditions of an urban Jewish family in mid-century America. Wise, talented, and quixotic as they all seem—their common background is defined not so much by a Jewish father and Irish mother as by the radio program which used to be called "It's a Wise Child"—they all deny themselves sexual preoccupations to lose themselves into an imaginative or altruistic ideal—Boo Boo is a Tuckahoe home-maker, Buddy a writer, Zooey an actor, Waker a monk, Seymour and Franny "mystics" of a kind.

In "Franny," Salinger succeeds far better in rendering the *experience* of Smith's conclusion: "Everybody is a nun." The story reveals the lacerated bonds between human beings when the intellect is proud and the self insatiate, and it hints at the availability of mercy. The surface is that of the bright, sophisticated expectancy of a college week end; the anguish is underneath. Almost entirely in dialogue, the narrative develops the rising antagonism between Lane, a somewhat cerebral college jerk, and his intuitive girl friend, Franny, the youngest and most engaging of the Glasses. The clarity and hysteria of Franny—she is capable of withering rejoinders—derive from her aversion to the egomaniac principle in her environment more than the possibility, vaguely and ambiguously hinted at, that she may be illicitly pregnant. "Everything everybody does," she exclaims helplessly, "is so—I don't know—not *wrong*, or even mean, or even stupid necessarily. But just so tiny and meaningless and—sad-making."[17] Like Holden Caulfield she is committed to intransigence; and it is characteristic that she can only practice her devotions—the incessant prayers of the Starets and Nembutsu Buddhists—in the seclusion of a lavatory, huddled in a foetal position, a work of mysticism clasped to her heart. And it is characteristic, too, that Franny's desire to burst the ego's shell does not confine itself to the action of an adolescent who, for the first time, reaches out beyond himself in sexual love.

Less perfect, perhaps, but certainly more ambitious in its formal intentions—this is the beginning of Salinger's parenthetical and digestive dialogue with himself—"Raise High the Roof Beam, Carpenter," takes us a step further in the Glass history. In Seymour Glass, the fictional descendant of Babe Gladwaller, Raymond Ford, and Vincent Caulfield, Salinger has no doubt created his fullest intelligence; in the story of his wedding and the record of his buried life Salinger has exercised his powers of spiritual severity and formal resourcefulness to their limit; and it is indicative of Salinger's recent predicament that in the story the powers of spirit overreach the resources of form. The ideas of normality and alienation, of imperviousness and vulnerability, of assertiveness and responsiveness, of squalid purpose and lovely inutility, of irreverent prejudice and holy indiscrimination are all released within an unwieldy frame of three concentric references. In the middle there are the actual characters, all strangers, crowded into a limousine on their way from a wedding which Seymour, the bridegroom, was "too happy" to attend, preferring later to elope with the bride. There is the formidable and indignant Matron of Honor, a "one-woman mob," raging away at the absent bridegroom; there is the narrator, Budd Glass, taking refuge in anonymity till the burden becomes intolerable; there is the quaint, tiny relative of the bride, steeped in the saving silence of his deaf-muteness; and there are other marginal characters which every society includes. But around this inhuman collocation of human beings press the organized forms of sentiment, cant, and even hate which crush Seymour's quixotic gesture before it can ever translate itself into meaning—note the gaudy wedding, the vicious rumors about Seymour's homosexuality or his brutality to Charlotte Mayhew, the obstructions of a street parade, and the very climate of the war which Salinger is anxious to preserve by referring often to the "crapulous" year of 1942. Between the private and the public response, between the impulse of love and the communal realization of it, language has traditionally acted as mediator. But it is Salinger's most final comment on our situation that language, in all its gradations, cannot fully redeem the tragic unavailability of the self. "It was a day, God knows, not only of rampant signs and symbols but of wildly extensive communication via the written word," Budd says ironically.[18] Thus the coarseness of the Matron's speech, the letters of Boo Boo or the Sapphic nuptial benediction she scrawls on the bathroom mirror, the diary of Seymour that Budd reads, again, in the bathroom, and even the eternal silence of the bride's relative, fall short of the spirit's ultimate intentions. In the end, it is only the holy indiscrimination of love that can be of any avail. "Followed purely," Seymour notes in his diary, "it's the way of Tao, and undoubtedly the highest way. But for a discriminating man to achieve this, it would mean that he would have to dispossess himself of poetry, go *beyond* poetry."[19] In the earlier stories Salinger had concerned himself with the *gesture* that is prior to poetry; in his latest work he is seeking, beyond poetry, beyond all speech, the *act* which makes communion possible. As action may turn to silence, so may satire turn to praise.

Praise is precisely what finally takes the place of satire in "Zooey." The novelette reverts to Franny's state of nausea with the world, and ends, via the action of Seymour on Zooey and Zooey on Franny, with her reconciliation to it. The story is narrated by Buddy Glass, official biographer of the family, who comes more and more to assume the persona of Salinger.

Buddy begins by confessing that his narrative is not a story at all but a "sort of prose home movie"; and in the process relieves himself of certain autobiographical remarks which identify him, in an arch and sophisticated way, with Salinger. But this tricky point of view is no sooner established than dropped; the rest of the story is told in the third person. The prologue ends, the curtain goes up on the Glass apartment in New York, and we see Zooey, the youngest brother, a beautiful and talented TV actor, sitting in a bathtub and reading a four-year-old letter of Buddy's who is now simply another invisible party in the play. By this device, the absent characters (Seymour, Buddy) and those present (Bessie, Zooey, Franny) are caught somewhat uneasily in a common perspective. The story continues in a witty dialogue of doting brutality, between Zooey and Bessie in the bathroom, between Zooey and Franny in her bedroom.

In the foreground of the action is Zooey who intercedes between Franny—she has gone on a hunger strike as the result of her religious crisis—and a bowl of chicken soup her earth-bound mother humbly wants to offer. Zooey's real purpose, however, is to mediate between Franny and the two elder brothers, Seymour and Buddy, who have acted as the spiritual conscience of the family, turning it, by their high and holy standards, as Zooey angrily feels, into freaks. The Four Great Vows on which the family is brought up read: "However innumerable beings are, I vow to save them; however inexhaustible the passions are, I vow to extinguish them; however immeasurable the Dharmas are, I vow to master them; however incomparable the Buddha-truth is, I vow to attain it." To which Zooey adds, "Yay, team. I know I can do it. Just put me in, coach."[20] Zooey's compulsive wit, it becomes clear, questions the workaday wisdom of Bessie, the arrogant idealism of Franny, and even the saintliness of the dead Seymour. He is in fact the most qualified member of the family to understand and rebuke his youngest sister because, like her, he holds in horror everything "campusy and phony," because, despite himself, he is forever sitting in judgment on his fellow men. (Does not this exaggerated terror of sham betray the self-hate men harbor for themselves?) When Franny objects to the tendency in our society to turn everything—knowledge, art, love—into "negotiable treasure," Zooey retorts that her own incessant use of the Jesus Prayer may not entirely escape the same stricture. He takes her to task for secretly preferring the engaging personality of St. Francis to the virile character of Jesus: "I *don't* see how you can go ahead with the Jesus Prayer till you know who's who and what's what. . . . You're constitutionally unable to love or understand any son of God who throws tables around. And you're constitutionally unable to love or understand any son of God who says that a human being, *any* human being . . . is more valuable to God than any soft, helpless Easter chick." And again: "You keep talking about *ego*. My God, it would take Christ himself to decide what's ego and what isn't. This is God's universe, buddy, not yours. . . ."[21] Man's duty in this life cannot be easily repealed by piety or continuous prayer. Franny's "tenth-rate" religious breakdown comes to an end when, after a phone conversation in which Zooey pretends unsuccessfully to be Buddy, she realizes that desirelessness is the heart of prayer, and understands that Seymour's ubiquitous Fat Lady, the eternal vulgarian, is Christ himself.

This is high praise of life. It is the sound of humility, calling us to *this* world. The vulgarian and the outsider are reconciled, not in the momentary flash of a quixotic gesture, nor even in the exclusive heart of a mystical revelation, but in the constancy of love. Franny's room, cluttered to the ceiling with bric-a-brac, full of things perishable and enduring, profane and holy, betokens that mixed, quotidian quality of grace which is perhaps the only quality grace can assume in our world. We cannot but feel that in this novelette Salinger has come close to realizing the full contradictions of his vision. If these contradictions seem to be still unexorcised, it is because the form of the novelette—its internal shifts and spurts—does not appear entirely conscious of its purpose. The improvised "home prose movie" ticks on in the dark.

The steady concerns of Salinger in the last decade came to an unhappy focus in "Seymour: An Introduction," which a good many readers hope may also prove to be Seymour's sprawling epitaph. The novelette starts with quotations from Kafka and Kierkegaard which proclaim the author's "steadfast love" for his fictional creations and apologize for his inability to do them full justice. But what starts as an effort on the part of Buddy Glass to appease once again the impossible ghost of his brother in a labor of love and art, turns out to be a monstrous amalgam of parenthetical remarks, a sermon in the form of description, a polemic autobiographical tract. The voice behind the piece is not entirely Buddy's nor exactly that of Salinger himself; it is a voice that can sound alternately rasping and contentious, engaging and coy; and it is one of the peculiarities of its tone that the reader sometimes gains the distinct impression he is being told to stop reading the author, to stop *bothering* him, since the author has nothing really to say. Prolixity born of irrelevance may be still another form of silence, it seems.

There is much in the piece to compound our discomfort. The autobiographical references to the reception of "Teddy," or the widespread rumor that Salinger had entered a Buddhist monastery—there is a variant which puts him in a mental institution —or to the speculations concerning the identity of Holden and Seymour seem more peevish than sly. Nor do the tirades, however justified, against critics, psychoanalysts, pedants, existentialists, and cultists of Zen appear convincing. Salinger returns to the satirical stance—indeed, he never found the way to escape it completely—but in making his exposé through a voice so uncomfortably close to his own, he is actually saying, rather disingenuously, what he only feigns to be saying as a character in a work of fiction. On the whole, we are made too keenly aware that Salinger has permitted his consciousness of rumor and his awareness of a specific audience—his "fair-weather friends," as he genially calls them—to dictate to his art. The artist's material should have proved a better dictator.

Having said this, one should add that Salinger's awareness of his audience, to which the singular qualities of his reticence and popularity have contributed, translates itself into a significant, dramatic theme: the Poet in American Society. Art and Sickness, we know, have been allied for some time in the popular imagination, but the Sick Poet, as Buddy argues, is also a Seer, and the Seer, like Seymour (See-More), is a man who in penetrating the substance of life suffers through his *eyes*. The gift of true vision requires more than artifice. Buddy puts it thus: "I say that the true artist-seer, the heavenly fool who can and does produce beauty, is mainly dazzled to death by his own scruples, the blinding shapes and colors of his own sacred human conscience."[22] True vision, we see, requires holiness; the artist is a saintly fool. In taking upon himself the burden of holiness, the artist also develops an attitude of holy indifference to his audience. Seymour's Chinese and Japanese poetry— Haikus and "double" Haikus—may not take its place in the American pantheon for decades to come. But this is immaterial. As Seymour reveals to Buddy during a game of marbles, the great Zen Master Archers are those who teach us not to aim at the target. Straining for aim is an invitation to chance; our willful involvement with ends blinds us to the means. And indeed, how can there be any goals to existence if, as Seymour maintains, "all we do our whole lives is go from one little piece of Holy Ground to the next." "Is he *never* wrong?" Buddy asks.[23]

The novella does not add much to our knowledge of Seymour as a character. The endless supercilious descriptions of his hair, ears, nose, eyes, etc., the scattered bouquets of parenthetical anecdotes concerning his behavior, do not finally amount to a credible dramatic image of an incredible genius—saint, poet, linguist, athlete, mentor, and Big Brother all in one. The piece, however, does show Seymour to be not only a *mukta*, a God-knower and ring-ding enlightened man, but also the infallible spiritual center of the Glass clan. Inbred in a common history of Fancies, the Glasses seem capable of looking outward beyond their bright familial circle only through the eyes of their dead brother who constantly mediates between their inner world and a world they find hard to endure. Because they are his brothers—"I can't be my brother's brother for nothing," Buddy exclaims—they are brothers to everyone.[24] And because they give themselves wholly to his imagination, they become part of all that his imagination commands. Intricately attuned and calibrated, they communicate with one another, past death itself, by letters, diaries, phone conversations, and a dialogue of deceptive simplicity. But their highest hope is to make language perform the impossible: to make it carry the full burden of love for which their family narcissism is only a guise. Seymour shoulders this burden. Scapegoat to vulgarians, the Seer is still to freaks a redeemer.

V

"It is the duty of the man of letters to supervise the culture of language, to which the rest of culture is subordinate," Allen Tate has said, "and to warn us when our language is ceasing to forward the ends proper to man. The end of social man is communion in time through love, which is beyond time."[25] The style J. D. Salinger has created shows clearly what human ends may be considered proper, and it carries its own warnings about the ways language may come to fail man. Beneath the tingling surface, the constant play of humor and perception, the ebullience of emotions, which are all part of Salinger's generosity, there always lurks the sad reality of human failure; and it is much as if the responsiveness, both spiritual and imaginative, of Salinger's language is constantly trying not only to reveal but also to expiate the burden of these failures.

Thus whimsey and humor, when they are not simply forms of facetiousness, prove themselves to be quixotic modes of communion or understanding. Vincent Caulfield, for instance, hits it off immediately with little Mattie Gladwaller when he says to her: "If A has three apples, and B leaves at three o'clock, how long will it take C to row five thousand miles upstream, bounded on the north by Chile?"[26] Seymour's funny comments on banana fish or Walt's quip about Uncle Wiggily—this is a standard Glass technique—are likewise little testaments of love. There are times, however, when Salinger's wit, itself a form of satiric awareness, seems more biting and hyperbolic—Franny describes a Bennington-Sarah Lawrence type of girl by saying that she "looked like she'd spent the whole train ride in the john, sculpting or painting or something, or as though she had a leotard under her dress."[27] The source of humor can also be found in the intimate and disconcerting gesture which reveals actor to witness, and witness to reader, in a peculiar light—Howie Croft suddenly takes the shoulder pads out of his coat, in the middle of a delicate conversation with Corinne, and Spencer picks his nose, making out "like he was only pinching it," while doling out advice to Holden Caulfield. But of the different kinds of humor Salinger uses, humor of contrast and situation, of action and characterization, of sudden perception and verbal formulation—Salinger seems to be fond of strung expressions like "the God-and-Walter Winchell section of the Stork Club"—of all these it may be said that their ultimate function is to sharpen our sense of the radical discrepancy between what is and what ought to be.[28]

The discrepancy is apparent in the verbal nature of his style which itself attempts to convey the difficulty of communication between human beings. Adolescents as well as adults are constantly groping for the life-giving Word. Their recourse to such expressions as "Oh, I don't know," and "You know what I mean," to oaths and obscenities, to trailing, fragmentary speeches and fierce emphases on neutral syllables, to solecisms, repetitions, clichés, and asides, betrays both the urgency of their need and the compulsion to save their utterances from the fate of mere ejaculation.

Even the structure of Salinger's stories—the obsessive use of first person narration or intimate dialogue, of epistolary and diary techniques, of the confessional tone—even the structure calls our attention to the tight, lucent caul from which the captive self seldom escapes. It is not accidental that the recording consciousness of the later stories, Buddy Glass, describes himself as "the odd man out," or that so many crucial experiences seem to take place within the tiled sanctum of the Glass bathrooms. The rambling, ranting, devotional forms of these narratives equally deny the classic precepts of the short story and the well-made novelette. As Buddy puts it, the short story form eats up fat little undetached writers like him whole. This is quite in keeping with Salinger's purpose, which is to discover the form of confession and communion, the way the self can be made available to another, the point at which the irrelevant fact and transcendental idea silently meet. The purpose is not easy to achieve. Two warring impulses of the soul distend the shape of Salinger's most recent fiction: one cries in outrage at a world dominated by sham and spiritual vulgarity, the other knows, as Seymour did, that Christ ordered us to call no man a Fool. Revulsion and holiness make up the rack on which Salinger's art still twitches.

In retrospect, the artistic identity of Salinger, which also may be called his limitation, appears clear enough. Despite his striking gifts for dialogue—Salinger had once expressed the hope of becoming a playwright—the broad sense of dramatic participation is lacking in his fiction. The lack is not occasioned by the refusal of Salinger's characters to engage reality; rather is it occasioned by their insistence to engage no more of reality than they can ultimately criticize. Their access to social facts remains limited. And their very identity, their recurrent types and their intransigence toward experience, often admits to their vision—and to ours, since no other vision qualifies theirs—such extremes of corruption and innocence as make the complex entanglements of life beyond their reach. Then, too, the cult they make of vulnerability, of amateurism in life, which is the very opposite of Hemingway's cult of professionalism, diffuses the pressure of Salinger's insight onto a rather thin surface. The quixotic gesture—Seymour searching for God by poking his finger into ashtrays—is made to carry a heavier burden of meaning than it can sustain. Love averts itself easily in whimsey or laughter. The highest candor requires us to praise things by adjectives no more complex than the word "nice."

288

But from the early search for innocence to the later testament of love, from the slick adequacy of his earlier style to the tense lyrical form of his later, if not latest, stories, Salinger has kept faith with the redeeming powers of outrage and compassion. His faith in these has not always allowed him to reconcile their shifting focus or to create the forms of dramatic permanence. When reconciliation is granted, when the rare, quixotic gesture, striking through, becomes the form of fiction, incarnate and ineluctable, we see Salinger at last for what he is: an American poet, his thin and intelligent face all but lost among the countless faces of the modern city, his vision, forever lonely and responsive, troubled by the dream of innocence and riddled by the presence both of love and of squalor. What saves Salinger's vision from sentimentality is the knowledge that no man can give an object more tenderness than God accords to it. His heroes, children, adolescents, or adult victims to the affluence of their own spirit, play upon our nostalgia for a mythic American past. They also manage to raise nostalgia to the condition of hope.

CHAPTER 11

SAUL BELLOW:

THE QUEST AND AFFIRMATION OF REALITY

"No doubt the world is entirely an imaginary
world, but it is only once removed from the true world."
ISAAC B. SINGER, *Gimpel the Fool*

I

SINCE the appearance of *The Adventures of Augie March* in 1953, the reputation of Saul Bellow no longer depends on the favors of the cognoscenti. His career is now a matter of public acclaim. We rejoice in him as a writer of the mind; a social critic who weathered the Depression years without benefit of dogma; a Jewish author who succeeds, as few others do, in defining what Fiedler called "the need of the Jew in America to make clear his relationship to that country in terms of belonging or protest"; a Chicagoan, free-style and city-bred, uninhibited by the naturalistic legacy Chicagoans risk to inherit.[1] We rejoice and are right to do so; for Bellow is both in a new and old-fashioned sense a sustained fantasist of the real.

This is a large order. Reality nowadays borrows the disguises of chaos, and the most significant contemporary facts still elude the full grasp of our imagination. It is as Bellow himself remarked, "People do not appear to respond as they once did to the various faces of reality. Innumerable things intervene to cloud or modify reactions."[2] Fact and fiction move to a grotesque corroboree; and some even think our dance to be the dance of death. Possibly so; but we are meanwhile free to note that Bellow's intuitions of reality have the authority of the

290

classic European novel behind them—the speculative earthiness
of Cervantes, the social scope of Balzac, the spiritual leanness
of Dostoyevsky—and possess at the same time a quality of hope
which we recognize as peculiarly American. What, then, does
the spirit of hope discover when it encounters the stubborn
modalities of our being?

The discovery of reality, in the end, is the discovery of the
limits we willfully impose on the real. Human knowledge is
always embarrassed by the presence of life. The sense of cosmic
wonder Bellow preserves through his novels lightens the solemnity of the spiritual quest his heroes undertake. The quest is
presumably for freedom, for knowledge, for love. This is old
hat. But true seekers, Bellow shows, never know where their
quest will come to rest. Freedom, knowledge, and love are
merely versions of the real; they give the quest its form without
determining its end. What we do recognize, in the *end*, is that
reality eludes the versions we make of it, eludes and transcends
them. What remains when all our seeking is done amounts to
this: the inestimable gift of awareness, of life willing and overreaching itself. An axiomatic statement beyond which the heroes
of Bellow cannot go.

It is true that Bellow's heroes finally learn to humble themselves before experience. But if they end with humility, they
begin in humiliation. They sink first to their knees by sullen
choice and sink again at last because they must. They cultivate
anger in perversity, suspicion and petulance in the spirit of
hope. The bilious or quixotic gesture saves them from a Pru-
frockian fate of genteel cynicism. Freedom is the provisional
goal of their quest, but freedom forces upon them a knowledge
of the self they did not bargain for, and self-knowledge discloses
to them a world intelligible only in love. The notion of love
is one that Bellow develops more acutely with each successive
work. Mediated constantly by the full play of reality, as it is
not, say, in Salinger's fiction, love entails on the part of the
hero an attitude of joyful acceptance; it answers the ego's need

291

for harmony, not sacrifice. The attitude is most engagingly, most accurately, expressed by Gimpel the Fool in a story Bellow translated from the Yiddish of Singer. It is no wonder that the earlier hero-victims of Bellow, detached, analytical, surly, give way to characters like Augie and Henderson who find their prototypes in the Jewish *schlimazl* and philosophical buffoon, the grieving, bouncing children of fate born under a lucky but crooked star.

Stars twinkle on the hero's birth but it is only in science fiction that quests are pursued in a void. Novels require a social atmosphere of some density. Bellow's novels richly evoke our cultural scene, convey its density, and penetrate it; in each work the narrative structure unites, with varying degrees of success, the philosophic and worldly purport of the hero's passion. The force of Bellow's worldly perceptions derives to some extent from the predicament of the contemporary writer in America, from the fact that his feelings must run counter to the general direction his culture has taken, and from his continuing awareness, as Bellow noted, that any "connection between art and authority has for some time been broken." The most affirmative of our novelists, *because* he is a novelist, must also dissent: "We must perfect ourselves, we must exhaust ourselves. Maybe, too, there is a perverse desire for freedom in this. Dominated by no single activity, we are free; free but not tranquil; at leisure but not idle, since all the while we strive for perfection. . . . By so doing we deny the power of death over us because as long as we're getting better there's no reason why we should die."[3]

The fetid distillation of our dream of perfection is nowhere more evident than in our great urban centers. Here the energy and despair, the softness and ferocity of American life, are projected in a thousand grotesque forms; here man and the civilization he has devised are prematurely on trial. In New York, the hero of *Seize the Day* feels the agonizing necessity "to translate and translate, explain and explain, back and forth, and it was the punishment of Hell itself not to understand or be understood, not to know the crazy from the sane, the wise from the fools, the young from the old or the sick from the well."[4] It is not on the high seas, on rolling plain or in wooded vale, that Bellow's American Adam is prepared to receive illumination. It is rather on Broadway: "The gassy air was almost motionless under the leaden spokes of sunlight, and sawdust footprints lay about the doorways of butcher shops and fruit stores. And the great, great crowd, the inexhaustible current of millions of every race and kind pouring out. . . ."[5]

The common element in this gigantic cauldron of illusions is not only the shiny white face of a movie star who smiles or cries to make a million others smile or cry with him. It is also—and Bellow persuades us of this in a hundred direct and oblique ways—*money*. Money, too, may be an arch illusion. If so, it is an illusion that assumes countless forms, and translates itself into our most secret wish. The conflict of class, the tensions of race, the tacit discriminations of power respond, each in its way, to the magic touch of gold; and so do love, freedom, and knowledge. This is not to say that Bellow, Midas-like, reduces everything to gold. What he attempts to show, as a character in his story, "A Father-to-Be," puts it, is that "money surrounds you in life as the earth does in death. Superimposition is the universal law. Who is free?"[6] The theme is picked up again and again, in the stories, in the novels. A Negro in "Looking for Mr. Green" exclaims, "That's the only sunbeams, money"; and the hero of a one-act play, "The Wrecker"—a piece, incidentally, which reveals a finer understanding of feminine psychology than most of Bellow's novels do—gives a symbolic focus to his whole life by turning down a money bonus.[7] If money is equated with any one thing in Bellow's fiction, it is with death, which is itself protean.

Bellow's concern with issues of social gravity does not put him, as Maxwell Geismar feels, in the ranks of "social realists" like Dreiser, Farrell, or Algren. By the accidents of age and environment—Bellow was born of Russian immigrants in 1915 and grew up in Chicago—his experience of the Depression might have been acute. The style and sensibility of his finished work, however, prove that he never surrendered to the "leftist" school of writing. His treatment of the Jew, compared to the pallid caricatures Irwin Shaw and Herman Wouk choose to draw, reveals once again how far the pieties of liberalism and doctrines of orthodoxy fall short of his intent. In one of those periodic symposia Jewish intellectuals use to examine their conscience, Bellow remarked, "For us the pain of Shylock may be greater than for others because we are Jews, but it has fundamentally the same meaning" we discover in the pain of Job or Lear.[8] This is a position that has not endeared Bellow to all our critics, but it is one that guarantees a more vital awareness of the contradictions which must inform morality when social order and metaphysical vision are caught in a single dramatic perspective.

II

Bellow's first novel, *Dangling Man*, 1944, owes more to the example of Kafka than Dreiser. Its awareness of things is acutely contemporary: hungry, bitterly ironic, introspective. The world it depicts is one in which man, seeking freedom, must finally deny it; in which the humanistic dictum "tout comprendre, c'est tout pardonner" is made unintelligible by the alliance of metaphysical absurdity with social regimentation; in which the flayed moral sense can only express itself by futile or nasty gestures.

It is these gestures, always unpleasant—there is no more adequate word for them—that redeem Joseph from the impotence to which he is prey: they are the weak, scratchy tokens of his rage. Joseph—he has no paternity beyond his crisis and no other name—seems a curious combination of Oblomov and Musil's Man Without Qualities, Hamlet and Prufrock, Kafka's

K. and Dostoyevsky's Man from Underground, the hero crippled and spiteful. He sits in his room awaiting the day's minor crises while his wife, Iva, earns their living. He considers himself a moral casualty of a war which denies him the possibilities both of freedom and commitment, a man condemned by a condemned age.

The plot is skeletal and simple; it reveals to us no experience we find hard to share. After giving up his job in a travel bureau, Joseph settles back to await his draft number. Ostensibly, he is at work, amidst the general madness, on the reasonable philosophers of the Enlightenment. Actually, he is taking a crack at *freedom,* the freedom to *be,* to *understand,* to disengage himself successfully from all that is conditioned. But nothing comes of it. Or rather, everything comes contrary to his expectations. His apparent disponibility serves only to accentuate his guilt, doubt, anxiety—what can be done with freedom? He snaps at friends, quarrels with relatives, clams up on his wife. Their affluence or apathy rattles him continually; their very presence forces him to admit that he is really of *their* world. A close friend of his renegade Communist days cuts him dead in the street. A party to which he goes seems to him, compared with the sacred Eleusinian rites of old, a travesty of human intercourse, a spectacle of everything "nasty, brutish, and short." And a Christmas dinner at the house of his wealthy brother, Amos, ends a vicious hassle with his snobbish teen-age niece —who physically resembles him! Everyone, he thinks, fails him; he is quite alone. And indeed Joseph is; for the questions to which he has addressed himself, counter to the rules of the game we play in culture, can only sharpen his solitude. Through his failures we begin to see the greater failures of his milieu. Irony and criticism involve both the hero and his world, and are rendered concurrently in spiritual and social terms.

Joseph claims, with the acrid naïveté which is the basis of his character, that his primary concern is to discover how a good man should live. The quest, no doubt, requires suffering and alienation. But Joseph also knows, by listening to Haydn, that he is "still an apprentice in suffering and humiliation," and he knows, too, that alienation is "a fool's plea," for the world lies within us.[9] How, then, does grace finally manifest itself to the weak? It is in keeping with the bold, bleak vision of this novel —in keeping with the destructive lucidity of intelligence with which Bellow begins his career as a novelist and which he gradually loses—that no spry or inspirational answer is proffered. Certainly Art, with all letters capitalized, can provide no substitute for the good life. After talking to John Pearl, the ivory tower artist, Joseph puts down in his diary: "Is there some sort of personal effort I can substitute for the imagination?"[10] (In this respect Joseph is not unlike Salinger's later heroes for whom saintliness comes before art.) We are not surprised; for Joseph has too much of a conscience, is always holding court on himself, and the ubiquitous nightmare of the war or the sight of a man sprawling in the street can prevent him from celebrating his wedding anniversary. Nor do his tortured debates with the Spirit of Alternatives—the spirit of unchosen choices —resolve his metaphysical doubts. Death, he agrees with Goethe, is the abolition of choices, but the greatest cruelty is life in death, the curtailment of choices while life, somehow, still persists. This is the meaning of the Dangling Man, the man who has no status in existence because his true self is governed not by Choice but Chance. The random and the inevitable act, pure Chance and pure Necessity, are alike in that they both cripple the will to be oneself. They limit freedom which is the end, as Joseph thinks, of all human striving, good and bad. But, paradoxical as it may seem, the difficulties of attaining freedom are the difficulties of transcending the narrow circle of personal fears and desires by which we are identified. "We are all drawn to the same craters of the spirit," Joseph meditates, "to know what we are and what we are for, to know our purpose, to seek grace. And, if the quest is the same, the differences in our personal histories, which hitherto meant so much to us, become of minor importance."[11] In this crucial statement, Joseph reveals the primary spiritual tension in Bellow's work: the tension between freedom and reconciliation, the first a personal and limited thing, the other, though individual still, attuned to the deeper harmonies of existence.

The spiritual action of the book engages the concrete social realities of the moment. To begin with, Joseph is a Jew, and a city Jew. He manifests certain qualities of abrasive intelligence, a knowledge of—even an urge for—suffering and humiliation, and an attitude toward enforced social norms, of which the war is a major symbol, that are relevant to his particular situation. Furthermore, his ambivalence toward friends and relatives within a recognizable ethnic community underscores the failure of family and tradition to provide an adequate buffer against the contemporary forces of chaos. Joseph is also an ex-Communist, a living testimony, that is, to the failure of another kind of ideology. This does not compel him, however, to deny his social conscience. Without resorting to the antics of the disabused Communist or the pieties of the sentimental liberal, he casts a cold eye on a culture debauched by its peculiar notions of affluence. Standing between the dead-beat Alf, and the arrogantly successful Abt, Joseph is subverted by his awareness of poverty and failure. As he puts it, the fear of lagging pursues and maddens us. It does more: by holding continually before us the promise of unlimited worldly rewards, it actively thwarts our quest for any other end. There is, for Joseph at least, no escape from the persuasions of society:

Great pressure is brought to bear to make us undervalue ourselves. On the other hand, civilization teaches that each of us is an inestimable prize. There are, then, these two preparations: one for life and the other for death. Therefore we value and are ashamed to value ourselves, are hard-boiled. . . . Who can be the earnest huntsman of himself when he knows he is in turn a quarry? Or nothing so distinctive as quarry, but one of a shoal, driven towards the weirs.[12]

There is no more illuminating statement on the predicament of the individual, and therefore of the fictional hero, in our time. The surrender of Joseph, his admission that he *needs* the leash, is inevitable; it takes the ironic form of an urgent note to his draft board, begging to be called up. "I had not done well alone," he writes at the end of this bitter experiment. "I doubted whether anyone could. To be pushed upon oneself entirely put the very facts of simple existence in doubt. Perhaps the war could teach me, by violence, what I had been unable to learn during those months in the room. . . . The next move was the world's."[13]

Dangling Man is a tight, speculative, and penetrating novel which nevertheless fails to find a sustaining form. The structure is not without interest, is vaguely avant-garde: it is the record of a spiritual defeat in diary form, written with an admixture of quotidian drabness and intensity. The style reflects the tedium and despair, the slovenliness and showy humiliations of Joseph's life, and reflects them often in sordid images—spilled orange juice or a half-plucked chicken in the sink. But the colorless style and rancid manner of confession, though apparently suited to the mood of the novel, insulate it from the currents of reality; they predetermine our attitude to the material and allow no contrary influence, no enriching substance, to enter in. This is another way of saying that the "objectivity" of the diary device is perhaps too obviously feigned, that Joseph does not remove himself sufficiently from authorial control to enlist our genuine sympathies. Joseph, unlike the heroes of Kafka, say, remains too much the puppet all the way around; his vitality as a *fictional* character is low. The brilliant inventiveness of Bellow is still muted here, and the vigor of his imagination exhibits itself mainly in a dance of ideas— though there are contradictions on the point of Personal Destiny he has not seen fit to purge—in grim irony, skull-like laughter, Mephistophelian comedy. Everyone and everything in the novel contains an element of the grim fantastic. Turned inward upon itself and thinly dramatic, the novel still leaves the ineradicable impression of a man who screams out in laughter to see his guts dangling from his belly.

III

In Bellow's first novel, the war, adroitly removed to a distance from the action, becomes both the cause and effect of moral detritus and personal defeat. Caught in its ugly toils, Joseph can only choose to be a victim rather than a beneficiary. In Bellow's second novel, *The Victim*, 1947, the focus of disorder is anti-Semitism; the quest is for self-knowledge rather than freedom. Anti-Semitism no doubt belongs to the pathology of culture. The disease, however, happens also to define a classic symptom of the human condition: the endless terrors of self-justification, darkness seeking light and light relapsing into darkness, a nightmare of ambiguities. Bellow sees the symptoms clearly, and treats the disease with a grotesque humor, for what indeed could be "funnier" than the monstrous mummery of guilt?

Defense and accusation, action and consequence make up the crazy, relentless dialogue of the novel. The narrative spins giddily around two characters, Asa Leventhal and Kirby Allbee, antagonists who turn out to be alter egos in the same bitter farce. Leventhal is the Jew, a burly, impassive, solitary man sprung from a background of tragedy—his mother dies insane in an asylum—failure, and erratic luck. He has, like Joseph, the gift of a dour, quarrelsome sensitivity, a measure of violence and self-pity, tenderness and strength—his natural tendency is to feel persecuted, a man bearing the world's weight, one who wrests a modest triumph against great odds. Allbee is the anti-Semite, a suffering and insufferable creep, endowed, at times, with an insane lucidity of perception. He appears from nowhere, down-and-out, to accuse Leventhal of having contrived his ruin in revenge for an anti-Semitic remark Allbee once made at a party. He blames Leventhal for all his ills, from the death of his wife to his inability to find employment, haunts Leventhal in parks and restaurants, and moves into his apartment where he finally attempts suicide. The two men are locked in a death struggle for the impossible meaning of innocence, for their own and each other's soul. On trial here are not only Jew and Gentile, but Man. It is a trial that can have no witnesses: Leventhal's wife, Mary, is away visiting her mother, his brother Max deserts his own family to work in a Texas shipyard, and his Jewish city friends come and go, bringing with them the irritations of easy counsel. Actually, most of the characters in the book are caught, like the two principal figures, in a conspiracy of parallel and ironic actions.

The first and most obvious irony of the novel is that Allbee, the Gentile, poses as the aggrieved party, the "victim." So long as Leventhal insists on his innocence—and it is with great subtlety that the ambiguous nature of his guilt is gradually unfolded—so long he remains wide of self-knowledge. But it is as Allbee says, " 'Know thyself'! Everybody knows but nobody wants to admit."[14] Only when Leventhal stops feeling wronged by this mad and repulsive intruder, only when he begins to see in Allbee an example of misery and desperation greater than his own, does he begin to admit. He, at least, had been able to "get away with it," to beat life's rap. Should he be forced then to become his brother's keeper? And how much may a man give of himself in a universe of "hot stars and cold hearts?" The answer to prevarication is this: " 'Why pick on me? I didn't set this up any more than you did.' Admittedly, there was a wrong, a general wrong. Allbee, on the other hand, came along and said, '*You!*' "[15]

But ironies beget ironies. Leventhal cannot easily rise to the spiritual exigencies of the situation because, as a Jew, he has been turned against himself: he has, that is, unconsciously surrendered to the anti-Semitic view of Jews. That he has an exacerbated sense of his Jewish destiny is evident not only in his inflamed conversations with Allbee but also in his talks with friends, Harkavy and Schlossberg, about Disraeli. Outrage against immemorial wrongs blends into the perverse *need* to be wronged; the rebel-victim seeks vindication in the same attitudes that perpetuate his agony. This is as true of Leventhal as it is of his unholy double, Allbee. But malice turned against the self can also turn outward. The paranoiac tendencies of Leventhal threaten to aggravate the domestic troubles of Max, who is married to a devout Italian Catholic; the errors of his partial judgments—the guilt, for instance, he feels at the death of his young nephew—penetrate into the lives of people he loves. Leventhal withers into the truth slowly: the old Christian truth —another irony still—that the power of love exceeds the requirements of justice.

Racial prejudice carries only part of the novel's meaning; its practical correlative is status. Raised in the school of hard knocks, Leventhal naturally feels resentful. Yet he shares the idea of success—that American compulsion to flash and excel —imposed by a society to which he must remain, in some ways, an outsider. Nor is success in America what it used to be. As Allbee puts it, "The day of succeeding by your own efforts is past. Now it's all blind movement, vast movement, and the individual is shuttled back and forth."[16] As personal effort comes to mean less in the contemporary world, group opinion comes to mean more and the confrontation of the victim with his oppressor becomes farce or phantasmagory. This is the situation of Leventhal and Allbee, both of whom assent to the rule of money, though they have both known failure, *because* they have known it. In this climate of unacknowledged opinion, the final crime is not the murder of a fellow man but the contrivance of his ruin. And indeed the symbolic equation of death and money is everywhere implied—in Harkavy's indictment of life insurance, in Allbee's feeling that his poverty and lost status are due to some kind of Hebraic retribution, something like the terrible darkness brought down by Moses on the Egyptians.

301

As the old aristocracy of America, which could claim—like Allbee!—descent from Governor Winthrop, breaks up and loses its economic grip on the country, wild accusations of class murder become as integral a part of the social process as the redistribution of wealth or power.

In the brilliant conception of this novel, reversal follows close on reversal. The final irony is the identification of the two antagonists with one another. For Leventhal not only submits to the spell of Allbee; he stands up for him in public and saves his life in private. His very fury when Allbee carries on a sordid affair with a woman in Leventhal's own apartment is the fury of a man who recognizes what *he* might have done in the absence of his wife. The identification, the marriage of opposites, is managed by Bellow with great tact. It is rendered physically in the weird sensation of a moment: Leventhal looking at Allbee's back in the zoo and experiencing the other's presence as one experiences one's own. It is suggested in the aftermath of dreams. Waking up from one of these dreams with a great sense of release, Leventhal thinks: "Admittedly, like others, he had been in the wrong. . . . Everybody committed errors and offences. But it was supremely plain to him that everything, everything without exception, took place as if within a single soul or person."[17] By coming to terms with his guilt, our hero discovers his identity, and discovering it he must relinquish it again to the common soul of human kind. Is this not love?

The ending of the novel is suspended as the ending of *Crime and Punishment*, say, must be. After seeing through Allbee a vision of "horror, evil, all that he had kept himself from," Leventhal goes back to a better life, a wiser and sadder man perhaps, certainly more affable and reconciled—which is exactly how Allbee turns out to be when they both meet in a theatre many years after. The defeat of *Dangling Man* gives way to the quiet stalemate of *The Victim*; the most affirmative note in the book is sounded by a minor character, old Schlossberg:

"If a human life is a great thing to me, it *is* a great thing. Do you know better? I'm entitled as much as you. And why be measly? Do you have to be? Is somebody holding you by the neck? Have dignity, you understand me? Choose dignity. Nobody knows enough to turn it down."[18]

Technically, too, the novel marks an advance over its predecessor. The grim comedy of humiliation, the terrible mockery of guilt, the absurdity of evil, the senselessness of sudden dread, the drabness of the spirit's sleep come alive in scene after scene, and the style acquires a certain concreteness of detail absent from the earlier novel. There is no doubt, however, that the novel tends to shuffle and drag, and that the ludicrous, nightmarish encounters with Allbee are so often repeated in the same key that they lose much of their intensity. Furthermore, Allbee as a figure tends to waver uneasily between a fictional character and thematic symbol. The details of his unprepossessing physique as of his wretched mental life are convincing enough, but the uncanny relevance of all his speeches forces upon him a different and symbolic presence, that of Mephisto perhaps, or the Darker Double. Even here, it seems, the energy of Bellow's mind overreaches his growing dramatic powers, and his creations remain somewhat in the shadowy realm between the "ideal" figures of Kafka and "real" characters of Dostoyevsky. This peculiar quality of Bellow's earlier work once again reminds us of the assumptions of romance as a form of fiction, albeit a kind of romance so ironic and intellectual as to bear greater resemblance to the European allegories of our time than to those fabulous evocations dear to the American imagination.

IV

It is not unfair to say that in his first two novels Bellow had not yet discovered the dramatic equivalent of *joy*. His heroes sweat continually, suffer from nausea and headaches, and their crotchety imagination broods on a spectacle of unrelieved moral sordor. They are heirs to a metaphysical drabness, their power, at best, is a pained, blistered power. The change to *The Adventures of Augie March*, 1953, seems therefore wondrous and staggering, so much so that critics whose pride is their sophistication must contrive to see in this trend-busting novel a subtle elaboration of Bellow's earlier concerns. Insofar as the concerns of this novel are still with personal character, social environment, and human destiny, the critics are no doubt right.

The character of Augie March is not merely the thread on which, picaresque fashion, the gay beads of events are strung; it is a character that directs these events. When Heraclitus says, and Augie concurs, that a man's character is his fate, he means that character is the *given* part of our nature and, also, that what we have been given determines what we are likely to hold and *receive*. Augie's character is a paradox. He seems at times too vague and easily diverted, a creature who shines only in the reflected light of others and is defined particularly by the affectionate glances of all the women he attracts. His brother Simon feels that Augie's wheels turn too freely, that he is hasty and too enthusiastic, "in few words, something of a *schlemiel*."[19] But Einhorn discerns early in the book the more essential quality of Augie. He says to him, "You've got *opposition* in you. You don't slide through everything. You just make it look so"; and Augie concurs: "I did have opposition in me, and great desire to offer resistance and to say 'No!' "[20] Augie does say No repeatedly, to the aggressive Simon, who wants to make a worldly success of him, to the Renlings, owners of a posh Evanston store, who want to adopt him, to the rich, intense Thea Fenchel, who wants to mold him to her idea of ruthless perfection. And yet Augie remains open to the highest bid of freedom and call of experience. His school is the world —later on, when he steals books to attend the University of Chicago for a time, he rejects academic knowledge as presenting too short a cut "from the brute creation to the sublime mind."[21] The incredible variety of jobs he holds, the motley company among whom he moves and odd influences to which he consents, do for him what the Hundred Great Books could never be expected to do. Schooled to the toughness of the world, he still retains a gift of vision, something like Gatsby's willingness of the heart: "If you want to pick your own ideal creature in the mirror coastal air and sharp leaves of ancient perfections and be at home where a great mankind was at home, I've never seen any reason why not."[22] It is this accountable dreaminess that sustains Augie through experiences that might have soured a stronger man in times of special disfigurement and "world-wide Babylonishness." The disposition of Augie is toward a kind of reserved and humane optimism—he wants, as Clem Tambow tells him, that there should be Man. Such faith does not prevent him, when he is thrown unjustly into a Pennsylvania clink, from realizing that "there is a darkness. It is for everyone. You don't . . . try it, one foot into it like a barbershop 'September Morn.' "[23] It does prompt him, however, to stand up against the scathing Mimi Villar for a high opinion of life, in whose name he tries to dissuade her from committing an abortion. Augie, we see, entertains a radical generosity toward the gratuities and gratuitousness of life, and yearns, somewhat indolently, for a "proud, independent fate," a "worthwhile fate." Hence his conception of himself as a "servant of love," a neophyte, that is, in the luminous mystery of acceptance. And hence, too, his instinctive desire to remain always in touch with the "axial lines" of existence: "Truth, love, peace, bounty, usefulness, harmony!"[24]

There is no doubt that the impact of the novel derives from its range of social perceptions. (Bellow's teeming images of our cultural life *specify*; they do not, like the images of Dreiser, say, or like those of Farrell, attempt to *determine*.) The social perceptions of the book find their centers within three widening circles of reference: the Jewish family, the big city, the spirit of American culture at mid-century. These, after all, make up the world in which Augie grows to his particular destiny.

The first impression we receive of the Marches is that of a broken-up family, a family still homeless in America—or perhaps homeless *because* in America. The father deserts his family and remains out of the picture; the "grandmother," the mother, and Augie's idiot brother, George, have to be put in special homes for the aged and retarded; and Simon, like Augie, goes his separate way. Augie confesses: "My own parents were not much to me, though I cared for my mother," and dreams repeatedly, in typical picaro, foundling fashion—for the picaro is a child of fate—of an illustrious father who will someday claim him for his own.[25] Grandma Lausch, from Odessa, who "played like Timur, whether chess or klabyasch," tells him, "If Kreindl's son can be a dentist, you can be governor of Illinois."[26] It is as if America, by promising to each a proud and independent fate, could play father to all the world's orphans. The orphanage is the city which gives concrete forms to the rootlessness peculiar to American life. Raised in a tough Polish neighborhood, Augie learns quickly—and this saves him later disillusionments—facts about which the Statue of Liberty is usually silent. What impresses us most, however, is not the denial of brotherhood, the crime and misery in Chicago slums, but rather the ability of the city, in its great, grim, pulsing motion, to transform death into life and life into death, so that Simon could still rise to be a latter-day baron full of power and darkness, and Augie attain to his particular state. Chicago may inspire no childhood memories of Sicilian pastoral "silken, unconscious, nature-painted times"; its "deep-city vexations" are all the Eden Augie recalls. Yet where but in Chicago or New York do petty thieves and readers of Spengler mix so freely and Einhorns or Mintouchians become the inspired mentors of youth? Augie raises at one point the question whether cities can exist without a civilization, since civilizations have never sprung without cities, and answers: "No, but it is not

possible, and the dreary begets its own fire. . . ."[27] And indeed
the civilization of cities is to a large extent the civilization of
mid-century America, where the fee of a dog's membership
in a club exceeds the amount Augie pays to keep his mother
in a home for the aged, and girls like Thea keep their money
in refrigerators. The old forms and conventions are exhausted,
Einhorn never tires of saying, and each grabs for himself as
best he can. Yet it is not the grabbiness of people that strikes
us in the novel; it is rather the abstract power of money, which
everywhere cuts across love, family, happiness, self-respect. In
a culture of abundance—the Depression notwithstanding—one
must either serve luxury or possess it. The dreams of the French
Revolution have been finally realized in the New World. Robey
stutters to Augie: "B-bread's almost free now in America.
What'll hap-happen when the struggle for bread is o-o. . . .
Will goods free man or enslave him?"[28] Serious misgivings,
these, and misgivings Bellow neither tries to shrug off nor
attempts to sentimentalize with indignation. His indignation
laughs, as does his hero, a "Columbus of those near-at-hand,"
who knows that though Columbus was sent back in chains,
and may have thought of himself as a flop in the bargain, it
all didn't "prove that there was no America."[29]

The last remark makes a sudden jab at the greater issues of
our historical destiny, and is but another instance of the pressure
Bellow constantly applies on character, action, and social comment to create new meanings. The coherence of these meanings
is what we call the world of the novel, and the first thing we
notice about that world is the leeway it provides for human
error. Free to err, the characters are also free to share in their
common humanity. Augie is first to admit that in any true
life one must be exposed outside the small circle that encompasses two or three heads in the same history of love. But
this too is love: the responsiveness to experience, the acceptance
of man. It is in the name of love, the affirmative capability,
that Augie refuses to believe we are living at the tail-end of

history, to believe that compared with the ancients—he himself does not hesitate to compare Einhorn with laureled caesars dead and gone—we are a fallen and dwarfed race. "How is it," he asks looking at Thea's eagle, "that human beings will submit to the gyps of previous history while mere creatures look with their original eyes?"[30] Accepting the claims of history as of nature to the full, he sees the freshness and fluidity of life in the possession of a bright moment. And why not? Everything lives in the face of its negative, and reality has no truck with the schemes which, in the arrogance of our discontent, we impose on it. As a realist, Augie accepts; as a dreamer who knows that human life is intolerable without some way of mediating its finitude, he advocates love. Yet the final note of the novel is not one of love, or freedom, or even endurance. The final note is sounded by the Norman maid, Jacqueline, and it is a note of *laughter*! Hence Augie's closing meditation: ". . . thinking of Jacqueline and Mexico, I got to grinning again. That's the *animal ridens* in me, the laughing creature, forever rising up. What's so laughable, that a Jacqueline, for instance, as hard used as that by rough forces, will still refuse to lead a disappointed life? Or is the laugh at nature. . . ? Nah, nah! I think. . . . But that probably is the joke, on one or the other, and laughing is an enigma that includes both."[31]

The high aim of comedy is to assimilate the contradictions of reality. This is what Bellow manages to do in the best scenes of the novel where thought and character are dramatized in the process of a single symbolic action. The Mexican episode, which marks a turning point in Augie's career, is in this connection particularly relevant. Augie, we remember, goes to Central America with Thea—they are passionately in love—to hunt giant lizards with an eagle she had desperately trained. The episode is not exotic: it stands in a meaningful and symbolic contrast to the teeming scenes of Chicago life. The atmosphere evokes obsidian knives and cruel Aztec rituals, a sky hard and blue, nature in the raw, death. Thea wants everything sharp and extreme, to the point of inhumanity; she passionately believes in the ferocity of nature. Augie humanizes everything and seems, in contrast to her deep-water nature, a creature "sculling a shallow bay." When the eagle turns out to be a craven bird, the rage of Thea is boundless. But Augie takes the eagle's side, for he sees that wild nature is also cowardly—humanity is mixed in it! He will have nothing to do with Thea's guns and cameras, her snakes and iguanas. What, then, Augie asks himself, is he doing in breeches and campaign hat down in Mexico? Augie could honestly say Love, but he is even more honest to admit, Money! For the latter, even though it may not unlock the secret of all our actions, remains "beside the secret, as the secret's relative, or associate or representative before the people."[32] Love, at any rate, does not last between them; their conception of it is too different. For Thea love is a preparation to a more exalted state; for him it is a worthy end. For Thea reality is something created in the burning depths of being. On reality Augie has this to say: "Everyone tries to create a world he can live in, and what he can't use he often can't see. But the real world is already created, and if your fabrication doesn't correspond, then even if you feel noble and insist on there being something better than what people call reality, that better something needn't try to exceed what, in its actuality, since we know it so little, may be very surprising."[33] Within the compass of a single action, we see, Bellow brings to life the ideas of love and death, illusion and reality, city and nature, social power and individual freedom. The encounter between two lovers transforms abstractions into felt experience.

Transformation, however, occurs more often on the level of style which has, alas, more admirers than the book itself can claim. Yet the style is far from blameless. It is ebullient, carnal, omnivorous; it bristles with neologisms, crackles with wit and references and asides. Its jostling compounds parallel the loose-strung structure of the narrative and testify to its guiding vision, and its mixture of racy lingoes—Polish, Yiddish, Midwestern, Underworld—celebrates the generosities of American life. The most striking instances of Bellow's writing are often the opening paragraphs of each chapter, which, read in succession, give some idea of the novel's pitch and motion. At its true best, the style circles round the ragged edge of poetry, refracting a thousand gay and broken lights. But it can also be turgid, obscure, knotted-up in philosophic ambiguities and Gordian syntax. Its major fault, however, is not that it seems too artless-cunning—Bellow likes, for instance, to begin his sentences with a preposition, a conjunction, or pronoun. The fault, which lies deeper in the structure of the novel, is that the style has to counteract the simplicity inherent in Augie's point of view. This is a criticism that warrants some elaboration.

The Adventures of Augie March is written in the first person; the voice we hear is Augie's, and the vision with which we see things is to a very great extent his own. But the comic flaw of the hero, by his own admission, is simplicity, enthusiasm. This is a classic picaresque trait, from Don Quixote to Parson Adams. Bellow's design, however, is ambitious, and his problem is to qualify the enforced simplicities of Augie's view with a more critical, a more ambiguous, vision which encompasses the whole action. The spirit of comedy, which is known to deflate all things but the true objects of excellence, is harbored by the style. Augie speaks, but as he speaks Bellow perceives and criticizes, too. The voice is Augie's, the style Bellow's, and it is the disparity between what Augie *can* see and Bellow *must* render that forces the style of the novel so heavily upon our attention.

This predicament of style reflects itself in some concrete ways. In a novel so large and rough-grained, there are things style cannot be expected to do alone. It cannot, for instance, convince us of Einhorn's greatness; in the end, we simply have to take Augie's word for it. Marvelously attuned to the resiliencies of experience, the style cannot make the sorrows of

Augie authentic as his joys—one is left with the impression that Augie's griefs are simply ballast to his nature. Nor does it finally persuade us that Augie *deserves* to be so generously sponsored by life. These are basic matters of dramatic vision and structure which Bellow, swinging as he does abruptly from early nausea to subsequent joy, must still resolve.

We have said that *The Adventures of Augie March* is a trend-busting book. We should add that it is a trend-making book in the great tradition of American novels. By reopening the form of the novel to the blatancy of American experience, it not only sets an example to writers who have surrendered their art to Jamesian refinements or Jungian archetypes, but also reaffirms the possibilities of *experience* itself at a time when the individual finds it easier to shrink in terror from the world he confronts. And yet if *Augie March* is a story of initiation, it is a story that, American style, can have no proper ending. Augie remains, like Huck, uncommitted, suspended, as it were, between native innocence and hard-earned knowledge, poised for the next adventure which, though it may not actually repeat a former escapade, guarantees no final knowledge or repose. Augie is no victim, and a rebel only in the most circumstantial way, but he no more belongs to the established forms of American life about him than Huck or Holden or Holly did.

V

In Bellow's work the quest for freedom is always qualified by the deeper need for reconciliation. The tension between these two elements is nowhere better realized than in *Seize the Day*, 1956, Bellow's only novelette to date and possibly his finest work. Tommy Wilhelm and Augie March, as we come quickly to perceive, are both children of fate. The life of one is ruled by error and ill-fortune as the other's is ruled by luck and grace. Both commit errors, but the difference, which is again the difference between the tragic and comic grammar of destiny, is that while the errors of Tommy *define* his situation those of Augie simply multiply his choices. The true difference between success and failure in our midst, how-ever, remains inscrutable as grace. This, at least, is what we are apt to feel when we move from *Augie March* to *Seize the Day*, a work that adumbrates those destructive elements of American culture which Augie managed to escape.

When we see Wilhelm he is already in his middle forties, an established failure in the business as in the private world, and the pattern of his past errors had worked itself out. His early "career" in Hollywood, for which he gives up college, culminates after seven years in a job as a movie extra. More recently, the company for which he works as a sales manager eases him out before he attains executive status. Separated from his wife, Margaret, and their two children, he is nevertheless bled re-morselessly by her constant demands. And his bland, egotistic father, once a distinguished physician, asks only that he be allowed to enjoy his retirement in affluent peace. The drama of the story derives from the close, ugly duel between father and son. At stake in this combat are the ideas of different generations on success, love, human dignity. The father's idea is generally one of self-sufficiency, stiff-backed and aggressive, an idea identified with a vanishing era of entrepreneurism. The son presents an image of candid failure, dependency, will-ing self-humiliation. Wilhelm may indulge himself in more self-pity than Dr. Adler would ever allow himself, but he is also far less selfish and hypocritical; he does not try to dodge the draft as his father recommends nor does he attempt to disguise his weaknesses behind a front of unctuous pride. But the contrast between the two men, between the two generations —terms like "inner" and "other-directed," "Protestant" and "Social" ethic come readily to mind—is best exemplified by the attitude each betrays toward his family. To the gelid courtesy, which masks a real indifference, Dr. Adler exhibits toward his son and daughter, Wilhelm manifests an agonized concern for his own children. Agonized, accountable, humiliated, begging often but never quite crawling, Wilhelm finally emerges as the kind of figure who gives to words like mercy and love a peculiar resonance.

The irony of the novella, of course, is that the only person to whom Wilhelm can turn in the great city is Dr. Tamkin, a charlatan and swindler, a combination healer, inventor, and sage. Tamkin manages to deprive Wilhelm of his last dollars on the stock market, but before vanishing from the scene, he leaves behind him strange words full of fakery and wisdom. It is a further irony that in Wilhelm's peculiar distress, separated as he is from father and child and wife, from society itself, since he has neither job nor money, Tamkin's rodomontades become part of a truer vision. Compelled all his life to make errors—and his errors are really gestures of hope, flickerings of innocence—and to suffer punishment, Wilhelm can find no past or future key to his existence. Comes Tamkin and says, "The real universe. That's the present moment. The past is no good to us. The future is full of anxiety. Only the present is real—the here—and now. Seize the day."[34] For Wilhelm, this is the beginning of an attitude which, however disingenuously it may have been presented by Tamkin, focuses human energy neither on the memory of failure nor on the presentiment of death, but on that intensity of perception, akin to love, which has the power to redeem past and future alike. For this quality of perception self-knowledge is required, and it is again behind Tamkin's rhetoric that Wilhelm finds the clue to his identity concealed. There are always two souls, Tamkin argues, the true and pretender soul. The pretender-soul is full of the world's vanity and uses altruism, even love, as a foil to its own insatiable egotism: "The interest of the pretender-soul is the same as the interest of the social life, the social mechanism."[35] Meanwhile, the true soul pays the price, suffers and becomes sick in its solitude, knowing that though its prime function must always be to love, the pretender-soul, of all things, is the most unlovable. Hence love turns into hate, and suicide becomes murder—we kill the enemy within. Reflecting on this, Wilhelm admits that he too has been party to this deadly game, that his pretender-soul must be the one called Tommy, the name he took out in Hollywood, and that Wilky, as his father insists on calling him, might not even be his true self: "Might the name of his true soul be the one by which his old grandfather had called him—Velvel?"[36] In this inner perspective, the fact of failure ceases to be a personal thing, and death itself no longer seems the final degradation, the apotheosis of all human errors. The climax of the novel comes when Wilhelm, feeling the full force of his predicament—when the lonely person begins to feel like an animal, and howls from his window like a wolf—stumbles into a funeral parlor. Earlier, we know, he had received an intimation of the meaning of love in an underground corridor off Times Square, a place dark and disfigured by desperate signs, echoing with a babel of broken voices and lurid human desires: "He was imperfect and disfigured himself, but what difference did that make if he was united with them by this blaze of love?"[37] But the vision of love is consummated only in the presence of the corpse he sees in the funeral parlor, a body composed and serene which could have been that of his father, but which in this particular moment of terrible illumination strikes Wilhelm as the body of Man himself, of Wilhelm or Wilhelm's children, the body of all desires composed by human mortality. The "great knot of ill and grief" in Wilhelm's throat bursts and he cries uncontrollably, but it is not, as some critics crassly believe, tears of self-pity he sheds. They are tears of piercing insight and release, a shuddering music: "He heard it and sank deeper than sorrow, and by the way that can only be found through the midst of sorrow, through torn sobs and cries, he found the secret consummation of his heart's ultimate need."[38]

The high solemn note on which the work ends gives us pause, and pausing we begin to wonder how Bellow, after all, brought us to face these ultimate verities. For the novelette starts by formulating the problem of success in America in worldly terms, continues to explore the predicament of Wilhelm in the light of the manners and morals of his particular milieu, and suddenly, as it were, resolves the question by rising to a more exalted level of perception. The difficulty Bellow encounters here is one that he must face and conquer in each of his works. It is essentially the difficulty of a novelist who, like some novelists of the Thirties, gives great credence to social facts yet, unlike them, finally embraces a meta-social view of man. It is this symbolic transition from manners to metaphysics that Bellow, to his very great credit, insists upon, and insisting upon it must find a way of performing.

In this particular respect, *Seize the Day* is a partial success as it is in other respects almost a complete one. The stages of Wilhelm's progress are well marked: humiliation, knowledge, love, reconciliation. And the theme of death is introduced early in the work: a reference to Milton's *Lycidas* which Wilhelm recollects from his college course, constant allusions to Wilhelm's age and his father's fear of death. Furthermore, the theme of death itself is more adroitly woven in the social fabric of the work than in any other Bellow has written. The equation is once again the Freudian equation of money and death, success and aggression. The abstract presence of the stock market dominates the novella, and it is given, by the ghostly figure of Mr. Rappaport, a distinctly macabre tone. On this subject Tamkin is quite explicit: " 'Money and Murder both begin with M. . . . Money-making is aggression. . . . People come to the market to kill. They say, 'I'm going to make a killing.' It's not accidental."[39] Death, we see, circulates in the golden arteries of our civilization; its hand moves silently over the city; and the dying reach out to pull the living into their walking graves. This Bellow sees with terrible clarity; the

315

abstract idea is rendered only too well. It is the specific event, however, the scene in the funeral parlor, coming where and when it does, coming to Wilhelm and to no other, that leaves us to wonder if the particular mode of his illumination does not seem rather gratuitous, rather foreign to the concerns he has most steadily expressed throughout the action. The thematic logic of Wilhelm's life remains convincing, the dramatic sequence of his actions not.

VI

Wilhelm is Augie's shabbier brother; his petty ailments, his furtive slovenliness and urge for humiliation remind us of Joseph and Leventhal. Wilhelm sees himself as "the man beneath," the eternal victim: "Tear me to pieces, stamp on me and break my bones."[40] Man's fate, in *Seize the Day*, is both ironic and tragic; social reality asserts itself with heavy, grimy hands.

The manner of *Henderson the Rain King*, 1958, is very different, and so is its hero equally different from Bellow's earlier victims and favored sons of fate. In the fabulous story of Henderson, Bellow goes farther than he ever did toward freeing the individual's spiritual quest from the enmeshing substance of society. To this end, the magic never-land of Africa is chosen for setting. The result, of course, is a work that reads like a romance and has, despite the author's warning to "those deep readers" forever engaged in a nervous quest of symbols, the universality only romance can bestow on action.[41] But the danger of romance is that, when it fails to awaken our sense of things permanent or large, it may appear no more than a happy use of fancy. This is a danger to which Bellow's novel is not entirely superior.

The hero of the book enjoys certain advantages of birth and power which the heroes of romance traditionally enjoyed. Henderson is not a Jew; he is the scion of an ancient American family distinguished for scholarship and public service. He is not poor, but many times a millionaire. And he is not defined by any particular urban role. Quite to the contrary, his roles and travels take him in the fifty-five years of his life over many strange grounds. Freed externally from necessity, he is thus forced to pursue the inner necessity of his being, to answer that unappeasable voice in him which constantly cries "I want, I want, I want," to burst his spirit's sleep and carry his life to a certain depth, to discover that service which, performed, may be the human retort to death. His travels are mental journeys, and the great turbulence of his spirit attests to the measure of his involvement with reality. A man of gigantic size and enormous strength, at once violent and tender, "an exceptional amalgam of vehement forces," he hauls his passionate bulk across the African wilderness like some buffoon or outlandish healer—his guiding image is that of men like Albert Schweitzer and Sir Wilfred Grenfell—seeking salvation and reflecting in his big suffering face, "like an unfinished church," all "the human passions at the point of doubt—I mean the humanity of them lying in doubt."[42] His search, first and foremost, is for reality, that same vibrant medley of fiction and fact which Eliot's celebrated bird pretended humankind could not bear too much of. But how much unreality can they bear, Henderson retorts? And though he claims to be on better terms with reality than most people—his second wife, Lily, for instance—it is in keeping with his spiritual progress, his humility and humiliation before life, that he discovers: "The physical is all there, and it belongs to science. But then there is the noumenal department, and there we create and create and create."[43]

Despite the archaic haze of fertility rituals, ceremonial hunts, and totemic cults through which the action of the novel flashes, the motive of Henderson's search and the stages of his spiritual progress remain clear. When Henderson leaves Lily behind, he leaves the only person with whom he has a struggling and irreplaceable relation. But in leaving her he also turns his back

317

on the passive morality she represents, dampened by social pieties and noble hypocrisy. (Society is precisely what Henderson, like so many heroes of the American novel, cannot fathom; all his deeds, heroic or clownish, transcend their social reference.) The true starting point of his quest is a quotation he discovers in his father's library: "The forgiveness of sins is perpetual and righteousness first is not required."[44] Because his disorderly life is so full of errors and remissions—a father he cannot reach though he takes up playing the violin with great hairy paws to do so, his own son alienated from him, a first wife, remote and neurotic, who can only laugh at his quixotic idealism, a career of false starts and frantic assertions —because of all this Henderson is compelled to seek redemption in a single act of charity, knowledge, and depth. The compulsion is as strong as death itself, the death of spirit and of matter too, that same death against which his hurtling soul is pitted and toward which it secretly moves. Bellow renders this fundamental antithesis of Henderson's character in a pattern of recurrent images: the octopus whose cold eyes and slow tentacles communicate to him a feeling of cosmic coldness, the dead man he has to carry on his back among the Wariri. In contrast to these intimations of death, the terrible fear of a traceless calm, there are the images of life to which Henderson responds with a singing soul: the wonder of a child in a world death has not yet touched, the rapture an African sunrise produces, "some powerful magnificence not human," pink light on a white wall with prickles and the whole physical universe wrinkling, heaving. Between life and death, turbulence and calm, reality beckons to Henderson, and the light of wisdom erratically gleams.

It is while Henderson is chopping wood at home—a log hits his face—that it first occurs to him truth must come in blows. Later, while he is wrestling with Prince Itelo, in a ritual gesture of acquaintance, he realizes once again that nothing but the *blows* of truth can burst the spirit's sleep. Yearning, he learns, is suffering, and suffering a kind of unhappy strength. But the latter is only a preamble to the wisdom which our experience already contains in fragments. With his unusual capacity to relate one fragment of experience to another—Bellow communicates this through a deft use of numerous flashbacks—Henderson, unlike Augie, gives the impression of creating the very destiny he seeks. Though he bungles the job of purifying the Arnewi cistern and lifting the "curse" on their cattle, he takes away, with his failure, the friendship of Itelo and the wisdom of Queen Willatale, who teaches him that a frenzied lust for living, "grun-tu-molani," not only affirms the basic value of human existence but further incarnates the desire to redeem its griefs. It is under the hypnotic influence of King Dahfu of the Wariris, however, that Henderson comes to realize that a rage for living is not enough. Man must also put an end to his *becoming* and enter the realm of *being*, the only realm in which love is possible. Between human beings, Henderson understands, there can be either brotherhood or crime, love or aggression. To attain the state of being man owes to his fellow man, human kind must turn to the beasts. This explains why the prophecy of Daniel—"They shall drive you from among men, and thy dwelling shall be with the beasts of the field" —is so constantly in Henderson's mind, and explains also why in the past Henderson raised pigs with such lavish care and performed with a bear in a roller coaster. The prophecy is actually consummated in a lion's den, under Dhafu's castle, where the king teaches Henderson in the dark, wordless presence of a lioness how to capture the emanations of a vital creature, how to be still and active, sufficient and attuned: how to *be* and how to *love*. It is not merely by journeying to Africa, with its strange kings and primitive rituals, nor is it merely by performing a serviceable act of extermination or rain-giving strength that Henderson begins to attain to wisdom. It is rather by learning how to absorb the pure moment which brings together the currents of life and death, ecstasy and numbness, absorb an animal presence, that he perceives the limits of human strife. The clamorous voice that used to cry, "I want, I want, I want," can now listen to other equally authentic voices: "He wants, she wants, they want."[45] Identity is found in communion and communion is reached not in the civilization to which we are born but out of it. Man must live with the rhythm of things, for he cannot *live* forever against it. In the last moving scene of the book, Henderson, on his way back to Lily, on his way to start medical studies at 55, clasps an orphan child to his chest and runs about the homebound plane with him, "leaping, leaping, pounding, and tingling over the pure white lining of the gray Arctic silence," knowing that though "for creatures there is nothing that ever runs unmingled," chaos does not run the whole human show, and ours is not "a sick and hasty ride, helpless, through a dream into oblivion."[46]

Precipitate, vigorous, candid as it is immensely colorful, the style of *Henderson the Rain King* leaps with the contortions of its hero's soul and sheds itself again on earth in a poetry of acceptance. Its exuberance is often controlled, and though it still rambles and digresses with the errant human spirit, it insinuates to us not the endless disponibility of Augie's life but a new idea of responsibility, namely, that man can never commit himself too late. The abstractness of a metaphysical romance is balanced everywhere by Bellow's awareness of the grotesque corporeality of spiritual experience—it is, for instance, while Henderson is wrestling with Itelo, and is tugged around prone on all fours, that he reveals to the prince the aim of his quest. But tragi-comedy, romance, and allegory sometimes add to a dubious mixture. We should be careful not to ascribe the uneasiness we feel about the novel to the conjured quality of the setting and action, for these remain within the realm of significant illusion. Our criticism, rather, must be that Bellow does not succeed in making us feel toward Henderson the detached and ironic sympathy which would have placed his

320

clownery and shenanigans in the right dramatic perspective. Henderson's posturing and garrulous sincerity promise more than they finally reveal; his peculiar admixture of bravado and self-deprecation seems at times too easy a substitute for the range of human emotions lying between laughter and tears. The effect is sometimes like that of a pantomime co-authored by Rider Haggard and Dostoyevsky. Nor is Henderson's play-acting limited to the roles of braggart and breast-beater. He plays too often the part of an obsequious straight man in a Socratic dialogue with African sages, and frequently echoes, like a great blubbering reverberator, thoughts which we would have liked to see developed rather than repeated—even so, the book could well stand some cutting. This is all to say that there is in Henderson a quality of emotional abundance or humility, Slavic or Hebraic perhaps but not entirely American, that puts a higher spiritual valuation on events than the events actually warrant. The result is that Henderson's quest, lacking the reticence of struggle, seems a little faked; his final reconciliation to life appears self-induced. Fate, to be sure, makes buffoons of us all, yet some consent more easily than others to dance the crazy tune.

Henderson the Rain King remains, in a genuine way, the most affirmative of Bellow's works. Starting with the familiar figure of the solitary American hero, unattached to father, wife, or son, fleeing civilization and in search of love, prodigal in his services to all, Bellow leads Henderson through reality's dark dream to a vision of light, and a commitment that can only bind man back again to life. Scapegoat, messiah, a king of plenty and of the spirit's drought—"He was despised and rejected, a man of sorrow and acquainted with grief," Henderson recites from Handel's *Messiah*—the American hero discovers at last that true innocence can be renewed only in the quixotic charity of pain.[47] And for once the American hero can go back home again.

An artist is always a pilgrim in progress. Bellow's artistic progress reveals itself in the stages his heroes mark. Joseph cried, in the sweet bitterness of surrender, "Long live regimentation." Asa Leventhal, discovering the ingenuity of human guilt, realizes that man is weak and yet accountable. Augie March, finding that every one must know bitterness in his chosen thing, manages still to keep fate and character responsive to the common touch of joy. And Henderson comes to salvation through service and love. The movement, we see, is toward a resolution of the conflict between self and world; the movement is from acid defeat to acceptance, and from acceptance to celebration. The querulous and ill-natured hero becomes prodigal and quixotic. In this process something of the dignity that the fictional hero has lost to history is restored to him. "It's obvious to everyone," Bellow wrote, "that the stature of characters in modern novels is smaller than it once was, and this diminution powerfully concerns those who value existence. I do not believe that human capacity to feel or do can really have dwindled or that the quality of humanity has degenerated. I rather think that people appear smaller because society has become so immense."[48] The immensity of society, luckily, can still be criticized or spoofed.

As the vision of Bellow expands in his novels, so does his style. Here are two city scenes, presumably "objective," one from *The Victim*, the other from *Augie March*:

This afternoon the cleaning woman had been in and there was a pervasive odor of soap powder. He got up and opened a window. The curtains waved once and then were as motionless as before. There was a moviehouse strung with lights across the street; on its roof a water tank sat heavily uneven on its timbers; the cowls of the chimneys, which rattled in the slightest air, were still.

We went through Gary and Hammond that day, on a trailer from Flint, by docks and dumps of sulphur and coal, and flames seen by their heat, not light, in the space of noon air among the

322

black, huge Pasiphae cows and other columnar animals, headless, rolling a rust of smoke and connected in an enormous statuary of hearths and mills. . . .[49]

The contrast of metaphor and syntax in the two scenes is evident, but the more arresting difference lies in the attitude of the observer to his surroundings implied by each passage. Beneath the objective surface of description, Augie exhibits a comic excess, a quality both of irony and acceptance, that is entirely missing from Leventhal's shrinking precision, as if the latter were trying to wipe the stain of the world off his eyes. Augie is a *witness* to the scene he describes, Leventhal an *alien*. A degree of comic excess is indeed present in all of Bellow's work as the profusion of ideas, put in the mouth of slightly "cracked" characters like Allbee, Einhorn, Tamkin, or Dahfu indicates. The distinction between the earlier and later works, however, is the distinction between ironic comedy ruled by the spirit of absurdity, which limits and bitterly denies, and romantic comedy informed by the spirit of compromise. The change is effectuated by opening the form of the novel to a dialogue between romance and picaresque. Such a dialogue, ludicrous or improbable as it may seem, plays chance against order, freedom against necessity, in the realm of human experience. It frees the hero's actions, and in so doing liberates the feelings and thoughts which make actions in an organized world still intelligible. Discovering how fluid experience can be, the hero pursues his quest, in reverence and intensity, to the point where the profound recalcitrance of reality asserts itself again. There freedom ends, and love begins. But love is an old familiar of comedy. "The presiding genius of comedy is Eros, and Eros has to adapt himself to the moral facts of society," Northrop Frye observes.[50] It is indeed the encounter of Eros with reality that guides Bellow's comic vision to its artistic end.

No end could be worthier of the challenges America presents to the fictional imagination. Conceived as a vision of love and violated by its lust for achievement, America has now moved, beyond innocence or guilt, to create a society in which certain basic human simplicities are satisfied only at the individual's peril. A comic vision as penetrating as Bellow's serves to redress the shuddering balance of our values, and it may even serve to foster values which fulfill man's lasting needs. "Imagination!" King Dahfu exclaims, "It converts to actual. It sustains, it alters, it redeems!"[51] Eden has now gone the dim abstract way of Utopia, as Bellow would be the first to agree, and the redemption of man, if redemption he needs, must come from the present acting upon itself. America is presences; this is what the versatile forms of Bellow's art proclaim. Like all things, like man himself, the "master of adaptations," the proclamation is mixed. It is in some ways a proclamation for radical innocence: the native No written in thunder. But it is also a proclamation of acceptance: the will and art to involve the radical dissent of the Self into the holiest equivocations of reality. This is the dialectic Bellow constantly tries to sustain.

EPILOGUE

I

WE end where we began. What is radical innocence? And why must we be still mindful of it in
America?

At bottom, all innocence amounts to a denial of death. It
is, therefore, a radical plea for the Self. The plea can be holy
or demonic; the Self is really the same. Deep down, where
things are stark yet fearfully deceptive, man always invents his
gods or becomes the gods he invents. Deep down, man always
disavows the reality his hands touch and his eyes see. This, too,
is innocence, the dangerous and outrageous kind conceived in
dreams.

The anarchy in the American soul is nourished on an old
dream: not freedom, not power, not even love, but the dream
of immortality. America has never really acknowledged Time.
Its vision of Eden or Utopia is essentially a timeless vision. Its
innocence is neither geographical nor moral: it is mainly
temporal, hence metaphysical. This is a radical innocence.

It is sometimes said of American literature that the most
significant works produced in the last two hundred years belong
in spirit to the twentieth century. The statement, no doubt,
was made by a modern. It suggests, nevertheless, that a certain
quality of American literature strikes deep in the modern consciousness. Many of us respond to Melville in a critical manner
which Dante, Shakespeare, and Goethe, however great and
however universal, do not encourage us particularly to elaborate.
The manner may be called existential, and it is predicated on a
sense both of the nudity and the terrifying aspiration of the
Self. For Europe has discovered in our century what America
seems to have been born knowing: that where the aboriginal
Self is concerned, nothing else appears to exist. This realization
is the source from which the broad stream of existential aware-

325

ness in Europe wells. After the death of God, proclaimed by Nietzsche, the dissolution of society was inevitable. Only the Self remained. And the Void all around it. The modern soul is eternally poised on the eve of Creation. This is the song American literature sings.

II

We end this study where we began, and move again to recapture a thread clumsily unraveled. A critic's statement should not end on an apocalyptic note. We see best when we see first what lies near at hand.

It is man who lies near at hand, seen darkly but with lucidity too in the images our fiction projects. If the broad existential view of this study amounts to anything, it amounts to an admission that a critique of the novel must ultimately seek the elusive boundaries between art and action, imagination and fact, order and disorder, the boundaries, that is, at which one form of human awareness blends into another. A critique of fiction is a criticism of dreams that have taken form, yearnings and denials that have taken shape. This is not a time for professors of literature to ignore the judgment of human passions.

Hence what may seem our inordinate attention to the hero in fiction. The conception of the hero lies at the point where action and art meet. He is an image of man's destiny, and also the focus of dramatic form in the novel. He unites the course of history and the stream of dreams. For the hero, since ancient times, has always embodied the collective wish of his race; through his agency, dreams are turned into history.[1] The act is one for which the hero, be he Oedipus or Theseus, two men who stand poles apart, must grievously pay. No one who has observed the refined hypocrisy of the chorus in a Greek play, the manner in which it wavers, backing the protagonist, then forsaking him, can deny that heroism makes every hero an outsider. Men seem to know by instinct that dreams are

326

monstrous, things that should never see the light of day. Men tempt the hero to realize their dreams, then punish him for his daring credulousness. (This seems particularly true of contemporary America, where hero worship conceals an abyssal distrust of prominence.) In a limited sense, therefore, every hero is a scapegoat, and a radical innocent. Thus was Prometheus chained to a rock and Oedipus banished from Thebes. Thus too, in more subtle fashion, was Faust self-damned and Christ crucified. These last still provide the effective prototypes of heroism in America, and still embody opposing images of immortality.

The modern hero, however, is an anti-hero. The term refers only to the quality of the hero's actions, not to his passions which hero and anti-hero share alike. The stature of the hero and the glory of his deed are secondary traits; the primary characteristic of the hero is his awareness of himself. Deep in his constitution, the hero incarnates the aboriginal Self. So long as it was possible to mediate between Self and World, the anarchy in the heroic soul remained covert; the hero appeared as a hero. But the World, in our time, seems to have either vanished or become a rigid and intractable mass. The anarchy of nihilism and the terror of statism delimit the extremes between which there seems to be no viable mean. Mediation between Self and World appears no longer possible —there is only surrender or recoil. In its modern recoil, the Self has bared its insatiable nature. The hero has become an anti-hero. And the latter, knowing that there is always an element of crime in freedom, that indeed freedom may be defined only in terms of rebellion, readied himself to pay the full price of immolation. The rebel-victim came of age.

"Where *is* this new bird called the true American?" D. H. Lawrence shrieks. "Show us the homunculus of the new era. Go on, show us him. Because all that is visible to the naked European eye, in America, is a sort of recreant European."[2] Lawrence did not see things as well by daylight as he could see in the dark; his fierce idea of what America might have been stood in his way. The "recreant European" of whom he speaks is the new rebel-victim, the Man from Underground in the soul of Huck Finn. He is old as America is and young as Europe is beginning to be. He is the anti-hero who, instead of turning dreams into history, converts history back into dreams. An archetypal figure, the anti-hero seeks to transcend Time or revert to the mythic innocence of the Self. This is why the anti-hero appears to us a peculiarly American creation, a recreant European perhaps, but only because he defies time and history, and denies death itself. A deep dreamer, a martyr and anarch, he is a clown too, a juggler whose game is to keep Eden and Utopia in airy balance.

The emergence of this type of hero in American culture, the homunculus of the new era, is best observed in the ordeals of initiation. Initiation has been defined as that critical encounter with experience the aim of which is confirmation into a social and moral order. Initiation, therefore, entails reconciliation to time, endeavor in history, the final acceptance of death. In the process of initiation, dreams surrender to reality. It is no wonder that initiation in America has seldom borne the fruits of completion. The process is either truncated or interminable. All the initiates we have met evade the full burden of confirmation; they cannot compromise with death.

In the last hundred years, the burdens of initiation have become heavier, the alternatives to compromise more crushing. The trend seems almost irreversible. The face of the initiate dissolves into the facial contours of the rebel-victim whose grimaces are legion. The latter now incarnates for us the eternal dialectic between the primary Yes and everlasting No. His appeal to the terrible imperatives of the Self overreaches the values coddled by his society. "It is not society that is to guide and save the creative hero, but precisely the reverse," Joseph Campbell concludes in his celebrated study of heroism. "And so every one of us shares the supreme ordeal—carries the cross

328

of the redeemer—not in the bright moments of his tribe's great victories, but in the silences of his personal despair."[3] In the secret smithies of the hero's conscience, new values are forged, annealed in pain or in the extremity of hope. By taking upon himself the intractable mysteries of existence, he offers himself, in this postindividual era, as a last exemplar of a vanishing conception of man. Denying death, the American hero shuts out a large part of life that men consider part of reality. But denying death, he also opens for us those gates of the Self which few men presume to unlock. The sound of these gates when they burst open is the thunder in Melville's utterance: No! Leslie Fiedler, who understands that fiction must be negative in order to fulfill its essential moral obligation, has made the following words of Melville the motto of his recent book:

There is the grand truth about Nathaniel Hawthorne. He says No! in thunder; but the Devil himself cannot make him say *yes*. For all men who say *yes*, lie; and all men who say *no*,—why they are in the happy condition of judicious, unincumbered travellers in Europe; they cross the frontiers into Eternity with nothing but a carpetbag—that is to say, Ego.[4]

No more succinct statement on the aspiration of the American Self could be found!

III

The function of American fiction, then as now, is to mediate between the hero's outrageous dream and the sadness of human mortality. But the novel does not merely recapitulate some immemorial rite beyond the recall of consciousness. It is a mode of our experience in and also out of time. It is a mode of our presence, and our presence is neither symbolic nor wholly unconscious. The fictional act of mediation is a feat of form. This is why critics brood over form.

If the energy of contemporary American fiction is the energy of opposition, its form is the form of irony. Irony implies distance, ambiguity, the interplay of views. It intercedes between poles of experience, unites the terrible and the ludicrous, and attempts to reconcile what remains, at bottom, irreconcilable: dream and fact. It is all the certainty we can allow ourselves where uncertainties prevail. Yet irony also commits itself to that which it criticizes. As Kenneth Burke has observed, "True irony, humble irony, is based upon a sense of fundamental kinship with the enemy. . . ."[5] True irony, which serves equally to engage the self with the other as insulate the ego from itself, may carry religious as well as secular connotations. It is viewed by Hopper as an esthetic equivalent to Original Sin, the Human Contradiction presented absolutely.[6] When ironic humility leads to its opposite, ironic superiority, the isolation of the ego becomes total, and man stands alone in an infernal void. The saintly and the demonic poles of irony thus are defined. Between these two poles, irony appears as the response of the human intelligence to absurdity, and, beyond absurdity, to death.

There is much in the past, and even more in the present, conditions of America to make irony the shaping spirit of our art. The discrepancy between the surface images of our mass society and the deep-seated urges of men provide large opportunities for ironic fiction. So does the interplay of manners and morals in marginal groups of our culture, cliques and fugitive movements stranded on the spiritual ebb of the times. For as there are pockets of resistance in our culture, there are still Bible, hibachi, and marijuana belts in it, too. Yet the voice of the Southern or Negro or Jewish writer must not be interpreted simply as a protest of hedged-in minorities; it is rather as a testament of contrariety, perhaps even of sheer perversity, rooted in the bitter complexities of heart and mind. Whatever the hero may now be a victim of, he is certainly not, as he was in the Thirties, a victim of systems or facts. Even romance, that native genre which entertains with such generosity a marvelous ideal on the sea coast of the soul's bohemia, is driven down to

Hades where it still thrives underground on a nightmare vision of Arcadian innocence. Irony, therefore, guides the novel on its way as it journeys, like Orpheus, to the bowels of the earth, bringing back forbidden knowledge; or fares, like the Ancient Mariner, to the antipodes of experience, returning to hold the Wedding Guest in the spell of a glittering eye; or yet scales the heights on which the gods take refuge and, like Prometheus, is fettered for its audacity.

The concept of the novel as a spiritual journey, a process, an existential encounter, allows us to discriminate between certain kinds of fiction without referring to contrasts between comedy and tragedy which no longer seem valid. The concept allows for distinctions but also points to a formal paradigm shared by a great many recent novels. Thus the closed encounter of the scapegoat, the qualified encounter of the humble hero, and the open encounter of the impostor or rogue reveal certain common traits which may be attributed to an ironic form. The three types of heroes around which these traits cluster, *pharmakos, eiron,* and *alazon,* are not envisaged as immutable archetypes. Their classical roles, it is true, define their character; but the particular use to which they lend themselves in contemporary fiction is not bound by tradition. The adaptation of an old myth to a new situation—the examples of Joyce, Gide, Mann, Lawrence, and Faulkner still overpower our imagination—is a profound comment on that situation; and the differences, say, between the classic and modern scapegoats of literature is itself a criticism of the meaning of outrage and atonement in our time. What remains of primary and formal importance, however, is the particular way a hero works out his concrete destiny in fiction. The "defeated" heroes of Styron, Swados, and Mailer are, in a sense, no less demonic than the "triumphant" heroes of Gold, Cheever, and Donleavy—and no more quixotic. Elements of defiance and sacrifice, crime and saintliness, are intermixed in their composition. If these two groups of heroes, who represent extremes on our scale, seem different, it is because the logic of necessity can still be distinguished from the logic of possibility in human actions. And if they seem, in some dim, half-forgotten way, very much the same, it is because they all share a vision of absurdity despite their radical apprehension of the Self.

IV

Sooner or later, critical insights become dogma, and dogma turns into platitude. This is a failing we have hoped to avoid by adopting the tripartite structure of this book. Our concern in Part One was with social and historical forces which point to a conceptual definition of the hero. In Part Two, we attempted to outline a generic form of fiction. The nine novels selected for discussion were chosen as exhibits of contemporary form; they were not intended to convey the full achievement of their respective authors. The focus of Part Three changes again, moving away from the general and closer to the specific. It is, after all, the confluence of gifted writers at a particular moment that gives the moment its character. Novelists like Styron, Ellison, and Mailer certainly deserve more attention than we have been able to accord them in the critical scheme of this study. Flannery O'Connor and Bernard Malamud, excellent writers both, may very well develop beyond the strict bounds prescribed by a compelling, if rather limiting, style. James Purdy, Philip Roth, and John Updike are indeed "promising newcomers," as reviewers like to say, on whom we have barely touched. And there are others. But our business is not to play the literary stockmarket; nor is it to assess reputations under the aspect of Dogma, Taste, or Intuition. It is enough if we can show that the spectacle of contemporary American fiction is not a mean or shabby spectacle. This is a statement of modest recognition, not liberal faith.

Modesty is often pragmatic, and it is pragmatism—which may verge on arbitrariness, as some readers, no doubt, will

think—that prompted us to view the works of Carson McCullers, Truman Capote, J. D. Salinger, and Saul Bellow not as
illustrations but rather as sources of the topics explored in our
discussions. Relatively speaking, these novelists have published
early and have published much. They reflect the rich diversity
of our fiction, a variety of subjects, styles, and background.
They tell us about Jew and Gentile, city dwellers and small-
town people, about the North and the South. And they tell
us about the pursuits of love or freedom in ways that must
seem radical to readers inured to soppy and sentimental views
of life.

Carson McCullers writes of love as the terrible form loneliness
takes. For her, loneliness is not a social condition but a function
of spiritual existence. The gothic metaphors of her novels invoke
a sealed and ghastly world, a set of ritual actions which make
of every lover a scapegoat. Yet what her characters secretly
seek is the immortality of the Self perpetuated as Absolute
Lover or God. Only in loving, without discrimination or hope
of reciprocity, can man transcend the isolation which, quite
paradoxically, he confirms by so loving.

Truman Capote begins his fictional career by projecting an
image of Narcissus, the essential Self beholding immortality in
a reflexive dream. Later, self-love yields to the less solipsistic
desire for freedom. Yet the freedom which Holly Golightly
suggests remains childlike: its exuberance depends on an evasion
of what others call responsibility. The function of the imagination—and this is the most central function in Capote's work—
is to rediscover the Self, and discover how Self and World
may be brought to a precarious balance.

The Self in Salinger's work is, above all, quixotic. Its true
strategy, therefore, is to give more than it takes. In giving so
freely of itself, it denies the cautionary ideas of measure and
proportion; denying the objective claims of reality, it denies its
own mortality. The quixotic gesture, overreaching itself, merges
into holy prayer; the natural successor of Holden Caulfield is

the saintly Seymour Glass. In the primitive and beautiful metaphors, Zen or Christian, evolved by the latter, immortality of the Self is insured by its total abnegation. The spiritual lover, by becoming one with creation, becomes also as indestructible. This is indeed a return to aboriginal innocence.

The old search for innocence is knotty and raddled in the novels of Saul Bellow. It is troubled by the pervasive presence of reality. His heroes, victims and picaresques alike, disclose secret images of the Self; but their dreams are so enmeshed in the tough substance of facts that nothing they do ever seems unmixed. The astonishing feat of Bellow's fiction is that to the extent that it acknowledges the complex pressures of reality, to that extent it appears to us genuinely affirmative. The ideas of freedom and love which motivate his characters—Wilhelm, Augie March, Henderson—are as extreme as any we have encountered; the true antagonist of these men is not so much society as implacable death. But their reconciliation to their fate in the real world—Wilhelm's vision of death is the most compelling example—brings the greatest imaginative release from tensions men are forced everyday to recognize. It is in Bellow's work that the fictional act of mediation between radical innocence and human mortality goes farthest. It is in his work, therefore, that we are likely to feel the consummation of an ironic form. This, if not praise of the highest, is praise enough.

V

Praise, as we conceive it, is an inherent function of criticism. In an age of mendacity, *kitsch* art, and counterfeit leisure, the pursuit of genuine excellence is a dangerous and noble pursuit. We must raise the standards on ourselves, and raise the price. We should tolerate arrogance in our novelists and encourage the kind of artistic courage and ruthlessness society calls subversive. We must always demand more. And still we must praise, for without praise criticism manages, somehow, to deny the values it sets out to preserve.

It would have been easy to take a more jaundiced view of the novelists reviewed in this work. It would have been easy to dwell on their limitations with more critical fervor. Their travails may have failed to produce that rare and outstanding novel which, in retrospect, seems to create the spirit of an era. The sense of a brave avant-garde hurtling headlong past the darkling plains of Philistinism does not possess them. New writers may write less and take longer to mature than their predecessors. And it may be true that our novelists, deprived of the impetus of disillusionment experienced by their elders, and lacking the formative experience of civil life, are readily seduced into exploring the narrow resources of their ironic sensibility. The evidence for these strictures is, to say the least, quite mixed; and the liabilities of a generation are often turned by the creative act to some enduring advantage. As in life, so in art: the limitations of human beings do not define their limits.

Praise, then, is due to the serious and dedicated novelist not because he has invariably achieved artistic perfection—the morality of style which Flaubert held up to his contemporaries as the only valid morality—but because, even in his honorable failures, he has shown men, as no priest or philosopher could, how they may actually live in the lion's mouth. This is a function which is neither exclusively literary nor entirely didactic. It is a function of the novel as novelists write it in our time, an ambiguous function perhaps, yet still a formal function. How, then, can a critic hope to describe it? Words like "radical," "innocence," "initiation," "encounter," "rebel," "victim," "irony," "dream," and "death," crowd into these pages not as shibboleths, we trust, but as metaphors of unappeasable desire. It is the national desire to placate the guilt and the arrogance of America's monstrous vision, a vision which broods over gothic horror and the blackness ten times black as symbolic expressions of the demonic aspirations of the Self. It is the novelist's desire to create order under the conditions of chaos, and possessing the energy thereof. It is the critic's desire to make of uncommon artifice a common performance, shared, intelligible, and ultimately disturbing. And it is the desire of all human beings alike to discover in literature images of their unacknowledged life.

VI

We end where we began, as everything ends in America, and end to begin again. If we have seemed at times too much obsessed by the idea of America, it is because our strange, mixed culture is obsessively unique. It is unique in time, in space, and in dream. A country without prehistory, it has suddenly entered history with the intention to rape and redeem time in its heart. A country of illimitable spaces, it has confronted men with nature in the raw, inducing in them permanent and atavistic loneliness, and it has been turned by them into the most profoundly denatured spectacle on record. Conceived as a dream, it has shown that dreamers may also awake in the cold sweat of a nightmare, and sleep to dream again. The novelist who writes of America earns his praise. The novelist who can write of America shows that the novel has not reached the end of its tether; nor is man both a creature and creator in vain.

We do not conclude with a doctrine of noble endurance, and despite Faulkner's spirited Nobel Prize speech, we do not conclude with a faith in the prevalence of man. There is simply no conclusion. The curse of Columbus is still with us: every one must rediscover America for himself—alone!

BIBLIOGRAPHIC NOTES

Where paperback editions have been found convenient to use, the date of publication refers to the paperback rather than to the original edition of the work.

Prologue

1. Quoted by Paul Darcy Boles, "The Vision Then and Now," in Granville Hicks, ed., *The Living Novel* (New York, 1957), p. 31.
2. See Flannery O'Connor, "The Fiction Writer and this Country," in *The Living Novel*, pp. 162f; and Norman Mailer, "The White Negro," in Gene Feldman and Max Gartenberg, eds., *The Beat Generation and the Angry Young Men* (New York, 1958), p. 344.
3. Lionel Trilling, *The Opposing Self* (New York, 1955), p. x.
4. Saul Bellow, *The Victim* (New York, 1947).
5. Wright Morris, "The Territory Ahead," in *The Living Novel*, p. 146.
6. Richard Chase, *The Democratic Vista* (New York, 1958), p. 30.
7. See Paul Radin, *The Trickster* (London, 1956), p. 200.

Chapter One
The Modern Self in Recoil

1. Oswald Spengler, *The Decline of the West*, 2 vols., (New York, 1926), Vol. 1, p. 48.
2. Arnold Toynbee, *A Study of History*, 2 vols., abridged by D. C. Somerwell (New York, 1947, 1957), Vol. 2, p. 328.
3. *ibid.*, Vol. 2, p. 349.
4. Roderick Seidenberg, *Posthistoric Man* (Boston, 1957), p. 180.
5. George Orwell, *Nineteen Eighty Four* (London, 1950), p. 268.
6. Friedrich Juenger, *The Failure of Technology* (Chicago, 1956), p. 177.
7. *Time*, December 8, 1958, p. 73.
8. *A Study of History*, Vol. 2, p. 334.
9. Hannah Arendt, *The Human Condition* (Chicago, 1958), pp. 45, 203, 204.
10. Erich Kahler, *The Tower and the Abyss* (New York, 1957), p. 45.
11. Quoted by Camus, *The Rebel* (New York, 1956), p. 182.
12. Bruno Bettelheim, "Individual and Mass Behavior in Extreme Situations," *The Journal of Abnormal and Social Psychology*, XXXVIII (1943).
13. Sigmund Freud, *Civilization and Its Discontents* (London, 1955), p. 123.
14. *ibid.*, p. 114.
15. Theodore Reik, *Of Love and Lust* (New York, 1957), p. 366.
16. Rollo May, Ernest Angel, and Henri F. Ellenberger, eds., *Existence* (New York, 1958), pp. 23-26.
17. Nathan A. Scott, Jr., "The Broken Center: A Definition of the Crisis of Values in Modern Literature," *Chicago Review*, XIII (Summer 1959), p. 196.
18. Quoted by Walter Kaufmann, ed., *Existentialism from Dostoyevsky to Sartre* (New York, 1957), p. 110.
19. See William Barrett, *Irrational Man* (New York, 1958), pp. 170f.
20. Kaufmann, *Existentialism from Dostoyevsky to Sartre*, p. 95. See

also Kierkegaard's analysis of collectivization in Robert Bretall, ed., *A Kierkegaard Anthology* (Princeton, 1951), pp. 262, 266, 267.

21. Albert Camus, *The Myth of Sisyphus* (New York, 1959), p. 90.

22. Lionel Trilling, *Freud and the Crisis of Our Culture* (Boston, 1955), pp. 58f.

23. Raymond Giraud, *The Unheroic Hero* (New Brunswick, 1957), p. 189. See also Harry Levin, "From Priam to Birotteau," *Yale French Studies*, VI (1950), 76.

24. Mario Praz, *The Hero in Eclipse in Victorian Fiction* (New York, 1956), p. 383.

25. Aldous Huxley, ed., *The Letters of D. H. Lawrence* (London, 1956), p. 198.

26. *The Short Novels of Dostoyevsky*, Introduction by Thomas Mann (New York, 1945), p. 137.

27. *ibid.*, p. 137.

28. *ibid.*, p. 140.

29. *ibid.*, p. 132.

30. Joseph Conrad, *Lord Jim* (New York, 1931), p. 214.

31. T. S. Eliot, "Ulysses, Order and Myth," in John W. Aldridge, ed., *Critiques and Essays on Modern Fiction* (New York, 1952), p. 426.

32. James Joyce, *Ulysses* (New York, 1946), p. 712.

33. *ibid.*, p. 284.

34. *Selected Stories of Franz Kafka*, Introduction by Philip Rahv (New York, 1952), p. 187.

35. Franz Kafka, *Dearest Father* (New York, 1954), p. 378.

36. Parallels between the two novelists are well elaborated by Renato Poggioli, "Kafka and Dostoyevsky," in Angel Flores, ed., *The Kafka Problem* (New York, 1946), pp. 97-107.

37. Thomas Mann, *The Magic Mountain* (New York, 1955), pp. 285f.

38. "Introduction," *The Short Novels of Dostoyevsky*, p. xv.

39. *The Human Condition*, p. 180.

40. See Colin Wilson, *The Outsider* (Boston, 1956), for an extended documentary more valuable for its recognition of the general problem and for its range of significant reference than for its particular insights into the crucial documents it uses.

41. Hermann Hesse, *Steppenwolf* (New York, 1929), p. 28.

42. *ibid.*, p. 77.

43. *ibid.*, p. 73.

44. *The Outsider*, p. 261. Also Colin Wilson, *Religion and the Rebel* (Boston, 1957).

45. Jean-Paul Sartre, *Nausea* (Norfolk, Conn., n.d.,), p. 91.

46. Erich Heller, *The Disinherited Mind* (New York, 1957), p. 202.

47. *Nausea*, pp. 135f.

48. Albert Camus, *The Plague* (Paris, 1948), 229.

49. *The Rebel*, p. 19.

50. *ibid.*, p. 22.

51. Ortega Y Gasset, *The Dehumanization of Art* (New York, 1956), p. 185.

52. Karl Jaspers, *Man in the Modern Age* (New York, 1957), p. 205.

53. *Matthew* 16:25.

Chapter Two
The Dialectic of Initiation in America

1. Leslie Fiedler, *An End to Innocence* (Boston, 1955), p. 128.
2. William Bradford, "Of Plymouth Plantation," in Perry Miller, ed., *The American Puritans* (New York, 1956), pp. 16f.
3. St. Jean de Crèvecoeur, *Letters from an American Farmer* (New York: E. P. Dutton and Co., n.d.), p. 55.
4. Loren Baritz, "The Sins of God's Country," Unpublished MS, p. 25.
5. *Letters from an American Farmer*, p. 58.
6. D. H. Lawrence, *Studies in Classic American Literature* (New York, 1951), p. 173.
7. Herman Melville, *Moby Dick* (New York, 1930), p. 777. Contrast the views of R.W.B. Lewis, *The American Adam* (Chicago, 1955), and Harry Levin, *The Power of Blackness* (New York, 1958). See also Frederic I. Carpenter, *American Literature and the Dream* (New York, 1955), pp. 9ff., for a fuller statement on this dichotomy of the American psyche.
8. F. G. Friedmann, "America: A Country Without a Pre-history," *Partisan Review*, xix (March-April 1952), 141-152. See also Hans Meyerhoff, "An American Odyssey," *Partisan Review*, xxv (Summer 1958), 443-453.
9. George Santayana, *Character and Opinion* (New York, 1955), p. 86. See also Merle Curti, *The American Paradox* (New Brunswick, N. J., 1956), pp. 54ff., and Van Wyck Brooks, *America's Coming-of-Age* (New York, 1958), pp. 15f.
10. "Somewhere in our mental constitution is the demand for life as pure spirit," Lionel Trilling noted, *The Opposing Self* (New York, 1955), p. 90. Trilling's point is anticipated by Robert S. and Helen M. Lynd, *Middletown, U.S.A.* (New York, 1929).
11. Jacques Maritain, *Reflections on America* (New York, 1958), p. 92.
12. *The Power of Blackness*, p. 7.
13. Quoted and discussed, respectively, by Henry B. Parkes, *The American Experience* (New York, 1955), p. 269, and Wright Morris, *The Territory Ahead* (New York, 1958), pp. 210f.
14. Mark Twain, *The Adventures of Huckleberry Finn* (New York, 1953), p. 91.
15. See W. H. Auden, "Authority in America," *The Griffin* (March 1955), p. 10. Howells reported of Twain: "He held himself responsible for the wrong which the white race had done the black race in slavery, and he explained, in paying the way of a Negro student through Yale, that he was doing it as part of the reparation due from every white man to every black man." See "My Mark Twain," in Henry Steele Commager, ed., *Selected Writings of William Dean Howells* (New York, 1950), p. 903.
16. *The Adventures of Huckleberry Finn*, p. 293.
17. F. W. Dupee, *Henry James* (New York, 1956), p. 95.
18. Malcolm Cowley, *Exile's Return* (New York, 1951); Frederick Allen, *Only Yesterday* (New York, 1931); Frederick J. Hoffman, *The*

Twenties (New York, 1955); John W. Aldridge, *After the Lost Generation* (New York, 1951).

19. Joseph Wood Krutch, *The Modern Temper* (New York, 1929). The later edition of this work (1956) acknowledges Krutch's revision of his earlier pessimism. See pp. xi ff.

20. Quoted by F. O. Matthiessen, *Theodore Dreiser* (New York, 1951), p. 188.

21. Theodore Dreiser, *An American Tragedy* (New York, 1925), p. 790.

22. Newton Arvin, "Individualism and the American Writer," in Morton D. Zabel, ed., *Literary Opinion in America* (New York, 1951), p. 548.

23. James T. Farrell, *The Young Manhood of Studs Lonigan*, in *Studs Lonigan* (New York, 1932), p. 411.

24. Justin O'Brien, *The Novel of Adolescence in France* (New York, 1937), p. 59.

25. For a thorough assessment of Freud's influence in America see Frederick J. Hoffman, *Freudianism and the Literary Mind* (Baton Rouge, 1957), chaps. 2, 3, 4, 8.

26. It is interesting that G. Stanley Hall, the man responsible for bringing Freud to lecture in this country at Clark University, should also be the author of a large, prophetic work called *Adolescence*. In the Preface to that work Hall wrote: "Never has youth been exposed to such dangers of both perversion and arrest as in our land today. Increasing urban life with its temptation, prematurities, sedentary occupations, and passive stimuli . . . early emancipation and a lessening sense for both duty and discipline, the haste to know all and do all befitting man's estate before its prime, the mad rush for sudden wealth and the reckless fashions set by its gilded youth—all these lack some of the regulations they still have in older lands with more conservative traditions." Quoted by Oscar Cargill, *Intellectual America* (New York, 1941), p. 601.

27. Hoffman, *Freudianism and the Literary Mind*, pp. 234ff.

28. "Letters to Van Wyck Brooks," in Edmund Wilson, ed., *The Shock of Recognition* (New York, 1955), p. 276.

29. Sherwood Anderson, *Winesburg, Ohio* (New York, 1946), p. 3.

30. Horace Gregory, ed., *The Portable Sherwood Anderson* (New York, 1956), p. 453.

31. *Winesburg, Ohio*, p. 28.

32. *ibid.*, p. 173.

33. John Dos Passos, *Three Soldiers* (New York, 1932), p. v.

34. F. Scott Fitzgerald, *This Side of Paradise* (New York, 1948), p. 288.

35. *ibid.*, p. 287.

36. Sigmund Freud, *Civilization and Its Discontents* (London, 1955), p. 14.

37. Thomas Wolfe, *Look Homeward, Angel* (New York, 1929), p. 192.

38. Thomas Wolfe, "The Story of the Novel," in Maxwell Geismar, ed., *The Portable Thomas Wolfe* (New York, 1946), pp. 588ff.

39. *Look Homeward, Angel*, pp. 544, 625.

40. Thomas Wolfe, *You Can't Go Home Again* (New York, 1940).

41. Ernest Hemingway, *The Short Stories of Ernest Hemingway* (New York, 1938), p. 218.

42. See William Van O'Connor, "Protestantism in Yoknapatawpha

County," in Louis D. Rubin, Jr., and Robert D. Jacobs, ed., *Southern Renascence* (Baltimore, 1953), pp. 153ff.

43. Arthur Mizener, "The Thin Intelligent Face of American Fiction," *Kenyon Review*, XVII (Autumn 1955), p. 524.

44. William Faulkner, "The Bear," in *Go Down, Moses* (New York, 1955), p. 192.

45. *ibid.*, p. 257.

46. Ernest Hemingway, *A Farewell to Arms* (New York, 1929), p. 259.

47. F. Scott Fitzgerald, *The Great Gatsby* (New York, 1951), pp. 119, 191.

Chapter Three
Contemporary Scenes:
The Victim with a Thousand Faces

1. Edmund Wilson, *The American Earthquake* (New York, 1958), p. 569.

2. Russell Lynes, *A Surfeit of Honey* (New York, 1957), p. 1.

3. Aldous Huxley, *Brave New World Revisited* (New York, 1958), p. 5.

4. William S. Whyte, Jr., *The Organization Man* (New York, 1956), p. 7.

5. James M. Gillespie and Gordon W. Allport, *Youth's Outlook on the Future* (New York, 1955), pp. 13ff. See also David Riesman, "The College Student in an Age of Organization," *Chicago Review*, XII (Fall 1958), 50-58; and "The Found Generation," *American Scholar*, XXV (Autumn 1956), 421-436.

6. "The first thing that distinguishes this generation of students is the way they whisper their hopes," R. J. Kaufmann notes. See *The Nation*, March 9, 1957, p. 210. The debate on "angry" and "unangry," "silent" and "unsilent," young men is far from settled. See Van Wyck Brooks, *The Writer in America* (New York, 1953), pp. 109-133; Leslie Fiedler, "The Un-Angry Young Men," *Encounter* (January 1958), pp. 3-12; John W. Aldridge, *In Search of Heresy* (New York, 1956), pp. 1-70; and Otto Butz, ed., *The Unsilent Generation* (New York, 1958).

7. Richard Frede, *Entry E* (New York, 1958), p. 244.

8. Norman Podhoretz, "Our Changing Ideals as Seen on TV," in Chandler Brossard, ed., *The Scene Before You* (New York, 1955), p. 99.

9. "For once our modern age has re-oriented itself, it will bring to the culture of the family a wealth of scientific and imaginative interests that our ancestors did not possess," Lewis Mumford hopefully writes in *The Human Prospect* (Boston, 1955), p. 272. The problem of leisure, on the other hand, is suggested by the forecast that a century hence America will be able to produce in a seven-hour day what now requires a forty-hour week. See Thomas R. Carshadon and George Soule, *U.S.A. in New Dimensions* (New York, 1957), p. 2.

10. Quoted by Eric Goldman, *The Crucial Decade* (New York, 1956), p. 291; William Faulkner, "On Privacy," *Harper's Magazine*, July 1955, p. 38.

11. Erich Fromm, *The Art of Loving* (New York, 1956), and *The Sane Society* (New York, 1955).

12. In Gene Feldman and Max Gartenberg, *The Beat Generation and the Angry Young Men* (New York, 1958), pp. 343, 346.

13. The capacity of art to reconcile opposites is intelligently discussed, in a psychoanalytic perspective, by Herbert Marcuse, *Eros and Civilization* (Boston, 1955), pp. 172-196.

14. Frank O'Connor, "And It's a Lonely Personal Art," *New York Times Review*, April 2, 1953.

15. Howard Nemerov, *Federigo, Or, The Power of Love* (Boston, 1954), p. 248.

16. *ibid.*, p. 209.

17. *ibid.*, p. 70.

18. *ibid.*, pp. 141f.

19. Robie Macauley, *The Disguises of Love* (New York, 1952), p. 282.

20. Alexis de Tocqueville, *Reflections on Democracy*, 2 vols. (New York, 1954), Vol. 2, pp. 202-222; Amaury de Riencourt, "Will Success Spoil American Women?" *New York Times Magazine*, November 10, 1957. See other statements on the subject by Lynes, *A Surfeit of Honey*, pp. 93f.; Jacques Maritain, *Reflections on America* (New York, 1957), pp. 583-611, 677-688; and the Editors of *Look* in *The Decline of the American Male* (New York, 1958).

21. One of the more serious of the new West Coast magazines, to which Henry Miller and Lawrence Lipton contribute, is actually called *Sex and Censorship*. See John Osborne "Sex and Failure," in *The Beat Generation and the Angry Young Men*, p. 318.

22. It has become suddenly fashionable to berate novelists—the more obscure they are, the more exuberant critics become—for the sexual offenses of their characters. See Robert Eliot Fitch, *The Decline and Fall of Sex* (New York, 1957) and Edmund Fuller, *Man in Modern Fiction* (New York, 1958).

23. Leslie Fiedler, *An End to Innocence* (Boston, 1955), pp. 146ff.; and "From Clarissa to Temple Drake: Women in Love in the Classic American Novel," *Encounter*, VIII (January 1957), 14-20.

24. Malcolm Cowley, *The Literary Situation* (New York, 1954), pp. 26ff, 6off.

25. Gore Vidal, *The City and the Pillar* (New York, 1948), p. 80.

26. James Baldwin, *Giovanni's Room* (New York, 1959), pp. 75, 121.

27. *ibid.*, p. 53.

28. James Leo Herlihy, *The Sleep of Baby Filbertson* (New York, 1959), p. 29.

29. Unpublished letter to the author, 25 January 1959.

30. Flannery O'Connor, *Wise Blood* (New York, 1952), p. 165.

31. *ibid.*, p. 232.

32. Ralph Ellison, *Invisible Man* (New York, 1953), p. 503.

33. James Baldwin, *Notes of a Native Son* (Boston, 1957), p. 172.

34. James Baldwin, *Go Tell It On the Mountain* (New York, 1954), pp. 168, 174, 179.

35. *ibid.*, pp. 170, 181.

36. *Notes of A Native Son*, pp. 113f.

37. James Jones, *From Here to Eternity* (New York, 1951), p. 248.
38. *ibid.*, p. 582.
39. *ibid.*, p. 276.
40. *ibid.*, p. 363.
41. Paul Bowles, *The Sheltering Sky* (New York, 1949), p. 51.
42. Paul Bowles, *Let It Come Down* (New York, 1953), p. 256.
43. *ibid.*, p. 156.
44. Lawrence Lipton, *The Holy Barbarians* (New York, 1959), p. 7.
45. Henry Miller, *Sunday After the War* (Norfolk, Conn., 1944), pp. 154, 155.
46. *ibid.*, pp. 158, 159.
47. *ibid.*, p. 160.
48. Henry Miller, *Big Sur and the Oranges of Hieronymus Bosch* (London, 1958), pp. 17, 21.
49. Alan W. Watts, *Beat Zen, Square Zen, and Zen* (San Francisco, 1959), p. 6.
50. Quoted by Eugene Burdick, "The Innocent Nihilists Adrift in Squareville," *The Reporter*, April 3, 1958, p. 32.
51. Robert M. Lindner, *Rebel Without A Cause* (New York, 1944), p. 13.
52. *The Beat Generation and The Angry Young Men*, p. 115; Jack Kerouac, *On the Road* (New York, 1957), p. 195.
53. Richard Stern, "Hip, Hell, and the Navigator: An Interview with Norman Mailer," *Western Review* (Winter 1959), p. 104.
54. See the statement of Kenneth Rexroth on this subject in Lipton, *The Holy Barbarians*, pp. 293ff.
55. John Clellon Holmes, *Go* (New York, 1952), p. 36.
56. *ibid.*, p. 90.
57. *ibid.*, p. 144.
58. *ibid.*, p. 245.
59. *On the Road*, p. 251.
60. *ibid.*, pp. 259, 193, 10.

Chapter Four

The Pattern of Fictional Experience

1. Van Wyck Brooks, *The Writer in America* (New York, 1953), p. 183.
2. Albert J. Guerard, "The Ivory Tower and the Dust Bowl," *New World Writing 3* (New York, 1953), p. 348.
3. Ralph Ellison, "Society, Morality and the Novel," in Granville Hicks, ed., *The Living Novel* (New York, 1957), p. 75.
4. Charles Fenton, "The Writer as Professor," *New World Writing 7* (New York, 1955), p. 169. For a more cantankerous view of the subject, see John W. Aldridge, *In Search of Heresy* (New York, 1956), chap. 2.
5. The other alternative to poetry which novelists have sometimes chosen is, as Podhoretz has noted, the article or essay form. Podhoretz' statement, however, that "the novel has taken over from poetry as the

sanctified genre," describes more nearly the trend we have in mind. See Norman Podhoretz, "The Article as Art," *Harpers Magazine*, 78, July 1958. The question is better stated by Earl Rovit when he says that "the novelist, like the poet, has been thrown back on the capacity of his individual imagination to create a metaphor . . . which will sustain itself reflexively without the prop of a conventional social myth." See Earl H. Rovit, "The Ambiguous Modern Novel," *The Yale Review* (Spring 1960), p. 422.

6. Stanley Edgar Hyman, "Some Trends in the Novel," *College English* (October 1958), p. 9.

7. As Swados put it, "Technological development, mass-media expansion, and suburban growth will make the novelist's America of the sixties more different from Scott Fitzgerald's America than Fitzgerald's America was from Edith Wharton's." See *The Living Novel*, p. 192.

8. Irving Howe, "Mass Society and Post-Modern Fiction," *Partisan Review* (Summer 1959), p. 428.

9. John W. Aldridge, *In Search of Heresy* (New York, 1956), p. 115.

10. Jean-Paul Sartre, "The Anti-Novel of Nathalie Sarraulte," *Yale French Studies* (Winter 1955-56), p. 43.

11. Alain Robbe-Grillet, "Une Voie pour le Roman futur," *Nouvelle Revue Française* (July 1956), p. 80. See also Jean Bloch-Michel, "The Avant-Garde in French Fiction," *Partisan Review* (Summer 1958), pp. 467-471.

12. Robbe-Grillet reproaches the American novel for remaining attached to an obsolete notion of its characters. See Alain Robbe-Grillet, "Le Réalisme, la Psychologie et l'avenir du Roman," *Critique* (August-September 1956), pp. 695-701.

13. A witty discussion of some formal characteristics of contemporary fiction may be found in Malcolm Cowley, *The Literary Situation* (New York, 1954), pp. 45-50.

14. See Arthur Mizener, "The Novel of Manners in America," *Kenyon Review* (Winter 1950), pp. 1-19; Lionel Trilling, "Manners, Morals, and the Novel," and "Art and Fortune," in *The Liberal Imagination* (New York, 1953); John W. Aldridge, "The Heresy of Literary Manners" in *In Search of Heresy*; and Delmore Schwartz, "The Duchess' Red Shoes," *Partisan Review* (January-February 1953), pp. 55-73.

15. *The Liberal Imagination*, pp. 201, 206.

16. *ibid.*, p. 257.

17. Marius Bewley, *The Eccentric Design* (London, 1959), p. 292.

18. Richard Chase, *The American Novel and Its Tradition* (New York, 1957), p. viiif.

19. *ibid.*, p. 7.

20. Sean O'Faolain, *The Vanishing Hero* (London, 1956), p. 14.

21. C. M. Bowra, *Heroic Poetry* (London, 1952), p. 5.

22. E. R. Dodds, *The Greeks and the Irrational* (Boston, 1957), p. 9.

23. Otto Rank, *The Myth of the Birth of the Hero* (New York, 1952), p. 82.

24. Lord Raglan, *The Hero* (New York, 1956), p. 193.

25. Joseph Campbell, *The Hero With a Thousand Faces* (New York, 1956), p. 386.

26. Hopper is right to say that "the artist's dilemma today has thrust

him inward upon himself in such a way that his journey has brought him round to the ultimate mysteries, where ethical and religious understandings take hold." See "The Problem of Moral Isolation in Contemporary Literature," in Stanley Romaine Hopper, ed., *Spiritual Problems in Contemporary Literature* (New York, 1952), p. 167. Also see, for a discussion of the Greek prototypes of the hero, Northrop Frye, *The Anatomy of Criticism* (Princeton, 1957), pp. 39-43.

27. Kenneth Burke, *Counter-Statement* (Los Altos, California, 1953), p. 143. Some cogent distinctions between types of form, such as are made by the Chicago critics, or neo-Aristotelians, do not seem appropriate to this discussion. See, for instance, Elder Olson, "William Empson, Contemporary Criticism, and Poetic Diction," in R. S. Crane, ed., *Critics and Criticism, Ancient and Modern* (Chicago, 1952), pp. 65ff.

28. R. P. Blackmur, *The Lion and the Honeycomb* (New York, 1955), p. 294.

29. A moderately instructive psychoanalytic discussion of fictional forms may be found in Simon O. Lesser, *Fiction and the Unconscious* (Boston, 1957), pp. 121-144. A preliminary effort to apply the criteria of Existentialism to modern American literature is undertaken by Richard Lehan, "Existentialism in Recent American Fiction: The Demonic Quest," *Texas Studies of Language and Literature* (Summer, 1959), 181-202.

30. See Wilbur M. Frohock, *The Novel of Violence in America* (Dallas, 1957), pp. 3-23.

31. Karl Jaspers, *Tragedy Is Not Enough* (Boston, 1952), p. 48.

32. See, for instance, Ursula Brumm, "The Figure of Christ in American Literature," *Partisan Review* (Summer 1957), pp. 403-413.

33. Wylie Sypher, *Comedy* (New York, 1956), p. 196.

34. Quoted by William Van O'Connor, "The Grotesque in Modern American Fiction," *College English* (April 1959), p. 342.

35. Cyrus Hay, "Comedy, Tragedy, and Tragicomedy," *Virginia Quarterly Review* (Winter 1960), p. 108. The tragi-comic nature of all fiction is also discussed with more insight than scope by Ortega. See Ortega Y Gasset, "The Nature of the Novel," *Hudson Review* (Spring 1957), pp. 39f.

36. *The Anatomy of Criticism*, p. 135. See also pp. 136, 33f.

37. *ibid.*, p. 42.

38. *ibid.*, p. 34.

39. *ibid.*, p. 42.

40. *ibid.*, pp. 41, 223; 45, 46, 185, 186, 187.

41. *ibid.*, p. 192.

42. *ibid.*, p. 223.

Chapter Five

Encounter with Necessity:
Three Novels by Styron, Swados, and Mailer

1. William Styron, *The Long March* (New York, 1952), pp. 55f.

2. William Styron, *Set This House on Fire* (New York, 1960), pp. 500f.

3. Malcolm Cowley, ed., *Writers at Work* (New York, 1959), p. 272.
4. *ibid.*, p. 273.
5. William Styron, *Lie Down in Darkness* (New York, 1957), p. 386.
6. Maxwell Geismar, *American Moderns* (New York, 1958), p. 243.
7. *Lie Down in Darkness*, pp. 9, 10, 68.
8. *ibid.*, p. 74.
9. *ibid.*, p. 363.
10. *ibid.*, pp. 184, 235.
11. *ibid.*, p. 377.
12. *ibid.*, p. 388.
13. *ibid.*, p. 397.
14. *ibid.*, p. 392.
15. *ibid.*, pp. 388f.
16. *ibid.*, p. 384.
17. *ibid.*, p. 386.
18. *ibid.*, p. 226.
19. *ibid.*, p. 152.
20. *ibid.*, p. 368.
21. Harvey Swados, "The Image in the Mirror," in Granville Hicks, ed., *The Living Novel* (New York, 1957), p. 174.
22. Harvey Swados, *Out Went the Candle* (New York, 1955), p. 338.
23. *ibid.*, pp. 347ff.
24. *ibid.*, p. 171.
25. *ibid.*, p. 341.
26. *ibid.*, p. 344.
27. *ibid.*, p. 349.
28. Norman Mailer, "Our Country and Our Culture," *Partisan Review* (May-June 1952), p. 299.
29. Norman Podhoretz, "Norman Mailer: The Embattled Vision," *Partisan Review* (Summer 1959), p. 371.
30. *American Moderns*, p. 179.
31. Norman Mailer, *Advertisements for Myself* (New York, 1959), p. 512.
32. Richard G. Stern, "Hip, Hell, and the Navigator: An Interview With Norman Mailer," *Western Review* (Winter 1959), pp. 104f.
33. Norman Mailer, *The Naked and the Dead* (New York, 1951), p. 152.
34. *ibid.*, pp. 153, 276.
35. *ibid.*, p. 277.
36. *ibid.*, p. 41.
37. *ibid.*, pp. 12, 142, 202.
38. *ibid.*, p. 592.
39. *ibid.*, p. 61.
40. *ibid.*, p. 302.
41. *ibid.*, p. 379.
42. *ibid.*, p. 598.
43. *ibid.*, p. 490.
44. *ibid.*, p. 493.
45. *ibid.*, p. 280.

46. *Advertisements for Myself*, p. 91.
47. *The Naked and the Dead*, p. 116.
48. Northrop Frye, *The Anatomy of Criticism* (Princeton, 1957), pp. 41f.

Chapter Six

The Qualified Encounter:
Three Novels by Buechner, Malamud, and Ellison

1. Frederick Buechner, *A Long Day's Dying* (New York, 1960), p. 10.
2. *ibid.*, pp. 158f.
3. *ibid.*, pp. 173f.
4. *ibid.*, p. 25.
5. See John W. Aldridge, *After the Lost Generation* (New York, 1951), pp. 219-230.
6. *A Long Day's Dying*, p. 210.
7. *ibid.*, pp. 257, 258, 263.
8. *ibid.*, p. 266.
9. *ibid.*, p. 3.
10. Leslie Fiedler, "Saul Bellow," *Prairie Schooner* (Summer 1957), p. 107.
11. *Current Biography Yearbook*, 1958, ed. Marjorie Dent Candee (New York, 1958), p. 272.
12. Earl H. Rovit, "Bernard Malamud and the Jewish Literary Tradition," *Critique* (Winter-Spring 1960), p. 5.
13. Bernard Malamud, *The Assistant* (New York, 1958), p. 25.
14. *ibid.*, p. 10.
15. *ibid.*, p. 32.
16. *ibid.*, p. 133.
17. *ibid.*, pp. 72f.
18. *ibid.*, p. 181.
19. *ibid.*, p. 189.
20. *ibid.*, p. 180.
21. *ibid.*, p. 173.
22. Ralph Ellison, "Richard Wright's Blues," in Paul Bixler, ed., *The Antioch Review Anthology* (New York, 1953), p. 267.
23. Ralph Ellison, *Invisible Man* (New York, 1960), p. 86.
24. *ibid.*, p. 10.
25. *ibid.*, pp. 379f.
26. *ibid.*, pp. 19f.
27. *ibid.*, pp. 137, 139.
28. *ibid.*, p. 463.
29. *ibid.*, p. 496.
30. *ibid.*, p. 497.
31. *ibid.*, p. 501.
32. *ibid.*, p. 495.
33. *ibid.*, p. 12.
34. *ibid.*, pp. 190, 231.

35. *The Antioch Review Anthology*, p. 264.
36. Ralph Ellison, "Change the Joke and Slip the Yoke," *Partisan Review* (Spring 1958), p. 218.
37. *Invisible Man*, p. 502.
38. Northrop Frye, *The Anatomy of Criticism* (Princeton, 1957), p. 40.

Chapter Seven
Encounter with Possibility:
Three Novels by Gold, Cheever, and Donleavy

1. Herbert Gold, ed., "Introduction," *Fiction of the Fifties* (New York, 1959), p. 12.
2. Herbert Gold, *The Optimist* (New York, 1959), p. 80.
3. *ibid.*, p. 127.
4. *ibid.*, p. 226.
5. *ibid.*, p. 43.
6. *ibid.*, pp. 174f.
7. *ibid.*, pp. 176f.
8. *ibid.*, p. 296.
9. *ibid.*, p. 329.
10. *ibid.*, p. 364.
11. *ibid.*, p. 365.
12. *ibid.*, p. 395.
13. Herbert Gold, "The Mystery of Personality in the Novel," in Granville Hicks, ed., *The Living Novel* (New York, 1957), p. 104.
14. *The Optimist*, p. 393.
15. Quoted by Robert Gutwillig, "Dim Views Through Fog," *The New York Times Book Review*, November 13, 1960, p. 68.
16. John Cheever, *The Wapshot Chronicle* (New York, 1958), pp. 308f.
17. *ibid.*, p. 54.
18. *ibid.*, p. 310.
19. *ibid.*, p. 48.
20. *ibid.*, p. 156.
21. *ibid.*, p. 288.
22. *ibid.*, p. 185.
23. J. P. Donleavy, *The Ginger Man* (New York, 1959), pp. 14f.
24. *ibid.*, pp. 43, 62.
25. *ibid.*, p. 54.
26. *ibid.*, p. 165.
27. *ibid.*, pp. 285f.
28. *ibid.*, p. 189.
29. *ibid.*, p. 271.
30. *ibid.*, p. 133.
31. *ibid.*, pp. 64f.
32. *ibid.*, p. 149.

33. See Northrop Frye's discussion of comedy, *The Anatomy of Criticism* (Princeton, 1957), pp. 163-186.

Chapter Eight
Carson McCullers

1. Robert B. Heilman, "The Southern Temper," in Louis D. Rubin and Robert D. Jacobs, eds., *Southern Renascence* (Baltimore, 1953), p. 6.

2. John Maclachlan, "No Faulkner in Metropolis," *ibid.*, p. 108.

3. Irwin Panofsky, *Gothic Architecture and Scholasticism* (New York, 1957), p. 16.

4. Allen Tate, *The Forlorn Demon* (Chicago, 1953), pp. 55, 59.

5. Carson McCullers, *The Ballad of the Sad Café: The Novels and Stories of Carson McCullers* (New York, 1951), p. 276. Subsequent references in this chapter are, unless noted otherwise, to this collection of the works of Mrs. McCullers.

6. Oliver Evans, "The Theme of Spiritual Isolation," *New World Writing I* (New York, 1952), p. 299.

7. *The Ballad of the Sad Café*, pp. 24f.

8. *The Heart Is A Lonely Hunter*, p. 273.

9. *The Forlorn Demon*, p. 76.

10. Denis de Rougemont, *Love in the Western World* (New York, 1940), pp. 64, 66.

11. *The Heart Is A Lonely Hunter*, p. 220.

12. *ibid.*, p. 493.

13. *ibid.*, p. 363.

14. *ibid.*, p. 174.

15. *ibid.*, p. 357.

16. *ibid.*, pp. 497f.

17. See Tennessee Williams, "Preface," in Carson McCullers, *Reflections in a Golden Eye* (Norfolk, Conn., 1940).

18. *Reflections in a Golden Eye*, p. 564.

19. *ibid.*, p. 584.

20. *The Member of the Wedding*, p. 640.

21. *ibid.*, p. 740.

22. *ibid.*, p. 599.

23. *ibid.*, p. 623.

24. *ibid.*, p. 646.

25. *ibid.*, p. 738.

26. *ibid.*, pp. 622, 599.

27. *ibid.*, pp. 622, 599, 789.

28. Frank O'Connor, *The Mirror in the Roadway* (New York, 1956), pp. 266f.

29. *The Ballad of the Sad Café*, p. 3.

30. *ibid.*, pp. 65f.

31. *ibid.*, p. 51.

32. Carson McCullers, "The Pestle," *Mademoiselle*, July 1953, p. 44.

Chapter Nine
Truman Capote

1. This and the previous autobiographical statement are quoted in *Current Biography Yearbook, 1951*, ed. Marjorie Dent Candee (New York, 1951), p. 92.
2. Quoted by Richard Chase, *The American Novel and Its Tradition* (New York, 1951), p. 26.
3. Truman Capote, *A Tree of Night and Other Stories* (New York, 1951), p. 57.
4. Truman Capote, *Other Voices, Other Rooms* (New York, 1949), p. 95.
5. Truman Capote, *The Grass Harp* (New York, 1953), p. 119.
6. Sigmund Freud, "The Uncanny," *Collected Papers*, IV (London, 1956), p. 398.
7. *Current Biography, 1951*, p. 93.
8. Henry James, *The Art of Fiction*, ed. R. P. Blackmur (New York, 1953), p. 253.
9. Sigmund Freud, "Humor," *Collected Papers* V (London, 1956), p. 217.
10. Wylie Sypher, *Comedy* (New York, 1956), p. 200.
11. Quoted by Chase, *The American Novel and Its Tradition*, p. 18.
12. *A Tree of Night*, p. 143.
13. *ibid.*, p. 24.
14. *ibid.*, p. 18.
15. *ibid.*, pp. 101f.
16. *ibid.*, p. 112.
17. See Carvel Collins, "Other Voices," *American Scholar* (Winter, 1955-56), pp. 114ff.; and John W. Aldridge, *After the Lost Generation* (New York, 1951), pp. 202-214.
18. *Other Voices, Other Rooms*, p. 10.
19. *ibid.*, p. 65.
20. *ibid.*, p. 74.
21. *ibid.*, p. 121.
22. *ibid.*, p. 125.
23. *ibid.*, pp. 139f.
24. *After the Lost Generation*, p. 219.
25. *Other Voices, Other Rooms*, p. 87.
26. *ibid.*, pp. 137ff.
27. Malcolm Cowley, ed., *Writers at Work* (New York, 1957), p. 290.
28. *The Grass Harp*, pp. 18, 20.
29. *ibid.*, p. 55.
30. *ibid.*, p. 61.
31. *ibid.*, p. 69.
32. *ibid.*, p. 121.
33. *ibid.*, p. 142.
34. *ibid.*, p. 137.
35. Truman Capote, *Breakfast at Tiffany's* (New York, 1958), p. 12.

36. *ibid.*, p. 19.
37. *ibid.*, p. 39.
38. *ibid.*, p. 83.
39. *ibid.*, pp. 39, 74.
40. *ibid.*, p. 109.
41. *ibid.*, p. 58.
42. *ibid.*, p. 12.
43. *The Grass Harp*, pp. 101f.
44. Theodore Reik, *Of Love and Lust* (New York, 1957), p. 27.

Chapter Ten
J. D. Salinger

1. Leslie Fiedler, *An End to Innocence* (Boston, 1955), p. 209.
2. See J. D. Salinger, "The Inverted Forest," *Cosmopolitan*, December 1947, pp. 73-109.
3. J. D. Salinger, "Backstage With Esquire," *Esquire*, October 1945, p. 34.
4. F. O. Matthiessen, *The Responsibilities of the Critic* (New York, 1952), pp. 136f.
5. Will Herberg, ed., *The Writings of Martin Buber* (New York, 1956), p. 44.
6. J. D. Salinger, *Nine Stories* (New York, 1954), p. 15.
7. *ibid.*, p. 65.
8. *ibid.*, p. 79.
9. J. D. Salinger, *The Catcher in the Rye* (New York, 1953), p. 130.
10. John W. Aldridge, *In Search of Heresy* (New York, 1956), p. 130.
11. *The Catcher in the Rye*, p. 129.
12. *ibid.*, p. 7.
13. *ibid.*, p. 159.
14. William Barrett, *Zen Buddhism: The Selected Writings of D. T. Suzuki* (New York, 1956), p. xiii.
15. *Nine Stories*, p. 129.
16. Frederick L. Gwynn and Joseph L. Blotner, *The Fiction of J. D. Salinger* (Pittsburgh, 1958), pp. 33f.
17. J. D. Salinger, "Franny," *The New Yorker*, January 29, 1955, pp. 30f.
18. J. D. Salinger, "Raise High the Roof Beam, Carpenter," *The New Yorker*, November 19, 1955, p. 95.
19. *ibid.*, p. 104.
20. J. D. Salinger, "Zooey," *The New Yorker*, May 4, 1957, p. 68.
21. *ibid.*, pp. 115f.
22. J. D. Salinger, "Seymour: An Introduction," *The New Yorker*, June 6, 1959, p. 45.
23. *ibid.*, p. 119.
24. *ibid.*, p. 119.
25. Allen Tate, *The Forlorn Demon* (Chicago, 1953), p. 17.

26. J. D. Salinger, "The Last Day of the Last Furlough," *Saturday Evening Post*, July 15, 1944, p. 61.
27. "Franny," *The New Yorker*, p. 25.
28. J. D. Salinger, "The Long Debut of Lois Taggett," *Story* (September-October 1942), p. 28.

Chapter Eleven
Saul Bellow

1. Leslie Fiedler, "Saul Bellow," *Prairie Schooner* (Summer 1957), p. 104.
2. Saul Bellow, "The Writer and the Audience," *Perspectives, U.S.A.*, 9 (Fall 1954), p. 101.
3. Saul Bellow, "Distractions of a Fiction Writer," in Granville Hicks, ed., *The Living Novel* (New York, 1957), pp. 4f.
4. Saul Bellow, *Seize the Day* (New York, 1956), pp. 83f.
5. *ibid.*, p. 115.
6. *ibid.*, p. 123.
7. *ibid.*, p. 152.
8. Saul Bellow, "The Jewish Writer and the English Literary Tradition," *Commentary* (October 1949), p. 366.
9. Saul Bellow, *Dangling Man* (New York, 1944), pp. 67, 137.
10. *ibid.*, p. 91.
11. *ibid.*, p. 154.
12. *ibid.*, p. 119.
13. *ibid.*, p. 190.
14. Saul Bellow, *The Victim* (New York, 1956), p. 227.
15. *ibid.*, p. 80.
16. *ibid.*, p. 70.
17. *ibid.*, p. 169.
18. *ibid.*, p. 134.
19. Saul Bellow, *The Adventures of Augie March* (New York, 1953), p. 194.
20. *ibid.*, p. 117.
21. *ibid.*, p. 286.
22. *ibid.*, p. 76.
23. *ibid.*, p. 175.
24. *ibid.*, p. 454.
25. *ibid.*, p. 3.
26. *ibid.*, pp. 5, 29.
27. *ibid.*, p. 159.
28. *ibid.*, p. 441.
29. *ibid.*, p. 536.
30. *ibid.*, p. 330.
31. *ibid.*, p. 536.
32. *ibid.*, p. 344.
33. *ibid.*, p. 378.
34. *Seize the Day*, p. 66.

35. *ibid.*, p. 70.
36. *ibid.*, p. 72.
37. *ibid.*, p. 84.
38. *ibid.*, p. 118.
39. *ibid.*, p. 69
40. *ibid.*, p. 105.
41. See Saul Bellow, "Deep Readers of the World, Beware," *New York Times Book Review*, February 15, 1959.
42. Saul Bellow, *Henderson the Rain King* (New York, 1959), p. 131.
43. *ibid.*, p. 167.
44. *ibid.*, p. 3.
45. *ibid.*, p. 286.
46. *ibid.*, pp. 175, 341.
47. *ibid.*, p. 84.
48. *Twentieth Century Authors, First Supplement*, ed. Stanley J. Kunitz (New York, 1955), p. 73.
49. *The Victim*, pp 22f.; *The Adventures of Augie March*, p. 90.
50. Northrop Frye, *The Anatomy of Criticism* (Princeton, 1957), p. 181.
51. *Henderson the Rain King*, p. 271.

Epilogue

1. I am indebted to Professor N. O. Brown's lecture on "The Hero," Wesleyan University, October 26, 1960, for this insight on which the rest of my discussion draws.
2. D. H. Lawrence, *Studies in Classic American Literature* (New York, 1955), p. 7.
3. Joseph Campbell, *The Hero With a Thousand Faces* (New York, 1956), p. 39.
4. Quoted by Leslie Fiedler, *No! in Thunder* (Boston, 1960), p. 6.
5. Kenneth Burke, *A Grammar of Motives* (New York, 1945), p. 512.
6. Stanley Romaine Hopper, "The Problem of Moral Isolation in Contemporary Literature," in Stanley Romaine Hopper, ed., *Spiritual Problems in Contemporary Literature* (New York, 1952), p. 166.

INDEX

Adams, Henry, 37
Agee, James, *Death in the Family*, 103
Aldridge, John, 45, 105, 106, 239, 244, 274
Algren, Nelson, 293; *A Walk on the Wild Side*, 91
Allen, Frederick, 45
Allport, Gordon, 65
Anderson, Sherwood, 49-51, 78, 170, 223; *Dark Laughter*, 49; "Death in the Woods," 49; "The Egg," 50; "I Want to Know Why," 49; "The Man Who Became a Woman," 49; *Many Marriages*, 49; *Winesburg, Ohio*, 50, 51
Arendt, Hannah, 27; *The Human Condition*, 11
Arvin, Newton, 47

Baldwin, James, *Giovanni's Room*, 77; *Go Tell It on the Mountain*, 8183; *Notes of a Native Son*, 81, 83
Balzac, Honoré, 21, 291
Baritz, Loren, 36
Barrett, William, 277
Baudelaire, Charles, 205
Beckett, Samuel, 194; *The Unnamable*, 27
Bellamy, Edward, 47
Bellow, Saul, 8, 106, 115, 161, 203, 229, 290-324, 333, 334; *The Adventures of Augie March*, 102, 187, 202, 290, 304-11, 312, 322-23; *Dangling Man*, 4, 152, 294-98, 302; "A Father-to-Be," 293; *Henderson the Rain King*, 105, 111, 202, 316-21; "Looking for Mr. Green," 293; *Seize the Day*, 108, 292, 311-16; *The Victim*, 4, 5, 179, 299-303, 322-23; "The Wrecker," 293
Berdyaev, Nicholas, 19
Berger, Tom, *Crazy in Berlin*, 102

Bergson, Henri, 48, 234
Bernanos, Georges, 28
Bettelhein, Bruno, 17
Bewley, Marius, 110
Blackmur, R. P., 116, 263
Blake, William, 91
Blotner, Joseph L., 278
Bourjaily, Vance, *The Violated*, 91
Bowen, Elizabeth, 153
Bowles, Paul, 115, 216; *Let It Come Down*, 87-88; *The Sheltering Sky*, 86-87, 152; *The Spider's House*, 86, 88
Bowra, C. M., 112
Bradford, William, 35
Brooks, Van Wyck, 50, 99; *America's Coming-of-Age*, 61
Brossard, Chandler, *Who Walk in Darkness*, 91
Brown, Norman O., 355n
Browne, Sir Thomas, 153; *Urn Burial*, 124, 125
Buber, Martin, 19, 67, 153, 260, 262, 267
Buechner, Frederick, 100, 153-61; *A long Day's Dying*, 4, 153-61, 178; *The Return of Ansel Gibbs*, 154; *The Season's Difference*, 153
Burke, Kenneth, 114, 330
Burns, John Horne, 266

Calvin, John, 35
Campbell, Joseph, 328; *The Hero with a Thousand Faces*, 113
Camus, Albert, 19, 31; *The Fall*, 30; *Myth of Sisyphus*, 20; *The Plague*, 30; *The Rebel*, 23, 30; *The Stranger*, 30, 88
Capote, Truman, 8, 76, 100, 153, 203, 226, 229, 230-58, 262, 333; "Beat the Devil," 230; *Breakfast at Tiffany's*, 202, 231, 233, 234, 250-55; "Children on Their Birthdays," 233, 239; "A Christmas Memory," 246; *The Grass Harp*, 231, 232, 233, 239, 245-